SUDAN

BUSINESS LAW HANDBOOK

VOLUME 1

STRATEGIC INFORMATION AND BASIC LAWS

International Business Publications, USA
Washington DC, USA - Sudan

SUDAN

BUSINESS LAW HANDBOOK

VOLUME 1 STRATEGIC INFORMATION AND BASIC LAWS

UPDATED ANNUALLY

We express our sincere appreciation to all government agencies and international organizations which provided information and other materials for this handbook

Cover Design: **International Business Publications, USA**

2017 Edition Updated Reprint International Business Publications, USA
ISBN 0-7397-2059-7

For additional analytical, business and investment opportunities information, please contact Global Investment & Business Center, USA at (703) 370-8082. Fax: (703) 370-8083. E-mail: ibpusa3@gmail.com Global Business and Investment Info Databank - www.ibpus.com

Printed in the USA

For additional analytical, business and investment opportunities information, please contact Global Investment & Business Center, USA at (703) 370-8082. Fax: (703) 370-8083. E-mail: ibpusa3@gmail.com Global Business and Investment Info Databank - www.ibpus.com

SUDAN

BUSINESS LAW HANDBOOK

VOLUME 1
STRATEGIC INFORMATION AND BASIC LAWS

TABLE OF CONTENTS

STRATEGIC AND DEVELOPMENT PROFILES

STRATEGIC PROFILE

Capital and largest city	Khartoum 15°38′N 032°32′E
Official languages	• Arabic, English
Religion	Islam
Demonym	Sudanese
Government	Dominant-party federal semi-presidential republic
• President	Omar al-Bashir
• Prime Minister	Bakri Hassan Saleh
• First Vice President	Bakri Hassan Saleh
• Second Vice President	Hassabu Mohamed Abdalrahman
Legislature	National Legislature
• Upper house	Council of States
• Lower house	National Assembly
Formation	
• Nubian kingdoms	3500 BC
• Sennar dynasty	1504
• Unified with Egypt	1820
• Anglo-Egyptian Sudan	1899
• Independence (from the United Kingdom and Egypt)	1 January 1956
• Current constitution	9 January 2005
• Secession of South Sudan	15 January 2011
Area	
• Total	1,886,068 km^2 (728,215 sq mi) (15th)
Population	
• 2015 estimate	40,235,000 (35th)
• 2008 census	30,894,000 (disputed)
• Density	21.3/km^2 (55.2/sq mi)
GDP (PPP)	2017 estimate
• Total	$186.715 billion
• Per capita	$4,578
GDP (nominal)	2017 estimate
• Total	$115.874 billion
• Per capita	$2,841
Gini	35.3 medium
HDI	▲ 0.490 low · 165th
Currency	Sudanese pound (SDG)
Time zone	EAT (UTC+3)
Date format	dd/mm/yyyy
Drives on the	right
Calling code	+249
ISO 3166 code	SD
Internet TLD	.sd, سودان.

Sudan also known as **North Sudan** since South Sudan's independence and officially the **Republic of the Sudan** is a country in Northern Africa. It is bordered by Egypt to the north, the Red Sea, Eritrea, and Ethiopia to the east, South Sudan to the south, the Central African Republic to the southwest, Chad to the west and Libya to the northwest. It is the third largest country in Africa. The River Nile divides the country into eastern and western halves. Before the Sudanese Civil War, South Sudan was part of Sudan but broke away in 2011. Its predominant religion is Islam.

Sudan was home to numerous ancient civilizations, such as the Kingdom of Kush, Kerma, Nobatia, Alodia, Makuria, Meroë and others, most of which flourished along the Nile. During the pre-dynastic period Nubia and Nagadan Upper Egypt were identical, simultaneously evolved systems of pharaonic kingship by 3300 BC. By virtue of its proximity to Egypt, the Sudan participated in the wider history of the Near East inasmuch as it was Christianized by the 6th century, and Islamized in the 15th.

As a result of Christianization, the Old Nubian language stands as the oldest recorded Nilo-Saharan language (earliest records dating to the 9th century). Sudan was the largest country in Africa and the Arab world until 2011, when South Sudan separated into an independent country, following an independence referendum. Sudan is now the third largest country in Africa (after Algeria and the Democratic Republic of the Congo) and also the third largest country in the Arab world (after Algeria and Saudi Arabia).

Sudan is a member of the United Nations, the African Union, the Arab League, the Organisation of Islamic Cooperation and the Non-Aligned Movement, as well as an observer in the World Trade Organization. Its capital is Khartoum, the political, cultural and commercial centre of the nation. It is a presidential representative democratic federal republic. The politics of Sudan are regulated by a parliamentary organization called the National Assembly. The Sudanese legal system is based on Islamic

GEOGRAPHY

Country name:
conventional long form: Republic of the Sudan
conventional short form: Sudan
local long form: Jumhuriyat as-Sudan
local short form: As-Sudan *former:* Anglo-Egyptian Sudan

forests and woodland: 19%
other: 30%

Irrigated land: 19,460 sq km
Natural hazards: dust storms
Environment - current issues: inadequate supplies of potable water; wildlife populations threatened by excessive hunting; soil erosion; desertification
Environment - international agreements:
party to: Biodiversity, Climate Change, Desertification, Endangered Species, Law of the Sea, Nuclear Test Ban, Ozone Layer Protection
signed, but not ratified: none of the selected agreements

Geography - note: largest country in Africa; dominated by the Nile and its tributaries

Location: Northern Africa, bordering the Red Sea, between Egypt and Eritrea

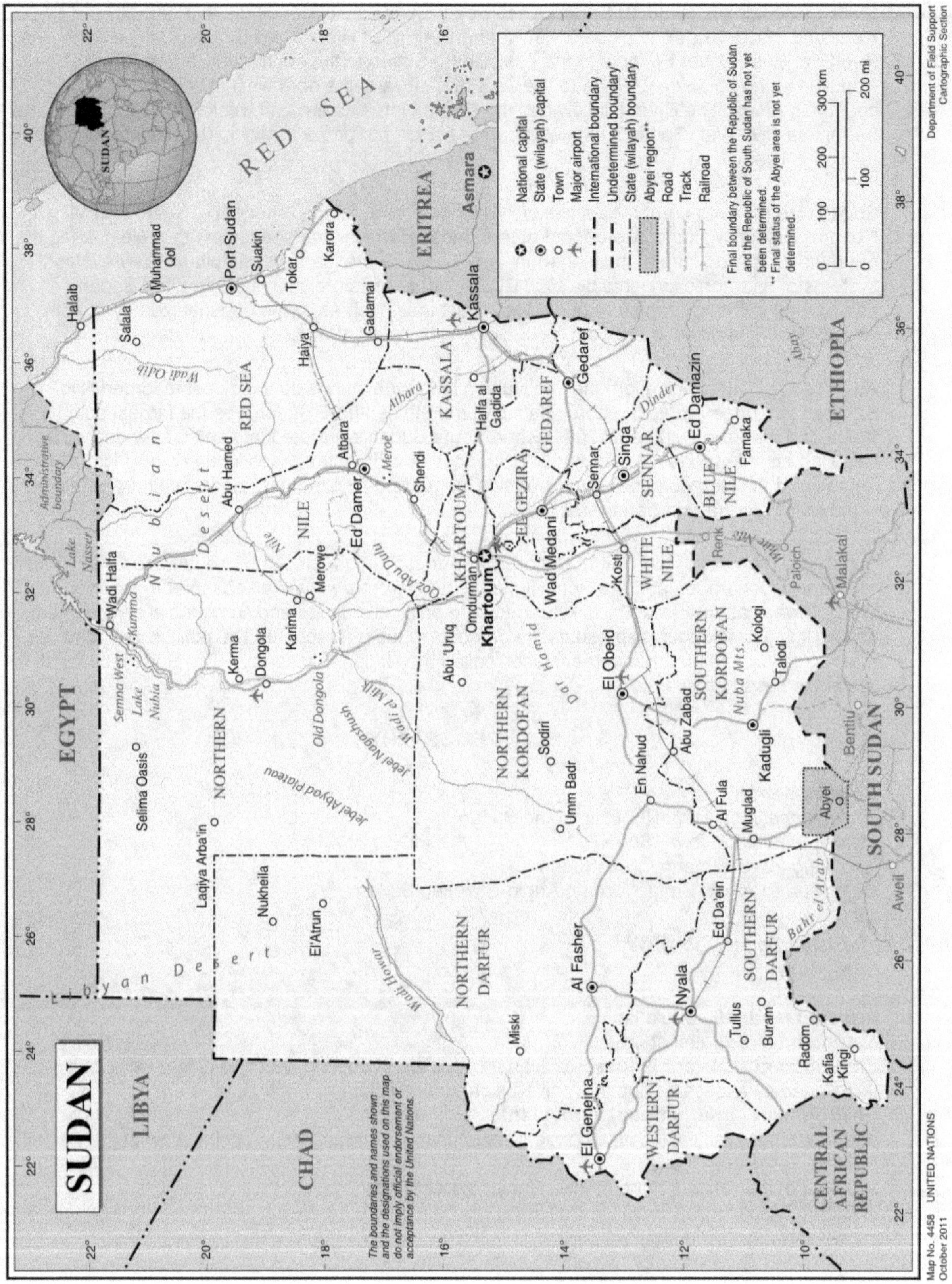
SUDAN
EGYPT
LIBYA
CHAD
ERITREA
ETHIOPIA
SOUTH SUDAN
CENTRAL AFRICAN REPUBLIC
RED SEA
NORTHERN
NILE
RED SEA
KASSALA
KHARTOUM
GEDAREF
GEZIRA
SENNAR
WHITE NILE
BLUE NILE
NORTHERN KORDOFAN
SOUTHERN KORDOFAN
NORTHERN DARFUR
WESTERN DARFUR
SOUTHERN DARFUR
Khartoum
Omdurman
Port Sudan
Kassala
Gedaref
Wad Medani
El Obeid
Al Fasher
Nyala
El Geneina
Kadugli
Ed Damazin
Singa
Kosti
Sennar
Ed Damer
Atbara
Shendi
Merowe
Karima
Dongola
Kerma
Wadi Halfa
Abu Hamed
Halaib
Suakin
Tokar
Karora
Haiya
Gadamai
Halfa al Gadida
Muhammad Qol
Salala
Selima Oasis
Laqiya Arba'in
Nukheila
El'Atrun
Miski
Umm Badr
Sodiri
Abu 'Uruq
En Nahud
Abu Zabad
Al Fula
Muglad
Abyei
Talodi
Kologi
Famaka
Ed Da'ein
Tullus
Buram
Radom
Kafia Kingi
Asmara
Malakal
Renk
Paloich
Bentiu
Aweil
Lake Nasser
Lake Nubia
Nubian Desert
Libyan Desert
Jebel Abyad Plateau
Nuba Mts.
National capital
State (wilayah) capital
Town
Major airport
International boundary
Undetermined boundary*
State (wilayah) boundary
Abyei region**
Road
Track
Railroad
* Final boundary between the Republic of Sudan and the Republic of South Sudan has not yet been determined.
** Final status of the Abyei area is not yet determined.
0 100 200 300 km
0 100 200 mi
The boundaries and names shown and the designations used on this map do not imply official endorsement or acceptance by the United Nations.
Map No. 4458 UNITED NATIONS
October 2011
Department of Field Support
Cartographic Section

Geographic coordinates: 15 00 N, 30 00 E
Map references: Africa

Area:
total: 2,505,810 sq km
land: 2.376 million sq km
water: 129,810 sq km

Area - comparative: slightly more than one-quarter the size of the US

Land boundaries: *total:* 7,687 km
border countries: Central African Republic 1,165 km, Chad 1,360 km, Democratic Republic of the Congo 628 km, Egypt 1,273 km, Eritrea 605 km, Ethiopia 1,606 km, Kenya 232 km, Libya 383 km, Uganda 435 km

Coastline: 853 km

Maritime claims: *contiguous zone:* 18 nm
continental shelf: 200-m depth or to the depth of exploitation
territorial sea: 12 nm

Climate: tropical in south; arid desert in north; rainy season (April to October)
Terrain: generally flat, featureless plain; mountains in east and west

Elevation extremes:
lowest point: Red Sea 0 m
highest point: Kinyeti 3,187 m

Natural resources: petroleum; small reserves of iron ore, copper, chromium ore, zinc, tungsten, mica, silver, gold, hydropower
Life expectancy at birth: *total population:* 56.55 years
male: 55.49 years *female:* 57.66 years
Total fertility rate: 5.47 children born/woman
Nationality:
noun: Sudanese (singular and plural)
adjective: Sudanese
Sudanic languages, English
note: program of Arabization in process
Literacy:
definition: age 15 and over can read and write
total population: 46.1% *male:* 57.7% *female:* 34.6%

ADMINISTRATIVE DIVISIONS

Sudan is divided into 18 states (*wilayat*, sing. *wilayah*). They are further divided into 133 districts.

Central and northern states

Darfur

Eastern Front

Abyei area

South Kurdufan and Blue Nile states

- Al Jazirah
- Al Qadarif
- Blue Nile
- Central Darfur
- East Darfur
- Kassala
- Khartoum
- North Darfur
- North Kurdufan
- Northern
- Red Sea
- River Nile
- Sennar
- South Darfur
- South Kurdufan
- West Darfur
- West Kurdufan
- White Nile

PEOPLE

Population: 35,079,814

Age structure:
0-14 years: 45% (male 8,064,592; female 7,712,839)
15-64 years: 53% (male 9,300,886; female 9,290,340)
65 years and over: 2% (male 406,034; female 305,123)

Population growth rate: 2.84%
Birth rate: 38.58 births/1,000 population
Death rate: 10.28 deaths/1,000 population
Net migration rate: 0.05 migrant(s)/1,000 population

Sex ratio:
at birth: 1.05 male(s)/female
under 15 years: 1.05 male(s)/female
15-64 years: 1 male(s)/female
65 years and over: 1.33 male(s)/female
total population: 1.03 male(s)/female

Infant mortality rate: 70.21 deaths/1,000 live births
Ethnic groups: black 52%, Arab 39%, Beja 6%, foreigners 2%, other 1%
permanent crops: 0%
permanent pastures: 46% **Religions:** Sunni Muslim 70% (in north), indigenous beliefs 25%, Christian 5% (mostly in south and Khartoum)
Languages: Arabic (official), Nubian, Ta Bedawie, diverse dialects of Nilotic, Nilo-Hamitic,

Data code: SU

Government type: transitional - previously ruling military junta; presidential and National Assembly elections held in March 1996; new constitution drafted by Presidential Committee, went into effect on 30 June 1998 after being approved in nationwide referendum

Capital: Khartoum

Administrative divisions: 26 states (wilayat, singular - wilayah); A'ali an Nil, Al Bahr al Ahmar, Al Buhayrat, Al Jazirah, Al Khartum, Al Qadarif, Al Wahdah, An Nil al Abyad, An Nil al Azraq, Ash

Shamaliyah, Bahr al Jabal, Gharb al Istiwa'iyah, Gharb Bahr al Ghazal, Gharb Darfur, Gharb Kurdufan, Janub Darfur, Janub Kurdufan, Junqali, Kassala, Nahr an Nil, Shamal Bahr al Ghazal, Shamal Darfur, Shamal Kurdufan, Sharq al Istiwa'iyah, Sinnar, Warab

Independence: 1 January 1956 (from Egypt and UK)
National holiday: Independence Day, 1 January (1956)

Constitution: 12 April 1973, suspended following coup of 6 April 1985; interim constitution of 10 October 1985 suspended following coup of 30 June 1989; new constitution implemented on 30 June 1998 partially suspended 12 December 1999 by President BASHIR

Legal system: based on English common law and Islamic law; as of 20 January 1991, the now defunct Revolutionary Command Council imposed Islamic law in the northern states; Islamic law applies to all residents of the northern states regardless of their religion; some separate religious courts; accepts compulsory ICJ jurisdiction, with reservations

Suffrage: NA years of age; universal, but noncompulsory

GOVERNMENT

Executive branch:

ote: the position of prime minister was reinstated in December 2016 as a result of the 2015-16 national dialogue process, and President al-BASHIR appointed BAKRI Hassan Salih to the position on 2 March 2017
chief of state: President Umar Hassan Ahmad al-BASHIR (since 16 October 1993); First Vice President & Prime Minister BAKRI Hassan Salih (first VP since 3 December 2013 and PM since 2 March 2017), Second Vice President Hasabu Mohamed ABDEL RAHMIN (since 3 December 2013); note - the president is both chief of state and head of government

head of government: President Umar Hassan Ahmad al-BASHIR (since 16 October 1993); First Vice President & Prime Minister BAKRI Hassan Salih (first VP since 3 December 2013 and PM since 2 March 2017), Second Vice President Hasabu Mohamed ABDEL RAHMIN (since 3 December 2013))

cabinet: Council of Ministers appointed by the president; note - the Natinal Congress Party or NCP, formerly the National Islamic Front or NIF, dominates al-BASHIR's cabinet
elections/appointments: president directly elected by absolute majority popular vote in 2 rounds if needed; last held on 13-16 April 2015 (next to be held in 2020); prime minister appointed by the president
election results: Umar Hassan Ahmad al-BASHIR reelected president; percent of vote - Umar Hassan Ahmad al-BASHIR (NCP) 94.1%, other (15 candidates) 5.9%

Legislative branch:
description: bicameral National Legislature consists of the Council of States or Majlis al-Wilayat (50 seats; members indirectly elected - 2 each by the 25 state legislatures to serve 6-year terms) and the National Assembly or Majlis Watani (426 seats; 213 members directly elected in single-seat constituencies by simple majority vote, 128 for women only directly elected by proportional representation vote, and 85 directly elected by proportional representation vote; members serve 6-year terms)

elections: last held on 13-15 April 2015 (next to be held in 2021)
election results: National Assembly - percent of vote by party - NA; seats by party - NCP 323, DUP 25, Democratic Unionist Party 15, other 44, independent 19
note: the mandate of the members from the south was terminated upon independence by the Republic of South Sudan effective 9 July 2011 and membership in Sudan's National Assembly was reduced to 354; it is unclear whether this total will be retained for the next election or whether the previous total of 450 will be reconstituted

Judicial branch:

highest court(s): National Supreme Court (consists of 70 judges organized into panels of 3 judges and includes 4 circuits that operate outside the capital); Constitutional Court (consists of 9 justices including the court president); note - the Constitutional Court resides outside the national judiciary

judge selection and term of office: National Supreme Court and Constitutional Court judges appointed by the president of the republic upon the recommendation of the National Judicial Service Commission, an independent body chaired by the chief justice of the republic and members including other judges and judicial and legal officials; Supreme Court judge tenure NA; Constitutional Court judges appointed for 7 years
subordinate courts: Court of Appeal; other national courts; public courts; district, town, and rural courts

Political parties and leaders:
Democratic Unionist Party or DUP
Democratic Unionist Party [Muhammad Uthman al-MIRGHANI]
Muslim Brotherhood or MB
National Congress Party or NCP [Umar Hassan al-BASHIR]
National Umma Party or UP [Saddiq al-MAHDI]
Popular Congress Party or PCP [Kamal UMARI]
Reform Now Party or RNP [Dr. Ghazi Salah al-DEEN]
Sudan National Front [Ali Mahmud HASANAYN]
Sudanese Communist Party or SCP [Mohammed Moktar Al-KHATEEB]
Sudanese Congress Party [Ibrahim Al-SHEIKH]
Unionist Movement Party or UMP

Political pressure groups and leaders:
Darfur rebel groups including the Justice and Equality Movement or JEM [Gibril Fidail IBRAHIM], Sudan Liberation Movement or SLM-AW [Abdel Wahid NUR, various factional leaders], Sudan Liberation Movement or SLM-MM [Minni Arkou MINAWI]
National Consensus Front or NCF [Farouq ABU ISSA]
Sudan People's Liberation Movement-North or SPLM-N [Yasir ARMAN]

International organization participation: ABEDA, ACP, AfDB, AFESD, AL, AMF, CAEU, CCC, ECA, FAO, G-77, IAEA, IBRD, ICAO, ICRM, IDA, IDB, IFAD, IFC, IFRCS, IGAD, ILO, IMF, IMO, Intelsat, Interpol, IOC, IOM, ISO (correspondent), ITU, NAM, OAU, OIC, PCA, UN, UNCTAD, UNESCO, UNHCR, UNIDO, UNU, UPU, WFTU, WHO, WIPO, WMO, WToO, WTrO (observer)

Diplomatic representation in the US:
chief of mission: Ambassador Mahdi Ibrahim MAHAMMAD (recalled to Khartoum in August 1998)
chancery: 2210 Massachusetts Avenue NW, Washington, DC 20008
telephone: (202) 338-8565
FAX: (202) 667-2406

Diplomatic representation from the US: US officials at the US Embassy in Khartoum were moved for security reasons in February 1996 and have been relocated to the US Embassies in Nairobi, Kenya and Cairo, Egypt; the US Embassy in Khartoum (located on Sharia Abdul Latif Avenue; mailing address - P. O. Box 699, Khartoum; APO AE 09829; telephone - [249] (11) 774611 or 774700; FAX - [249] (11) 774137) is kept open by local employees; the US Embassy in Nairobi, Kenya is located in the Interim Office Building on Mombasa Road, Nairobi; mailing address - P. O. Box 30137, Box 21A, Unit 64100, APO AE 09831; telephone - [254] (2) 751613; FAX - [254] (2) 743204; the US Embassy in Cairo, Egypt is located at (North Gate) 8, Kamel El-Din Salah Street, Garden City, Cairo; mailing address - Unit 64900, APO AE 09839-4900; telephone - [20] (2) 3557371; FAX - [20] (2) 3573200

Flag description: three equal horizontal bands of red (top), white, and black with a green isosceles triangle based on the hoist side

ECONOMY

Sudan has experienced protracted social conflict, civil war, and, in July 2011, the loss of three-quarters of its oil production due to the secession of South Sudan. The oil sector had driven much of Sudan's GDP growth since 1999. For nearly a decade, the economy boomed on the back of rising oil production, high oil prices, and significant inflows of foreign direct investment. Since the economic shock of South Sudan's secession, Sudan has struggled to stabilize its economy and make up for the loss of foreign exchange earnings.

The interruption of oil production in South Sudan in 2012 for over a year and the consequent loss of oil transit fees further exacerbated the fragile state of Sudan's economy. Ongoing conflicts in Southern Kordofan, Darfur, and the Blue Nile states, lack of basic infrastructure in large areas, and reliance by much of the population on subsistence agriculture, keep close to half of the population at or below the poverty line.

Sudan is also subject to comprehensive US sanctions. Sudan is attempting to develop non-oil sources of revenues, such as gold mining, while carrying out an austerity program to reduce expenditures. The world's largest exporter of gum Arabic, Sudan produces 75-80% of the world's total output. Agriculture continues to employ 80% of the work force.

Sudan introduced a new currency, still called the Sudanese pound, following South Sudan's secession, but the value of the currency has fallen since its introduction. Khartoum devalued the currency in June 2012 and November 2016, in both cases to accompany austerity measures that included gradually repealing fuel subsidies. Sudan also faces high inflation, which reached 20% on an annual basis in October 2016.

GDP (purchasing power parity):

$176.3 billion (2016 est.)
$171.1 billion (2015 est.)
$163.1 billion (est.)
note: data are in 2016 dollars
country comparison to the world: 67

GDP (official exchange rate):
$94.3 billion (2016 est.)

GDP - real growth rate:

3.1% (2016 est.)
4.9% (2015 est.)
1.6% (est.)
country comparison to the world: 92

GDP - per capita (PPP):
$4,500 (2016 est.)
$4,500 (2015 est.)
$4,400 (est.)
note: data are in 2016 dollars
country comparison to the world: 172

Gross national saving:
10.7% of GDP (2016 est.)
9.3% of GDP (2015 est.)
10% of GDP (est.)
country comparison to the world: 150

GDP - composition, by end use:
household consumption: 82.6%
government consumption: 7.4%
investment in fixed capital: 14.1%
investment in inventories: 1.3%
exports of goods and services: 7.1%
imports of goods and services: -12.5% (2016 est.)

GDP - composition, by sector of origin:
agriculture: 27.5%
industry: 20.7%
services: 51.8% (2016 est.)

Agriculture - products:
cotton, groundnuts (peanuts), sorghum, millet, wheat, gum Arabic, sugarcane, cassava (manioc, tapioca), mangoes, papaya, bananas, sweet potatoes, sesame seeds; animal feed, sheep and other livestock

Industries:
oil, cotton ginning, textiles, cement, edible oils, sugar, soap distilling, shoes, petroleum refining, pharmaceuticals, armaments, automobile/light truck assembly, milling

Industrial production growth rate:
2.5% (2016 est.)
country comparison to the world: 93

Labor force:
11.92 million (2007 est.)
country comparison to the world: 49

Labor force - by occupation:
agriculture: 80%
industry: 7%
services: 13% (1998 est.)

Unemployment rate:

13.6% (est.)
14.8% (est.)
country comparison to the world: 147

Population below poverty line:
46.5% (2009 est.)
Household income or consumption by percentage share:
lowest 10%: 2.7%
highest 10%: 26.7% (2009 est.)

Budget:
revenues: $7.301 billion
expenditures: $11.28 billion (2016 est.)

Taxes and other revenues:
7.7% of GDP (2016 est.)
country comparison to the world: 215

Budget surplus (+) or deficit (-):
-4.2% of GDP (2016 est.)
country comparison to the world: 142

Public debt:
68.8% of GDP (2016 est.)
68.9% of GDP (2015 est.)
country comparison to the world: 48

Fiscal year:
calendar year

Inflation rate (consumer prices):
17.6% (2016 est.)
17.3% (2015 est.)
country comparison to the world: 217

Stock of narrow money:
$9.711 billion (31 December 2016 est.)
$9.511 billion (31 December 2015 est.)
country comparison to the world: 83

Stock of broad money:
$15.64 billion (31 December 2016 est.)
$15.42 billion (31 December 2015 est.)
country comparison to the world: 97

Stock of domestic credit:
$17.41 billion (31 December 2016 est.)
$17.34 billion (31 December 2015 est.)
country comparison to the world: 93

Current account balance:
-$5.545 billion (2016 est.)
-$6.386 billion (2015 est.)
country comparison to the world: 172

Exports:
$3.703 billion (2016 est.)
$3.169 billion (2015 est.)
country comparison to the world: 118

Exports - commodities:
gold; oil and petroleum products; cotton, sesame, livestock, peanuts, gum Arabic, sugar

Exports - partners:
UAE 23.4%, Macau 23.3%, Saudi Arabia 20.8%, Egypt 9.6%

Imports:
$9.345 billion (2016 est.)
$8.368 billion (2015 est.)
country comparison to the world: 99

Imports - commodities:
foodstuffs, manufactured goods, refinery and transport equipment, medicines, chemicals, textiles, wheat

Imports - partners:
Macau 22.7%, UAE 8.8%, India 8.4%, Egypt 6%, Saudi Arabia 4.6%, Turkey 4.3 % (2015)
Reserves of foreign exchange and gold:
$167.3 million (31 December 2016 est.)
$173.5 million (31 December 2015 est.)
country comparison to the world: 161
Debt - external:
$51.1 billion (31 December 2016 est.)
$49.42 billion (31 December 2015 est.)
country comparison to the world: 62

Stock of direct foreign investment - at home:
$24.41 billion (31 December 2015 est.)
$24.41 billion (31 December 2015 est.)
country comparison to the world: 72

Exchange rates:
Sudanese pounds (SDG) per US dollar -
6.32 (2016 est.)
6.03 (2015 est.)
6.03 (est.)
5.74 (est.)
3.57 (2012 est.)

ENERGY

Electricity access:
population without electricity: 24,700,000
electrification - total population: 35%
electrification - urban areas: 63%

electrification - rural areas: 21%

Electricity - production:
12 billion kWh (est.)
country comparison to the world: 95

Electricity - consumption:
9.9 billion kWh (est.)
country comparison to the world: 93

Electricity - exports:
0 kWh (est.)
country comparison to the world: 117

Electricity - imports:
0 kWh (est.)
country comparison to the world: 131

Electricity - installed generating capacity:
3.7 million kW (est.)
country comparison to the world: 92
Electricity - from fossil fuels:
30.7% of total installed capacity (2012 est.)
country comparison to the world: 182

Electricity - from nuclear fuels:
0% of total installed capacity (2012 est.)
country comparison to the world: 64

Electricity - from hydroelectric plants:
66.3% of total installed capacity (2012 est.)
country comparison to the world: 31

Electricity - from other renewable sources:
3% of total installed capacity (2012 est.)
country comparison to the world: 72

Crude oil - production:
64,770 bbl/day (est.)
country comparison to the world: 50

Crude oil - exports:
2,060 bbl/day (est.)
country comparison to the world: 74

Crude oil - imports:
0 bbl/day (est.)
country comparison to the world: 109

Crude oil - proved reserves:
5 billion bbl (1 January 2016 es)
country comparison to the world: 25

Refined petroleum products - production:
88,180 bbl/day (est.)
country comparison to the world: 72

Refined petroleum products - consumption:
108,000 bbl/day (est.)
country comparison to the world: 79

Refined petroleum products - exports:
5,984 bbl/day (est.)
country comparison to the world: 92

Refined petroleum products - imports:
24,800 bbl/day (est.)
country comparison to the world: 109

Natural gas - production:
0 cu m (est.)
country comparison to the world: 121
Natural gas - consumption:
0 cu m (est.)
country comparison to the world: 196

Natural gas - exports:
0 cu m (est.)
country comparison to the world: 86

Natural gas - imports:
0 cu m (est.)
country comparison to the world: 176

Natural gas - proved reserves:
21.24 billion cu m (1 January 2016 es)
country comparison to the world: 75

Carbon dioxide emissions from consumption of energy:
14 million Mt (est.)
country comparison to the world: 93

COMMUNICATIONS

Telephones - fixed lines:
total subscriptions: 118,954
subscriptions per 100 inhabitants: less than 1 (July 2015 est.)
country comparison to the world: 102

Telephones - mobile cellular:
total: 27.939 million
subscriptions per 100 inhabitants: 77 (July 2015 est.)
country comparison to the world: 46

Telephone system:
general assessment: well-equipped system by regional standards and being upgraded; cellular communications started in 1996 and have expanded substantially with wide coverage of most major cities
domestic: consists of microwave radio relay, cable, fiber optic, radiotelephone communications, tropospheric scatter, and a domestic satellite system with 14 earth stations

international: country code - 249; linked to the EASSy and FLAG fiber-optic submarine cable systems; satellite earth stations - 1 Intelsat (Atlantic Ocean), 1 Arabsat

Broadcast media:
the Sudanese Government directly controls TV and radio, requiring that both media reflect government policies; TV has a permanent military censor; a private radio station is in operation

Internet country code:
.sd

Internet users:
total: 9.61 million
percent of population: 26.6% (July 2015 est.)
country comparison to the world: 48

TRANSPORTATION

Railways:
total: 5,311 km
narrow gauge: 4,595 km 1.067-m gauge; 716 km 1.6096-m gauge plantation line
note: the main line linking Khartoum to Port Sudan carries over two-thirds of Sudan's rail traffic

Highways:
total: 11,900 km
paved: 4,320 km
unpaved: 7,580 km

Waterways: 5,310 km navigable
Pipelines: refined products 815 km
Ports and harbors: Juba, Khartoum, Kusti, Malakal, Nimule, Port Sudan, Sawakin

Merchant marine:
total: 4 ships (1,000 GRT or over) totaling 38,093 GRT/49,727 DWT
ships by type: cargo 2, roll-on/roll-off 2

Airports: 61
Airports - with paved runways:
total: 12
over 3,047 m: 1
2,438 to 3,047 m: 8
1,524 to 2,437 m: 3
Airports - with unpaved runways:
total: 49
1,524 to 2,437 m: 15
914 to 1,523 m: 24
under 914 m: 10
Heliports: 1

MILITARY

Military branches:

Sudanese Armed Forces (SAF): Land Forces, Navy (includes Marines), Sudanese Air Force (Sikakh al-Jawwiya as-Sudaniya), Rapid Support Forces, Popular Defense Forces (2016)

Military service age and obligation:
18-33 years of age for male and female compulsory or voluntary military service; 1-2 year service obligation; a requirement that completion of national service was mandatory before entering public or private sector employment has been cancelled

TRANSNATIONAL ISSUES

Disputes - international:

the effects of Sudan's almost constant ethnic and rebel militia fighting since the mid-20th century have penetrated all of the neighboring states; Chad wishes to be a helpful mediator in resolving the Darfur conflict, and in 2010 established a joint border monitoring force with Sudan, which has helped to reduce cross-border banditry and violence; as of mid-2013, Chad, Egypt, Ethiopia, Israel, the Central African Republic, and South Sudan provided shelter for more than 600,000 Sudanese refugees; during the same period, Sudan, in turn, hosted about 115,000 Eritreans, 32,000 Chadians, and smaller numbers of Ethiopians and Central Africans; Sudan accuses Eritrea of supporting Sudanese rebel groups; efforts to demarcate the porous boundary with Ethiopia proceed slowly due to civil and ethnic fighting in eastern Sudan; Sudan claims but Egypt de facto administers security and economic development of the Halaib region north of the 22nd parallel boundary; periodic violent skirmishes with Sudanese residents over water and grazing rights persist among related pastoral populations along the border with the Central African Republic; South Sudan-Sudan boundary represents 1 January 1956 alignment, final alignment pending negotiations and demarcation; final sovereignty status of Abyei Area pending negotiations between South Sudan and Sudan

Refugees and internally displaced persons:

refugees (country of origin): 98,676 (Eritrea); 8,894 (Chad) (2015); 375,719 (South Sudan) (2017)

IDPs: 3,218,234 (civil war 1983-2005; ongoing conflict in Darfur region; government and rebel fighting along South Sudan border; inter-tribal clashes) (2016)

Trafficking in persons:

current situation: Sudan is a source, transit, and destination country for men, women, and children who are subjected to forced labor and sex trafficking; Sudanese women and girls, particularly those from rural areas or who are internally displaced, or refugees are vulnerable to domestic servitude in country, as well as domestic servitude and sex trafficking abroad; migrants from East and West Africa, South Sudan, Syria, and Nigeria smuggled into or through Sudan are vulnerable to exploitation; Ethiopian, Eritrean, and Filipina women are subjected to domestic servitude in Sudanese homes, and East African and possibly Thai women are forced into prostitution in Sudan; Sudanese children continue to be recruited and used as combatants by government forces and armed groups

tier rating: Tier 2 Watch List - Sudan does not fully comply with the minimum standards for the elimination of trafficking; however, it is making significant efforts to do so; the government increased its efforts to publically address and prevent trafficking, established a national anti-trafficking council, and began drafting a national action plan against trafficking; the government acknowledges cross-border trafficking but still denies the existence of forced labor, sex trafficking, and the recruitment of child soldiers domestically; law enforcement and judicial officials struggled to apply the national anti-trafficking law, often relying on other statutes with lesser penalties; authorities did not use systematic procedure to identify victims or refer them to care and relied on international organizations and domestic groups to provide protective services; some foreign victims were penalized for unlawful acts committed as a direct result of being trafficked, such as immigration or prostitution violations (2015)

LARGEST SUDANESE CITIES

ATBARA (Atbarah -- The main draw of Atbara is that it's near the Nile's Fifth Cataract. Plan only a few hours there -- enough time to see the cataract and the old steam locomotives that died and are rusting in railyards. 172 mi/277 km northeast of Khartoum.

DINDER NATIONAL PARK -- This medium-sized reserve 16,000 acres/6,475 hectares) is in eastern Sudan, on the border with Ethiopia. Lions, monkeys, giraffes, leopards, bushbucks, kudus, antelope and many kinds of birds can be seen there, but you'll need your own vehicle. The park's main season is January-April. 250 mi/400 km southeast of Khartoum.

DONGOLA (Dunqulah) -- On the Nile in northern Sudan, this town lies in a noted date-growing area. Across the river are the ruins of the Temple of Kawa. Dongola is served by bus and steamer (during winter months only). 284 mi/457 km northeast of Khartoum.

EL OBEID (Al Ubayyid) -- The self-proclaimed "gum arabic capital of the world," El Obeid is a fairly large desert city (pop. 140,000). It has a small history museum, two markets and, interestingly enough, one of the largest cathedrals in Africa (attend a Sunday service, even if you're not particularly religious). Plan one night. 228 mi/367 km southwest of Khartoum.

ERKOWIT -- Located in the beautiful Red Sea Hills, Erkowit was once a cool retreat for the British. There are, however, few original buildings left; it's just a place to go to get out of the heat for a while. The area is reached by private vehicle. 62 mi/100 km south of Port Sudan.

IMATONG MOUNTAINS (Matong) -- When reopened, this area on the border with Uganda will be worth a visit for its cool climate and interesting tribal people. Like Erkowit (see separate paragraph), Matong was also a British hill station. Currently, the region is in rebel territory and considered unsafe to visit. 80 mi/129 km southeast of Juba.

JEBEL MARRA (Jabal Marah) -- This splendid region of small mountains in Darfur Province (western Sudan) is popular with trekkers. In the center of Jebel Marra is an extinct volcanic crater with a lake called the "Eye of Jebel Marra." Most visitors pay for a truck ride to the area from Nyala (see separate paragraph). 60 mi/120 km northwest of Nyala.

JUBA -- Capital of Equatoria Province and terminus for Nile steamers, Juba (pop. 116,000) is a place to visit just to say you've been there. Although the government has control of the city, we would be wary of flights into the airport since rebels control the surrounding countryside (an Air Sudan jetliner was shot down in Juba a few years ago). 745 mi/ 1,200 km south of Khartoum.

KARIMA (Kuraymah) -- This small market town on the Nile north of Khartoum is near the ruins (small pyramids and a temple) of Jebel Bakal. Farther south in Kurru are other interesting antiquities (underground tombs with paintings). And just across the Nile by ferry are the ruins of Merowe (not to be confused with Meroe -- see separate paragraph), the site of the ancient capital of Napata. Karima cannot be reached by road, but it is on the railway. 210 mi/338 km north-northeast of Khartoum.

KASSALA -- Surrounded by strange jebels (rounded hills), Kassala (pop. 149,000) has an active suq (market) selling locally made handicrafts (jewelry, knives, swords). Women of the Rashida tribe (descendants of 19th-century immigrants from Saudi Arabia) make the silver jewelry. Kassala can be reached by bus from Khartoum or Port Sudan. 252 mi/405 km east of Khartoum.

KHARTOUM -- The arid capital city (pop. 800,000) of Sudan, at the junction of the White Nile and Blue Nile, merits a stay of at least two nights. It's an interesting place to walk around, snoop in shops and people-watch. Also take a ride on the Nile (in Khartoum or in nearby Omdurman -- see separate paragraph), then visit the National Museum (antiquities from around the country), ethnological museum (tribal artifacts), natural-history museum (local bird and wild-game displays) and Sunt Forest (near the Hilton -- a favorite spot for picnics). The most fascinating sight is the juncture of the White and Blue Niles. Al Mogran Family Park, an amusement park, is located at the point where the rivers flow together. After spending time at the confluence, take a ferry to Tuti Island for a look at a typical rural village. Consider excursions to Jebel Aulia Dam (great spot for bird-watching, fishing, picnics and people-watching) and the Sabaloka Gorge (the Nile's Sixth Cataract -- it's a three- or four-hour drive each way). Other trips -- by four-wheel-drive vehicles or local buses -- can be made to the ruins at Meroe and Shendi; they can be seen on a day trip, but we really recommend taking them in during a three-day trip.

KOSTI (Kusti) -- South of Khartoum on a new road, Kosti sits in an area that's usually considered safe. Visit the Kenana Sugar Project, as well as the Mahdi's Mosque on nearby Gezira Aba Island. Try the local fish from the Nile at one of the restaurants. The Nile steamer that used to travel from Kosti to Juba is not currently in service. 193 mi/310 km by road south of Khartoum.

MEROE -- On the east bank of the Nile northeast of Shendi, these ruins of pyramids, temples and palaces are remnants of the Meroitic era (350 BC to AD 350). The kingdom was influenced by Egyptian art and religion, but it became isolated, developing its own script and art. After weathering attacks by several tribes, the city was destroyed by the Christian kingdom of Axum (Ethiopia). Between the railway and the Nile, you'll see ruins of the Amon Temple, and 1 mi/2 km east of Meroe is the Temple of the Sun. The pyramids lie 3 mi/5 km from town. The nearest train station is in Kabushiya. 44 mi/70 km north of Shendi.

NUBA MOUNTAINS -- This region southwest of Khartoum is in an area that may be even more dangerous to visit, so check locally before venturing in. It's a beautiful region, and the resident Nuba tribe has managed to maintain many of its traditional ways (although the government has a campaign under way to clothe them). If the opportunity arises, see one of the local dances (and, if you have the stomach, one of their rather violent wrestling matches). Among the more interesting towns in the region are Rashad, Heiban, Kadugli and El Odaiya. Anyone visiting this area must have a lot of time; the roads are rough and transportation is unreliable. Take supplies, as food is scarce at some times of the year. 75 mi/120 km southeast of El Obeid.

YALA -- At the end of the western railway from Khartoum, Nyala is the nearest rail station to Jebel Marra (see separate paragraph). Pack animals may be purchased there for treks through Jebel Marra. There's also a government rest house. 569 mi/915 km west-southwest of Khartoum.

OMDURMAN -- The holiest site in Sudan is located across the Nile from Khartoum. Omdurman (pop. 526,000) makes a nice day trip to see the site of the Mahdi's Tomb (nonbelievers aren't permitted to enter), as well as Khalifa's House (relics of the Mahdi and British Sudan). The Old Dervishes Fort Museum (exhibits from colonial times) and a huge, fascinating market (excellent silver jewelry) are worth seeing. Don't miss the Hamed al Niel Mosque (Sufi "whirling" dervishes dance there an hour before sunset on Fridays). Omdurman presents quite a contrast to modern Khartoum. At the base of the Nile bridge, boat builders can be seen plying their trade. We consider Omdurman a must-see. 6 mi/10 km northwest of Khartoum.

PORT SUDAN -- The nation's principal port (pop. 207,000) on the Red Sea, Port Sudan doesn't have many attractions, though there are some good beaches. The ancient port of Suakin (see separate paragraph) lies 35 mi/58 km south, and the nearby resort of Arusa is a good place to snorkel. 411 mi/661 km northeast of Khartoum.

SHENDI (Shandi) -- On the Nile northeast of Khartoum, Shendi was a large 18th-century market town. Now it's mainly visited on the way to the Meroitic ruins of the Naqa and Musawwarat temples. Frequent bus service departs Khartoum. 109 mi/175 km by road northeast of Khartoum.

SHOWAK -- In eastern Sudan, Showak is the Sudanese headquarters of the United Nations High Commission for Refugees. Many refugee settlements may be found in this area. 85 mi/137 km southwest of Kassala.

SUAKIN -- This ancient Red Sea port is now inhabited mostly by cats. The town, best visited as a trip from Port Sudan, is on an island connected to the mainland by a causeway. Of interest are the ruined buildings, made of coral. 40 mi/64 km south of Port Sudan.

WADI HALFA -- The transit point of Wadi Halfa is to be endured, rather than enjoyed, while entering or leaving Egypt. There's really not much to see; the "highlight" of the area is a Chinese fish-processing plant. 578 mi/930 km by road north of Khartoum.

WAU -- Founded at its present site by the French in the 1890s, this capital of Bhar El-Ghazal Province (pop. 116,000) sits at the end of the southwest branch of the railway. Wau is in a largely Dinka tribal area that's been the longtime center of famine and war. There's a Catholic mission in Wau. 310 mi/500 km northwest of Juba.

IMPORTANT INFORMATION FOR UNDERSTANDING SUDAN

PROFILE

Geography
Area: 1.8 million sq. km. (695,000 sq. mi.); the third-largest country in Africa (after having been the largest until the July 2011 secession of South Sudan) and slightly less than a quarter the size of the continental U.S.
Cities: *Capital*--Khartoum (pop. 1.4 million). *Other cities*--Omdurman (2.1 million), Port Sudan (pop. 450,000), Kassala, Kosti.
Land boundaries: Central African Republic, Chad, Egypt, Eritrea, Ethiopia, Libya, and South Sudan.
Terrain: Generally flat with mountains in east and west. Khartoum is situated at the confluence of the Blue and White Nile Rivers. The southernmost region is inundated during the annual floods of the Nile River system.
Climate: Desert and savanna in the north and central regions and tropical in the south.

People
Nationality: *Noun and adjective* (sing. and pl.)--Sudanese.
Population (July 2011 est.): 33,419,625; 49% urban.
Annual population growth rate (2011 est.): 2.8%.
Ethnic groups: Sudanese Arab (approximately 70%, including Shaigiyya, Ja'alin, Misseriya,

Kababish and Rizegat), Fur, Zaghawa, Massalit, Beja, Nuba, and Dinka Ngok.
Religions: Islam (official), indigenous beliefs, Christianity.
Languages: Arabic (official), English (official), tribal languages (Nubian, Ta Bedawie, Fur, Zaghawa, Masalit).
Education: *Years compulsory*--8. *Attendance*--35%-40%. *Literacy*--69%.
Health: *Infant mortality rate*--71/1,000. *Life expectancy*--55.42 years.
Work force: *Agriculture*--80%; *industry and commerce*--7%; *government*--13%.

Government
Independence: January 1, 1956.
Type: Constitutional democracy in form. The last national elections took place from April 11-15, 2010. The next national elections are scheduled for 2014.
Constitution: The Interim National Constitution was adopted on July 6, 2005. It was drafted by the National Constitutional Review Commission, as mandated by the January 2005 Comprehensive Peace Agreement (CPA). The government is establishing a process to write a new constitution following the end of the CPA period.
Branches: *Executive*--Executive authority is held by the president, who also is the prime minister, head of state, head of government, and commander in chief of the armed forces. The executive branch also includes a first vice president and a vice president. As stipulated by the Doha Document for Peace in Darfur, the second vice president position is held by a person of Darfuri origin. *Legislative*--National Legislature. The National Assembly, the lower house, has 354 elected members. There is also an upper house, the Council of States, which is composed of two representatives from each of the nation's 15 states, and two observers from the Abyei Area. *Judicial*--High Court, Minister of Justice, Attorney General, civil and special tribunals.
Administrative subdivisions: Fifteen states, most with an elected governor, along with a state cabinet and elected state legislative assembly. States are divided into districts, with 133 districts comprising the 15 states.
Political parties: Seventy-two parties registered to take part in the April 2010 elections. Following the secession, there are many political parties, 70 of which are registered. All political parties were banned following the June 30, 1989 military coup. Political associations, taking the place of parties, were authorized in 2000. Some parties are in self-imposed exile. The principal national parties are the National Congress Party (NCP) and the Sudan People's Liberation Movement-North (SPLM-N), which is an offshoot of the South Sudan-based party and is currently banned by the Sudanese Government.
Central government budget (2010 est.): $13.35 billion.
Defense (2005 est.): 3% of GDP.

Economy
Natural resources: Modest reserves of oil, natural gas, gold, iron ore, copper, and other industrial metals.
Agriculture: *Products*--cotton, peanuts, sorghum, sesame seeds, gum arabic, sugarcane, millet, livestock.
Industry: *Types*--motor vehicle assembly, cement, cotton, edible oils and sugar refining.
Trade: *Exports* (2009 est.)--$10.29 billion f.o.b.: crude oil and petroleum products, cotton, gold, sorghum, peanuts, gum arabic, sugar, meat, hides, live animals, and sesame seeds. *Major markets*--China, Japan, Indonesia, Egypt, United Arab Emirates, Saudi Arabia, Malaysia, and South Korea. Imports (2010 est.)--$9.176 billion f.o.b.: oil and petroleum products, oil pipeline, pumping and refining equipment, chemical products and equipment, wheat and wheat flour, transport equipment, foodstuffs, tea, agricultural inputs and machinery, industrial inputs and manufactured goods. *Major suppliers*--European Union, China, Malaysia, Saudi Arabia, Egypt, United Arab Emirates, and India.
Fiscal year: January 1-December 31.

PEOPLE

Sudan's population is one of the most diverse on the African continent. Within two distinct major cultures--Arab and sub-Saharan African--there are hundreds of ethnic and tribal subdivisions and language groups, which make effective collaboration among them a major political challenge.

The Sudanese are predominantly Arabic-speaking Muslims, though many also use a non-Arabic mother tongue--e.g., Nubian, Beja, Fur, Nuban, Ingessana, etc. Among these are several distinct tribal groups: the Kababish of northern Kordofan, a camel-raising people; the Ja'alin and Shaigiyya groups of settled tribes along the rivers; the semi-nomadic Baggara of Kordofan and Darfur; the Hamitic Beja in the Red Sea area and Nubians of the northern Nile areas, some of whom have been resettled on the Atbara River; and the Nuba of southern Kordofan and Fur in the western reaches of the country. Following the secession of South Sudan, there remain some small factions of Dinka (particularly the Dinka Ngok in Abyei), Shilluk, and the Nuer from the Nilotic tribes.

According to post-secession figures based on census results released in early 2009, Sudan's population has reached an estimated 33.4 million.

HISTORY

Sudan was a collection of small, independent kingdoms and principalities from the beginning of the Christian era until 1820-21, when Egypt conquered and unified the northern portion of the country. However, neither the Egyptian nor the Mahdist state (1883-1898) had any effective control of the southern region outside of a few garrisons.

In 1881, a religious leader named Muhammad ibn Abdalla proclaimed himself the Mahdi, or the "expected one," and began a religious crusade to unify the tribes in western and central Sudan. His followers took on the name "Ansars" (the followers) which they continue to use today and are associated with the single largest political grouping, the Umma Party, led by a descendant of the Mahdi, Sadiq al Mahdi.

Taking advantage of dissatisfaction resulting from Ottoman-Egyptian exploitation and maladministration, the Mahdi led a nationalist revolt culminating in the fall of Khartoum in 1885. The Mahdi died shortly thereafter, but his state survived until overwhelmed by an invading Anglo-Egyptian force under Lord Kitchener in 1898. While nominally administered jointly by Egypt and Britain, Britain exercised control, formulated policies, and supplied most of the top administrators.

Independence

In February 1953, the United Kingdom and Egypt concluded an agreement providing for Sudanese self-government and self-determination. The transitional period toward independence began with the inauguration of the first parliament in 1954. With the consent of the British and Egyptian Governments, Sudan achieved independence on January 1, 1956, under a provisional constitution. This constitution was silent on two crucial issues for southern leaders--the secular or Islamic character of the state and its federal or unitary structure. However, the Arab-led Khartoum government reneged on promises to southerners to create a federal system, which led to a mutiny by southern army officers that launched 17 years of civil war (1955-72).

Post-Independence

Sudan has been at war with itself for more than three-quarters of its existence. Since independence, protracted conflict rooted in deep cultural and religious differences have slowed Sudan's economic and political development and forced massive internal displacement of its people. Northerners, who have traditionally controlled the country, have sought to unify it along the lines of Arabism and Islam despite the opposition of non-Muslims, southerners, and marginalized peoples in the west and east. The resultant civil strife affected Sudan's neighbors, as they alternately sheltered fleeing refugees or served as operating bases for rebel movements.

In 1958, General Ibrahim Abboud seized power and pursued a policy of Arabization and Islamicization for both North and South Sudan that strengthened Southern opposition. General Abboud was overthrown in 1964 and a civilian caretaker government assumed control. Southern leaders eventually divided into two factions, those who advocated a federal solution and those who argued for self-determination, a euphemism for secession since it was assumed the south would vote for independence if given the choice.

Until 1969, there was a succession of governments that proved unable either to agree on a permanent constitution or to cope with problems of factionalism, economic stagnation, and ethnic dissidence. These regimes were dominated by "Arab" Muslims who asserted their Arab-Islamic agenda and refused any kind of self-determination for southern Sudan.

In May 1969, a group of communist and socialist officers led by Colonel Gaafar Muhammad Nimeiri, seized power. A month after coming to power, Nimeiri proclaimed socialism (instead of Islamism) for the country and outlined a policy of granting autonomy to the South. Nimeiri in turn was the target of a coup attempt by communist members of the government. It failed and Nimeiri ordered a massive purge of communists. This alienated the Soviet Union, which withdrew its support.

Already lacking support from the Muslim parties he had chased from power, Nimeiri could no longer count on the communist faction. Having alienated the right and the left, Nimeiri turned to the south as a way of expanding his limited powerbase. He pursued peace initiatives with Sudan's hostile neighbors, Ethiopia and Uganda, signing agreements that committed each signatory to withdraw support for the other's rebel movements. He then initiated negotiations with the southern rebels and signed an agreement in Addis Ababa in 1972 that granted a measure of autonomy to the South. Southern support helped him put down two coup attempts, one initiated by officers from the western regions of Darfur and Kordofan who wanted for their region the same privileges granted to the south.

However, the Addis Ababa Agreement had no support from either the secularist or Islamic Northern parties. Nimeiri concluded that their lack of support was more threatening to his regime than lack of support from the south so he announced a policy of national reconciliation with all the religious opposition forces. These parties did not feel bound to observe an agreement they perceived as an obstacle to furthering an Islamist state. The scales against the peace agreement were tipped in 1979 when Chevron discovered oil in the south. Northern pressure built to abrogate those provisions of the peace treaty granting financial autonomy to the south. In 1983, Nimeiri abolished the Southern region, declared Arabic the official language of the South (instead of English) and transferred control of Southern armed forces to the central government. This was effectively a unilateral abrogation of the 1972 peace treaty. The second Sudan civil war began in January 1983 when southern soldiers mutinied rather than follow orders transferring them to the North.

In September 1983, as part of an Islamicization campaign, President Nimeiri announced that traditional Islamic punishments drawn from Shari'a (Islamic law) would be incorporated into the penal code. This was controversial even among Muslim groups. Amputations for theft and public lashings for alcohol possession became common. Southerners and other non-Muslims living in the north were also subjected to these punishments.

In April 1985, while out of the country, Nimeiri was overthrown by a popular uprising in Khartoum provoked by a collapsing economy, the war in the south, and political repression. General Suwar al-Dahab headed the transitional government. One of its first acts was to suspend the 1983 constitution and disband Nimeiri's Sudan Socialist Union.

Elections were held in April 1986, and a civilian government took power. There were tentative moves towards negotiating peace with the south. However, any proposal to exempt the south from Islamic law was unacceptable to those who supported Arabic supremacy. In 1989, an Islamic army faction led by General Umar al-Bashir mounted a coup and installed the National Islamic Front. The new government's commitment to an Islamic state intensified the North-South conflict.

The Bashir government combined internal political repression with international Islamist activism. It supported radical Islamist groups in Algeria and supported Iraq's invasion of Kuwait. Khartoum was established as a base for militant Islamist groups: radical movements and terrorist organizations like Osama Bin Laden's al Qaida were provided a safe haven and logistical aid in return for financial support. In 1996, the UN imposed sanctions on Sudan for alleged connections to the assassination attempt on Egyptian President Hosni Mubarak.

Meanwhile, the 1990s saw a growing sense of alienation in the western and eastern regions of Sudan from the Arab center. The rulers in Khartoum were seen as less and less responsive to the concerns and grievances of both Muslim and non-Muslim populations across the country. Alienation from the "Arab" center caused various groups to grow sympathetic to the southern rebels led by the Sudan People's Liberation Movement/Army (SPLM/A), and in some cases, prompted them to flight alongside it.

The policy of the ruling regime toward the South was to pursue the war against the rebels while manipulating tribal divisions. Ultimately, this policy resulted in the rebels' uniting under the leadership of John Garang. During this period, the SPLM/A rebels also enjoyed support from Ethiopia, Eritrea, and Uganda. The Bashir government's "Pan-Islamic" foreign policy, which provided support for neighboring radical Islamist groups, was partly responsible for this support for the rebels.

The 1990s saw a succession of regional efforts to broker an end to the Sudanese civil war. Beginning in 1993, the leaders of Eritrea, Ethiopia, Uganda, and Kenya pursued a peace initiative for Sudan under the auspices of the Intergovernmental Authority for Development (IGAD), but results were mixed. Despite that record, the IGAD initiative promulgated the 1994 Declaration of Principles (DOP) that aimed to identify the essential elements necessary to a just and comprehensive peace settlement; *i.e.*, the relationship between religion and the state, power sharing, wealth sharing, and the right of self-determination for the south. The Sudanese Government did not sign the DOP until 1997 after major battlefield losses to the SPLA. That year, the Khartoum government signed a series of agreements with rebel factions under the banner of "Peace from Within." These included the Khartoum, Nuba Mountains, and Fashoda Agreements that ended military conflict between the government and significant rebel factions. Many of those leaders then moved to Khartoum where they assumed marginal roles in the central government or collaborated with the government in military engagements against the SPLA. These three agreements paralleled the terms and conditions of the IGAD agreement, calling for a degree of autonomy for the south and the right of self-determination.

End to the Civil War

In July 2002, the Government of Sudan and the SPLM/A reached a historic agreement on the role of state and religion and the right of southern Sudan to self-determination. This agreement, known as the Machakos Protocol, named after the Kenyan town where the peace talks were held, concluded the first round of talks sponsored by IGAD. The effort was mediated by retired Kenyan General Lazaro Sumbeiywo. Peace talks resumed and continued during 2003, with discussions focusing on wealth sharing and three contested areas.

On November 19, 2004, the Government of Sudan and the SPLM/A signed a declaration committing themselves to conclude a final comprehensive peace agreement by December 31,

2004. The declaration came in the context of an extraordinary session of the United Nations Security Council (UNSC) in Nairobi, Kenya--only the fifth time the Council had met outside of New York since its founding. At this session, the UNSC unanimously adopted Resolution 1574, which welcomed the commitment of the government and the SPLM/A to achieve agreement by the end of 2004, and underscored the international community's intention to assist the Sudanese people and support implementation of the comprehensive peace agreement. In keeping with their commitment to the UNSC, the Government of Sudan and the SPLM/A initialed the final elements of the comprehensive agreement on December 31, 2004. The two parties formally signed the Comprehensive Peace Agreement (CPA) on January 9, 2005. The U.S. and the international community welcomed this decisive step forward for peace in Sudan.

In January 2011, the South voted in a referendum to secede from Sudan. Ninety-eight percent of voters cast ballots for secession in mostly orderly and peaceful balloting. International and national observers hailed the referendum process as consistent with international standards and representing the free expression of voters. On July 9, 2011, the Republic of South Sudan officially declared independence, seceding from Sudan. Several violent conflicts flared up in 2011, including continued conflict in Darfur and in the three border states of Abyei, Southern Kordofan, and Blue Nile (the "Three Areas").

GOVERNMENT AND POLITICAL CONDITIONS

Officially, the politics of Sudan takes place in the framework of a federal presidential representative democratic republic, where the President of Sudan is head of state, head of government and commander-in-chief of the Sudan People's Armed Forces in a multi-party system. Legislative power is vested in both the government and the bicameral parliament—the National Legislature, with its National Assembly (lower chamber) and the Council of States (upper chamber). The judiciary is independent and obtained by the Constitutional Court. It is part of the Northern Africa grouping of the UN geoscheme.

However, following the Second Sudanese Civil War (1983–2005) and the now-low-scale war in Darfur, Sudan is widely recognized as an authoritarian state where all effective political power is obtained by President Omar al-Bashir and the ruling National Congress Party (NCP).

In 1993, Sudan was transformed into an Islamic authoritarian one-party state as al-Bashir abolished the Revolutionary Command Council and created the National Islamic Front (NIF) with a new parliament and government obtained solely by members of the NIF. At the same time, the structure of regional administration was replaced by the creation of twenty-six states, each headed by a governor, thus making Sudan a federal republic.

Executive posts are divided between the NCP, the SPLA, the Sudanese Eastern Front and factions of the Umma Party and Democratic Unionist Party (DUP).

According to the new 2005 constitution, the bicameral National Legislature is the official Sudanese parliament and is divided between two chambers—the National Assembly, a lower house with 450 seats, and the Council of States, an upper house with 50 seats. Thus the parliament consists of 500 appointed members altogether, where all are indirectly elected by state legislatures to serve six-year terms.

Despite his international arrest warrant, al-Bashir was a candidate in the 2010 Sudanese presidential election, the first democratic election with multiple political parties participating in twenty-four years. In the build-up to the vote, Sudanese pro-democracy activists say they faced intimidation by the government and the International Crisis Group reported that the ruling party had gerrymandered electoral districts. A few days before the vote, the main opposition candidate, Yasir Arman from the SPLM, withdrew from the race. The U.S.-based Carter Center, which helped monitor the elections, described the vote tabulation process as "highly chaotic, non-transparent and vulnerable to electoral manipulation." Al-Bashir was declared the winner of the election with sixty-eight percent of the vote.

SHARIA LAW

The legal system in Sudan is based on Islamic Sharia law. The 2005 Naivasha Agreement, ending the civil war between north and south Sudan, established some protections for non-Muslims in Khartoum. Sudan's application of Sharia law is geographically inconsistent.

Stoning remains a judicial punishment in Sudan. Between 2009 and 2012, several women were sentenced to death by stoning. Flogging is a legal punishment. Between 2009 and 2014, many people were sentenced to 40–100 lashes. In August 2014, several Sudanese men died in custody after being flogged. 53 Christians were flogged in 2001. Sudan's public order law allows police officers to publicly whip women who are accused of public indecency.

Crucifixion is a legal punishment. In 2002, 88 people were sentenced to death for crimes relating to murder, armed robbery, and participating in ethnic clashes, Amnesty International wrote that they could be executed by either hanging or crucifixion.

International Court of Justice jurisdiction is accepted, though with reservations. Under the terms of the Naivasha Agreement, Islamic law did not apply in South Sudan. Since the secession of South Sudan there is some uncertainty as to whether Sharia law will now apply to the non-Muslim minorities present in Sudan, especially because of contradictory statements by al-Bashir on the matter.

The judicial branch of the Sudanese government consists of a Constitutional Court of nine justices, the National Supreme Court, the Court of Cassation, and other national courts; the National Judicial Service Commission provides overall management for the judiciary.

FOREIGN RELATIONS

Sudan has had a troubled relationship with many of its neighbours and much of the international community, owing to what is viewed as its radical Islamic stance. For much of the 1990s, Uganda, Kenya and Ethiopia formed an ad-hoc alliance called the "Front Line States" with support from the United States to check the influence of the National Islamic Front government. The Sudanese Government supported anti-Ugandan rebel groups such as the Lord's Resistance Army (LRA).

As the National Islamic Front regime in Khartoum gradually emerged as a real threat to the region and the world, the U.S. began to list Sudan on its list of State Sponsors of Terrorism. After the US listed Sudan as a state sponsor of terrorism, the NIF decided to develop relations with Iraq, and later Iran, the two most controversial countries in the region.

From the mid-1990s, Sudan gradually began to moderate its positions as a result of increased U.S. pressure following the 1998 U.S. embassy bombings, in Tanzania and Kenya, and the new development of oil fields previously in rebel hands. Sudan also has a territorial dispute with Egypt over the Hala'ib Triangle. Since 2003, the foreign relations of Sudan had centered on the support for ending the Second Sudanese Civil War and condemnation of government support for militias in the war in Darfur.

Sudan has extensive economic relations with China. China obtains ten percent of its oil from Sudan. According to a former Sudanese government minister, China is Sudan's largest supplier of arms.

In December 2005, Sudan became one of the few states to recognize Moroccan sovereignty over Western Sahara.

In 2015, Sudan participated in the Saudi Arabian-led intervention in Yemen against the Shia Houthis and forces loyal to former President Ali Abdullah Saleh, who was deposed in the 2011 uprising.

ARMED FORCES

The Sudan People's Armed Forces is the regular forces of Sudan and is divided into five branches: the Sudanese Army, Sudanese Navy (including the Marine Corps), Sudanese Air Force, Border Patrol and the Internal Affairs Defense Force, totalling about 200,000 troops. The military of Sudan has become a well-equipped fighting force, thanks to increasing local production of heavy and advanced arms. These forces are under the command of the National Assembly and its strategic principles include defending Sudan's external borders and preserving internal security.

Since the Darfur crisis in 2004, safe-keeping the central government from the armed resistance and rebellion of paramilitary rebel groups such as the Sudan People's Liberation Army (SPLA), the Sudanese Liberation Army (SLA) and the Justice and Equality Movement (JEM) have been important priorities. While not official, the Sudanese military also uses nomad militias, the most prominent being the Janjaweed, in executing a counter-insurgency war. Somewhere between 200,000 and 400,000 people have died in the violent struggles.

INTERNATIONAL ORGANIZATIONS IN SUDAN

Several UN agents are operating in Sudan such as the World Food Program (WFP); the Food and Agriculture Organization of the United Nation (FAO); the United Nations Development Program (UNDP); the United Nations Industrial Development Organizations (UNIDO); the United Nations Children Fund (UNICEF); the United Nations High Commissioner for Refugees (UNHCR); the United Nations Mine Service (UNMAS), the United Nations Office for the Coordination of Humanitarian Affairs (OCHA) and the World Bank. Also present is the International Organization for Migration (IOM).

Since Sudan has experienced civil war for many years, many Non-Governmental Organisations (NGOs) are also involved in humanitarian efforts to help internally displaced people. The NGOs are working in every corner of Sudan, especially in the southern part and western parts. During the civil war, international nongovernmental organizations such as the Red Cross were operating mostly in the south but based in the capital Khartoum. The attention of NGOs shifted shortly after the war broke out in the western part of Sudan known as Darfur. The most visible organization in South Sudan is the Operation Lifeline Sudan (OLS) consortium.

Even though most of the international organizations are substantially concentrated in both South Sudan and Darfur region, some of them are working in the northern part as well. For example, the United Nations Industrial Development Organization is successfully operating in Khartoum, the capital. It is mainly funded by the European Union and recently opened more vocational training. The Canadian International Development Agency is operating largely in northern Sudan.

HUMAN RIGHTS

Since 1983, a combination of civil war and famine has taken the lives of nearly 2 million people in Sudan. It is estimated that as many as 200,000 people had been taken into slavery during the Second Sudanese Civil War.

Sudan ranks 172 of 180 countries in terms of freedom of the press according to Reporters Without Borders, yet more curbs of press freedom to report official corruption are planned.

Muslims who convert to Christianity can face the death penalty for apostasy, see Persecution of Christians in Sudan and the death sentence against Mariam Yahia Ibrahim Ishag (who actually was raised as Christian). According to a 2013 UNICEF report, 88% of women in Sudan had undergone female genital mutilation. Sudan's Personal Status law on marriage has been criticized for restricting women's rights and allowing child marriage. Evidence suggests that support for female genital mutilation remains high, especially among rural and less well educated groups, although it has been declining in recent years. Homosexuality is illegal and is a capital offense in Sudan.

DARFUR

A letter dated 14 August 2006, from the executive director of Human Rights Watch found that the Sudanese government is both incapable of protecting its own citizens in Darfur and unwilling to do so, and that its militias are guilty of crimes against humanity. The letter added that these human-rights abuses have existed since 2004. Some reports attribute part of the violations to the rebels as well as the government and the Janjaweed. The U.S. State Department's human-rights report issued in March 2007 claims that "*[a]*ll parties to the conflagration committed serious abuses, including widespread killing of civilians, rape as a tool of war, systematic torture, robbery and recruitment of child soldiers."

Over 2.8 million civilians have been displaced and the death toll is estimated at 300,000 killed. Both government forces and militias allied with the government are known to attack not only civilians in Darfur, but also humanitarian workers. Sympathizers of rebel groups are arbitrarily detained, as are foreign journalists, human-rights defenders, student activists and displaced people in and around Khartoum, some of whom face torture. The rebel groups have also been accused in a report issued by the U.S. government of attacking humanitarian workers and of killing innocent civilians. According to UNICEF, in 2008, there were as many as 6,000 child soldiers in Darfur.

DISPUTED AREAS AND ZONES OF CONFLICT

- In mid-April 2012, the South Sudanese army captured the Heglig oil field from Sudan.
- In mid-April 2012 the Sudanese army recaptured Heglig.
- Kafia Kingi and Radom National Park was a part of Bahr el Ghazal in 1956. Sudan has recognized South Sudan independence according to the borders for 1 January 1956.
- The Abyei Area is disputed region between Sudan and South Sudan. It is currently under Sudan rule.
- The states of South Kurdufan and Blue Nile are to hold "popular consultations" to determine their constitutional future within the Sudan.
- The Hala'ib triangle is disputed region between Sudan and Egypt. It is currently under Egyptian administration.
- Bir Tawil is a terra nullius occurring on the border between Egypt and Sudan, claimed by neither state.

REGIONAL BODIES AND AREAS OF CONFLICT

In addition to the states, there also exist regional administrative bodies established by peace agreements between the central government and rebel groups.

- The Darfur Regional Authority was established by the Darfur Peace Agreement to act as a co-ordinating body for the states that make up the region of Darfur.
- The Eastern Sudan States Coordinating Council was established by the Eastern Sudan Peace Agreement between the Sudanese Government and the rebel Eastern Front to act as a coordinating body for the three eastern states.
- The Abyei Area, located on the border between South Sudan and the Republic of the Sudan, currently has a special administrative status and is governed by an Abyei Area Administration. It was due to hold a referendum in 2011 on whether to join an independent South Sudan or remain part of the Republic of the Sudan.

PRINCIPAL GOVERNMENT OFFICIALS - CURRENT NATIONAL MINISTERS

Office	Incumbent	Website
Prime Minister		
First Lieu. General S.G Bakri Hassan Saleh	Minister of the Presidency Affairs	http://www.presidency.gov.sd/
Dr. Luka Biong	Minister of the Council of Ministers	http://www.sudan.gov.sd/
Lieu. General. Ahmed Awad Ibn Auf	Minister of National Defense	http://www.mod.gov.sd
Mr. Ibrahim Mahmoud Hamad	Minister of Interior	http://moi.gov.sd/
Mr. Ibrahim Ghandour	Minister of Foreign Affairs	http://www.mfa.gov.sd/
Mr. Mohammed Bushara Dousa	Minister of Justice	http://www.moj.gov.sd/
Mr. Ali Mahmoud Abdul-Rasool	Minister of Finance & National Economy	http://www.mof.gov.sd/
	Minister of Science and Communication	http://msc.gov.sd/ (down)
Mr. Kamal Abdul-Latif Abdul-Rahim	Minister of Human Resources Development	
Dr. Abdul-Halim Ismail Al- Mutaafi	Minister of Agriculture	http://agri-khs.gov.sd/indexen.php
Dr. Awad Ahmed Al- Jaz	Minister of Industry	
Dr. Azhari Al-Tigani Awad Al-Sayid	Minister of Guidance and Endowments	
Mr. Kamal Mohamed Obeid	Minister of Information	http://mininfo.gov.sd/en
Kamaladdin	Minister of International	

Hassan Ali	Cooperation	
Mr. Lual Achuil Deng	Minister of Petroleum	
Dr. Peter Adok Nyaba	Minister of High Education & Scientific Research	
Mr. Farah Mustafa Abdalla	Minister of Public Education	http://moekh.gov.sd/en/
Mr. Kamal Ali Mohammad Ahmed	Minister of Irrigation & Water Resources	http://wre.gov.sd/en/
Eng Mr. Osama Abdalla Mohamed Al - Hassan	Minister of Electricity	http://wre.gov.sd/en/
	Minister of Dams	http://diu.gov.sd/en/
Mr. Eissa Bashari Mohamed	Minister of Science & Technology	
Mr. Al - Samawa'al Khalafalla Al-Quraish	Minister of Culture	
Dr. Abdalla Tiya Juma	Minister of Health	http://www.fmoh.gov.sd/ (down)
Ustaza\ Amira Al-Fadil Mohamed Ahmed	Minister of Welfare & Social Security	
Mr. Haj Magid Siwar	Minister of Youth And Sports	
Mr. Chol Ram Pang	Minister of Transportation	
Dr. Mostafa Osman Ismail	Minister of Investment	http://minv.gov.sd/en
Professor / Elias Nyamlel Wakoson	Minister of Foreign Trade	http://www.tpsudan.gov.sd/index.php/en/
Dr. Abdul-Bagi Al-Jailani	Minister of Minerals	http://minerals.gov.sd/en
Dr. Ahmed Babekir Nahar	Minister of Antiquities, Tourism & Wildlife	
Eng. Joseph Malwal Dong	Minister of Environment, Forestry & Physical Development	
Mr. Abdul - Wahab Mohamed Osman	Minister of Roads & Bridges	
Ustaza / Halima Hassaballah Al-Naeem	Minister of Parliamentary Affairs	
Mr. Dak Dob Bishok	Minister of Labor	

Dr. Faisal Hassan Ibrahim	Minister of Animal Resources & Fisheries	http://agri-khs.gov.sd/indexen.php
Mr. Joseph Lual Achuil	Minister of Humanitarian Affairs	
Dr. Yahiya Abdallah Mohamed Hamad	Minister of Communications & Information Technology	

Sudan maintains an **embassy** in the United States at 2210 Massachusetts Ave. NW, Washington, DC 20008 (tel: (202) 338-8565; fax: (202) 667-2406); and a Consular Office at 2612 Woodley Place, NW, Washington, DC 20008 (tel: (202) 232-1492; fax: (202) 232-1494).

ECONOMY

Overview

In 2004, the cessation of major north-south hostilities in Sudan and expanding crude oil exports resulted in 6.4% GDP growth and a near doubling of GDP per capita since 2003. The aftereffects of the 21-year civil war and very limited infrastructure, however, presented obstacles to stronger growth and a broader distribution of income. The country continued taking some steps toward transitioning from a socialist to a market-based economy, although the government and governing party supporters remained heavily involved in the economy.

The July 2011 secession of South Sudan had an immediate and profound impact on Sudan's economy, and the reverberations from the split will continue to resound in the coming years. While the composition of what the "new" Sudanese economy will be is unclear, the country will not be able to rely on the oil production and export that had served as the principal driver of growth since 2000. With much of its oil production having come from what is now South Sudan, Sudan has suffered a dramatic decline in its oil revenues. The government has targeted agriculture, mining, and enhanced oil production as sectors for development. With conflicts continuing on its southern borders, a virtual cessation in cross-border trade with the new South Sudan, and unresolved issues with both oil revenue sharing and an arrangement for transporting South Sudan oil to Port Sudan, Sudan and its people are not able in the near future to reap the benefits from its natural resources, rebuild its infrastructure, increase oil production and exports, and be able to attain its export and development potential.

Background

Sudan's oil production began in the late 1990s and grew rapidly starting in July 1999 with completion of an export pipeline that runs from South Sudan through the North to the Port of Sudan. Sudan produced an estimated 401,000 barrels per day (b/d) in 2005, which brought in about $1.9 billion and provided 70% of the country's total export earnings. As of 2007, oil production in Sudan was at 466,100 barrels per day. In 2010, oil accounted for over 90% of Sudan's foreign exchange earnings. Prior to South Sudan's July 2011 secession, roughly 75% of Sudan's oil production, representing almost 36% of government revenues, came from fields located in the South. Remaining production in Sudan barely covers domestic use.

Agriculture, which was the economy's mainstay prior to oil, accounted for about a third of GDP prior to secession. It represented 90% of Sudan's 2009 non-oil exports, and the sector employed about 80% of the labor force. Sudan's authorities are looking at increasing agricultural production in an effort to diversify growth; only an estimated 15%-20% of Sudan's arable land is cultivated. The authorities have launched an Agricultural Revitalization Plan to invest some $5 billion in the sector through 2012, and hope to attract strategic foreign investors. Cotton and gum arabic remain its major agricultural exports. Grain sorghum (dura) is the principal food crop, and millet and wheat are grown for domestic consumption. Sesame seeds and peanuts are cultivated for domestic consumption and increasingly for export. Livestock production has vast potential, and many animals, particularly camels and sheep, are exported to Egypt, Saudi Arabia, and other Arab countries. However, Sudan remains a net importer of food. Problems of irrigation and transportation remain the greatest constraints to a more dynamic agricultural economy.

Sudan's non-oil private sector remains nascent. Sudan ranked 154 in the Doing Business survey in 2010. Firms identify the top three constraints holding back growth and investment as political instability, corruption, and economic uncertainty. Transparency International ranked Sudan as 172 out of 180 countries in its 2010 corruption perception index. Competitiveness remains low due to high transaction costs, poor market institutions, lack of infrastructure, and high administrative barriers.

Sudan's growth has historically been unbalanced, with the majority of its manufacturing firms and irrigated land concentrated in the northern states of Khartoum and Gezira. The World Bank reports that there is a large disparity in development indicators between the best- and worst-performing states. Sudan's capital city Khartoum consumes nearly a third of Sudan's total electricity production, while less than 7% of households in the country have access to the national grid. Sudan's limited industrial development consists of agricultural processing and various light industries located in Khartoum North. In recent years, the GIAD industrial complex introduced the assembly of small autos and trucks, and some heavy military equipment such as armored personnel carriers and the proposed "Bashir" main battle tank. Although Sudan is reputed to have great mineral resources, exploration has been quite limited, and the country's real potential is relatively unknown. Small quantities of asbestos, chromium, and mica are also exploited commercially.

Since the global financial crisis of 2008 and the collapse of crude oil prices, Sudan has faced a severe foreign exchange reserves shortfall. While data is not made public on a regular basis, the International Monetary Fund reported that reserves at the Central Bank of Sudan fell below 2 weeks of import coverage at one point. As a result of the shortage of foreign currency, the Government of Sudan has significantly tightened conversion and transfer policies. Domestic businesses have no assurance of obtaining needed levels of foreign currency for international transactions. Foreign companies operating in Sudan must have the permission of the Central Bank of Sudan to repatriate profits and foreign currency. Changes to policies are introduced without warning and generally become effective immediately upon announcement.

Debt and Aid

Sudan has a severe external debt burden, with large and protracted arrears that limit both its relations with the international financial institutions (IFIs) and integration into the world economy. The country has not serviced the majority of its external debt since the early 1990s, although some creditors, including some offering more recent financing, are receiving repayments. The United States accounts for $2.2 billion, of which $2.0 billion is in arrears. Sudan is subject to a variety of legal sanctions and legislative mandates that would complicate U.S. Government participation in IFI normalization and debt relief. Reducing U.S. claims would also require significant appropriations. Sudan's ruling NCP party views the provision of debt relief as critical for the North's economic prospects in view of Southern secession and closely links debt relief to the division of the country's oil revenues.

Historically, the U.S., the Netherlands, Italy, Germany, Saudi Arabia, Kuwait, and other Organization of Petroleum Exporting Countries (OPEC) have supplied most of Sudan's economic assistance. Sudan's role as an economic link between Arab and African countries is reflected by the presence in Khartoum of the Arab Bank for African Development. The World Bank had been the largest source of development loans but is currently unable to lend.

During the late 1970s and 1980s, the International Monetary Fund (IMF), World Bank, and key donors worked closely to promote reforms to counter the effect of inefficient economic policies and practices. By 1984, a combination of factors--including drought, inflation, and confused application of Islamic law--reduced donor disbursements, and capital flight led to a serious foreign-exchange crisis and increased shortages of imported inputs and commodities. More significantly, the 1989 revolution caused many donors in Europe, the U.S., and Canada to suspend official development assistance, although not humanitarian aid.

As Sudan became the world's largest debtor to the World Bank and IMF by 1993, its relationship with the international financial institutions soured in the mid-1990s and has yet to be fully rehabilitated. The government fell out of compliance with an IMF standby program and accumulated substantial arrearages on repurchase obligations. A 4-year economic reform plan was announced in 1988 but was not pursued. An economic reform plan was announced in 1989 and implementation began on a 3-year economic restructuring program designed to reduce the public sector deficit, end subsidies, privatize state enterprises, and encourage new foreign and domestic investment. In 1993, the IMF suspended Sudan's voting rights and the World Bank suspended Sudan's right to make withdrawals under effective and fully disbursed loans and credits. Lome Funds and European Union agricultural credits, totaling more than 1 billion euros, also were suspended.

DEFENSE

The Sudan People's Armed Forces is a 100,000-member army supported by a small air force and navy. Irregular tribal and former rebel militias and Popular Defense Forces supplement the army's strength in the field. This is a mixed force, having the additional duty of maintaining internal security. During the 1990s, periodic purges of the professional officer corps by the ruling Islamist regime eroded command authority as well as war-fighting capabilities. Indeed, the Sudanese Government admitted it was incapable of carrying out its war aims against the SPLA without employing former rebel and Arab militias to fight in support of regular troops. During the CPA period, Joint Integrated Units were formed to unite Sudanese Armed Forces and former SPLM rebels. After the secession of South Sudan, people of Southern descent were let go from the army and the Joint Integrated Units were dissolved.

Sudan's military forces historically have been hampered by limited and outdated equipment. In the 1980s, the U.S. worked with the Sudanese Government to upgrade equipment with special emphasis on airlift capacity and logistics. All U.S. military assistance was terminated following the military coup of 1989. Oil revenues have allowed the government to purchase modern weapons systems, including Hind helicopter gunships, MiG 23 fighter aircraft, mobile artillery pieces, and light assault weapons. Some military techniques are improvised, such as using Antonov transport aircraft as crude and inaccurate bombers. Sudan now receives most of its military equipment from China, Russia, and (until 2011) Libya.

FOREIGN RELATIONS

Solidarity with other Arab countries has been a feature of Sudan's foreign policy. When the Arab-Israeli war began in June 1967, Sudan declared war on Israel. However, in the early 1970s, Sudan gradually shifted its stance and was supportive of the Camp David Accords.

Relations between Sudan and Libya deteriorated in the early 1970s and reached a low in October 1981, when Libya began a policy of cross-border raids into western Sudan. After the 1985 coup in Sudan, the military government resumed diplomatic relations with Libya, as part of a policy of improving relations with neighboring and Arab states. In early 1990, Libya and the Sudan announced that they would seek "unity," but this unity was not implemented.

During the 1990s, as Sudan sought to steer a nonaligned course, courting Western aid and seeking rapprochement with Arab states, its relations with the U.S. grew increasingly strained. Sudan's ties with countries like North Korea and Libya and its support for regional insurgencies such as Egyptian Islamic Jihad, Eritrean Islamic Jihad, Ethiopian Islamic Jihad, Palestinian Islamic Jihad, Hamas, Hezbollah, and the Lord's Resistance Army generated great concern about its contribution to regional instability. Allegations of the government's complicity in the assassination attempt against the Egyptian President in Ethiopia in 1995 led to UNSC sanctions against Sudan. By the late 1990s, Sudan experienced strained or broken diplomatic relations with most of its neighboring countries. However, since 2000, Sudan has actively sought regional rapprochement that has rehabilitated most of these relations.

U.S.-SUDANESE RELATIONS

Sudan broke diplomatic relations with the U.S. in June 1967, following the outbreak of the Arab-Israeli War. Relations improved after July 1971, when the Sudanese Communist Party attempted to overthrow President Nimeiri, and Nimeiri suspected Soviet involvement. U.S. assistance for resettlement of refugees following the 1972 peace settlement with the south added further improved relations.

On March 1, 1973, Palestinian terrorists of the "Black September" organization murdered U.S. Ambassador Cleo A. Noel and Deputy Chief of Mission Curtis G. Moore in Khartoum. Sudanese officials arrested the terrorists and tried them on murder charges. In June 1974, however, they were released to the custody of the Egyptian Government. The U.S. Ambassador to the Sudan was withdrawn in protest. Although the U.S. Ambassador returned to Khartoum in November, relations with the Sudan remained static until early 1976, when President Nimeiri mediated the release of 10 American hostages being held by Eritrean insurgents in rebel strongholds in northern Ethiopia. In 1976, the U.S. decided to resume economic assistance to Sudan.

In late 1985, there was a reduction in staff at the U.S. Embassy in Khartoum because of the presence in Khartoum of a large contingent of Libyan terrorists. In April 1986, relations with Sudan deteriorated when the U.S. bombed Tripoli, Libya. A U.S. Embassy employee was shot on April 16, 1986. Immediately following this incident, all non-essential personnel and all dependents left for 6 months. At this time, Sudan was the single largest recipient of U.S. development and military assistance in sub-Saharan Africa. However, official U.S. development assistance was suspended in 1989 in the wake of the military coup against the elected government, which brought to power the National Islamist Front led by General Bashir.

U.S. relations with Sudan were further strained in the 1990s. Sudan backed Iraq in its invasion of Kuwait and provided sanctuary and assistance to Islamic terrorist groups. In the early and mid-1990s, Carlos the Jackal, Osama bin Laden, Abu Nidal, and other terrorist leaders resided in Khartoum. Sudan's role in the radical Pan-Arab Islamic Conference represented a matter of great concern to the security of American officials and dependents in Khartoum, resulting in several draw downs and/or evacuations of U.S. personnel from Khartoum in the early-mid 1990s. Sudan's Islamist links with international terrorist organizations represented a special matter of concern for the U.S. Government, leading to Sudan's 1993 designation as a state sponsor of terrorism and a suspension of U.S. Embassy operations in Khartoum in 1996. In October 1997, the U.S. imposed comprehensive economic, trade, and financial sanctions against the Sudan. In August 1998, in the wake of the East Africa embassy bombings, the U.S. launched cruise missile strikes against Khartoum. The last U.S. Ambassador to the Sudan, Ambassador Tim Carney, departed post prior to this event and no new ambassador has been designated since. The U.S. Embassy is headed by a Charge d'Affaires. The Embassy continues to re-evaluate its posture in Sudan, particularly in the wake of the January 1, 2008, killings of a U.S. Agency for International Development (USAID) employee and his Sudanese driver in Khartoum.

The U.S. and Sudan entered into a bilateral dialogue on counterterrorism in May 2000. Sudan has provided concrete cooperation against international terrorism since the September 11, 2001, terrorist strikes on New York and Washington. However, although Sudan publicly supported the international coalition actions against the al Qaida network and the Taliban in Afghanistan, the government criticized the U.S. strikes in that country and opposed a widening of the effort against international terrorism to other countries. Sudan remains on the state sponsors of terrorism list.

In response to the Government of Sudan's continued complicity in unabated violence occurring in Darfur, President Bush imposed new economic sanctions on Sudan in May 2007. The sanctions blocked assets of Sudanese citizens implicated in Darfur violence, and also sanctioned additional companies owned or controlled by the Government of Sudan. Sanctions continue to underscore U.S. efforts to end the suffering of the millions of Sudanese affected by the crisis in Darfur.

Despite policy differences the U.S. has been a major donor of humanitarian aid to the Sudan throughout the last quarter-century. The U.S. was a major donor in the March 1989 "Operation Lifeline Sudan," which delivered 100,000 metric tons of food into both government and SPLA-held areas of the Sudan, thus averting widespread starvation. In 1991, the U.S. made major donations to alleviate food shortages caused by a 2-year drought. In a similar drought in 2000-2001, the U.S. and the international community responded to avert mass starvation in the Sudan. In 2001 the Bush administration named a presidential envoy for peace in the Sudan to explore what role the U.S. could play in ending Sudan's civil war and enhancing the delivery of humanitarian aid. Andrew Natsios and subsequently Ambassador Richard Williamson served as presidential envoys to Sudan during the Bush administration. On March 18, 2009 President Obama announced the appointment of J. Scott Gration as the U.S. Special Envoy to Sudan.

On October 19, 2009, Secretary Clinton, accompanied by Special Envoy Gration and U.S. Ambassador to the United Nations Susan Rice, announced the Obama administration's new Sudan strategy. U.S. strategy in Sudan is comprised of three core principles: 1) Achieving a definitive end to conflict, gross human rights abuses, and genocide in Darfur; 2) Implementation of the North-South Comprehensive Peace Agreement (CPA) that results in a peaceful post-2011 Sudan, or an orderly path toward two separate and viable states at peace with each other; and 3) Ensuring that Sudan does not provide a safe haven for international terrorists.

In January 2011, Dane Smith was appointed Senior Advisor for Darfur. In March 2011, Princeton N. Lyman was appointed U.S. Special Envoy for Sudan.

Principal U.S. Officials

Chargé d'Affaires Steven Koutsis
A career member of the Senior Foreign Service, Mr. Koutsis was most recently Director of the Special Envoy's Office for Sudan and South Sudan. Prior to that, he was Deputy Chief of Mission in Ouagadougou, Burkina Faso. He has also served as Deputy Director and interim Director in the Office of Central African Affairs, and as Team Leader of the Provincial Reconstruction Team in Diyala Province, Iraq. Other tours include Political and Economic Counselor in Monrovia, Liberia, and Deputy Chief of Mission in Nouakchott, Mauritania. He was Consular Section Chief in Damascus, Syria and in Abidjan, Cote d'Ivoire. His other assignments include Washington, D.C., Marseille, France, and Port-au-Prince, Haiti.

Charge d'Affaires--Mary C. Yates
Deputy Chief of Mission--Dennis Hankins
USAID Director--Barry Primm
Political-Economic Chief--Howell Howard
Public Affairs Officer--William Bellis

The **U.S. Embassy** in Sudan is located at Embassy Road, Kilo 10, Soba, off Wad Medani

Highway, Khartoum (tel. 249-187-022000). Hours are 8 a.m. to 4:30 p.m. Sunday through Thursday.

TRAVEL AND BUSINESS INFORMATION

Travel Alerts, Travel Warnings, Trip Registration
The U.S. Department of State's Consular Information Program advises Americans traveling and residing abroad through Country Specific Information, Travel Alerts, and Travel Warnings. **Country Specific Information** exists for all countries and includes information on entry and exit requirements, currency regulations, health conditions, safety and security, crime, political disturbances, and the addresses of the U.S. embassies and consulates abroad. **Travel Alerts** are issued to disseminate information quickly about terrorist threats and other relatively short-term conditions overseas that pose significant risks to the security of American travelers. **Travel Warnings** are issued when the State Department recommends that Americans avoid travel to a certain country because the situation is dangerous or unstable.

For the latest security information, Americans living and traveling abroad should regularly monitor the Department's Bureau of Consular Affairs Internet web site at http://travel.state.gov, where current Worldwide Caution, Travel Alerts, and Travel Warnings can be found. The travel.state.gov website also includes information about passports, tips for planning a safe trip abroad and more. More travel-related information also is available at http://www.usa.gov/Citizen/Topics/Travel/International.shtml.

The Department's Smart Traveler app for U.S. travelers going abroad provides easy access to the frequently updated official country information, travel alerts, travel warnings, maps, U.S. embassy locations, and more that appear on the travel.state.gov site. Travelers can also set up e-tineraries to keep track of arrival and departure dates and make notes about upcoming trips. The app is compatible with iPhone, iPod touch, and iPad (requires iOS 4.0 or later).

The Department of State encourages all U.S. citizens traveling or residing abroad to enroll in the State Department's Smart Traveler Enrollment Program (STEP). A link to the registration page is also available through the Department's Smart Traveler app. U.S. citizens without internet access can enroll directly at the nearest U.S. embassy or consulate. By enrolling, you make your presence and whereabouts known in case it is necessary to contact you in an emergency and so you can receive up-to-date information on security conditions.

Emergency information concerning Americans traveling abroad may be obtained by calling 1-888-407-4747 toll free in the U.S. and Canada or the regular toll line 1-202-501-4444 for callers outside the U.S. and Canada.

Passports
The National Passport Information Center (NPIC) is the U.S. Department of State's single, centralized public contact center for U.S. passport information. Telephone: 1-877-4-USA-PPT (1-877-487-2778); TDD/TTY: 1-888-874-7793. Passport information is available 24 hours, 7 days a week. You may speak with a representative Monday-Friday, 8 a.m. to 10 p.m., Eastern Time, excluding federal holidays.

SUDAN LEGAL SYSTEM BASICS

As Africa's largest country, Sudan includes many religious, ethnic and socio-economic groups. Prevailing issues of access to resources, economic opportunity and power against the background of such diversity has unfortunately resulted in some of Africa's longest-running conflicts since the country became independent in 1956. These conflicts have included those between Muslim-Christian, Arab-African and nomad-farmer groups, e.g. The rule of law is but one of many casualties resulting from the permanent presence of conflict (or threat thereof) in the South, West and Eastern regions. Not surprisingly, historical, social and political factors have largely shaped Sudanese laws in terms of substance and application, including colonial legacies, a historically Arab-dominated central government and the presence of an intricate network of informal laws that are based upon religious, ethnic and/or tribal communities. The complexity of these factors renders it extremely difficult to distil a comprehensive overview of formal and informal Sudanese laws that are currently in operation. Rather, this article will attempt to present an elementary overview of principle Sudanese laws, as well as some contextual background as to the nature of the informal justice mechanisms that operate outside the formal legal mechanisms.

The laws includes criminal (Criminal Act, 1991; Criminal Procedure Act, 1991); civil (Muslim Law Act 1991); commercial (Banking; Investment Encouragement; National Petroleum Commission, Telecommunications, Copyright); public laws (Khartoum Public Order Act; Labour Act, 1997); as well as gender issues, and child rights and duties (Child Act 2004). A final section is included that lists important domestic legislation; as well as primary treaty law to which Sudan is a signatory. A list of useful electronically available resources is also provided, in particular, links to extensive reporting on human rights practices in Sudan.

CURRENT POLITICAL LANDSCAPE

Prior to independence in 1956, Sudan was jointly administered by Anglo-Egyptian forces following their capture of Khartoum in 1898. The north and southern regions of Sudan were administered separately until 1947, after which political power was placed within the hands of a northern elite that was composed largely of Arab ethnicity. Following independence, the North and South have been in almost constant conflict; the first civil war lasting from 1956 - 1972 and the second from 1983 to 2005. At present, "Sudan has an authoritarian government in which all effective political power lies in the hands of President Omar Hassan al Bashir and the National Congress (NC) Party inner circle, who have been in power since a 1989 military coup (that was) instigated and supported by the fundamentalist National Islamic Front (NIF). . In 2000, Bashir was re-elected, and his NC/NIF political party won 340 out of 360 seats in the Parliament in deeply flawed elections boycotted by all major opposition parties. NC/NIF members and supporters continued to hold key positions in the Government, security forces, judiciary, academic institutions, trade unions, professional associations, and the media."

According to International Crisis Group, Sudan is divided by religion (70 per cent Muslim, 25 per cent animist, 5 per cent Christian), ethnicity (between African and Arab origin Sudanese), tribe and economic activity (between nomadic and sedentary cultures). The principal conflict between the northern and southern parts of Sudan was borne out during 1956 - 72 and 1983 - 2005 and has cost an estimated 2 million lives, while displacing over 4 million people. The origins of what developed into a national conflict between the North and South have been said to lie in Sudan's colonial past; however, economic and political disparities, the discovery of oil-rich areas in the South, as well as regional power politics have also fuelled the conflict.

Not surprisingly, the early mixture of British and Arab rule, combined with more recent assertions of Islamisation by political forces in Khartoum, have had significant implications upon the composition of Sudanese laws. Indeed, the religious composition of the warring groups has also influenced the nature of laws administered in areas controlled by the Muslim-dominated central government and the Christian rebel movement in the South.

THE COMPREHENSIVE PEACE AGREEMENT (CPA)

A cease-fire was eventually declared between the Sudanese government and the Sudan People's Liberation Movement / Army (SPLM/A) in July 2002. Peace talks were carried on through 2003, though fighting also continued on both sides; eventually in 2005, a peace agreement between the Government of Sudan and the SPLM/A was reached. Highlights of the Comprehensive Peace Agreement include a Power Sharing Agreement, a Wealth Sharing Agreement and Security Protocol; and special power and wealth sharing agreements for the areas of Abyei, Southern Kordorfon and Blue Nile (also referred to as the Three Areas), which individually possess specific factors that precipitated and prolonged the conflict - including and especially resource wealth).

Despite the death of SPLM leader and Vice-President elect John Garang in August 2005, the peace process continued with the ratification of a new constitution in October 2005, the swearing-in of a new government (that divided executive posts between the ruling parties of the North and South) and the functioning of an autonomous Southern legislature and government. Much of Sudan's laws will undergo amendment following the new Constitution, which seek to balance interests and power between the South Sudanese and Central Governments.

The UN has deployed a multilateral peacekeeping observer mission to the South that is mandated to monitor the implementation of the agreement and support the building of national capacity until a referendum on the sovereignty of the south can be held in 2011. Despite all of this progress, tensions between the Government of National Unity (GONU), i.e. the National Congress, and the Sudan People's Liberation Movement (SPLM) remain live. The SPLM has accused the GONU of slowing down implementation of the Comprehensive Peace Agreement (CPA). The issues in dispute included the designated commissions by agreement, Abyei borders, withdrawal of the government army beyond the Independence border of January 1956, the volume and revenue of oil production, and the democratic transition, which had been extremely sluggish.

CURRENT CONFLICTS - DARFUR AND THE EAST

The peace between the North and the South remains fragile, while other conflicts or threats thereof loom elsewhere in Sudan, notably in Darfur and Eastern Sudan. The central government continues to wage war in Darfur, since the taking-up of arms by the Sudan Liberation Army/Movement (SLA) and Justice and Equality Movement (JEM) rebels (predominantly African sedentary tribes of the Fur, Zaghawa and Massaleit) in February 2003. The central government responded by arming Arab "Janjaweed" militia, in addition to deploying the Sudanese army. Some estimate that Darfur conflict has displaced almost 2 million and taken anywhere from 200,000 - 400,000 lives. With much of the civilian population permanently displaced, the rule of law appears virtually non-existent. Humanitarian agencies such as International Rescue Committee together with the United Nations Development Fund have undertaken efforts to build "Justice Confidence Centres" in displacement camps, which aim to create community spaces for resolving disputes as well as information on human rights and local laws. To the East, a third conflict may escalate between the Government and the opposing "Eastern Front", who are in negotiations towards a peace agreement. The Islamist Ruling Party (known as the NCP - National Congress Party) is alleged to maintain dominance over the region by measures not unknown in Darfur - undercutting support for the opposition through patronage, divide-and-rule policies, and the creation of tribal militias. International Crisis Group reports that some fear that humanitarian levels in the East have dropped lower than those in Darfur. Both situations bode poorly for rule of law and access to justice for local populations.

THE JUDICIAL SYSTEM

Arbiters of disputes and administrators of formal and informal laws come in various forms throughout Sudan, depending on ethnic, religious and political factors. Judicial courts are provided for under both statute *and* customary law while informal community practices also rely upon local chiefs, known as Sultans, to resolve disputes between community members. Indeed, "(t)he judiciary relies greatly on popular justice for solving disputes through methods of conciliation and the application of tradition." Customary laws generally consist of non-state dispute resolution systems that are usually based upon local customary, traditional or tribal systems of justice. Given Sudan's ethnic and religious plurality, customary laws and practice are diverse, differing from tribe-to-tribe and community-to-community. Case reporting of decisions by the formal courts is published in the *Sudan Law Journal and Reports*, whilst laws are published in the *Sudan Gazette*.

According to Y. Sherif, Northern "judiciary structures are more developed but the independence of the judiciary seems to have been compromised - as evidenced by the arbitrary dismissal of qualified judges, attorneys-general and law officers. Existing legislation fails to guarantee the full spectrum of human rights and fundamental freedoms, while military decrees and emergency laws undermine those rights currently protected by statutory law." Indeed, thought the "Constitution provides for an independent judiciary; however, the judiciary (is) largely subservient to the President or the security forces, particularly in cases of crimes against the state."

Questions of independence reach beyond the judiciary to practising lawyers. Lawyers throughout Sudan must belong to the National Bar Association, which is based in Khartoum. Outside of Khartoum, the Association is viewed as being overly urban in both composition and its substantive focus and therefore removed from the daily needs and challenges outside of the capital. However, it is unfair to characterize an entire bar; indeed, the Association has endured its own difficulties even within Khartoum. In 1992, "the government amended the Advocate Act of 1983 in such a drastic way as to totally abrogate the Association's independence. For the first time in its history, the SBA has been reduced to another trades union. the Association has now been registered with the Registrar of Trades Union." According to the U.S. Department of State, members of the legal profession are harassed by the Government viewed as political opponents; some have been detained, including the Director of the Darfur Lawyers Association, Mohamed Adomo, who was later released.

THE SUPREME COURT

The Supreme Court is composed of seventy judges and operates through panels that are composed of three judges, which are presided over by the most senior of the three. Decisions are reached by a majority of opinion and are subject to revision only if and when the chief justice deems that an infringement of (*shari'a* laws) has taken place. In this case the Chief Justice convenes a five member panel, the majority of whom must not have participated in reaching the disputed decision in order to receive the matter. The court disposes of appeals against the judgments of the courts of appeal in civil, criminal and personal matter cases." The Court also has "preliminary jurisdiction of a single judge to consider appeals against the administrative decision of the president of the republic of the governors and of the federal and state ministers. Appeals from the decision of this single judge's court are dealt with by panel of three Supreme Court judges." Four circuits of the Supreme Court operate outside the capital in the western, central and eastern states.

THE CONSTITUTIONAL COURT

In addition to the Supreme Court, the Sudanese judicial system includes four types of courts: regular courts, which primarily consider criminal and civil matters; special mixed security courts, military courts and tribal courts, which apply customary law to resolve disputes over land and water rights and family matters. The regular courts include Court of Appeal, the Public Courts and District Courts (courts of first instance). The Constitutional Court considers:

a. Interpretation of the constitution when requested to do so by the President of the Republic, the National Assembly, half of the Governors of the states or half of the State Assemblies.

b. Suits from any aggrieved person to protect the freedoms and rights guaranteed by the Constitution after exhausting the executive and administrative remedies available.
c. Suits concerning jurisdictional conflicts between national and federal bodies.
d. Criminal procedures against the President of the Republic and the Governors under the Constitution or the laws.
e. Objections concerning the acts of the President of the Republic, the Council of Ministers or a National or Federal Minister if the objection concerns any infringement of the national constitutional system or the constitutional inviolable freedoms or rights.
f. Any other matters determined to be within the competence of the Constitutional Court.

During a campaign of Islamisation in 1983, the central government reunified the civil and *shari'a* courts, which had earlier been made separate during colonialism. Subsequent constitutional reform did not alter the ability of formal courts to consider *shari'a* law.

MILITARY INTELLIGENCE/SECURITY CASES

"In addition to the regular police and the Sudan People's Armed Forces, the Government maintain(s) an external security force, an internal security force, a militia known as the Popular Defense Forces (PDF), and a number of police forces. The security forces (are) under the effective control of the Government. Members of the security forces (commit) numerous, serious human rights abuses." Arrests and detention can occur extra-legally or under emergency powers. For example, individuals associated with armed forces rebelling against the government can be accused of crimes against the state (Chapter 5, Criminal Act 1991). Created under the Special Courts Act, **security courts** constituted of three civilian judges convene to hear such cases. Those in military intelligence custody who later find their case before such courts are not permitted representation by a lawyer, though they may be accompanied by a 'friend.' Accordingly, lawyers have attended security cases as such, though are not permitted to address the court. Overall, due process is not ensured in military or civilian courts. Sentences are usually severe and implemented immediately; death sentences are referred to the Chief Justice and the Head of State. It has been reported that children used by armed groups as spies have later been tortured to death in Military Intelligence custody.

ISLAMIC *HADD* CASES

Individuals may also be convicted of crimes defined in Islamic *shari'a* law, which can include Islamic *hadd* punishments of amputation and death. It has been noted that girls alleging rape can in turn be themselves accused of adultery in such courts. Charging women with adultery is not unique to North Sudan. Indeed, in a prison in the town of Wau, South Sudan, many women were in detention under the charge of adultery - either for having relations with a man before marriage and/or refusing marriage arranged by her family.

POPULAR OR TRIBAL COURTS

Popular courts are staffed by respected community elders and enforce customary law that is not considered to be inconsistent with the law or public policy. Generally, judges are citizens of good conduct who are "well known, well reputed and reasonably well off in rural areas"; membership includes tribal chiefs, Omdas, sheikhs, and Nazirs. Due process in customary courts does not appear to be clearly defined, rendering them vulnerable to arbitrary application of the laws. Cases in customary courts can be referred to statutory courts; such courts also have powers of detention.

SOUTHERN SUDAN

The parallel operation of formal laws with informal laws is particularly strong in Southern Sudan. During the civil war, "units of the armed forces and militias ruled by force of arms, and in many cases the accused were summarily tried and punished, especially for offences against public order." Within the former SPLM controlled areas, SPLM de facto laws and decrees were undermined by a severe lack of judicial facilities and lack of trained personnel in the judiciary and law enforcement. These institutional short-comings remain today and pose serious challenges to justice reform and access. For example, in the Southern Kordofan state, there are less than 30 well-qualified judges and about 50 lawyers. Here, *shari'a*- based laws remained applicable during the war in those areas formerly-held by the Government of Sudan, while a common law system was administered in former SPLM/A rebel-controlled areas. Indeed, under the terms of the recent peace agreement for Sudan, customary law will dominate in the South Sudan. It is presently unclear how the customary law system will in the future formally interact with the development of a formal legal system in the South, as well as with the justice system in the north of the country. Recent outcry over the continued application of strict Islamic *shari'a* Law in Southern Courts that remain adjudicated by Northern judges suggests that law reforms required under the CPA are not being to the liking of Southerners.

"The SPLM has a judicial system of county magistrates, county judges, regional judges, and a court of appeals." A High Court is located in each Southern State whilst the Supreme Court is situated in Rumbek. Southern States will generally continue to have the two systems of formal and customary law operating until the new Government undertakes to merge them. The formal courts are located mainly in towns; their role is not well understood by the public. Public access to the courts has been criticized by outside observers as practically non-existent due to high user charges, cumbersome formal procedures and their distance from the people, especially poor rural communities. Limited operational budgets prevent courts to hear cases in rural areas or for judges/legal administration officers to monitor and guide traditional courts on points of law and procedures.

CUSTOMARY LAW

Justice John Wuol Makec writes in "*Legal Aid and its Problems in Sudan: Proposed Supplementary Mechanisms*":

> One of the main objectives of customary law is the establishment of peace and harmony between the parties and society as a whole through compromise, conciliation, and compensation or restoration of social imbalance created by the commission of wrong or criminal acts.

The largely dualistic legal structure in Sudan results in several stages being passed before a matter reaches any formal justice institution (such as the police or statutory Courts) - if at all. Indeed, there exists a strong customary law network through which personal problems are dealt with.

THE OPERATION OF CUSTOMARY LAW

Personal matters are generally governed by the religious laws of the particular individuals concerned: Muslims are usually governed by local interpretations of *shari'a* law, whilst Christians are governed by local understandings of sectarian laws. If an individual is of no formal religion, then personal issues are governed by the customary laws of his/her particular tribe. For example, the tribal laws of the Dinkas in the South are in fact codified and held by the local Mullah. Other local tribes rely upon an oral tradition that is according to custom.

For family disputes, often the father or the head of the extended family will resolve matters within the family unit. Beyond the family, people who are party to disputes, whether they are husband and wife or neighbours, will go to the local Sultan to resolve the issue. The Sultan applies local customary laws and tribal practices in reaching a resolution of the issues presented before him. In cases of dissatisfaction with his decision, either party will apply to the District Court Judge and appeal. However, the decision of the Sultan is usually respected by the District Court Judge in deference to his sound knowledge and practice of local customary law.

Mediating disputes is generally the means by which conflicts are handled within the community. Fully outlining the myriad of local practices requires deep knowledge and access to individual communities, which is beyond the scope of this introduction. Given the dire need for capacity-building of local police, the office of the attorney general and judiciary throughout Sudan - especially in post-conflict areas (and outside the capital), the dominance of the community/customary network holds much potential for justice advocacy. Naturally, customary law is weak in terms of human rights protections for women and children; nonetheless, individual interventions by local justice actors can serve to slowly improve and strengthen customary laws.

FORMAL LAWS

Sudan's formal legal system is grounded in British common law and Islamic law. Sources of law are Islamic law, constitutional law, legislation, judicial precedent, and custom. In family law, judicial circulars (*manshurat*) issued by the Qadi al-Quda (first issued in 1916) served to institute reforms or instruct the application of particular interpretations.

CRIMINAL LAW

Sudanese criminal law includes elements from British colonial penal law, Egyptian civil code and more recently, what are known as the "September Laws," otherwise referred to as *hudud* (sing., *hadd*) or penalty prescribed by Islamic law. The applicable criminal laws include: Criminal Act, 1991 and Criminal Procedure Act, 1991 (CPA); as well as *shari'a* and local custom. The following is an overview of general due process provisions

- Arrests under the CPA: An arrest may be undertaken in two modes: arrest by prosecution attorney or magistrate's warrant (s. 67) or arrest by a policeman or "People's administrator" (that is, chairman of a state-sponsored local committee for order) (s. 68). In Darfur, a "People's administrator" is usually a tribal leader, appointed by the Government under the 1991 Native Administration Act. People can be arrested without warrant if found in suspicious circumstances, or if found with property suspected as stolen, or for not giving their name and address.
- Recording arrest: Police must record arrests made without a warrant in a register of arrests (s. 75.2, s. 82), and inform the prosecution attorney or magistrate (s. 77).
- Interrogation: Investigations are carried out by the General Crimes Police (s. 39) and should be recorded in writing (s. 41) and include statements of the accused and

decisions taken regarding charges (s. 42). Suspects may undergo medical examination for purposes of gaining evidence, not for protection (s. 49). If an accused confesses, a magistrate should immediately assess the voluntariness of confession and record his judgement (s. 60). Lawyers are not present at interrogation.

- Powers of detention: The CPA allows police to detain people for no more than 24 hours for inquiry; the prosecution attorney can renew detention for no more than 3 days for inquiry; the magistrate can renew detention weekly, for up to two weeks; the superior magistrate can renew detention weekly, for up to six months (s. 79). CPA allows for police supervision or restriction of movement of accused persons (ss. 84, 85).
- Records of detention: Magistrates need to record reasons for arrests in the Case Diary (*mahdar al-taharri*) (s. 79), and detainees can appeal detention (s. 179). Prosecution attorneys are required to inspect all people in custody daily (s. 81).
- Powers of detention in the CPA: Only a court can order detention for trial (s. 80). Courts can order detention for up to one month, renewable weekly, and superior magistrates can order detention for up to six months, renewable monthly.
- Bail: The CPA allows for bail against different guarantees (s. 105) for offences not involving compensation (*diyya*) or Islamic *hadd*punishments (ss. 107, 108). Any reasons for not releasing persons accused of bailable offences must be recorded (s. 108).
- Free legal representation: The CPA allows for free legal representation only for people facing the gravest charges (s. 135).
- Language: The CPA gives a right to translation of trial proceedings, but not other proceedings (s. 137).
- Sentencing: Sentencing may consist of physical punishment (such as lashings), compensation (for homicide or injury) and death. It is the trial judge's responsibility to explain the sentence and any appeal rights that are available to the convicted person and to other interested parties (CPA 171).

The amended Law of Criminal Procedure 1991 added additional powers to law-enforcement to investigate, arrest, interrogate or detain irrespective of magisterial investigation, as was lawfully required to guarantee the rights of persons in contact with the law. Notwithstanding both of these acts, the National Security Act includes a provision authorizing solitary detention from nine months to a year, which has been alleged to be largely used to harass political opponents. Against this legal backdrop, human rights organizations allege routine arbitrary detentions, extrajudicial killings and torture by central government agents. Despite a Constitutional guarantee of fair and prompt trials, trials in "regular courts nominally (meet) international standards of legal protections. The accused normally have the right to an attorney, and the courts are required to provide free legal counsel for indigent defendants accused of crimes punishable by death or life imprisonment; however, there (are) reports that defendants frequently did not receive legal counsel and that counsel in some cases could only advise the defendant and not address the court."

CIVIL MATTERS

Civil matters are formally governed by statute, but outside the capital are in practice resolved at through informal laws and long-standing community justice mechanisms. Disagreement over the outcome of such will lead the parties to then appeal to the formal justice system, though much discretion is generally accorded to the decision rendered by a local Sultan or popular court. Relevant formal laws include the Civil Transactions Act, the Family Code, 1991. Passed in 1991, the Family Code includes *shari'a* principles as well as interpretations of some*manshurat*, though the Supreme Court (*Shari'a* Circuit) is vested with the power to issue interpretations of Code. Hanafi *fiqh* is also established as a residual source of law.

MUSLIM PERSONAL LAW ACT

The Muslim Personal Law Act 1991 requires that both parties to a marriage be past the age of puberty and consent to the marriage. A male guardian marries adult women with their consent, although the qadi is empowered to act in this capacity if her guardian refuses his consent without justification. The guardian retains entitlement to seek dissolution on the grounds of lack of kifa'a of the husband, where kifa'a is defined in religion and morals. The wife is entitled to maintenance, assessed according to the circumstances of the husband; however, the wife loses the right to maintenance if she refuses to move to the marital home or leaves it without a shari'a justification. Right to maintenance may be lost if the wife works outside the house without the husband's consent, provided he is not being arbitrary in such.

Reforms standard to the region to the rules on talaq have been introduced. These reforms include the validity of talaq in terms of its number in word or sign; talaq in the form of an oath; and talaq intended to induce someone to do something. As a further reform to what is known as classical law, the wife must be informed of her husband's revocation of a revocable talaq during her 'idda period in order for the revocation to be valid. A judicial divorce may be sought by the wife on the following grounds: a husband's incurable physical or mental illness rendering it impossible for the wife to continue to live with him without harm; a husband's impotence not curable within one year; a husband's cruelty, or discord between the spouses; a husband's inability to pay maintenance. Finally, a divorce by 'ransom' may be instigated where a wife who is held disobedient by the court may waive her rights in return for a divorce; arbitrators must be appointed if the husband refuses to agree to such, and if the wife establishes that she suffers from remaining with him, a talaq will be ordered by the court.

After divorce, the wife is entitled to maintenance for the `idda period and to mut`a, which is assessed according to the means of her ex-husband - but only to a maximum of six months of maintenance. Maintenance will not be accorded in such a manner if the divorce was a judicial divorce by reason of the man's poverty and inability to pay maintenance, or for some physical reason arising in the wife, or unless the divorce was by khul.' A divorced mother is entitled to custody of her male children till they are 7 years old and females till they are 9. This period may be extended by the court if it can be proven to be in the interests of the wards, in which case, custody will extend until the sons reach puberty and the daughters consummate marriage. The father or other male guardian is to maintain scrutiny of all matters related to the raising of the children in the custody of their mother. Child support is the responsibility of the father until the daughter is married and the son is of an age when he is able to earn his own living.

GENDER ISSUES

Women's community-based groups voice serious concerns with the prevalence of gender-based violence, which is considered to include: Early (forced) marriage of girls; Domestic violence; Rape; Female circumcision; Forced marriages of widows. Additional prevailing gender issues include the right to own property; freedom of choice to enter into marriage; payment of dowry - bride wealth; wife inheritance; ghost marriages. Of note, the Convention on the Elimination of All Forms of Discrimination Against Women has not been signed and ratified by Sudan.

CHILD RIGHTS AND DUTIES

While Sudan ratified the Convention on the Rights of the Child (CRC) without reservation, the prevalence of key child rights issues remain of concern, including child labour; choice of education; rights to own property; right to care and protection; and juvenile justice concerns. The Child Act 2004 prescribes laws for child welfare, juvenile justice issues (including children's rights during arrest and imprisonment), health, education, 'working child', and the broader subject of 'satisfying child cultural needs.' The legislation is due to be revised after the signing of the Interim Constitution and consequently, it is in force but not being implemented. As such, the act is seen more to serve as an advocacy tool.

JUVENILE JUSTICE

All children under seven are below the age of criminal responsibility. All those above 15 have reached the age of criminal responsibility. Children between seven and 15 are criminally responsible if they have reached puberty. The Criminal Procedure Act 1991 (CPA) - which has few special protections for children in arrest and detention - is the law under which children are arrested and tried, and together with other legislation such as the Child Act provides the following:

- Children's arrest in the Child Act: The Child Act states that where a warrant is issued for children's arrest, they should be arrested by Children's Police (s. 51.1)
- Special provisions for children: The Juvenile Care Act 1983 says that parents/guardians or lawyers should be informed of any procedures involving children, as far as possible (s. 17b). Child Act: a parent/guardian and social welfare officer must be present (s. 50).
- Confidentiality: Children's trials are supposed to be in private Child Act (s. 64).
- Sentencing: Section 58 prescribes broad measures of 'corrective arrangements', which range from placing in the custody of family member or other adult, to being prevented from frequenting certain places or practicing certain jobs; the Act confers broad powers on the courts to prescribe measures it considers necessary for delinquent children or those 'susceptible to delinquency'; Article 85 stipulates that if a child between 15 and 18 years of age is found guilty of an offence punishable by death sentence, that child shall be sentenced to no less than 6 years, and no more than 10 years.
- Alternatives to imprisonment: The Criminal Act (s. 33.3) states that children should not be sentenced to jail except for the Islamic-defined crime of *haraba* (waging war against society). Child Act (ss. 60, 62) allow for a wide variety of non-custodial dispositions. The Criminal Procedure Act allows for suspension of sentence (s. 170). The Criminal Act alternatives to imprisonment include reprimand; awarding custody to the parent or other adult; or sending to a reform institution for a period between 2-5 years (s. 47).

THE CHILD ACT 2004

The Child Act 2004 repealed Juvenile Welfare Act 1983. Here, a child is defined as any individual below the age of 18, unless the more applicable law stipulates that the child has reached age of maturity. The Act establishes that the protection and best interests of the child will have priority in all decisions or measures concerning "childhood, family or environment' (Chapter Two, s. 5(b)).

In terms of education, 'free education in the basic stage' is affirmed as a fundamental right for child upon age 6, for which 'the state shall create a conducive atmosphere' (s. 27). Section 32 provides for a school record that contains a birth certificate as well as notation as to 'health condition, type of disability and social status' and level of education. Corporal punishment is prohibited (section 30(a)); however, amongst objectives of education of Sudanese child is the building of character in the child that shall 'worship Allah in Freedom.' This objective is clearly problematic in light of Sudan's ethnic and religious pluralism.

In relation to what is termed as 'child culture' and 'satisfying child cultural needs', the act maintains a broad prohibition of any publications and literary works that "appeal to child's instincts or urging (sic) him to indulge in behaviours contrary to society's values and traditions or encouraging delinquency" (s. 36). The state is obliged to establish bookshops for children, which are to be associated with children's clubs mandated under the Act.

With respect to child labour, children under age 15 are prohibited from employment in industrial work; however, children between the ages of 14 and 18 may participate in agricultural work that is not harmful to health, as well as apprenticeships - both of which are subject to Ministerial regulations (s. 39(2)(a)). Notably, section 41 prohibits the use of children in armed conflict, forced labour, illicit trade and sexual exploitation; and section 84(1)(d) establishes penal consequences for employers or manages for violations of such with max imprisonment of one year, or fine, or both. The Act also establishes labour requirements for the employment of children between 14 and 18 under the legislated exceptions. These include: medical checks by employers (s. 42), working hours not exceeding 6 hours daily with one hour break (s. 43(1)), prohibition of working between 8pm and 7 am (s. 43(3)).

The Act also prescribes government obligations in relation to child welfare. These include the establishment of "alternative welfare families" and institutions (s. 22 and 23 respectively); as well as correction houses for delinquent children (s. 24), and the employment of disabled children in state organs and public utilities (s. 55).

KHARTOUM PUBLIC ORDER ACT 1998

This Act governs certain activities within the Khartoum State. First, private or public parties are subject certain permissions (s. 5) and prohibitions, including "no dancing between men and women and women shall not dance in front of men" (s. 7(1)(b)). Other areas subjected to restrictions under the act include the use of public transportation (s. 9); a prohibition of begging and vagrancy (s. 10); license requirements for places of women's hairdressers (Ch. 5); and a prohibition of using loud speakers (Ch. 6). Penalties for infractions include fines, whipping and imprisonment (Ch. 7).

LABOUR ACT 1997

This Act applies to all workers except civil servants, members of the armed forces, domestic servants, agricultural workers, family members of an employer, and casual workers.

The Act establishes a Manpower Committee (Ch. II), which is responsible for *inter alia,* coordinating manpower-related issues within executive organs and the collection of related data.

The Act also addresses the Organization of Employment (Ch. III) through provisions governing employment agencies, private employment agencies, recruitment, apprenticeships, and registration of workers. Chapter Three includes a requirement that all Sudanese seeking employment outside of Sudan seek permission of the Federal Minister of Labour. (s. 14) Chapter Four's "Employment of Women and Young Persons" includes a prohibition of the employment of women in hazardous or arduous working conditions and during the night - save foradministrative or health-care jobs. In relation to children, Chapter IV forbids the employment of children (defined as persons under 12 years of age) and the employment of young persons (persons under 16 years of age) in specified tasks that are listed under section 21.

Chapter Five's "Contracts of Employment" regulates the types and contents of employment contracts and permitted modes of renewal. The sixth chapter, "Wages, advances and other allocations" governs the payment of wages while the seventh chapter, "Hours of work and leave" regulates the calculation of official hours of work, overtime work, types of leave (annual, maternity - four weeks prior to and following birth, sick, religious - namely, Hadj and Idda). The remaining chapters address "Termination of contract or employment" (Ch. VIII); "Severance pay" (Ch. IX); "Industrial Safety" - i.e. occupational health and safety (Ch. XI); "Labour disputes and stages of their settlements" (Ch. XII); and the "Stages of settling labour disputes" - i.e. negotiation and arbitration (Ch. XIII) and other general provisions concerning penalties, validity of contracts with successor employers, and labour inspection. (Ch. X). Despite the laws concerning workplace health and safety,working conditions are generally poor, and enforcement by the Ministry of Labour minimal.

Additional legislation relating to labour issues include the Public Service Act (No. 5 of 1991) and its accompanying Public Service Regulations, 1995; as well as the Peasants' Organizations Act of 1976, which includes the treatment of agricultural workers. Relevant to broader public welfare are the Health Insurance Act, 2000, which addresses medical care and sickness benefit; and the Social Security Act of 1990, which addresses old age security, and survivor's benefits.

COMMERCIAL LAWS

BANKING LAW

Banking is governed by the Law on the Regulation of Banking and the Money Laundry Combating Act. The Bank of Sudan Act 2000 establishes the Bank of Sudan and provides for its objectives in relation to setting monetary and credit policy, currency and exchange rates as well as economic and social development (s. 6). The functions and powers of the Bank are executed through the Bank's Board (Ch. III) and the Governor (s. 10). The Act governs "Capital, Reserves and Profits" (Chapter IV); "Currency" (Ch. V); "Foreign Exchange - Operations" (Ch. VI); "Relations with other Banks" (Ch. VII)'; "Relations with the Government" (Ch. VIII); "Other Operations of the Bank" (Ch. IX); and "Accounts" (Ch. XI).

INVESTMENT ENCOURAGEMENT ACT, 1999 AMENDED (2003)

Laws such as the Investment Encouragement Act have likely much facilitated the ability of the ruling Islamists "to privatize most of the State's infrastructural establishments and key production units, including tanneries, textile factories, and railways." This Act in particular aspires to "encourage investment in projects in the fields of agricultural, animal and industrial activities, energy and mining, transport, communication, tourism and environment, storage, housing, contracting, infrastructure, economic, administrative and consultative services, information technology, education, health, water and culture and information services and any such other field, as the Council of Ministers may specify." It consists of five parts, which include: "Encouragement of Investment"; "Privileges and Guarantees"; "Safeguard of Investment"; "Investment Organs"; and "Final Provisions." An anti-discrimination clause is provided for at the outset, which states that "no discrimination shall be made between invested money, by reason of its being local, Arab or alien, or by reason of its being public, private, co-operative or mixed sector" (s. 8(1)).

Certain fields are deemed strategic investment, namely those relating to infrastructure, roads, ports, electricity, dams, communications, energy, transport, contracting business, education, health and tourist and information technology services and water projects; relating to extraction of subterranean and deep seas wealth; agricultural, animal and industrial production; crossing more than one state; and any such other fields, as the Council of Ministers may prescribe (s. 9(1)). Those considered strategic projects are exempted from taxes from the business profits tax for a period of ten years (s. 10(1)(a)); as well as exempted from customs duties, or "customs privileges", as prescribed by the Minister (s.11(1)). State projects may also be exempted from taxes and fees (s. 13); likewise, federal projects also enjoy certain privileges, including exemption from local state taxes and fees (s. 14, 15).

Most notably, the Act provides for an explicit rule concerning expropriation. Specifically, the Act provides for the "non-nationalization, or non-confiscation of his project, non-acquisition of all, or part of the estates of the project thereof, or his investments, for public interest", with the exception that any such expropriation would have to be committed under the law and with "just compensation. (Emphasis added)" (s. 17(1)(a) - Investment Guarantees). Also noteworthy is a provision requiring that all investment projects require a licence (s. 19); the process for the granting of such licenses is governed under Chapter 4 - Safeguard of Investment, which includes a provision concerning "duties of the investor" (s. 25). The fifth and final chapter explains the relevant government bodies overseeing the Act, including the formation of a "Committee of Commissioners" (s. 27 - 30). The Act is unclear as to accountability for the granting of such licenses, which is problematic given the breathtaking breadth of investment activity that the Act potentially encapsulates.

NATIONAL PETROLEUM COMMISSION (NPC)

Since the discovery of oil in the South of Sudan, development and control over such has remained a difficult issue for some time, especially in relation to the conflict in South Sudan. Following the Sudan Interim National Constitution Presidential Decree No. 37 (2005) was formulated concerning the establishment of the National Petroleum Commission (NPC). The Commission is primarily responsible for formulating policies and guidelines in relation to the development and management of the petroleum sector and to monitor the implementation of these policies to ensure that they "serve the best interest of the people of Sudan".

THE TELECOMMUNICATION ACT 2001

The Telecommunication Act establishes the National Telecommunication Corporation, which regulates and licenses the provision of telecommunications services. The National Telecommunication Corporation has suspended on-line publications, including internet site "Sudanonline" in March 2006. The Act ought to be considered against the broader efforts to curtail freedom of expression and freedom of the press by Sudanese authorities. Examples of such include: journalists being routinely subject to interrogation by the security prosecutor of crimes against the state; foreign journalists generally being denied access to the region of Darfur; and members of the media are usually urged on by government security officials to support foreign policy decisions by the President.

The Act is applicable to those "licensed hereto, to install and operate a broadcast station, a public or private telecommunication network, or use frequencies or import or trade in telecommunication equipment, shall adapt their positions according to the provisions of this Act in a period not exceeding three months from the date of signature of this Act." (s. 3) The Act addresses issues such as the National Telecommunications Corporation's Establishment, the Headquarters and Supervision of the Corporation (Ch. II); the Management of the Corporation Establishment And Constitution of the Board (Ch. III); the establishment of Telecommunications, Equipment and Radio Stations, Possession and Use Of Telecommunication Network (Ch. IV); Licensing and Fees Licensing (Ch. V); Public Telecommunication Services Submission of Reports (Ch. VI); Inspection and Supervision Adherence to the License Conditions (Ch. VII); and General Provisions Connectivity of Licensed Telecommunications Networks (Ch. VIII).

COPYRIGHT AND NEIGHBOURING RIGHTS PROTECTION ACT 1996

This Act establishes intellectual property standards in relation to works, performances, etc. in Sudan. The Act establishes the "Scope of Copyright Protection," including Works Covered by the Protection (s.5), Works Not Covered by the Protection (ss.6 - 7), Copyright (s.8); "Ownership of Copyright" (Part III), including Author's Name (s.10), Joint Works (s.11). Cinematograhic and

Analogous Work (s.12), Duration of Author's Protection (s.13), Restrictions on Copyright (s.14); the Transfer of Ownership of Copyright (Part IV), including Transfer of Moral and Financial Rights (s.15), Use of Copyright (s.16), Publishing Contract (s.17), Public Performance Contract (s.18), Vesting of Ownership of Copyright on Author's Death (s.19), Order of Publication and Falling of Works into the Public Domain (s.20), Invalidity of Acts of Third Party for Lack of Consent (s.21). Finally, the "Registration of Works and Contracts" (Part V) is provided for, as is Protection of Neighbouring Rights of Performers (Part VI); and the Infringement of Copyright and Legal Consequences Thereof (Part VII).

Treaties

Sudan is signatory to the following treaties:

- ICCPR & ICESCR (Accession 1986, without reservations)
- CRC (Signature & ratification 1990, without reservations)

STRATEGIC ND LEGAL INFORMATION FOR CONDUCTING BUSINESS

BASIC INDUSTRIAL SECTORS IN SUDAN

AGRICULTURAL SECTOR:

It is the most important sector. It provides about45 % of the GDP and also provides employment opportunities for more than53 % of the labour force. This sector supplies the country with the green and cash crops. For instance sorghum (pure); millet and wheat; cotton; sesame; ground nuts. As a whole, the agricultural sector provides the domestic industries with raw material.. Cultivable lands in the Sudan are approaching2000 million feddans (about 840 million hectors). Only 30 million feddans has so far been exploited, ie15 % of the total cultivable area.

FOREST SECTOR:

22% of the total area of the Sudan is covered by forests of Mahogany, Teak, Acacia, Ebony and various other kinds. Gum Arabic is the most important of all forests products in the Sudan besides the wood. Forests are situated in the Northern State, Southern part of Kordofan, Darfur, Blue Nile, Kassala and Elgdariff state sector:

The Sudan possesses a huge livestock ,which consists of 30 million heads of cattle.37 million heads of sheep. 33 million heads of goats & 29 million heads of camels. Rich& open natural pastoral areas cover more than 57 million feddans.

INDUSTRIAL SECTOR:

It is the third in order of importance. The animal and agricultural products provide raw materials for food industry such as sugar, vegetable oil, mutton, beef and poultry products, vegetable and fruits, canning, leather and the spinning and weaving industries. While mining and extracted minerals act as raw materials for cement, gypsum, marble, and glass industries. Some of the major industries in this sector are:

SUGAR INDUSTRY:

there are five sugar factories in the Sudan:

1. Sennar sugar factory.
2. Elgined sugar factory.
3. Asalaya sugar factory.
4. New halfa sugar factory.

The above mentioned factories are owned by the public sector.
The fifth factory is Kenana sugar factory that belongs to (Kenana sugar company) a joint- venture between Arab, Sudanese and foreign capitals.

THE FOOD INDUSTRY:

The food factories function in areas where production of the raw materials, food packing, canning and processing takes place. Most of these factories belong to the private sector. This sector includes the fruit and vegetable canning industries and vegetable oils industries, which extract oil from sesame, groundnuts and sun flower seeds.

THE LEATHER INDUSTRIES:

Fur, and other sorts of animal skins are raw materials for the tanning and leather industries; and the recycling of the tanneries remnants geletine and lubber. There are seven modern tanneries in the Sudan beside many other conventional ones. There are also alot of leather factories for shoes.

BUILDING MATERIAL INDUSTRIES:-

There are two cement factories in Sudan, one in the white Nile state and the other is in Atbara . There are also many factories for firebrick, marble, gypsum, titles and granite industries. Nearly most of these apply conventional methods.

CHEMICAL AND PHARMACEUTICAL INDUSTRIES:-

The chemical and pharmaceutical comprise various industries such as insecticide, sulphur, perfume, pharmaceutical industries, fertilizers, paints, plastic and tyre. There are other industries, which are, light industry wise such as fodder, giarelte, flour- packing and paper timber industries.

TEXTILE SECTOR:-

The weaving and spinning industry in the Sudan include the production to yarn cloth, ready-made cloth. Blankets and medical cotton. This sector consist of:
Spinning, weaving, ready made cloth, knitting.
The public sector owns eight integrated spinning and weaving factories while the private sector owns seven integrated factories.

ENERGY SECTOR

Oil and natural gas have been discovered in western and southern Sudan, but only a small amount have been topped and refined.

MINERAL SECTOR:

Minerals based in Sudan are mica, marble, chromium, Asbestos, manganese, iron, lead, zinc, nickel, silver, gypsum, copper, uranium, and tin. Gold has been explored in eastern Sudan. Sudan exported gold of43 . 781million dollars in1998 .

THE SERVICE SECTOR:

The service sector accounts for40 % of the GDP. Its main sub sectors are:
Transport sector
the Sudan railway has 7484 km of major railway and729 km of roads.
The land transport sector is owned by private sector.

TOURISM SECTOR:

Sudan has many tourists' attraction sites, such as ancient civilization sites.
There are some resorts in the east of Sudan on the red sea coast ,such as (Arous resort)and (Arkawit resort) on the red sea hills . There is also the Blue Nile Dinder natural animal reserve.

In the North and the River Nile states, there are a lot of archeological sites on the banks of the Nile from Dongola along the Nile up to wadi halfa. Also the "Bijrawia "area near shendi which has attractive pyramids .

In the north of Dar fur , there is "jabal marra" a striking resort and "El radom" park which is famous for wild life.

Transport sector:

The Sudan shipping line public sector is equipped with 12 vessel. Port Sudan and Osman Digna (Swakin) are major ports in the Sudan. Also Swakin port is considered as the third main port in the Sudan. Bashair is a special port for Sudan's oil export. The Sudan airways is one of the oldest companies in Africa. There are three international air ports in Sudan, Khartoum international Airport, Port Sudan international Airport and Dongla international Airport.

Communication sector:-

Sudan has one of the most advanced companies in this field. It is sudatel. It is conducting highly perfect means of communications.

FREE TRADE ZONES

The Sudanese Free Zones and Markets Co. (SFZ)

The Sudanese Free Zones (SFZ) is one of Pioneering Economic Institutions in the country. It is one of the companies which guarantees freedom of capital movement and provides suitable investment climate for both the local and foreign investors. It is one of basic pillars of Sudanese Liberalization Policy.

The Sudanese Free Zones & Markets Co. was established in 1993 to adopt, enhance and implement the Free Zones concept in Sudan in addition it its commitment to a wide range of Duty Free Business & Exhibition Industry.

THE RED SEA FREE ZONE:
Located at a focal point connecting the port of Sudan, Port Sudan international Airprt, Kharloum-Port Sudan Highway and Suakin Harbour, a 26 sq. km, coastal area at the Red Sea has been planned as the Red Sea Free Zone. The Master Planning of this area was earned out and concluded by the NCCC of Tian Jin Economic Development Area of China. The RSFZ is now prepared to host all kinds of investment activities. The inclusive planning of this area is very much qualified to host:

. Free Zone Port
. Infrastructure Investment Projects
. Multi-economic activities
. Exports Processing Industries
. Industries and Assembling investments
. Banking and Insurance activities
. A wide range of related services/investments

AL GAILI FREE ZONE
Located (60) km. north of Khartoum (Capital of Sudan). This area is allotted and is now being planned to cover (20) sq.km. This area is significant since it is:

. Located within a fast economic booming circle accessed to the country's main Oil Refinery Station.
. Linked with active business and industrial communities in Khartoum, the heart of the nation's economy.
. Well connected with traffic networks of air, highways and railways extending beyond Sudan's boundaries into the African markets.

INVESTMENT GUARANTEES
Sudan is a signatory to the conventions on Arbitration and Investment Guarantees and is a member of:
a) The Arab Agency for Investment Guarantees,
b) The International Agency for Investment Guarantees.

The Sudanese Free Zones Act of 1994 stipulates:
□ No property, assets, funds or other possessions are subject to nationalization or confiscation.
□ The right of IMPORT EXPORT DATA and profits at any stage of duly met obligations.

INCENTIVE & FACILITIES

. 100% ownership.
. 100% IMPORT EXPORT DATA & profits.
. No personal income tax
. No corporate tax for 12 years renewable.
. No currency restriction
. No restrictions on entry & stay permits.
. Cost effective labour supply.
. Freedom of labour recruitment.
.Abundant & cost effective raw material and production resources.

MAJOR SFZ ACTIVITIES

Trade

Import of varied commodities and goods for wholesale and retail distribution through the duty free and other outlets and shops in all major towns of Sudan.

Managing a Bond Area

Export of raw material and other Sudanese products such as: groundnuts, sesame and other oil seeds. cotton, wood products, water-melon seeds, vegetables & fruits, edible oils, animal fodder, meat and livestock.

Fairs and Exhibitions:

Organizing of local and international fairs including the annual International Fair of Khartoum in addition to participation and representation in fairs organized abroad.

Hotels and Catering:

To build and manage hotels and recreation facilities and to provide various catering services.

FAIRS AND EXHIBITIONS

The SFZ Fair Grounds was opened early in 1978 and is considered as one of the best exhibition facilities in Africa and the Middle East. SFZ was able to organize outstanding international and local exhibitions during the year.

The Fair Location:

The 475,000 square metres Fair Grounds lies on the western bank of the Blue Nile in eastern Khartoum. It is about seven kilometres from the city centre and the International Airport, The SFZ main offices are located within the Fair Grounds.

The Pavilions:

The Fair has three pavilions of international standard each with an area of 1800 square metres. Additional covered spaces can be provided at short notice if the need arises. The open exhibition area covers more than 40,000 square metres.

Annual Fairs:

. The International Fair of Khartoum-
. Slates of Sudan Fair,
. Khartoum Information Technology Exhibition.
. Sudan Industrial Fair.
. Sudan Agricultural Fair.
. Eid Consumer Fair.
. School & Family Needs Fair.

THE RED SEA FREE ZONE

Name of Project:	The Red Sea Free Zone.
Location:	38 kms to the South of Port Sudan town.
Area:	600 kms – 26 kms are prepared as a first stage.
Date of Inauguration:	February 2000.
Cost of the implementation of the first stage:	US$ 12 millions.
Total Operating Investments:	US $ 45 millions.
The Investment Map:	Includes Several activities; such as: 41% Industrial Activities. 15% Commercial Activities. 44% service Activities. The preparation of export industries comes at the top of the set objectives.
The operating investments in the Zone:	- The number of licences granted to investors is 415 licences. The commercial system forms a ratio of 80%. These include the import, export, re-export, and transit trade to neighbouring states. - The total invested area is 600,000 m^2. - The industrial activity started to assume an important role, by the entry of some companies in the plastic products industry and some Sudanese exports processing industries; such as, gum Arabic and oil seeds (like sesame).For increasing the investment capacities, Dubai Islamic Bank implemented depots, by an area of 40,000m^2, at high quality specifications.
Contact Address:	The Sudanese Free Zones and Markets Co. The General Administration for Free Zones,
Internet site:	. www.sudanfreezones.com

GARRI (AL-GAILI) FREE ZONE

Name of Project:	Garri (Al-Gaili) Free Zone
Location:	70 Kms North of Khartoum the Capital
Area:	26 kms^2 near the main station of petroleum refining. The infrastructures are complete.
Date of Inauguration:	End of December 2004
Cost of the implementation of the first stage:	US$ 9 millions.
The Available Investment Opportunities:	- Industrial investment and assembly industries. - Supporting services., logistic centres and distribution services. - Food industries trade centres. - Light transformational industries. - Packing and packaging requirements industry. - Petrochemicals and plastic products industry. - Financial and consultancy services.
Contact Address:	The Sudanese Free Zones and Markets Co. The General Administration for Free Zones, Tel: 249-183-481814/481811.
Internet site:	www.sudanfreezones.com

THE FREE PORT PROJECT

Name of Project:	The Free Port Project
Location:	Red Sea State

Objectives:	Expansion of sea transport vessels
Current Situation:	- A study and preliminary indicators have been completed for the establishment of the port. - Specialized bodies have been contacted for preparing the technical and economic feasibility study; together with the detailed and comprehensive plant.
Contact Address:	The Sudanese Free Zones and Markets Co. The General Administration for Free Zones, Tel: 249-183-481814/481811.
Internet site:	www.sudanfreezones.com

MINISTRY OF FINANCE & NATIONAL ECONOMY

The Ministry of Finance and National Economy is the principal competent agency assigned the functions and responsibilities for managing and directing the national economy to achieve its goals and objectives within the federal system of rule and market-oriented economy enshrined in the country's philosophy, strategy and programs.

MAIN FUNCTIONS & RESPONSIBILITIES OF THE MINISTRY:

Overall Functions:

Play a major role in the economic front to spawn socio-economic resilience and economic health through:

- Upgrading the economic capacities of the country through designing intellectual policies and instruments capable of stimulating resource mobilization.
- Liberalizing the national economy from various forms of restrictions and distortions inhibiting economic activities and competitiveness,
- Realizing a balanced national socio-economic development,
- Allocating economic resources in a way that raises standards of living, generates prosperity and engenders gracious livelihood,
- Building and maintaining a strategic food grains stock and achieve food security, and.
- Serving as a custodian of the public funds.

Management of the National Economy:

- Formulating development strategies, programs and policies in order to achieve economic growth and development.
- Introducing modern scientific techniques and methodologies of macro-economic modelling, analysis, review and monitoring mechanisms necessary for improving economic management and performance and rational use of resources.
- Spearheading the national development process.
- Monitoring economic progress and performance in view of the rapidly changing international environment and remove impediments to impeccable strategic path to growth and development with transformation.

FINANCIAL & ECONOMIC PLANNING:

- Ensuring coordination and integration between financial and economic management and development planning and improvising coherent policies and procedures required to achieve the desired objectives and targets thereof.

- Maintaining effective institutional mechanisms and modalities to ensure coordination and consolidation between development plans and programs at the Federal, State, Local and scrotal levels in order to realize national objectives.
- Developing and maintaining effective monitoring and evaluation systems to analyze Federal and State plans and programs in a comparative fashion.

FINANCIAL MANAGEMENT:

- Drawing and executing financial, monetary and developmental policies, plans and strategies.
- Introducing modern techniques and systems for budget preparation and management.
- Developing standards and regulations to ensure optimum utilization of national resources.
- Developing sound policies and appropriate instruments and measures to restore financial balance through increased revenues and rational use of public expenditure and ensuring that such expenditure is fairly distributed and in accordance with priorities.

FINANCIAL & ACCOUNTING CONTROL:

- Developing appropriate policies that sharpen the institutional structure of the financial and accounting systems and introducing requisite rules and regulations to ensure and realize effective custody of public funds.
- Strengthening the accounting system and applying modern techniques to ensure accurate recording of public assets and financial resources in systematic registers.
- Developing and upgrading human and administrative capacities of accounting and internal audit.

EXTERNAL FINANCE & ECONOMIC COOPERATION :

- Drawing strategies, policies, modalities and procedures for external financial cooperation and granting final approval of external cr agreements.
- Upgrading capacities and skills in the fields of management, implementation and loan negotiation and efficiently deal with external economic agencies.
- Effectively represent the country in the annual meetings of international and regional financial and economic institutions.

SUDAN DEVELOPMENT CORPORATION

ADDRESS:

Sudan Development Corporation
SDC Building Complex
Street 21 Al Amarat (New Extension) Khartoum
P.O.Box 710
Khartoum –Sudan
Cables :DECORP
Telex :24078 SDC SD
Tel. :472186-472195(10 Lines)
Fax : 249-11-472148

ESTABLISHMENT DATE : March 1974 (Act Mo. 93)
AUTHORIZED CAPITAL : US $ 500 million
PAID UP CAPITAL : US $ 200 million
LEGAL STATUS : An autonomous Corporate body,
Financially independent, and wholly owned by
The Government of Sudan.

LINE OF BUSINESS: SDC is the leading National Development Finance Institution (MDFI) in the country.

OBJECTIVES:

To identify, formulate, prepare, appraise, implement, and monitor and evaluate joint-venture projects between Sudanese and foreign technical and financial parties in various sectors particularly agriculture, industry and services.

To act as catalyst by combining in joint-venture projects local funds and entrepreneurship with foreign appropriate technology and capital for the acceleration of socio-economic development of Sudan.

To provide finance, technical and management skills to technically sound, financially feasible and economically viable new and existing projects/companties in both public and private sectors.

SALIENT FINANCIAL FEATURES AS AT 31 DECEMBER 1995:

Total assets: US $ 133.9 million
Total Investment Portfolio: 104 projects/companies
Total Value of the Portfolio: 126.9 million.
Total Equity/Musharaka
Investment: US $ 53.2

MANAGEMENT & ORGANIZATION:

Board of Directors:
Eng. Al Saeed Osman Mahgoub - Chairman
Dr. Mohamed Kheir El Zubair - Member
Eng. Monier Yousif El Hakim -Member
Mrs. Bedour Osman Abu Affan - Member
Mr. George Moris Lomoro -Member
Dr. Babiker Mohamed Tom -Member
Mr. Khogali Abu Bakr -Member
Mr. Abdalla Ali Abdalla -Member
Mr. Nasr El Din Mohamed Omer -Member
Mr. Mahmoud Yousif Ismail -Secretary

TOP MANAGEMENT:

NAME	NATIONALITY	ACADEMIC QUALIFICATION	STATUS	DEPT./SECTION
Dr. Mohamed Kheir EL Zubair	Sudanese	Ph.D. Degree	Managing Director	
Mr. Awad Abdalla Higazi	Sudanese	M.Sc.Degree	Project Director	Project
Mr. Farouk Mohamed Abderahman	Sudanese	M.Sc.Degree	Manager	Project-Preparation

Mr. Abdalla Karamalla Babiker	Sudanese	B.Sc.(Hon).Degree	Manager	Follow-up
Mr. Stephen Pitya Lako	Sudanese	M.Sc.Degree	Manager	Planning Research & Foreign Relation
Mr.Nafee Mahmoud Hamid	Sudanese	M.Sc.Degree	Manager	Administration
Mr. Nasr El din Satti Badi	Sudanese	Accounting Experience	Manager	Finance
Mr. Ibn El-Haj Mohamed Salih	Sudanese	M.Sc.Degree	Manager	SDC Building Complex

STATUS AND OWNERSHIP

Sudan Development Corporation (SDC), established in 1974, is the leading financial institution involved with investment and the provision of finance for development in the Sudan. SDC, as defined by its Act, is an autonomous corporate body having perpetual succession, a common seal, and may sue and be sued in its own name.

Authorized Capital = U.S.$500 Million
Paid Up Capital = U.S. $200 Million
SDC is wholly owned by the Government of the Sudan and is managed by a Board of Six Directors.

OBJECTIVE

I. Contribute to the promotion and acceleration of the economic development of the Sudan through the provision of financial and technical assistance to new and existing revenue-bearing projects/companies.
II. Encourage the participation of capital and skills - domestic and foreign - for the economic development of the Sudan with the objective of contributing directly or indirectly to the increase in earning and / or saving of foreign exchange through export promotion or import substitution.
III. Initiate and encourage the extension of technical and managerial assistance in the promotion and development of revenue-bearing projects, whether or not such projects shall be financed by SDC.
IV. Act as a coordinating agent in projects or joint ventures; by providing local currency components of the financing and / or entrepreneurship and supplementing the appropriate technology and foreign finance from Arab, Asian and other international sources.

FUNCTIONS

In pursuance of its objectives the Corporation may:
I. Promote and identify opportunities in new development projects in the Sudan.
II. Invest directly in any project, which proves to be financially sound, commercially viable and technically feasible.

III. Provide administrative, technical and financial assistance for the development, expansion or operatin of projects/companies.
IV. Assist in streamlining the operation of existing development projects to achieve optimum utilization of planned capacities.

INVESTMENT CRITERIA

Sudan Development Corporation within the context of its investment policy :-
I. Manages its participations and capital assets in accordance with the principles of sound business practice within the framework of national development policies.
II. Uses its best endeavours to attract foreign finance and mobilize internal financial resources.
III. Seeks to diversify its portfolio of investment among different economic sectors and endeavours to extend its range of activity to cover the different regions of the country.
IV. Extends its assistance to revenue-bearing projects and companies in the fields of agriculture, industry, agro-industry, mining and services.
V. Accords priority to projects aiming at import-substitution and export promotion.
VI. Participates only in projects, which prove through feasibility studies and appraisal reports, to be technically feasible, commercially viable, economically sound and contribute to the development of the National Economy.
VII. Renders assistance only to projects, which demonstrate the availability of competent management and the commitment of adequate finance including cost over-runs.

FINANCIAL POLICY

I. SDC requires sponsors to make sufficient contribution to the financing of projects to ensure their commitment to the success of the projects.
II. SDC conducts its operations on a self-sustained and profitable basis.
III. SDC normally acquires a share in the equity capital of any one project.
IV. SDC shareholding shall not exceed 40% of the total capital of the project.
V. SDC may dispose of its shares or fade out its investment in any one project whenever if deems appropriate.
VI. The total amount of SDC's financial assistance in the form of equity, guarantees and other forms, to any one project shall not exceed 50% of the total cost of the project and 10% of the net worth of the Corporation.
VII. Loans shall be repayable in the currency or currencies in which they are extended or in any other currency or currencies acceptable to SDC,
VIII.SDC shall make adequate provisions against potential losses and build up reserves to a level consistent with sound financial practices taking into account the size and quality of its portfolio of equity participation, loans and guarantees. Within these limitations, SDC shall seek to pay fair dividends to the Government while maintaining satisfactory prospects for the continuation of a sound liquidity situation in local and foreign currencies.
IX. SDC shall not bear the risks resulting from foreign exchange fluctuations in respect of loans. The borrower(s) shall bear the costs of such risks.
X. SDC shall not incur or permit any of its subsidiaries to incur any long-term debt from outside sources whereby the total indebtedness of SDC and all its subsidiaries exceeds three times the capital and reserves of SDC and its subsidiaries.
XI. SDC shall seek to obtain the best return on its short-term investments while reasonably diversifying their maturities in accordance with financial projection.
XII. SDC shall be reimbursed for all its preinvestment expenses.

FINANCIAL ASSISTANCE

SDC provides loans and other forms of financial assistance as follows ;-
a) Equity Participation in Project Capital.
b) Islamic Modes of Finance.
Murabaha - Financial assistance in which a client desirous of purchasing equipment, goods, raw materials etc., requests the financial institution to acquire these items on his behalf at cost and sells them to the client on a cost-plus negotiable profit margin basis. Capital and profit will be payable on terms and conditions to be agreed upon.

Musharaka (Participation) - Financial assistance, which is formally a limited partnership, whereby both the financial institution and the customer provide capital for a specific project. Another possibility is the participation of the financial institution in an existing enterprise by means of a capital contribution. The pro-rata distribution of profits between the financial institution and the customer is subject to a contract between the parties. Losses are shared by the partners in direct proportion to their capital contribution. The financial institution may participate in the management of the venture but it may also waive this right.

Musharaka is based on either permanent or diminishing participation. In the latter form the participation of the financial institution diminishes through time.

Leasing - This is a mode of financial assistance under which production and/or services facilities are provided by SDC and leased to the client on terms and conditions to be agreed upon. Normally, this includes rentals, operational costs and maintenance charges to be paid by the client.

Guarantees - In certain circumstances the Corporation may further assist a project by acting as a guarantor within the limits of total finance indicated above.

THE ROLE OF SDC

In addition to the financial assistance listed above, the Corporation plays a leading role in all stages of the project cycle including the operational stage. The continuous support of the corporation may include:

I. Assistance during the negotiation stages to ensure that the project company will be structured on a sound economic, financial and legal basis.
II. Participation on the Board of Directors of these project companies.
III. Participation in the promotion, formulation, establishment and commissioning of these project companies-
IV. Provision of contracts inside and outside the Sudan to facilitate and expe implementation of projects.
V. Spearheading of reappraisal and market surveys and studies during the operational stage.
VI. Monitoring and reviewing of operations throughout the project life,
VII. Provision of technical assistance to new or operational projects whether or not financed by SDC.

RELATIONS WITH FOREIGN INSTITUTIONS

SDC maintains a wide network of relationships with foreign finance institutions, which permits it to serve as a link between Sudanese project sponsors and foreign technical or management partners, investors and financial sources.

THE LOCAL SPONSOR

I. Several projects co-financed by the Corporation are initiated by local sponsors seeking assistance. In cases where a project is identified by the Corporation, one of the first steps is to find a suitable local sponsor. Such a local sponsor may be an individual, a group of individuals, partnership, or a corporate body.
II. The local sponsor should be ready to participate in the development of the project and ultimately to become the owner of the project.
III. In cases where 3 project is initiated by a local sponsor, he / she must submit a preferability study outlining the principal characteristics of the proposed project, on the basis of which the corporation shall decide the further steps to be taken.
IV. The local sponsor will also be expected to assist the technical partner in planning the project and to acquire a reasonable stake in the share capital of the project company to be established

FEES AND CHARGES

Financial assistance is advanced at a profit margin determined from time to time by the Board of Directors.

Fees chargeable by SDC include: "Murabaha" margin; an investigation fee of 1/2 percent charged on total financial assistance to a project; a commitment fee of 1 percent payable on the undisbursed portion of a loan; guarantee fees at a rate to be determined by the Board of Directors; charges in respect to technical assistance are determined on the basis of mutual agreement.

LEGAL DOCUMENTS
a) All financial assistance rendered by SDC should be evidenced by authenticated documents.
b) SDC assists projects implemented by enterprises having distinct legal entity.
c) Subject to the type of assistance rendered, any of the following legal documents are required wherever relevant: Memorandum and Articles of Association; Certificate of Registration; Shareholder's Agreement; "Murabaha" Agreement; "Musharaka" Agreement; Lease Agreement; Loan Agreement; Technical Cooperation Agreement; and Management Agreement.

Security To protect its own financial position, SDC shall take adequate security measures towards any loan, murabaha, or guarantees and in this respect shall ascertain that any of the following requirements for collateral security are fulfilled:-

a) First mortgage on the borrower's registered property including land, buildings, machines and other fixed assets and / or a lien on the floating assets.
b) Bank guarantee from a reputable bank acceptable to SDC or counter guarantee.
c) In addition SDC may in its absolute discretion: Demand collateral security from a third party or a counter guarantee; Earmark certain present or future assets of the borrower as security with regard to the claims of the Corporation;
Demand post-dated cheques.

HOW TO APPROACH THE CORPORATION FOR SUPPORT

Initial contacts with the Corporation should be made by way of a formal letter supported by: Prefeasibility study on the marketing, technical and financial aspects of the project; Name of the applicant's bankers and, if a company or a Partnership, the Registration Certificate, Memorandum and Articles of Association or Partnerships Deed; Licences, permits and concessions which will be available to the project; Audited accounts for previous years if any. (for existing companies); Other information and documents SDC may deem necessary.

EL-NILEIN INDUSTRIAL DEVELOPMENT BANK GROUP:

P.O. Box 1722
KHARTOUM - SUDAN
Tels: 780082-773939-780750
Tlx: 22456-22243
Fax: 780776

NIDBG is a pioneering developmental banking institution in financing industrial development projects in all sectors (food industry, chemical industry, textile, construction materials, medicines, engineering workshops etc.)

1- The group extends its funding services through all Islamic formulas of financing.

2- Special concern and easy funding terms are extended to the small scale, rural handicraft, and productive families industries.

3- Through its branches spreading in all the states of the Sudan, the group presents its advanced banking and investment services the country- wide in realization of the balanced comprehensive development goal, besides its branches in the United Arab Emirates (UAE).

4- NIDBG is the only banking institution which has introduced the automatic teller system, and work is currently underway to generalize the system in all the group's branches.

5- The group presents comprehensive investment projects for the expatriates, and developing the export sector.

6- Our correspondents network covers the biggest capitals of the world.

The group's affiliated company (the Industrial Bank;s Company) provides production inputs and equipment to craftsmen and the small scale producers and productive families with the aim of stabilizing the price and encouraging the productive sectors.

8- NIDBG following incorporation of former Nilein Bank and the Sudanese Bank for Industrial Development, has become more capable of realizing the comprehensive industrial development.

9- NIDBG is the only bank in Sudan that has branches outside the country.

10- NIDBG has capital contributions in many of the regional financing institution and companies (funding program), Arab trade, Arab financial services company and Kenana Sugar Company .

11- NIDBG has broad relation with much of the regional and international development financing institutions.

(NIDBG The Pioneering Name in Banks' World).

The NIDBG Was constituted on the 8th of March 1993 as a consequence of a merger process between the Nilein Bank and the previous industrial Bank of Sudan. The new organ embodies the mission of the two banks, respectively commercial banking and development banking.

THE GROUP OBJECTIVES:

1- Mobilizing internal and external resources in the development process.
2- Providing financial assistance for industrial sector.
3- Providing technical assistance for industrial enterprises.
4- Supporting small-scale industries both financially and technically.
5- Providing finance to different economic sectors in Sudan.
6- Providing banking services to enhance foreign trade.

THE GROUP ACTIVITIES:

The group performs all the activities of commercial bank among which are:
- Accepting different kinds of deposits.
- Opening letters of cr and issuing letters of guarantee.
- Dealing in foreign exchange.
- Extending cr to different economic sector.
- Establishing correspondent network with foreign banks and in international financial institutions.

THE GROUP NETWORK OF BRANCHES:

NIDBG Comprises about 42 banking branches inside Sudan and one branch in Abu Dhabi abroad. These branches provide all banking activities.

THE CORRESPONDENTS NETWORK:

The group enjoys a wide range of correspondents all over the world, the network intensively correspondents covers the different parts of the world and assists in promoting foreign trade in Sudan.

THE NIDBG'S MAIN SUBSIDIARY:

The group has its own subsidiary company, the industrial Bank company for development and trade . The company tended to support industrial enterprises, both large scale and small scale. Within its activities, the company also work in the field of foreign trade, it is engaged in the import and export of goods.

General features of the group:

Authorized capital	Is. 10.000.000.000
Paid- up capital	Is. 7.000.000.000
Number of branches	42
Planned branches	8
Number of employees	2000

Finally the NIDBG seeks to extend cooperation with all institution and corporation ... etc, in different fields of banking activities, hoping that this cooperation would develop the mutual interest of all parties.
All correspondents should be sent to the following address:

NILEIN INDUSTRIAL DEVELOPMENT BANK GROUP,
P.O BOX 1722
KHARTOUM SUDAN
TELEX ; 22456 - 22243, FAX : 780776
PHONE : 771992 - 780750 - 780082
TELEGRAPH ADDRESS : NILEIN BANK OR SENAIE

AGRICULTURE BANK OF SUDAN

Head office : Al Mugran area, to the west and Gamhoriya Avenu.
P.O.Box : 1263

Tel : 777432 – 770150 – 779413
Fax : 778296
Tel : 22610
The Bank's capital is L.S 2 billion. It has 114 branches spreading at the state levels.
The Bank welcomes its clients and presents them its quick and advanced services:

1. Opening of accounts in foreign currencies which allow the opportunity of depositing and withdrawing along with easy procedures.
2. Saving facilities in local and foreign currencies with high satisfactory returns, at hand deposit, saving accounts and investment deposits.
3. Buying and selling of foreign currencies and providing legal banking facilities.
4. Financing of internal and external trade, issuing of Bank cheques and cr statements and opening of cr document.
5. Correspondents all over the world.

Distinguished services for the expatriates.

INVESTMENT

Investment is a renewed economic activity governed by the renewed ambitions of man, with the changing demands of life and with its unstable conditions.
due to the availability of information, the world has become one village with resources competitively sought by big, international companies.

These companies seek the best conditions for the investment of their funds, especially that the development of stock markets and the increase in their number, along with the diversity of high technology contributed to ensuring a quick turnover.
Sudan realized the need for investment, now that the country has great potentialities, and its unexploded resources prevail its wide area. These resources included crude oil, valuable minerals,

arable land and conducive atmospheric conditions secured by its tropical location.
Sudan also realized the necessity of providing an investment atmosphere with the most stable conditions to attract investors who are no larger barred by barriers of time and place.

So it (SUDAN) hastened to regulating and encouraging investment, now and kept coping with its quickening pace.
Promotion for investment now comes on top of economic researchers' concern, and has even become the most important marketing factor in the field of economic infrastructure.
Sudan was successfully during the previous decade in promoting investment in the various fields and scored notable successes on the investment domain.
Sudan enacted in 1999 a law for the regulation and encouragement of investment and determined privileges and guarantees.

The law exempted strategic investment from direct fax. And granted non-strategic investment a tax exemption not exceeding five years.
It also cut short investment procedures and determined where each procedure can be carried out to save time.

The law further stated that no state nor local duties should be imposed on any commercial investment project.
Investment is guaranteed against nationalization and confiscation as investors are entitled to restore their investment after obtaining an agreement from the authority that issued the license. they can hence get their funds and profits accruing from the investment.

Widened during the 1990s and included agriculture, industry, animal production, electricity, oil and minerals.

Multi-national companies entered Sudan and competition started owing to Sudan's adoption of the economic liberalization policy.
The stability of this policy, along with the government trend towards modernizing the structure of the Sudanese economy to cope with developments, at the international level boosted the channel of investment in the country. Globalization led to a radical change in the economic dealings.

Some of the most prominent fields of investment in Sudan include projects of infrastructures, electricity, water, strategic projects, heavy petro-chemical projects, along with projects of rehabilitation, modernization, expansion, implementation of quality programmes and international standard specifications.

The investment in oil prosecution was widely undertaken to attract local and foreign investment.

Many international companies embarked on the prospecting , refinement and transportation of oil.

The oil transportation sector received the concern of local investors rather than investment in the field of oil storage and other concomitant oil-production industries.
In the field of processing industries, greater concern was given to this sector on the domain of investment.

Many industries based on the local agricultural raw materials were adopted and promoted. Such being the case, sugar, meat, animal production and cotton industries became popular. This is in addition to the spread of small-scale industries throughout the country. Sudanese expatriates were even inclined to invest in many investment projects and contributed to the establishment of passenger and goods transportation companies under the umbrella of this attractive investment atmosphere.

OFFSHORE INDUSTRY, GOVERNMENTAL AND RELATED ORGANISATIONS IN SUDAN

Institute of Energy Research
PO Box 2649, Khartoum
Sudan
Tel: +249 11 80 137

Ministry of Energy, National Energy Administration
PO Box 2087, Khartoum
Sudan
Tel: +249 11 75 595

Sudan Exploration and Production Authority
PO Box 2986, Khartoum
Sudan
Tel: +249 11 79 366
Fax: +249 11 73 663

BANKING SYSTEM CONTACTS

There are many commercial and specialized banks, which have branches in 26 states. Also there are foreign exchange bureau's (Sirafat). The exchange rates are determine according to the demand and supply factors (market forces).

The banks in the Sudan:

Bank of the Sudan Tel: 778064-778594 Fax: 778547

1st) Governmental Banks

Bank of Khartoum

Tel: 779924-770198-780137
Fax: 772880-774528

Sudanese Saving and Social Development
Tel: 774358- 775157

SPECIALIZED BANKS

Elnilein Industrial Development Group Bank

Tel: 7712109-771984-773939
Fax: 774686-772638

Agricultural Bank of Sudan

Tel: 777401-776975-770150-774049
Fax: 779081-778296

Farmer's Commercial Bank

Tel: 774960-783005-779836
Fax: 779907

Animal Resources Bank

Tel: 472025-472026-449383
Fax: 471533

3rd) Private Sharing Banks

Tadamon Islamic Bank
Tel: 781709-771505-771845
Fax: 771073

Elbaraka Bank
Tel: 783962-784911-780688
Fax: 788948

Omduman National Bank
Tel: 770400-777221-7770360779306
Fax: 770392

Elgharb Islamic Bank
Tel: 779583-777110-779583-788472-772529

Faisal Islamic Bank
Tel: 773566-773401-774716-781848-772800
Fax: 781830

Ialamic Co-operation and Development Bank
Tel: 775234-775366-774081-780505-777706
Fax: 777715

Islamic Bank of Sudan
Tel: 780759-780142-774554-774552
Fax: 779545

Sudanese - Saudi Bank
Tel: 781708-775049-776700
Fax: 771505

Sudanese French Bank

Tel: 770403-778600-773794-779542
Fax: 771740-773696

ElShamal Islamic Bank
Tel: 774728-779078-782190-782186
Fax: 773585-774277

Almashriq Bank
Tel: 779840-778777
Fax: 772743

Customs

Customs Tariff structure For Imports To Sudan
Products imported to Sudan are Subject to four banks to tariff rate a follows (in 2001)

Rate	Example of products
0%	Rice, rentals, computer system of accessories, animal production inputs
6%	Raw matenals, capital goods, pharmaceuticals, fertilizers.
20%	Intermediate goods foodstuffs.
40%	Household machinese, passenger cars, Tobacco cement, Sugar

EXILE DUTINGOR IMPORTS

The following products are subject to excise duty in addition to the import tariff rate.

Product	Exile Rate
Crenate	25%
Saloon cars	40%

Pickup cars	40%
Tobacco and cigarettes	200%
Mineral water softdrinks	10%
Parts	10%
Sugar	10%

VAT on Imports

All imports to Sudan are subject to VAT with 10% except the following products.
(1) Agricultural inputs (seeds, fertilizers, and presticides)
(2) Cultural inputs papers for printing News papers of magazines and printing equipment's.
(3) Capital goods

Export Duties
All produced of Sudan origin when exported to any country are not subject to any export duty with the exception of raw hides of skins which are subject to 15% export duty. All exports are exported from the VAT.

SSMO

SUDANESE STANDARDS AND METROGY ORGANIZATION
P.O. Box: 13574 Khartoum Fax: 774852 Tel: (249)-11-775247
E-mail: ssmo@Sudantel.net

SSMO IN BRIEF LEGAL IDENTITY AND FOUNDATION:

Sudanese Standards & Metrology Organization low was issued in 1992 and indorsed by the National Assembly
SSMO Headquarters based in Khartoum where it opeates the following offices:

States Office:

1. Port sudan Harbour Office
2. Al Obied Office
3. Al Gedarif Office
4. SSMo s Objectives
5. Protection of consumer
6. Protection of National Economy
7. Promotion of efficiency and maintining quality control of local product
8. Training the required cadre to run the job related to standard.
9. Awarding certificates for imports and exports according to standard requirements
10. Linking Sudan's Stardards & metrology with international and regional Organizations
11. Linching orientation to enlighten the public and local institution.

For the first is to realize which of the best quality and for later must have to follow the total quality management.

SSMo Facilities. Head Quarter Khartoum:

1. cereal lab
2. Dairly lab
3. Mineral water lab

4. Paints lab
5. High performance liquid
6. Chromatography lab
7. Microbiology lab
8. Gas chromatography lab.
9. Analysis and Hall marking of Gold and precious Metal lab.
10. Port Sudan lab.

Information Center(1.c)

SSMO information center in Khartoum work in coordination to exchange up-to-date with international and regional standards & metrology organizations such as ISO, CODEX, ARSO & ADIMO in additions SSMO coordinates with British, Japan, India, Australia, South Africa, Germany, Saudi Arabia and Tunisia, In the field of standards in these respected countries. Further.

More, in response to the requirements and needs of integration with world to boost business however SUDAN adopted as active policy to restore quality control system related to regional and international standards organization. As a result Sudan has obtained the fully accred membership of the following

1. CODEX
2. ISO
3. ARSO
4. ASMO
5. International Institute for Standards and Metrology of Islamic countries based in Turkey
6. Mycotoxin lab
7. Microbiology lab.
8. Gas chromatography lab
9. Analysis and Hall marking of Gold and Precious Metal lab.
10. Port Sudan lab

SCIENTIFIC RESEARCH

SSMocooperates with Sudanese Universities and scientific research center to make technical standards data of commodities which needed. Blow are number of researches conducted by SSMO collaboration with universities and research centers.

1. GUM Arabic (Hashab) and rest of Sudanese gum varieties
2. All Karkdi varieties (the process includes picking, drying and packing methods)
3. aflatoxins and ocratoxins researches on groundnuts Cakes and grain
4. Poultry and animal seeds industry in Khartoum
5. Promotion of local bricks including up grading of a hand used machine.
6. Promotion of jaguar Sugar and its applications in local industry
7. Using of solar energy for drying vegetable and fruits.
8. Use of solar energy for production distilled water
9. separation of impurities from the drinking water
10. Improvement of town bus to the standard required
11. Promotion of hides and skins production.

INVESTMENT 30 REASONS TO INVEST IN THE SUDAN

1. Investors should not miss the privilege to invest in Sudan, the largest country in Africa and the Middle East, and number ten in size in the world, with its unmatched investment opportunities in all Sectors.

2. Sudan is a country with great potentialities whether in form of the extensive uncultivated farmland or the plentiful water resources, differing climatic zones; its huge animal wealth and limitless natural pastureland, forests or the mineral wealth, particularly its large oil reserves, which have not been fully exploited yet. The diversities in wealth are an added advantage.

3. There are countless and various investment opportunities in the different economic sectors such as the agricultural sector, the industrial sector, energy and mining and in fields of economic services. There are also investment opportunities in the fields of air, and road transport, warehousing and the infrastructure sectors. In all these areas the Investment Authority will do the homework and finalize necessary steps on behalf of the investor.

4. With its abundant resources and immense potential, investors in the Sudan are assured of great benefits and successful partnerships.

5. In addition to the availability of raw material, Sudan is home to the most secure and stable environment. It is an ideal climate for investors and businessmen.

6. An unprecedented investment Encouragement Act enacted with its huge incentives and privileges.

7. There are well-identified economic, social and investment plans and sectoral programmes embodied in the "Comprehensive National Strategy for the Sudan".

8. The most recent reformatory steps taken by the state have freed investment in Sudan from all restrictive acts. The Sudanese economy is a market-driven economy, and there is a rapid shift towards privatization in all sectors.

9. Stable policies, easy access to all cities, quick movement to the different parts of the country.

10. With its strategic location, Sudan is a gateway to African and Middle-Eastern markets and beyond.

11. All procedures pertaining to investment in Sudan are prompt and of a simple nature. There shall be facilities, adequate assurances and incentives for both the investor and the invested capital without any hindrances.

12. Transactions in hard currency shall not be restricted, and there shall be an extraordinary freedom of trade with the outside world and at the national level; assured flexibility in the pricing policies.

13. Availability of a highly trained and qualified manpower in the agricultural, industrial, mining, energy and the economic services sectors.

14. The banking sector in Sudan is firmly established and banking services are accessible in all the states of the country. Moreover there are some specialized banks which are solely devoted to spur investment and development to greater efficiency in particular fields. There are also some state-owned institutions and private companies that finance investment activities. Partners to all are invited.

15. Big market at home and abroad to the nine neighbouring countries. The unique geographical location of the country makes it an ideal marketing center and traverse point for supplying neighbouring countries with commodities and services.

16. Cheap labour.

17. Organized business sector ready for joint ventures.

18. Examples of success stories in local and foreign direct investment such as the giant projects in sugar, telecommunication and oil can be emulated.

19. More than thirty universities and research centers as reservoir for highly trained and qualified personnel.

20. Sudan is the largest and key member of the Common Market for East and South Africa (COMESA), in addition to its membership in other international, regional and sub-regional economic and financial institutions. Sudan is also party to regional and international investment protection regimes.

21. Advanced telecommunication networks... easy access to and from Sudan to any place in the world.

22. Affordable destination with easy air connections to and from Sudan to Africa, the Middle East, Europe and beyond.

23. Different varieties of hotel services with affordable prices for tourists and investors.

24. Roads, seaports and airports connecting the national capital with the regional states and production centers.

25. Enchanting locations... the Nile which is the longest river in the world-the confluence in Khartoum of the Blue and White Niles- the Sahara desert, the mountains and the valleys with unmatched scenery... Wealth in wildlife and game viewing□The country is an ideal destination for tourists and filmmakers.

26. An investment regime that does not discriminate between foreigners and nationals; complete ownership with guarantees against any form of nationalization or confiscation.

27. Well-established stock markets as well as insurance and re-insurance companies.

28. Easy and quick visa procedure.

29. The country is well known for the traditions of hospitality and warmth of its people.

30. Pleasant climate in most parts of the year including the Merranean, poor savannah, rich savannah and equatorial.

The historical, deep-rooted, cordial and warm relations that characterize Indo-Sudanese ties for thousands of years is an added incentive, indeed a solid foundation of economic, trade and investment relations.

SUDAN ECONOMIC POTENTIAL & DEVELOPMENT PROSPECTS

Sudan is an Afro-Arab country of multi-ethnic, multi-cultural and multi-lingual society. It enjoys a remarkable strategic location in the center of the African continent that marks a melding point between Arabs and sub-Saharan peoples. The country shares extensive boarders with nine countries of Northern, Central, Eastern and Western Africa. Such juxtaposition engenders a mix of trade, culture, social, ethnic and other human ties built through history.

The country enjoys a total area of 2.5 million km^2, the largest in Africa. It extends from the hot arid North to West tropics in the South with diversified ecosystems that provide immense fertile land of about 80 million hectares (about 20% of this land space is cultivated), natural pastures of about 24 million hectares, forest area of about 64 million hectares and the remaining land is desert or semi-desert. Considerable water resources is available from the River Nile and its tributaries, seasonal streams and rains with annual amount of 109 billion m^3 of water in addition to the underground water underlay the Nubian Sand-Stone Aquifer which is one of the the largest water reservoirs in the world of estimated potential rechargeable 29 billion m^3 of water. Sudan also enjoys a long coastal line at the Red Sea.

Current estimates put the population in excess of 30 million with estimated annual growth rate of 2.6% and a population density of 10.2 per km^2, though this figure masks wide variation with respect to effective population density on arable land which exceeds 50 persons per km^2. About 67% of the population live in rural areas while 33% live in urban areas. The demographic characteristics of the country indicate a young population structure with the number of population under 15 years accounts for about 45% of total population, according to the last Census of 1993. Total estimated labor force accounts for 9 million with increasing female participation in economic activities. Unemployed people represent about 15% of the total labor force. Employment structure since 1996 is dominated by agriculture followed by services, industry, transport and construction with 55%, 10%, 5%,6% and 3% respectively. Broad agriculture and rural sector espouse about 77% of the labor force.

Agriculture remains the leading sector in the economy with an estimated contribution of 45% of GDP, and 85% of export earnings before the year 2000. The main export commodites are livestock (having potential animal wealth of about 128 million heads of sheep, goats, cattle and camels), sesame, groundnuts, cotton, vegetables, fruits, sugar and gum Arabic. Oil exports started in August and refined oil products and natural gas in July 2000.

In addition to its natural, agricultural and animal resources, Sudan abounds with potential mineral wealth of which petroleum, now exploited, is the most important with commercially proven and prospects for additional reserves. Gold mining and exports are on a rising trend while numerous minerals such as iron ore, copper, mica, zinc, chromate and manganese together with non-ferrous resources such as plaster, lime and black sand are also available in appreciable quantities and potentially tradable. This could pose a real base for industrial development.

The industrial sector still depends on agricultural raw materials inputs such as vegetable oil, sugar cane, cotton, hides, skins etc.. With more development of these natural resources agro-industrial potential investment opportunities will thrive and encourage manufacturing of agricultural-related means of production required for improving productivities of both plant and animal sectors.

PEACE AND SOCIO-ECONOMIC STABILITY:

The daunting civil strife inflicting the South continues to impend national security and the very texture of the society in its various political, economic and social fabrics. The ramification of this war, flaring over since 1950s, has a devastating impingement not only at the war fields but on other areas in the form of influx of displaced people with the consequences of wide spread of poverty and pauperism. However, the quest for peace continues to be the main concern of the

Government with commitment to building confidence through devolution of power and wealth sharing among all the States particularly the Southern States.

The Government has assiduously engaged in efforts to end the war. It believes that stopping the war is a moral obligation to unravel the human tragedy of the people of the South and restore economic, social and security situations. The Government has announced its readiness to make peace through preparing the climate for talks, announcing repeatedly a ceace-fire from one side, granting general amnesty for all those who carried arms against the Government and agreeing on Operation Life-line to safe the citizens exposed to hunger and diseases. Since 1989, the Government and the rebels have entered into more than twelve rounds of talks outside the framework of IGAD Initiative. In a parallel line to the external mediation, the Government has doubled its efforts to achieve peace from-within. In April 1997 the Khartoum Peace Agreement was signed between the Government and a number of Southern rebel factions. This agreement recognizes for the first time in contemporary Sudan the right of self-determination for the South. It was followed by Fashoda and the Nuba Mountains Agreements. These agreements feature in the Permanent Constitution. A recent development was the signing of the new Nuba Mountains Agreement with the main rebel stream following the United States special envoy initiative. It is expected that with the successful implementation of this agreement the peace process will continue to cover the South.

ISSUES OF GOVERNANCE:

The Sudan Government is committed to adhere to the basic human rights enshrined in the divine laws and international covenants, ensuring the supremacy of society and its legitimate right to developing own indigenous democracy and peaceful exchange of power among the various partisan movement within the Federal System and united Sudan. Enforcing peace, restoring security and the rule of law, building confidence among all people and ensuring fair distribution of wealth and power are the main policy agenda of the Government. However, the rehabilitation of society's political, social and economic infrastructure are basic issues necessary to achieve peace, decent livelihood, fairness and justice together with fostering democracy among all citizens having different social, ethnic, religious and cultural background without discrimination.

REGIONAL AND INTERNATIONAL COOPERATION

Sudan is a member of a number of regional and international organizations of which the following are the most important with respect to economic, financial, investment and trade flows:

- Member of the the Arab League and its Economic and Social Council.
- Member of IMF, WB/IDA.
- Member and Founder of the Arab Monetary Fund.
- Member and host country of the Arab Bank for Economic Development in Africa.
- Member and host country of the Arab Corporation for Agricultural Investment and Development.

Member of the Arab Investment Guarantee Agency.

- Member of the Inter-Arab Trade Development Agreement (now called the larger Arab Free Trade Zone).
- Member and founder of the Organization of African Unity.
- Member and founder of the Common Market for Eastern and Southern Africa and its Preferential Trade Bank. Trade has been liberalized within this market following the abolition of custom duties between member states.
- Member of the Islamic Conference Organization and its affiliates.
- Member of the Islamic Development Bank.
- Member of the African, Caribbean and Pacific Group and the European Union

(ACP/EU).

- Member of the African Development Bank.
- Member of the International Fund for Agricultural Development.
- Member of Food Agricultural Organization.

Sudan has managed to normalize its relations with international, regional and bilateral financial institutions. In this respect, the IMF's declaration that Sudan is a cooperative country has been a major incentive for Sudan to continue its efforts to normalize relations with other financial institutions. Most of them resumed their financial activities with the Sudan particularly the Arab funds and the OPEC Fund. Presently Sudan is witnessing a remarkable flow of technical missions from the world Bank, Arab funds, China, Russia, Malaysia, Turkey, Egypt, the Gulf states, Iran and others. Financial agreements for financing major projects in the fields of electricity, agriculture, irrigation, health and education were signed including crs to the private sector from available financial windows of external financial institutions.

EFFORTS TO JOIN THE WORLD TRADE ORGANIZATION (WTO):

Sudan has presented its offer to join the WTO since 1994. Measures have been taken to meet the requirements of membership terms and conditions especially in the fields of economic, trade and investment liberalization and revision of laws and regulatory framework.

STRATEGIC AND PRACTICAL INFORMATION FOR CONDUCTING BUSINESS

ECONOMY & ECONOMIC DEVELOPMENT

Cooperation between Sudan and the IMF continues within the framework of a medium-term staff-monitored program (MTSMP) for the period of 1999-2001. The MTSMP is based on the government's economic recovery strategy and builds on the progress achieved in the implementation of the 1997-98 annual staff-monitored programs (SMP), including in reducing financial imbalances, strengthening taxation, improving public expenditure management, financial deepening, exchange rate unification, foreign trade liberalization, and privatization.

The objective of the MTSMP is to lay a solid foundation for sustained economic growth through a further improvement in the macroeconomic situation supported by implementation of structural reforms to enhance resource allocation and encourage private sector activity. The program establishes medium-term targets of annual real growth of 5-6 percent, a reduction in average inflation to 5 percent, a further narrowing of the current account deficit, and a substantial buildup of gross usable reserves.

In 1999, the Sudanese authorities broadly achieved the macroeconomic objectives of the first annual program under the MTSMP. Based on solid performance of rainfed and non-traditional crops, livestock, and the new oil sector, growth is estimated to have reached about 6 percent. Tight fiscal and monetary policies allowed the government to successfully reduce inflationary pressures and to bring the average inflation rate down, for the third consecutive year, to 16 percent. After averaging about 8 percent of GDP in recent years, the external current account deficit contracted to 3.5 percent of GDP (excluding interest due and public transfers) as higher than projected oil prices helped to offset the weaker performance of traditional exports. By end-1999 the Bank of Sudan (BOS) doubled its usable foreign exchange reserves, to US$53 million, exceeding the target by US$6 million.

Structural reforms moved forward in 1999 and early 2000. The tax authority has finalized preparations for the June 1, 2000 start date for the Value Added Tax (VAT). Implementing regulations for the revised Investment Encouragement Act have been passed. Exchange market reforms continue. The BOS has introduced instruments for indirect monetary management, although their monetary impact remains limited. The BOS has announced a new bank restructuring strategy and is addressing the issue of nonperforming loans.

Despite the progress achieved, the overall economic situation remains fragile and susceptible to exogenous shocks. Determined policy implementation by the government is needed if the objectives of the MTSMP are to be met. Public expectations and political pressures for immediate use of oil revenues are high. However, the oil revenue windfall by itself will not be enough to sustain even required increases in spending, such as in the social and development sectors. For the near future, Sudan will remain a predominantly agricultural economy, facing financing shortages, a deteriorated infrastructure, recurrent problems with flooding, an inappropriate institutional framework in the irrigated sector, and a secular decline in world commodity prices. The banking system is weak, with many banks undercapitalized, and is not capable of supporting private sector growth. Poverty, especially in the South, is extremely high. Finally, Sudan's external debt, estimated at US$24 billion at end-1999 and most of it in arrears, is unsustainable.

Against this background, the program for 2000 aims at cementing the macroeconomic gains of the previous years, while expanding the breadth and depth of the structural reforms. Real GDP growth is targeted to reach 6.5 percent. New oil revenue will allow the government to reduce its borrowing from the BOS and leave more room for cr to the private sector. The resulting lower monetary expansion will help to relieve inflationary pressures and to achieve the 9 percent end-of-year inflation target. In line with expected improvements in the balance of payments, Sudan's gross usable reserves will increase by US$45, doubling the level at end-1999. On the structural side, the program pursues the goal of strengthening the budget by introducing a VAT and improving expenditure management through establishing accounts classification compatible with international standards.

The government intends to start automatic adjustments of domestic oil prices in line with international prices. Financial sector reforms include bank consolidation and restructuring, enforcing capital adequacy requirements, reduction of nonperforming loans, and further development of indirect monetary management instruments. The program also envisages a wide range of other structural reforms, such as further trade and exchange market liberalization and privatization. The government has committed to US$60 million in payments to the IMF in 2000. The authorities are also working with the World Bank to develop policies that would eventually enhance the social safety net, strengthening health and education systems and reducing poverty.

EXECUTIVE BOARD ASSESSMENT

Executive Directors noted the progress achieved by Sudan over the past three years in stabilizing the macroeconomic situation, moving forward the structural reform agenda, and improving relations with crors against a background of a difficult domestic and international environment. Directors generally considered that Sudan's performance under the staff-monitored program (SMP) in 1999 had been satisfactory both in terms of policy implementation and payments to the Fund. Nevertheless, they noted that the overall macroeconomic policy stance had not yet succeeded in reducing inflation adequately, and there had been delays in implementing some of the key reforms. Looking ahead, Directors urged the authorities to consolidate and sustain the improvement in the macroeconomic situation, to push forward their agenda of structural reforms in order to enhance confidence and the expansion of the private sector, and to ensure careful management of Sudan's new oil resources. Directors also emphasized the contribution that a peaceful resolution of the armed conflict would make to poverty alleviation and improvements in social indicators.

In considering the outlook for 2000, Directors urged the authorities to be vigilant against the possible reversal of the recent improvements in the inflation rate and to proceed with caution in implementing the program by minimizing central bank financing of the budget and restraining expenditure as needed to keep inflation on track. Directors strongly emphasized the importance of ensuring that higher oil revenues not undermine budgetary discipline, and, in this regard, they welcomed the commitment to use excess oil revenues to reduce net borrowing from the Bank of Sudan. Moreover, they cautioned against increasing entitlement programs, which would be difficult to unwind should oil prices weaken. Directors also noted the need to continue to broaden the tax base and improve collection of non-oil revenue. In this connection, they welcomed the indication that the VAT will be put in place as planned on June 1. Directors underscored that cuts in nonproductive, and especially military expenditures would greatly facilitate the achievement of social objectives consistent with overall strength in the fiscal position.

Directors observed that no major pressure on the exchange rate was evident, despite the virtual stability in the rate in recent months. However, in view of the many challenges and risks facing Sudan's economy and the still low level of international reserves, Directors encouraged the authorities to allow the exchange rate to move flexibly in response to market forces and not to allow any perception to develop in the market that the rate was effectively fixed. In this regard, Directors considered that efforts should be stepped up to further develop the interbank foreign exchange market. Directors encouraged the authorities to closely monitor developments in external competitiveness, and, in particular, to avert any threat of oil-induced strength in the exchange rate undermining the competitiveness of the non-oil sector.

Directors welcomed the recent measures taken by the Bank of Sudan to strengthen the financial and banking sector, including the recent unification of the reserve requirements on domestic and foreign currency deposits, and urged the authorities to continue their program on an accelerated basis. They drew attention to the recent decline in cr to the private sector, observing that its reversal—in line with the program—would be an essential prerequisite for future economic growth. To that end, Directors agreed with the package of measures prepared by the authorities to address this problem, including the updating of laws to remove impediments to the extension of cr, strengthening provisioning and compliance with prudential regulations, and improving performance with respect to loan recovery. Directors encouraged the provision of Fund technical assistance to assist the authorities in these areas.

In other structural reform areas, Directors were encouraged by the measures taken recently—in particular, the approval of the implementing regulations for the Investment Encouragement Act—but urged the authorities to avoid any further delays in implementation. Directors were concerned with the continuing delays in adjusting petroleum product prices and recouping the remaining losses of the Sudan Petroleum Company. They stressed that it would be important for the authorities to utilize the agreed automatic petroleum price mechanism. Directors advised the authorities to move to full market liberalization in the petroleum product sector as quickly as possible.

The commitment to transparency in the oil sector to date was welcomed, and Directors strongly urged the authorities to build on this by full public disclosure of oil revenue data and periodic internal audits.

Taking a longer-term perspective, Directors were in general agreement with the medium-term macroeconomic targets for the SMP, noting that these were based on continued structural reforms across many sectors, and in particular the financial and agricultural sectors. At the same time, they recognized the risks to the program from structural weaknesses in the economy, such as low investment in physical and human capital, deteriorating infrastructure in the agricultural sector, and an unsustainable debt burden.

Directors noted Sudan's adherence to the schedule of payments to the Fund through April 2000, and urged the authorities to continue this performance. Welcoming the continued improvement in relations with external crors, they also urged that further progress be made toward an eventual resolution of Sudan's external debt problem.

Directors welcomed the authorities' intention to strengthen the statistical database, especially regarding monetary statistics where some problems had emerged.

Sudan: Selected Economic and Financial Indicators, 1996-1999

	1996	1997	1998	1999
	(Annual changes in percent)			
Domestic economy				
Real GDP growth	4.0	6.7	5.0	6.0[1/]
End-of-period CPI inflation	114.2	32.0	7.9	17.0
Average CPI inflation	132.8	46.7	17.1	16.0

	(In percent of GDP)				
Financial variables					
Total revenue		6.3	6.6	7.9	8.5
Total expenditure		9.8	7.4	8.6	9.3
Current expenditure		9.2	6.8	7.8	8.0
Capital expenditure		0.6	0.6	0.8	1.3
Overall balance (cash)		-3.5	-0.7	-0.7	-0.9
Broad money (change in percent)		6.5	37.0	29.6	24.6
Reserve money (change in percent)	81.8	34.3	29.4	35.1	
	(In millions of U.S. dollars)				
External sector					
Exports, f.o.b.		620	594	596	780
Imports, c.i.f.		-1,547	-1,580	-1,925	-1,412
External current account balance [2/]	-579.6	-330	-338	-236	
In percent of GDP		-7.6	-4.0	-3.9	-2.4
Real effective exchange rate (change in percent)		6.7	22.0	-25.8	18.8

Sources: Data provided by the Sudanese authorities, IMF staff estimates.
1/ Preliminary
2/ Excluding interest due, public transfers, and oil pipeline imports.

[1]Under Article IV of the IMF's Articles of Agreement, the IMF holds bilateral discussions with members, usually every year. A staff team visits the country, collects economic and financial information, and discusses with officials the country's economic developments and policies. On return to headquarters, the staff prepares a report, which forms the basis for discussion by the Executive Board. At the conclusion of the discussion, the Managing Director, as Chairman of the Board, summarizes the views of Executive Directors, and this summary is transmitted to the country's authorities. In this PIN, the main features of the Board's discussion are described.

THE ECONOMY IN THE EARLY AND MID-1990S

The Economy of Sudan continued to be in disarray in 1994. The principal causes of the disorder have been the violent, costly civil war, an inept government, an influx of refugees from neighboring countries, as well as internal migration, and a decade of below normal annual rainfall with the concomitant failure of staple food and cash crops.

The economic and political upheavals that characterized Sudan in the 1980s have made statistical material either difficult to obtain or unreliable. Prices and wages in the marketplace fluctuated constantly, as did the government's revenue. Consequently, information concerning Sudan's economy tends to be more historical than current.

In the 1970s, economic growth had been stimulated by a large influx of capital from Saudi Arabia and Kuwait, invested with the expectation that Sudan would become "the breadbasket" of the Arab world, and by large increments of foreign aid from the United States and the European Community (EC). Predictions of continuing economic growth were sustained by loans from the World Bank and generous contributions from such disparate countries as Norway, Yugoslavia, and China. Sudan's greatest economic resource was its agriculture, to be developed in the vast arable land that either received sufficient rainfall or could be irrigated from the Nile. By 1994 Sudan had not yet claimed its full water share (18.5 billion cubic meters) under the 1959 Nile Waters Agreement between Egypt and Sudan.

Sudan's economic future in the 1970s was also energized by the Chevron Overseas Petroleum Corporation's discovery of oil on the borderlands between the provinces of Kurdufan and Bahr al Ghazal. Concurrently, the most thoroughly researched hydrological project in the Third World, the Jonglei Canal (also seen as Junqali Canal), was proceeding ahead of schedule, planned not only to provide water for northern Sudan and Egypt, but also to improve the life of the Nilotic people of the canal zone. New, large agricultural projects had been undertaken in sugar at Kinanah and cotton at Rahad. Particularly in southern Sudan, where the Addis Ababa accords of March 27, 1972, had seemingly ended the insurgency, a sense of optimism and prosperity prevailed, dashed, however, when the civil war resumed in 1983. The Khartoum government controlled these development projects, but entrepreneurs could make fortunes through the intricate network of kinship and political relations that has traditionally driven Sudan's social and economic machinery.

In the early 1970s, public enterprises dominated the modern sector, including much of agriculture and most of large-scale industry, transport, electric power, banking, and insurance. This situation resulted from the private sector's inability to finance major development and from an initial government policy after the 1969 military coup to nationalize the financial sector and part of existing industry. Private economic activities were relegated to modern small- and medium-scale industry. The private sector dominated road transport and domestic commerce and virtually controlled traditional agriculture and handicrafts.

In the 1980s, however, Sudan underwent severe political and economic upheavals that have shaken its traditional institutions and its economy. The civil war in the south resumed in 1983, at a cost of more than £Sd11 million per day. The main participant in the war against government was the Sudanese People's Liberation Army (SPLA, the armed wing of the Sudanese People's Liberation Movement (SPLM)), under John Garang's leadership. The SPLA made steady gains against the Sudanese army until by 1992 it controlled nearly one-third of the country.

The dearth of rainfall in the usually productive regions of Sahel and southern Sudan added to the country's economic problems. Refugees, both Sudanese and foreigners from Eritrea, Ethiopia, Uganda, and Chad, further strained the Sudanese budget. International humanitarian agencies have rallied to Sudan's aid, but the government rejected their help.

When Jaafar an Nimeiri was overthrown in April 1985, his political party disappeared, as did his elaborate security apparatus. The military transitional government and the democratically elected coalition government of Sadiq al Mahdi that succeeded the exiled Nimeiri failed to address the country's economic problems. Production continued to decline as a result of mismanagement and natural disasters. The national debt grew at an alarming rate because Sudan's resources were insufficient to service it. Not only did the SPLA shut down Chevron's prospecting and oil production, but it also stopped work on the Jonglei Canal.

On June 30, 1989, a military coup d'état led by Colonel (later Lieutenant General) Umar al Bashir overthrew the government of Sadiq al Mahdi. Ideologically tied to the Muslim Brotherhood and dependent for political support on the Brotherhood's party, the National Islamic Front, the Bashir regime has methodically purged those agencies that dealt primarily with the economy--the civil service, the trade unions, the boards of publicly owned enterprises, the Ministry of Finance and Economic Planning, and the central bank. Under Bashir's government, Sudan's economy has been further strained by the most severe famine of this century, the continuation of the war in the south, and a foreign policy that has left Sudan economically, if not politically, isolated from the world community.

ECONOMIC DEVELOPMENT BACKGROUND

Historically, the colonial government was not interested in balanced economic growth and instead concentrated its development efforts on irrigated agriculture and the railroad system throughout the Anglo-Egyptian condominium. Incidental government investment had gone mainly into ad hoc projects, such as the construction of cotton gins and oilseed-pressing mills as adjuncts of the irrigation program. A limited amount of rainfed mechanized farming, similarly on an ad hoc basis, had also been developed during World War II.

After the war, two development programs-- actually lists of proposed investments--were drawn up for the periods 1946-50 and 1951-55. These plans appear to have been a belated effort to broaden the country's economic base in preparation for eventual Sudanese independence. Both programs were seriously hampered by a lack of experienced personnel and materials and had little real impact. Independently, the private sector had expanded irrigated agriculture, and some small manufacturing operations had been started, but only three larger industrial enterprises (meat and cement plants and a brewery) had been constructed, all between 1949 and 1952. As a result, at independence the new Sudanese government's principal development inheritance was the vast irrigated Gezira Scheme (also seen as Jazirah Scheme) and Sudan Railways.

Not until 1960 did the new government attempt to prepare a national development plan. Since that time, three plans have been formulated, none of which has been carried through to completion. Work on the first of these, the Ten-Year Plan of Economic and Social Development, for the fiscal years 1961-70, began in late 1960, but the plan was not formally adopted until September 1962, well over a year after its scheduled starting date. The total ten-year investment was set at £Sd565 million, at the time equivalent to more than US$1.6 billion. The private sector was expected to provide 40 percent of the amount. Unfortunately, the goals were overly ambitious, and the government had few experienced planners.

The plan as prepared was not adhered to, and implementation was actually carried out through investment programs that were drawn up annually and funded through the development budget. Projects not in the original plan were frequently included. Investment was at a high rate in the first years, well beyond projections, and a number of major undertakings had been completed by mid-plan, including the Khashm al Qirbah and Manaqil irrigation projects, a sugar factory at the former site, another at Al Junayd irrigation project, and the Roseires (also called Ar Rusayris) Dam.

As the 1960s progressed, a lack of funds threatened the continuation of development activities. Government current expenditure had increased much faster than receipts, in part because of the intensification of the civil war in the south, and government surpluses to finance development vanished. At the same time, there was a shortfall in foreign investment capital. The substantial foreign reserves held at the beginning of the plan period were depleted, and the government resorted to deficit financing and foreign borrowing. The situation had so deteriorated by 1967 that implementation of the Ten-Year Plan was abandoned. Sudan's international cr worthiness became open to question.

Despite major financial problems, real economic gains were nevertheless made during the Ten-Year Plan, and per capita income rose from the equivalent of US$86 in 1960 to about US$104 at the end of the decade. Late in the 1960s, the government prepared a new plan covering FY 1968 to FY 1972. This plan was discarded after the military coup led by Nimeiri in May 1969. Instead, the government adopted a Five-Year Plan of Economic and Social Development, 1970-74. This plan, prepared with the assistance of Soviet planning personnel, sought to achieve the major goals of the May revolution (creation of an independent national economy; steady growth of prosperity; and further development of cultural, education, and health services) through socialist development.

During the plan's first two years, expenditures remained low, affected largely by uncertainties that stemmed from the civil war. After the war ceased in early 1972, the government felt that the plan failed to provide for transportation improvements and large-scale productive projects. In 1973, the government therefore established in the Interim Action Program, which extended the original plan period through FY 1976. New objectives included the removal of transportation bottlenecks, attainment of self-sufficiency in the production of several agricultural and industrial consumer items, and an increase in agricultural exports.

To accomplish these goals, proposed public sector investment increased from £Sd215 million to £Sd463 million (however, actual expenditures during the five years, excluding technical assistance, were £Sd250 million). Private sector projected investment was estimated at £Sdl70 million originally, but the nationalizations carried out in 1970 and 1971 discouraged private investment in productive undertakings. Foreign private capital investment became negligible, and domestic private capital was put mostly into areas considered less subject to takeover, such as service enterprises, housing, traditional agriculture, and handicrafts.

The denationalizations since 1972 resulted in increased private foreign investment in development. The final investment total during the first five years was considerably above the original plan projection. The plan failed to achieve its goal of a 7.6 percent annual growth rate in gross domestic product, however, and was extended to 1977.

From FY 1973, after introduction of the Interim Action Program, through 1977, development expenditures grew to more than 1 billion Sudanese pounds. The government initiated several irrigation projects at Rahad, Satit southeast of Khashm al Qirba, Ad Damazin, and Kinanah; and established factories at Sannar, Kinanah, at Shandi on the Nile northeast of Khartoum, Kusti, Kaduqli, Nyala, and Rabak on the White Nile south of Khartoum. Roads between Khartoum and Port Sudan were paved with tarmacadam. Excavation began on the Jonglei Canal. Chevron discovered oil. The original plan called for almost half of investment to be provided by surpluses in the central government budget. Although this assumption appeared highly optimistic in view of the modest surpluses attained during the last half of the 1960s, tax revenues did increase as projected.

Earnings from public corporations, however, fell short of projections, and growth in government current expenditures greatly exceeded revenue growth. As a result, not only were there no surpluses in the public sector, but the government had to borrow from the Bank of Sudan to cover the current expenditure account. Foreign capital, although abundant, also did not equal the spending on development, and, contrary to the expectations of the plan's drafters, the government had to resort to domestic borrowing to proceed with project implementation.

In early 1977, the government published the successor Six- Year Plan of Economic and Social Development, 1977-1982. Its goals and projections also appeared optimistic because of the worsening domestic economic situation, which was marked by growing inflation. The inflation stemmed in large part from deficit development financing (printing money), increasing development costs because of worldwide price rises, and rising costs for external capital. During the plan's second year, FY 1978, there was no economic growth as the deficit development financing in the mid- and late 1970s led the Sudan into a deepening economic crisis. At the same time, external debt pressures mounted, and Sudan failed to meet its scheduled payments A substantial cutback in further development expenditures became unavoidable. The result was an abandonment of Six-Year Plan projections, a restriction of expenditures generally to the completion of projects under way, improvement of the performance of existing operational projects, elimination of transport constraints, and a series of short-term "rolling" programs that particularly emphasized exports.

In October 1983, the government announced a three-year public investment program, but efforts to Islamize the economy in 1984 impeded its implementation, and after the Nimeiri overthrow in April 1985, it was suspended. In August 1987, an economic recovery program was initiated. This program was followed, beginning in October 1988, by a three-year recovery program to reform trade policy and regulate the exchange rate, reduce the budget deficit and subsidies, and encourage exports and privatization. There was little possibility for early economic recovery offered by the military government of General Umar al Bashir that took office on June 30, 1989. The government's economic policies proposed to Islamize the banking system, but foreign business interests viewed this measure as a disincentive to do business in Sudan, because no interest would be paid on new loans.

Furthermore, Islamic banks and other economic supporters of the regime were to be granted disproportionate influence over the economy, which led to widespread resentment among other sectors. Finally, the government did not go far enough to satisfy the International Monetary Fund or other major crors that it had sufficiently reduced subsidies on basic commodities, thus reducing its budget deficit. Bashir had announced an economic recovery program in mid-1990, but in 1991 its results were still awaited.

The late 1970s had seen corruption become widespread. Although always present, corruption never had been a major characteristic of the Sudanese economic scene. The enormous sums that poured into Sudan in the late 1970s from the Arab oil- exporting countries, the United States, and the European Community, however, provided opportunities for the small clique that surrounded Nimeiri to enrich themselves. This corruption fell into three principal categories: embezzlement of public funds, most of which left the country, agricultural acquisition schemes, and investment in the mercantile sphere.

The most common ways of embezzling public funds were acquiring liquid assets from banks or government agencies, selling the state's assets, selling state land, and smuggling. The siphoning off of liquid assets usually required the connivance of a high government official. Between 1975 and 1982, more than 800 cases were reported of embezzlement of, on the average, more than £Sd1,000. In one case, principal bank officials embezzled £Sd3 million; another bank made a loan of £Sd200 million to a businessman whose business was fictitious.

State property sold by embezzlers included gasoline and medicines. State officials also sold real estate in residential areas at below the market price. An impressive residence would then be built on the property for rental to diplomatic officials or executives of multinational companies. In the past, small operators penetrating the vast and unpatrolled borders of Sudan carried out smuggling, but in the late 1980s it became a vast and sophisticated business. Of the smuggling operations uncovered, one involved £Sd2.5 million in cloth, another £Sdl million in matches, and a third £Sd0.5 million in automobiles.

Another highly profitable form of corruption was the selling of state farmlands, each about 30,000 *feddans* (1 *feddan* is equivalent to 0.42 hectares). Mechanized Farming Corporation (MFC) officials sold large numbers of *feddans* at low prices to senior officials in Khartoum; many of the latter exploited the land for profit at the expense of the peasantry and caused profound ecological deterioration.

As corruption ran rampant during the late 1970s until Nimeiri was overthrown, commercial companies, particularly in the export- import trade, profited through their influence on public policy and through special permits they received. The Islamic institutions that dominated Sudanese banking facilitated this corruption. These banks, of which the most important was the Faisal Islamic Bank, possessed privileges not enjoyed by Sudanese national banks, such as exemption from taxation and the right to transfer profits abroad. An example of the combination of political power and financial capital was the Islamic Development Company. Established in 1983 as a limited shareholding company with an authorized capitalization of US$1 billion, the company was chartered to invest in agriculture, industry, services, construction, and Islamic banks. In practice, it concentrated on the export-import trade, where high profits could be made quickly and easily, in contrast to the slow returns of agricultural development projects.

The board of directors consisted of ten persons, four Sudanese and six foreign nationals, mostly Saudis, including a son of the late King Faisal ibn Abd al Aziz Al Saud. Of the Sudanese, three belonged to the National Islamic Front, and the fourth was the son of the leader of the Khatmiyyah, a Muslim religious group associated with the National Unionist Party. All had connections with Islamic banks and the Sudanese parliament. Their purpose was to strengthen the Islamist movement's economic power by tying their commercial enterprise to the state in order to achieve a privileged position in the marketplace. They accomplished this aim by granting shares valued at US$100,000 to founding members and to prominent persons, ranging from the republic's president to wealthy Muslim businessmen.

Between 1978 and 1985, agricultural and industrial production had declined in per capita terms. Imports during much of the 1980s were three times the level of exports. By 1991 the value of the Sudanese pound against the dollar had sunk to less than 10 percent of its 1978 value, and the country's external debt had risen to US$13 billion, the interest on which could be paid only by raising new loans.

Two reasons for this decline were the droughts and accompanying famine occurring in the 1980s and 1991, and the influx of more than 1 million refugees from Eritrea, Ethiopia, Chad, and Uganda, in addition to the persons displaced by the continuing war in southern Sudan who were estimated to number between 1.5 million and 3.5 million. Nevertheless, the decline in Sudan's agricultural and industrial production had begun before these calamities. Few development projects were completed on time and those that were failed to achieve projected production. After 1978 the GDP steadily fell so that the vast sums of money borrowed could not be repaid by increased productivity. Sudan found itself in a cycle of increasing debt and declining production.

These economic problems had two fundamental causes. First, in planning little thought was given to the impact of any one project on the whole economy and even less to the burden such huge projects would place on a fragile infrastructure. Some ministries undertook projects by unilaterally negotiating loans without reference to the Central Planning Agency. Second, remittances by Sudanese laborers in the Persian Gulf (thousands of workers were based in Kuwait and Iraq, until many of them were expelled) placed a stress on Sudan's economy, because the government was forced to relax its stringent currency controls to induce these workers to repatriate their earnings. Such funds were largely invested in consumer goods and housing, rather than in development projects.

AGRICULTURE, LIVESTOCK, FISHERIES, AND FORESTRY

In the early 1990s, agriculture and livestock raising were the main sources of livelihood in Sudan for about 61 percent of the working population. Agricultural products regularly accounted for about 95 percent of the country's exports. Industry was mostly agriculturally-based, accounting for 15 percent of GDP in 1988. The average annual growth of agricultural production declined in the 1980s to 0.8 percent for the period 1980-87, as compared with 2.9 percent for the period 1965-80. Similarly, the sector's total contribution to GDP declined over the years, as the other sectors of the economy expanded. Total sectoral activities, which contributed an estimated 40 percent of GDP in the early 1970s, had fluctuated during the 1980s and represented about 36 percent in 1988. Crop cultivation was divided between a modern, market-oriented sector comprising mechanized, large-scale irrigated and rainfed farming (mainly in central Sudan) and small-scale farming following traditional practices that was carried on in the other parts of the country where rainfall or other water sources were sufficient for cultivation.

Large investments continued to be made in the 1980s in mechanized, irrigated, and rainfed cultivation, with their combined areas accounting for roughly two-thirds of Sudan's cultivated land in the late 1980s. The early emphasis on cotton growing on irrigated land had decreased. Although cotton remained the most important crop, peanuts, wheat, and sugarcane had become major crops, and considerable quantities of sesame also were grown. Rainfed mechanized farming continued to produce mostly sorghum, and short-fiber cotton was also grown. Production in both subsectors increased domestic supplies and export potentials. The increase appeared, however, to have been achieved mainly by expanding the cultivated area rather than by increasing productivity. To stimulate productivity, in 1981 the government offered various incentives to cultivators of irrigated land who were almost entirely government tenants. Subsistence cultivators produced sorghum as their staple crop, although in the northerly, rainfed, cultivated areas millet was the principal staple. Subsistence farmers also grew peanuts and sesame.

Livestock raising, pursued throughout Sudan except in the extremely dry areas of the north and the tsetse-fly-infested area in the far south, was almost entirely in the traditional sector. Because livestock raising provided employment for so many people, modernization proposals have been based on improving existing practices and marketing for export, rather than moving toward the modern ranching that requires few workers.

Fishing was largely carried out by the traditional sector for subsistence. An unknown number of small operators also used the country's major reservoirs in the more populated central region and the rivers to catch fish for sale locally and in nearby larger urban centers. The few modern fishing ventures, mainly on Lake Nubia and in the Red Sea, were small.

The forestry subsector comprised both traditional gatherers of firewood and producers of charcoal--the main sources of fuel for homes and some industry in urban areas, and a modern timber and saw milling industry, the latter government owned. Approximately 21 million cubic meters of wood, mainly for fuel, were cut in 1987. Gum Arabic production in FY 1986-87 was about 40,000 tons. In the late 1980s, it became in most years the second biggest export after cotton, amounting to about 11 percent of total exports.

LAND USE

By 1991 only partial surveys of Sudan's land resources had been made, and estimates of the areas included in different landuse categories varied considerably. Figures for potentially arable land ranged from an estimate of 35.9 million hectares made in the mid-1960s to a figure of 84 million hectares published by the Ministry of Agriculture and Natural Resources in 1974. Estimates of the amount actually under cultivation varied in the late 1980s, ranging from 7.5 million hectares, including roughly 10 or 11 percent in fallow, to 12.6 million hectares.

Substantial variations also existed in land classified as actually used or potentially usable for livestock grazing. The ministry and the United Nations Food and Agriculture Organization (FAO) have classified about 24 million hectares as pastureland. The 1965 estimate of land use classified 101.4 million hectares as grazing land, and in 1975 an ILO-United Nations Development Programme (UNDP) interagency mission to Sudan estimated the total potential grazing land at between 120 million and 150 million hectares.

Forestland estimates also differed greatly, from less than 60 million hectares by staff of the Forestry Administration to about 915 million hectares by the Ministry of Agriculture and Natural

Resources and the FAO. Dense stands of trees only covered between 20 million and 24 million hectares of the total forestland. Differences in land classification may have been accounted for by use of some woodland areas for grazing and some traditional grazing lands for raising crops. Given the dearth of rainfall during the 1980s and early 1990s, the ecological damage from mechanized farming, and the steady march of desertification, discrepancies in these statistics had little meaning in 1991.

It was generally agreed, however, that in the late 1980s Sudan still had a substantial amount of land suitable for future cropping. The ILO-UNDP mission believed that two-thirds of the potential area for livestock grazing, however, was already in use. In addition to land suitable for cultivation and livestock grazing, Sudan also had about 76 million to 86 million hectares of desert. Additionally, an area of about 2.9 million hectares was covered by swamps and inland water, and about 280,000 hectares were occupied by urban settlements and other man-made features.

LAND TENURE

The right to own property, to bequeath it to heirs, and to inherit it was established by the Permanent Constitution of 1973; this right was suspended in 1985. Sudan had long had a system of land registration through which an individual, an enterprise, or the government could establish title to a piece of land. Such registration had been extensive in northern Sudan, especially in Al Khartum, Al Awsat, and Ash Shamali provinces. Before 1970 all other land (unregistered) belonged to the state, which held ownership in trust for the people, who had customary rights to it. In 1970 the Unregistered Land Act declared that all waste, forest, and unregistered lands were government land. Before the act's passage, the government had avoided interfering with individual customary rights to unregistered land, and in the late 1980s it again adhered to this policy.

The government owned most of the land used by the modern agricultural sector and leased it to tenants (for example, the Gezira Scheme) or to private entrepreneurs, such as most operators of large-scale mechanized rainfed farming. In the late 1980s, however, the great area of land used for pasture and for subsistence cultivation was communally owned under customary land laws that varied somewhat by location but followed a broadly similar pattern. In agricultural communities, the right to cultivate an area of unused land became vested in the individual who cleared it for use. The rights to such land could be passed on to heirs, but ordinarily the land could not be sold or otherwise disposed of. The right was also retained to land left in fallow, although in Bahr al Ghazal, Aali an Nil, and Al Istiwai there were communities where another individual could claim such land by clearing it.

Among the transhumant communities of the north, the rights to cultivated land were much the same, but the dominant position of livestock in community activities had introduced certain other communal rights that included common rights to grazing land, the right-of-way to water and grazing land, the right to grass on agricultural land unless the occupier cut and stacked it, and the right to crop residues unless similarly treated. In the western savannas, private ownership of stands of *hashab* trees could be registered, an exception to the usual government ownership of the forests. But dead wood for domestic fuel and the underlying grass were common property. Water, a matter of greatest importance to stock raisers, was open to all if free standing, but wells that had been dug and the associated drinking troughs were private property and were retained by the digger season after season. In northern Sudan, especially in the western savanna where increasing population and animal numbers have placed pressure on the land, violations of customary laws and conflicts between ethnic groups over land rights have been growing. Resolution of these problems has been attempted by local government agencies but only on a case-by-case basis.

IRRIGATED AGRICULTURE

In 1991 Sudan had a large modern irrigated agriculture sector totaling more than 2 million hectares out of about 84 million hectares that are potentially arable. About 93 percent of the irrigated area was in government projects; the remaining 7 percent belonged to private operations. The Nile and its tributaries were the source of water for 93 percent of irrigated agriculture, and of this the Blue Nile accounted for about 67 percent. Gravity flow was the main form of irrigation, but about one-third of the irrigated area was served by pumps.

The waters of the Nile in Sudan have been used for centuries for traditional irrigation, taking advantage of the annual Nile flood. Some use of this method still continued in the early 1990s, and the traditional *shaduf* (a device to raise water) and waterwheel were also used to lift water to fields in local irrigation projects but were rapidly being replaced by more efficient mechanized pump systems. Among the first efforts to employ irrigation for modern commercial cropping was the use of the floodwaters of the Qash River and the Baraka River (both of which originate in Ethiopia) in eastern Sudan to grow cotton on their deltas. This project was started in the late 1860s by the Egyptian governor and continued until interrupted by the turbulent period of the 1880s, leading to the reconquest of the country by the British in 1899. Cultivation was resumed in 1896 in the Baraka Delta in the Tawkar area, but in the Qash Delta it only resumed after World War I. Between 1924 and 1926, canals were built in the latter delta to control the flood; sandstorms made canals unfeasible in the Baraka. Between the 1940s and the 1970s, various projects were developed to irrigate land. In 1982 both deltas yielded only one crop a year, watered by the flood. Adequate groundwater, however, offered the eventual possibility of using pump irrigation from local wells for additional cropping or for supplementing any flood shortages.

The drought that affected Sudan in the 1980s was a natural disaster that had a crushing effect on the country's irrigation systems. In 1990-91, for instance, water was so scarce in the Tawkar area that for the first time in 100 years the crops failed.

As of 1990, the country's largest irrigation project had been developed on land between the Blue and White Nile rivers south of their confluence at Khartoum. This area is generally flat with a gentle slope to the north and west, permitting natural gravity irrigation, and its soils are fertile cracking clays well suited to irrigation. The project originated in 1911, when a private British enterprise, Sudan Plantations Syndicate, found cotton suited to the area and embarked on what in the 1920s became the Gezira Scheme, intended principally to furnish cotton to the British textile industry. Backed by a loan from the British government, the syndicate began a dam on the Blue Nile at Sannar in 1913. Work was interrupted by World War I, and the dam was not completed until 1925. The project was limited by a 1929 agreement between Sudan and Egypt that restricted the amount of water Anglo-Egyptian Sudan could use during the dry season. By 1931 the project had expanded to 450,000 hectares, the maximum that then could be irrigated by the available water, although 10,000 more hectares were added in the 1950s. The project was nationalized in 1950, and was operated by the Sudan Gezira Board as a government enterprise. In 1959 a new agreement with Egypt greatly increased the allotment of water to Sudan, as did the completion in the early 1960s of the Managil Extension on the western side of the Gezira Scheme. By 1990 the Managil Extension had an irrigated area of nearly 400,000 hectares, and with the 460,000 hectares eventually attained by the original Gezira Scheme, the combined projects accounted for half the country's total land under irrigation.

In the early 1960s, the government set up a program to resettle Nubians displaced by Lake Nubia (called Lake Nasser in Egypt), which was formed by the construction of the Aswan High Dam in Egypt. To provide farmland for the Nubians, the government constructed the Khashm al Qirbah Dam on the Atbarah River and established the Halfa al Jadidah (New Halfa) irrigation project. Located west of Kassala, this project was originally designed to irrigate about 164,000 hectares.

In 1982 it was the only large irrigation project in the country that did not use the waters of the Blue Nile or White Nile. The resettlement was effected mainly after completion of the Khashm al Qirbah Dam in 1964. Part of the irrigated area was also assigned to local inhabitants. The main commercial crops initially introduced included cotton, peanuts, and wheat. In 1965 sugarcane was added, and a sugar factory having a design capacity of 60,000 tons was built to process it. The project enabled 200,000 hectares of land to be irrigated for the first time. Heavy silting as well as serious problems of drainage and salinity occurred. As a result, by the late 1970s the reservoir had lost more than 40 percent of its original storage capacity and was unable to meet the project water requirements. These problems persisted in the early 1990s.

The multipurpose Roseires Dam was built in 1966 and power- generating facilities were installed in 1971. Both the water and the power were needed to implement the Rahad River irrigation project located east of the Rahad River, a tributary of the Blue Nile. The Rahad entered the Blue Nile downstream from the dam and during the dry season had an insufficient flow for irrigation purposes. Work on the initial 63,000 hectares of the project began in the early 1970s, the first irrigation water was received in 1977, and by 1981 about 80 percent of the prepared area was reported to be irrigated. (In May 1988, the World Bank agreed to provide additional funding for this and other irrigation projects). Water for the project was pumped from the Blue Nile, using electric power from the Roseires plant, and was transported by an eighty-kilometer-long canal to the Rahad River (en route underpassing the Dindar River, another Blue Nile tributary). The canal then emptied into the Rahad above a new barrage that diverted the combined flow from the two sources into the project's main irrigation canal. Irrigation was by gravity flow, but instead of flat field flooding, furrow irrigation was used, because it permitted more effective use of machinery.

In the 1920s, private irrigation projects using diesel pumps also had begun to appears in Al Khartum Province, mainly along the White Nile, to provide vegetables, fruit, and other foods to the capital area. In 1937 a dam was built by the Anglo-Egyptian condominium upstream from Khartoum on the White Nile at Jabal al Awliya to regulate the supply of water to Egypt during the August to April period of declining flow. Grazing and cultivated land along the river was flooded for almost 300 kilometers. The government thereupon established seven pump irrigation projects, partially financed by Egypt, to provide the area's inhabitants with an alternative to transhumance.

This irrigation project eventually proved successful, making possible large surpluses of cotton and sorghum and encouraging private entrepreneurs to undertake new projects. High cotton profits during the Korean War (1950-53) increased private interest along the Blue Nile as well, and by 1958 almost half the country's irrigated cotton was grown under pump irrigation. During the 1960s, however, downward fluctuations in world cotton prices and disputes between entrepreneurs and tenants led to numerous failures of pump irrigation projects. In 1968 the government assumed ownership and operation of the projects. The government established the Agricultural Reform Corporation for this purpose, and the takeover began that year with the larger estates. Subsequently, as leases expired, the corporation acquired smaller projects, until May 1970 when all outstanding leases were revoked. A considerable number of small pump operations that developed on privately owned land, chiefly along the main Nile but also on the Blue Nile, continued to operate.

Since the 1950s, the government has constructed a number of large pump projects, mostly on the Blue Nile. These have included the Junayd project on the right bank of the Blue Nile east of the Gezira Scheme. This project, with an irrigated area of about 36,000 hectares, went into operation in 1955 to provide an alternative livelihood for nomadic pastoralists in the area. It produced cotton until 1960, when about 8,400 hectares were converted to sugarcane. A sugar factory built to process the crop (with a potential capacity of 60,000 tons of sugar a year) opened in 1962. In the early 1970s, the Japanese-assisted As Suki project, also of 36,000 hectares, was established upstream from Sannar to grow cotton, sorghum, and oilseeds. In the mid-1970s, the government constructed a second project near Sannar of about 20,000 hectares. In addition to cotton and other crops such as peanuts, about 8,400 hectares of the area were devoted to raising sugarcane. The cane-processing factory, with a design capacity of 110,000 tons of sugar a year, opened in 1976. Several smaller Blue Nile projects added more than 80,000 additional hectares to Sudan's overall irrigated area during this time.

In the 1970s, when the consumption and import of sugar grew rapidly, domestic production became a priority, and two major pump-irrigated sugar plantations were established on the White Nile in the Kusti area. The Hajar Asalaya Sugar Project, begun in 1975, had an irrigated area of about 7,600 hectares. The sugar factory, completed in 1977, had a potential annual capacity of 110,000 tons. The Kinanah Sugar Project, which had almost 16,200 hectares under irrigation in 1981 and had a future potential of over 33,000 hectares, was one of the world's largest sugar-milling and refining operations. In 1985-86 production reached more than 330,000 tons a year. This project, first proposed in 1971, was beset with funding problems and overruns that increased overall costs from the equivalent of US$113 million estimated in 1973 to more than US$750 million when the plant opened officially in early 1981.

The Kinanah Sugar Project, unlike the country's four other government-owned sugar projects, was a joint venture--among the governments of Sudan, Kuwait, and Saudi Arabia, and the Arab Investment Company, the Sudan Development Corporation, Kinanah Limited, and the AAAID, including local Sudanese banks. An initial trial run in the 1979-80 cane season produced 20,000 tons of sugar. Yield increased to an estimated 135,000 to 150,000 tons the following season. Production at the Hajar Asalaya factory did not get under way until the 1979-80 season because of cane and sugar-processing difficulties. Problems have also affected the other three state sugar factories, but as a result of proposed World Bank management, the output total of these four government operations for the 1984-85 season improved to nearly 200,000 tons. Output declined to 159,000 tons in 1985-86 because of the drought. In 1989 sugarcane production reached 400,000 tons.

RAINFED AGRICULTURE

Cultivation dependent on rainfall falls into two categories. Most Sudanese farmers always have relied on rainfed farming. In addition to these traditional farmers, a large modern mechanized rainfed agriculture sector has developed since 1944-45, when a government project to cultivate the cracking clays of central Sudan started in the Al Qadarif area of Ash Sharqi Province, largely to meet the food needs of army units stationed in the British colonies in eastern Africa (present-day Kenya, Tanzania, and Uganda).

An average of about 6,000 hectares a year was cultivated between 1945 and 1953, producing chiefly sorghum, under a sharecropping arrangement between the government and farmers who had been allocated land in the project. These estates proved costly, however, and in 1954 the government began encouraging the private sector to take up mechanized farming in the area, a policy that continued after Sudan gained independence in 1956. Under the new approach, the government established several state farms to demonstrate production methods and to conduct research. Research activities have been very limited, however, because of staffing and funding problems, and the farms have been operated essentially as regular production units.

The private sector response was positive, and by 1960 mechanized farming had spread into other areas of the cracking clay zone in Ash Sharqi and Al Awsat provinces. The government set aside rectangular areas that were divided into plots of 420 hectares (later raised in places to 630 hectares) each. Half of these plots were leased to private farmers, the other half left in fallow. After four years, the originally leased land was to be returned to fallow and the farmer was to receive a new lease to an adjacent fallow area. When the demand for land grew faster than it could be demarcated, areas outside the designated project limits were taken over by private individuals. The four-year lease proved unpopular because it meant new investment in clearing land every four years, and apparently much of the worked land continued to be cultivated while fallow land was also placed under cultivation. By 1968 more than 750,000 hectares were being cultivated, of which it was estimated that more than 200,000 hectares constituted unauthorized holdings. The average agricultural production growth rate declined, however, from 2.9 percent in the period between 1965 and 1980, to 0.8 percent in the period between 1980 and 1987, the latest available figures. Reportedly, for the 1992-93 season, the Ministry of Agriculture and Natural Resources planned for about 7.3 million hectares of food crops to be planted, with about 1.6 million hectares planted in the irrigated sector and about 5.7 million hectares in the rain-fed areas.

The investment requirements for mechanized farming favored prosperous cultivators, and eventually most farms came to be operated by entrepreneurs who raised capital through mortgageable property or other assets in the urban centers. Through arrangements with other individuals, these entrepreneurs frequently managed to control additional plots beyond the legal limit of two. Their ability to obtain capital also permitted them to abandon depleted land and to move into newly demarcated uncleared areas, a practice that had a deleterious impact upon the environment, deprived the indigenous inhabitants of work opportunities, and increased desertification. In 1968, to expand the operator base and to introduce more control over land allocation, crops, and farming methods, the government established the Mechanized Farming Corporation (MFC), an autonomous agency under the Ministry of Agriculture and Natural Resources. From 1968 through 1978, the IDA made three loans to the government to enable the MFC to provide technical assistance, cr for landclearing and machinery, and marketing aid to individual farmers and cooperative groups. The MFC also became the operator of state farms.

In the late 1970s, about 2.2 million hectares had been allocated for mechanized farming, and about 420,000 hectares more had been occupied without official demarcation. About 1.9 million hectares in all were believed to be under cultivation in any one season. Of the officially allocated land, more than 70 percent was held by private individuals. Private companies had also begun entering the field, and some allocations had been made to them. State farms accounted for another 7.5 percent. About 15 percent of the total allocated land was in MFC-IDA projects.

The largest proportion of mechanized farming was in Ash Sharqi Province, 43 percent; the next largest in Al Awsat Province, 32 percent; and about 20 percent was in Aali an Nil Province. Mechanized farming had also been initiated in southern Kurdufan Province through a project covering small-scale farmers in the area of the Nuba Mountains, but under a different government program. Proposals also have been made for MFC projects using mechanized equipment in other areas of southern Kurdufan (some have already been tried) and southern Darfur provinces. There were serious feasibility problems in view of competition for land and conflicts with traditional farming practices, difficult soil conditions, and the probable negative effect on the large numbers of livestock of nomads.

Only a few crops had been found suitable for cultivation in the cracking clay area. Sorghum had been the principal one, and during the early 1980s it was planted on an average of about 80 percent of the sown area. Sesame and short-fiber cotton were also grown successfully but in relatively smaller quantities, sesame on about 15 percent of the land and cotton on about 5 percent. Soil fertility has reportedly been declining because of the continued planting of sorghum and the lack of crop rotation. Yields have apparently decreased, but in view of the area's greatly varying climatic conditions and the uncertain production data, definitive conclusions on trends appeared premature.

LIVESTOCK

In the early 1990s, drought caused a dramatic decline in livestock raising in Sudan, following a period in the early 1980s when livestock provided all or a large part of the livelihood of more than 40 percent of the country's population. Livestock raising was overwhelmingly in the traditional sector, and, although initial steps had been taken to improve productivity and develop market orientation, for the modern monetized economy the sector represented largely a potential asset. In 1983 Sudan's more than 50 million animals comprised the second largest national herd in Africa, next in size to that of Ethiopia.

An FAO estimate in 1987 indicated that there were about 20.5 million cattle, 19 million sheep, 14 million goats, and 3 million camels. Other animals included 660,000 donkeys, 21,000 horses, a small number of pigs (kept by such non-Muslim peoples as the Nuba) and 32,000 chickens. By 1991 these numbers had been reduced by perhaps one-third by the drought of 1990-91; the August 1988 floods in the south, described as the worst in Sudan's history; and the ravages of civil war in the south. Poultry was raised mainly by farm families and villagers. A small modern sector consisted of limited government commercial operations and a few semicommercial private ventures.

Sudanese cattle are of two principal varieties: Baqqara and Nilotic. The Baqqara and two subvarieties constituted about 80 percent of the country's total number of cattle. This breed was found chiefly in the western savanna regions and in fewer, although significant, numbers farther to the east from Aali an Nil to Kassala in Ash Sharqi. The Nilotic, constituting approximately 20 percent of all cattle, were common in the eastern hill and plains areas of southeastern Al Istiwai, which were free of the tsetse fly, and in those parts of the Bahr al Ghazal and Aali an Nil lying outside the tsetse-fly zone. Because of periodic rinderpest epidemics, the total number of cattle was relatively small until about 1930, when it stood at an estimated 2 million. A vaccination program begun about that time and mass inoculations during the succeeding decades resulted in a great increase in numbers, which by 1970 had reached about 12 million. In the vast areas used by pastoral herders (estimated to be 80 million to 100 million hectares), cattle husbandry was conducted in an economic, cultural, and social context that had evolved over generations.

This included an emphasis on increasing herd size as an investment for future family security. Small surpluses (usually bulls) were available for subsistence use, exchange, or sale for local consumption or export. Cattle were also used for marriage payments and among the Nilotes for rituals. Numbers of cattle also helped to establish or increase status and power in a social system in which cattle were the measure of wealth.

Most Nilotic cattle were kept by transhumant groups. Migrations , related to the wet and dry seasons, usually did not exceed 150 to 160 kilometers. The majority of the Baqqara strain of cattle belonged to the Baqqara Arabs. The latter were largely nomadic, but since at least the early 1900s had a settled base on which crop cultivation was practiced. The farmers, their relatives, or their agents moved the cattle over traditional migratory routes northward during the rainy season and southward to the area of the Bahr al Arab as the dry season progressed. Migrations in either direction might amount to 400 kilometers. The expansion of mechanized rainfed agriculture in the region used by the Baqqara, continued government efforts to enlarge the cultivated area, and pressures on the land from the growing population have gradually reduced grazing areas. At the same time, traditional cultural forces have brought about a steady increase in cattle numbers.

The result has been increasing overstocking and pasture depletion until the outbreak of civil war in 1983 and the devastating droughts of the 1980s and early 1990s decimated not only the Nilotic herds but livestock throughout Sudan. Many families and indeed whole ethnic groups who have traditionally survived on their cattle, sheep, goats, or camels, lost all of their herds and were forced to migrate to the Three Towns (Omdurman, Khartoum, and Khartoum North) in search of sustenance.

Sheep were herded chiefly by transhumants in Darfur and Kurdufan. Large numbers were found in the drier areas at greater elevations than the usual cattle zone. Several breeds were raised, but the predominant and preferred one was the so-called desert sheep, which had both good weight and good milk yield. Villagers in Al Awsat also raised large numbers of sheep, mostly on a nonmigratory basis. Fodder was obtained from crop residues on irrigated and rainfed farms and from vegetation along the rivers and canals. Goats, of which there were three principal breeds (desert, Nubian, and Nilotic), were found throughout the country south of the northern desert areas. They were raised mainly by sedentary families for milk and meat. Goat meat, although less popular than mutton, formed part of the diet of most families, particularly those having low incomes. Goat milk was an important source of protein, and many families in urban areas kept a few goats for their milk.

Camels were largely concentrated in the desert and subdesert regions of northern Darfur, northern Kurdufan, and southern Ash Sharqi. They were kept almost entirely by nomadic and seminomadic peoples, for whom the animal represented the preferred mode of transport. Camels were also important for milk and for meat. Camel ownership and numbers were sources of prestige in nomadic societies.

FISHERIES

Sudan's total production of fish, shellfish, and other fishing products reached an estimated 24,000 tons per year in 1991, the latest available yearly figures. This compared with estimates of a potential yearly catch exceeding 100,000 tons. The principal source of fish was the Nile River system. In central and northern Sudan, several lakes and reservoirs have been formed by the damming of the river and its branches: the 180-kilometer section of Lake Nubia on the main Nile in Sudan and the reservoirs behind the Roseires and Sennar dams on the Blue Nile, the Jabal al Awliya Dam on the White Nile, and the Khashm al Qirbah Dam on the Atbarah tributary of the main Nile. These bodies of water accounted for about 11,000 tons of fish against a calculated potential of about 29,000 tons.

Production from Lake Nubia through 1979, the latest figures available in 1991, was only 500 tons a year, or about one-tenth of the estimated potential. Inhabitants around the lake, which had formed gradually in the 1960s, had no previous experience in fishing, and the first significant commercial exploitation of the lake's resources had been undertaken by the government's Fisheries Administration. In 1973 a private company also started operations. In the mid- and late 1970s, an ice plant and a cold storage facility were built at Wadi Halfa with assistance from China. China also furnished thirty-five two-ton fishing vessels, a number of transport launches, and other fishing equipment. Cooling plants were constructed at Khartoum and Atbarah to hold fish that were brought from Wadi Halfa by railroad. Although ice was used in the shipments, substantial loss occurred, especially during the hotter months. To what extent fish production from the lake and availability to consumers were increased by these new facilities was not known in 1991.

The largest potential source of freshwater fish was southern Sudan whose extensive river network and flooded areas in As Sudd were believed able to provide 100,000 to 300,000 tons annually on a sustained basis. Statistics on actual production were unavailable in 1991; much was consumed locally, although limited quantities of dried and salted fish were exported to Zaire where it was in great demand.

The country's second source of fish, the Red Sea coastal area, was relatively unexploited until the late 1970s. Annual production toward the end of the decade amounted to about 500 tons of fish, shellfish (including pearl oysters), and other marine life. In 1978 the British Ministry of Overseas Development began a joint project with the government Fisheries Administration to raise output by making boats, motors, and equipment available to fishermen. Included was an ice plant built at Sawakin to furnish local fishermen with ice for their catch. By 1982 the project was well advanced, and about 2,000 tons of fish were taken annually. A sustained catch of 5,000 tons might eventually be possible.

FORESTRY

Since the early 1900s, extensive areas of woodland and forest have been converted to agricultural use. Large amounts of land classifiable as woodland have been cleared in the development of large-scale mechanized rainfed farming in Ash Sharqi and Al Awsat states, and smaller amounts in Aali an Nil and southern Kurdufan states. Although Sudan had a large quantity of natural forest, by 1994 much of it remained almost totally unexploited. In the late 1970s, FAO estimated that the country's forests and woodlands totaled about 915,000 square kilometers, or 38.5 percent of the land area.

This figure was based on the broad definition of forest and woodland as any area of vegetation dominated by trees of any size. It also included an unknown amount of cleared land that was expected to have forest cover again "in the foreseeable future." An estimate in the mid-1970s by the Forestry Administration, however, established the total forest cover at about 584,360 square kilometers, or 24.6 percent of the country's land area. More than 129,000 square kilometers (about onequarter) of this amount were located in the dry and semiarid regions of northern Sudan. These forests were considered valuable chiefly as protection for the land against desertification, but they also served as a source of fuel for pastoral peoples in those regions.

The continued population pressure on the land has resulted in an accelerated destruction of forestland, particularly in the Sahel, because charcoal remained the predominant fuel. The loss of forestland in the marginal areas of the north, accelerated by mechanized farming and by drought, resulted in a steady encroachment of the Sahara southward at about ten kilometers a year in the 1980s.

The productive forest extended below the zone of desert encroachment to the southern border. It included the savanna woodlands of the central and western parts of the country, which were dominated by various species of acacia, among them *Acacia senegal*, the principal source of gum arabic. Gum arabic was Sudan's second largest export product, accounting for 80 percent of the world's supply. It is nontoxic, noncalorific, and nonpolluting, having no odor or taste. It is used widely in industry for products ranging from mucilage (for postage stamps) to foam stabilizers to excipient in medicines and dietetic foods. In 1986-87 Sudan produced more than 40,000 tons marketed through the Gum Arabic Company. In the late 1980s the drought severely curtailed production.

The principal area of productive forest and woodland, however, was in the more moist southern part of the country. Covering an area of more than 200,000 square kilometers and consisting mainly of broadleaf deciduous hardwoods, it remained largely undeveloped in 1990. Timber processed by government mills in the area included mahogany for furniture and other hardwoods for railroad ties, furniture, and construction. Domestic production of timber fell far short of local needs in the 1970s, and as much as 80 percent of the domestic requirement was met by imports.

Plantations established by the government Forestry Administration in the mid-1970s totaled about 16,000 hectares of hardwoods and 500 to 600 hectares of softwoods, most were in the south. They included stands of teak and in the higher elevations of the Imatong Mountains, exotic pines. Eucalyptus stands had also been established in the irrigated agricultural areas to serve as windbreaks and to supply firewood. A gradually increasing forest reserve has been developed, and by the mid1970s it covered more than 13,000 square kilometers. Additional protection of forest and woodland areas was provided by several national parks and game reserves that encompassed 54,000 square kilometers in the mid-1970s.

Since 1983 the civil war virtually halted forestry production in southern Sudan, from which came the overwhelming amount of forestry products. According to FAO estimates, however, in 1987 Sudan produced 41,000 cubic meters of sawn timber, 1,906,000 cubic meters of other industrial roundwood, and more than 18 million cubic meters of firewood. Each of these categories showed a substantial increase from production levels in the 1970s. The insatiable demand was for charcoal, the principal cooking fuel, and the one major forest product not dependent upon the south. Because wood of any kind could be turned to charcoal, the acacia groves of the Sahel have been used extensively for this purpose, with a resulting rapid advance of deforestation. To improve government forestry conservation and management policy, as well as the issue of land use, in 1990-91 plans were underway to establish a forestry resource conservation project, funded and cofinanced by several international development agencies and donors.

MANUFACTURING

The development of modern manufacturing received little direct encouragement in Sudan during the condominium period. British economic policies were aimed basically at expanding the production of primary products, mainly cotton, for export. Imports and traditional handicraft industries met the basic needs for manufactured goods. Indirectly, however, the vast Gezira Scheme cotton-growing project induced the construction of ginneries, of which more than twenty were in operation by the early 1930s. A secondary development was the establishment of several cottonseed oil-pressing mills. During World War II, small import substitution industries arose, including those manufacturing soap, carbonated drinks, and other consumer items. These operations did not survive the competition from imports after the war's end. Foreign private interests invested in a few larger enterprises that included a meat-processing factory, a cement plant, and a brewery, all opened between 1949 and 1952.

At independence the Sudanese government supported an industrial development policy to be effected through the private sector. To facilitate this process, Khartoum adopted the Approved Enterprises (Concessions) Act of 1956, to encourage private Sudanese and foreign investment. The act placed few restrictions on foreign equity holdings. By 1961, however, the government had concluded that the private sector lacked interest or funds to establish enterprises important to the national economy, and so it entered the manufacturing field. The first government project was a tannery opened that year, and this was followed in 1962 by a sugar factory. In 1962 Khartoum formed the Industrial Development Corporation (IDC) to manage government plants.

During the decade, several additional government enterprises were built, including a second sugar factory, two fruit and vegetable canneries, a date-processing plant, an onion-dehydrating plant, a milk-processing plant, and a cardboard factory. During this time, the private sector also made substantial investment, which resulted in factories making textiles and knitwear, shoes, soap, soft drinks, and flour. Other private enterprises included printing facilities and additional oil-pressing mills. Among the largest private undertakings was the foreign-financed and foreign-built oil refinery at Port Sudan, which opened in 1964. Well over half the private sector investment during the decade came from foreign sources.

Government participation in the manufacturing sector increased dramatically after the 1969 military coup and the adoption of a policy aimed at placing the country's economic development in government hands, although private ownership continued. During 1970 and 1971 Khartoum nationalized more than thirty private enterprises. In 1972, however, to counter the drop in foreign private investment that followed, Nimeiri announced that private capital would again be accorded favorable treatment, and the government passed the Development and Promotion of Industrial Investment Act of 1972, containing even more liberal provisions than precoup legislation.

As the economy remained dependent on private capital, as well as capital investment from developed nations, the government incorporated further incentives for the favorable treatment of such capital in a 1974 revision of the industrial investment act, and added provisions against arbitrary nationalization. Moreover, in 1972 Khartoum denationalized some enterprises nationalized earlier, and returned them to their former owners under an arrangement for joint government-private ownership. One of the largest of these enterprises was the Bata Shoe Company, which was returned in 1978 as a reorganized joint company in which Bata held a 51 percent interest and the government 49 percent. The most successful such enterprise, however, was the Bittar Group, which in 1990 had become the largest undertaking in Sudan. Begun in the 1920s, nationalized in 1969 but returned to its owners in 1973, it has diversified into products ranging from exports of vegetable oils to imports of wheat, sugar, and insecticides. The firm has been active in a wide range of projects involving agriculture, electricity, and such industrial products as household and office equipment, soap, and detergents.

Throughout the 1970s, the government continued to establish new public enterprises, some state-owned, others in conjunction with private interests, and some having foreign government participation, especially by the Arab oil-producing states. The new plants included three sugar factories, among which was the Kinanah sugar-milling and refining factory; two tanneries; a flour mill; and more than twenty textile plants. A joint venture with United States interests built Sudan's first fertilizer plant south of Khartoum, which was in operation by 1986. Private investment continued, particularly in textiles. About 300 million meters of cloth were produced annually in the 1970s, but output fell to 50 million meters in 1985. In 1988, the textile industry functioned at about 25 percent of capacity. The latter figure reflected the effects of the civil war, the dearth of hard currency for spare parts to maintain machinery, and the debt crisis.

Since independence Sudan's modern manufacturing establishment has emphasized the processing of agricultural products and import substitution. The production of foodstuffs, beverages, and clothing has accounted for a large part of total output. Significant import substitution industries included cement, chemicals, and dry battery manufacture; glass-bottle-making; petroleum refining; and fertilizer production. In the late 1980s, estimates of the contribution of modern manufacturing to GDP varied from about 7 to 8 percent a year, including mining (compared to about 2 percent in 1956). Employment in the sector had risen during that period from possibly 9,000 in 1956 to 185,000 in 1977, including wage earners in government enterprises. Almost three-quarters of large-scale modern manufacturing was located in Al Khartum, attracted by market size, higher per capita income, better transportation and power infrastructure, and access to financial and government services.

Total manufacturing output, however, had not met expectation by the end of the 1970s and steadily declined in the 1980s. Overall output in some subsectors had grown as new facilities began operating, but the goal of self-sufficiency had generally not been attained. Shortages of domestic and imported raw materials, power failures, transportation delays, lack of spare parts, and shortages of labor ranging from qualified managerial staff and skilled workers to casual laborers had been drawbacks to effective operations and increased output. Losses of skilled labor and management to the Persian Gulf states have been particularly debilitating. In the 1980s, many factories operated below capacity--frequently at well under 50 percent of their potential. In some instances, low production also was related to poor project planning.

For example, the government cannery at Kuraymah in Ash Shamali was already constructed when scientists found that the surrounding farming area could not produce the quantity of crops the plant could process. The milk-processing facility at Babanusah south of Khartoum had a similar record of poor planning. Efforts to improve the transportation and power infrastructure, whose deficiencies have been major contributors to the manufacturing problems, and rehabilitation of existing plants were among the basic goals of the 1977-82 Six-Year Plan of

Economic and Social Development. That plan was never effectively implemented. Some progress has been reported, but in 1990 the production problems faced earlier by manufacturing persisted.

MINING

In 1992 the mining industry accounted for less than 1 percent of the total GDP. A wide range of minerals existed in Sudan, but the size of reserves had not been determined in most cases. The discovery of commercially exploitable quantities of petroleum in the late 1970s offered some hope that the sector would play an increased role in the economy in the future. However, from February 1984, some months after concessions were allotted, oil exploration operations had been suspended in the south, where the largest deposits were located, as a result of the region's security problems. Nonhydrocarbon minerals of actual or potential commercial value included gold, chrome, copper, iron, manganese, asbestos, gypsum, mica, limestone, marble, and uranium. Gold had been mined in the Red Sea Hills since pharaonic times. Between 1900 and 1954, several British enterprises worked gold mines in the area, and extracted a considerable quantity of the metal--one mine alone reportedly produced three tons of gold between 1924 and 1936. Gold also has been mined along the borders between Sudan and Uganda and Zaire, but not in commercially profitable amounts. During the 1970s, the government's Geological Survey Administration located more than fifty potential gold-producing sites in different parts of the country. Several joint ventures between the Sudanese Mining Corporation, a government enterprise, and foreign companies were launched in the 1980s; these undertakings produced gold at Gebeit and several other mines near the Red Sea Hills beginning in 1987. In 1988, about 78,000 metric kilograms of gold ore were mined in Sudan. In late 1990, Sudan and two French mining companies formed a joint venture company to exploit gold reserves in the Khawr Ariab wadi in the Red Sea Hills.

Chrome ore was mined in the Ingessana Hills in Al Awsat. In the late 1970s, output was reportedly more than 20,000 tons a year, of which more than four-fifths were produced by the Ingessana Hills Mines Corporation, a subsidiary of Sudanese Mining Corporation. A private operation produced the remainder. The ore was exported, chiefly to Japan and Western Europe. In the 1980s, the establishment of ferrochrome processing facilities had been discussed with Japanese interests, but the estimated 700,000 tons of reserves were insufficient for profitable longterm operations. By 1983, when the civil war brought a halt to all production in the Ingessana Hills, chrome production had declined about 50 percent to only 10,000 tons per year. In 1988, production of chromium ore was estimated at 5,000 metric tons. Asbestos had also been found in the Ingessana Hills area. It was reportedly of good commercial grade, and mining possibilities were under study by a Canadian subsidiary of the United States firm of Johns-Manville. A small pilot extraction plant had been built, but larger scale operations were dependent on locating adequate reserves and on the ending of the civil war.

Large gypsum deposits, estimated to contain reserves of 220 million tons, were found along the Red Sea coast. Reportedly of high purity, the ore was mined mainly north of Port Sudan. In the late 1980s, about 20,000 tons were produced annually, about 6,000 tons by the Sudanese Mining Corporation and the remainder by private operations. Gypsum was used mostly in the production of cement. Limestone, found in substantial quantities in Sudan, was mined both for use in making cement and for other construction materials. Marble was also quarried for the latter purpose.

There has been some commercial mining of mica, exploitable deposits of which had been located in Ash Shamali Province by a UN mineral survey team between 1968 and 1972. The Sudanese Mining Corporation produced about 1,000 tons of scrap mica in FY 1978, but output reportedly slumped thereafter to about 400 tons annually. Manganese and iron ore, of which several large deposits exist in different parts of the country, have been mined at times but only on a small basis by international standards. There were more than 500 million tons of iron ore deposits in the

Fodikwan area of the Red Sea Hills, and beginning in the late 1980s a project had been planned to produce between 120,000 and 200,000 tons a month. Exploitation of Sudan's mineral deposits, however, depended in large part on foreign companies willing to undertake such risks in the face of the country's mounting problems, and on international market factors.

Uranium ores have been discovered in the area of the Nuba Mountains and at Hufrat an Nahas in southern Kurdufan. Minex Company of the United States obtained a 36,000-square-kilometer exploratory concession in the Kurdufan area in 1977, and the concession was increased to 48,000 square kilometers in 1979. Uranium reserves are also believed to exist near the western borders with Chad and Central African Republic. Another potential source of mineral wealth was the Red Sea bed. In 1974 officials established a joint Sudanese-Saudi Arabian agency to develop those resources, which included zinc, silver, copper, and other minerals. Explorations below the 2,000-meter mark have indicated that large quantities of the minerals are present, but as of 1990 no actual extraction had been undertaken.

ENERGY SOURCES AND SUPPLY

In the early 1990s the chief sources of energy were wood and charcoal, hydroelectric power, and imported oil. Wood and charcoal were principally used by households for heating and cooking. Substantial quantities of wood fuels, amounting to roughly onefifth of the country's annual consumption, were also used by commercial operations--chiefly baking and brickmaking and, to a lesser extent, tobacco curing. Some use was also made of other vegetable matter including sugarcane bagasse, which met a significant part of the energy needs of the sugar mills, and cotton stalks, used locally by households. Consumption of wood and charcoal has continued to increase as the population has grown, and some concern has been voiced at the gradual depletion of forest and woodland resources serving the large towns. Overuse of the sparser vegetation in the semidesert grazing areas reportedly was resulting in some fuel deficiencies in those regions, as well as in desertification.

The country's hydroelectric potential has been only partially exploited. Major undeveloped hydropower sources existed at the several cataracts on the main Nile downstream from Khartoum. Natural gas was discovered in the early 1960s along the Red Sea coast in a fruitless search for petroleum. In the mid-1970s, further quantities were found during additional oil explorations, but development was not considered at the time to be commercially feasible. In October 1988, Sudan announced that natural gas production would start in one year; presumably this would come from the 85 billion cubic meters of gas reserves Chevron had earlier estimated. The 1979 and later petroleum discoveries in southern and southwestern Sudan added a new potential domestic energy source. However, these deposits to date have yielded little oil because petroleum companies, such as Chevron, had suspended oilfield explorations in these regions because of the civil war. Sudan had no known deposits of coal or lignite as of the early 1990s.

ELECTRIC POWER

The only sizable area of the country having electric power available to the public was the central region along the Blue Nile from Khartoum south to Ad Damazin. The central region in the early 1990s accounted for approximately 87 percent of Sudan's total electricity consumption. The area was served by the country's only major interconnected generating and distributing system, the Blue Nile Grid. This system provided power to both the towns and the irrigation projects in the area, including the Gezira Scheme. Another small, local, interconnected system furnished power in the eastern part of the country that included Al Qadarif, Kassala, and Halfa al Jadidah. The remaining customers were in fewer than twenty widely scattered towns having local diesel-powered generating facilities: Shandi, Atbarah, and Dunqulah in the north; Malakal, Juba, and Waw in the south; Al Fashir and Nyala in Darfur; Al Ubayyid and Umm Ruwabah in Kurdufan; a few towns along the White Nile south of Khartoum; and Port Sudan. About fifty other urban centers in outlying regions, each having populations of more than 5,000, still did not have a public electricity supply in 1982, the latest year for which statistical information was available. Rural electrification was found only in some of the villages associated with the main irrigation projects.

Approximately 75 percent of the country's total electric power was produced by the Public Electricity and Water Corporation (PEWC), a state enterprise. The remaining 25 percent was generated for self-use by various industries including foodprocessing and sugar factories, textile mills, and the Port Sudan refinery. Private and PEWC electricity generation increased about 50 percent in the 1980s, to an estimated 900 gigawatt hours in 1989 in attempts to counter frequent cuts in electric power. PEWC also handled all regular electricity distribution to the public. In 1989 PEWC power stations had a total generating capacity of 606 megawatts, of which about 53 percent was hydroelectric and the remainder thermal.

The largest hydroelectric plant was at Roseires Dam on the Blue Nile; it had a capacity of 250 megawatts. Other hydroelectric stations were located at the Sennar Dam farther downstream and at Khashm al Qirbah Dam on the Atbarah River; the latter was part of the small power grid in the Al Qadarif-Kassala area. The Sennar and Roseires dams were constructed originally to provide irrigation, Sennar in 1925 and Roseires in 1966. Electric-power generating facilities were added only when increasing consumer demands had made them potentially viable (Sennar in 1962 and Roseires in 1971), yet power generation in Sudan has never satisfied actual needs.

The Blue Nile Grid, in addition to its Roseires and Sennar hydroelectric plants, had thermal plants at Burri in eastern Khartoum, where work on a 40-megawatt extension began in 1986, and in Khartoum North, where a 60-megawatt thermal station began operation in 1985. In the late 1980s, two additional stations producing 40 to 60 megawatts each were under consideration for Khartoum North.

The demand for electricity on the Blue Nile system increased greatly in the late 1970s, and power shortages have been acute from 1978 onward. Shortages have been blamed in part on management inefficiency and lack of coordination between the PEWC and irrigation authorities and other government agencies. Demand continued to grow strongly during the 1980s as development projects were completed and became operational and the population of the Three Towns increased dramatically. New generating facilities were completed in 1986 under the Power III Project, almost doubling generating capacity in the Blue Nile Grid. The project included work on the Roseires units, funded by IDA, and on the Burri and Khartoum North installations, funded by the British Overseas Development Administration. In 1983, recognizing the need for more electricity the government began seeking support for the Power IV Project to be funded by the World Bank, the African Development Bank, and the Federal Republic of Germany (West Germany) to bring the entire electrical system up to its full generating capacity. The plan was later scaled back from the initial cost of US$100 million and renamed Power V Project.

PETROLEUM USE AND DOMESTIC RESOURCES

In 1982 roughly four-fifths of the nation's energy requirement for industry, modern agriculture, transportation, government services, and households (in addition to wood fuel, charcoal, and the like) was provided by imported petroleum and petroleum products. Approximately 10 percent of these imports were used to generate electricity. Foreign exchange costs for oil imports rose dramatically after 1973 and by 1988 amounted to almost 46 percent of earnings from merchandise exports. Dependence on external sources might lessen when the security situation permits Sudan's domestic petroleum resources to be exploited.

The search for oil began in 1959 in the Red Sea littoral and continued intermittently into the 1970s. In 1982 several oil companies were prospecting large concessions offshore and on land from the Tawkar area near the Ethiopian border to the northern part of the Red Sea Hills. No significant discoveries were reported. In 1974 Chevron, a subsidiary of Standard Oil Company of California, began exploration of a 516,000-square-kilometer concession (later reduced to 280,000 square kilometers by voluntary relinquishment) in southern and southwestern Sudan. Drilling began in 1977, and the first commercial flow was obtained in July 1979 at Abu Jabirah in southern Kurdufan Province. In 1980 major finds were made at the company's Unity Field near Bentiu in Aali an Nil Province, where further drilling by early 1981 had brought in forty-nine wells having a combined flow of more than 12,000 barrels a day.

The company has estimated this field's reserves at from 80 to 100 million barrels, but exploration farther south placed the reserves at more than 250 million barrels. Other oil companies--including some from the United States, Canada, and France--have also obtained concessions, and by 1982 almost one-third of Sudan had been assigned for exploration. Oil exploration and production have been hampered, however, by the almost total lack of infrastructure and by the civil war in the south of the country. Chevron had found small aircraft and helicopters essential for transport, the latter for moving portable rigs and equipment and for general use during the rainy season when all roads and locally constructed air strips were washed out.

The domestic processing of crude petroleum began in late 1964 when the Port Sudan oil refinery went into operation. The refinery, which was financed, built, and managed by the British Petroleum and Royal Dutch Shell companies--from July 1976 as a joint equal shareholding project with the government--had a capacity of about 21,440 barrels per day. Its capacity was well in excess of Sudan's needs at the time it was built, and refined products were exported. Local demand had quintupled by 1990, well beyond the plant's capacity. As a result, more than one-third of the gas oil (used in diesel motors and for heating) and well over two-fifths of the kerosene required for domestic use had to be imported. A substantial quantity of other products refined by the plant in excess of Sudan's own needs were exported.

The domestic petroleum discoveries led to intensive discussion within the government concerning the establishment of a new refinery. Southern Sudan pressed for construction near the oilfields in the south, but it was decided finally to locate the refinery at Kusti on the White Nile about 315 kilometers south of Khartoum. In August 1981, the White Nile Petroleum Company (WNPC) was set up by the central government as a subsidiary of the Sudanese National Oil Company to handle the undertaking. The government held a two-fifths share in WNPC, Chevron Overseas Petroleum Corporation another two-fifths, and the International Finance Corporation the remaining one-fifth. Plans called for a 550-kilometer pipeline to be built from the oilfields to the new refinery. By early 1982, however, the estimated costs of the refinery and pipeline had risen to at least the equivalent of US$1 billion as against an earlier project allotment of about one-third that figure.

The Kusti refinery was predicated on production for domestic consumption. Its estimated capacity (in early 1982) of between 15,000 and 25,000 barrels a day would meet only part of Sudan's overall requirements, however, and the quality of the petroleum would restrict economic production to certain products, so the Port Sudan refinery would have to continue operating. In view of the greatly increased cost estimates of the new plant, the World Bank in 1982 undertook a study of an alternative plan that might be more attractive to foreign capital. Under this plan, the proposed pipeline would run to Port Sudan, and an extension to the existing refinery would make it possible to export surplus refined products and even earn foreign-exchange crs. Contracts were let for the construction of the pipeline, but the government canceled them in September 1986. Further seismic studies were undertaken in the swamps (As Sudd) of Aali an Nil, but all of Chevron's exploration and development activities came to an abrupt end in February 1984 when guerrillas from the southern Sudanese insurgent group known as Anya Nya II attacked the main forward Chevron base across the Bahr al Ghazal River from Bentiu, killing four Chevron employees. Chevron immediately terminated its development program and, despite repeated demands by successive Sudanese governments, has refused to return to work its concession until the safety of its personnel can be guaranteed by a settlement of the Sudanese civil war. Total, the French oil company, shut down its operations several months later.

The Nimeiri government pressured foreign oil companies to resume exploration and drilling and hoped to encourage them to do so in part by forming the National Oil Company of Sudan (NOCS) in a joint venture with Saudi Arabian entrepreneur Adnan Khashoggi. After Nimeiri was overthrown, the new government dissolved NOCS but continued to press companies to renew work. As a result, Chevron stated in late 1987 that it would begin a sixty-day, twowell drilling program in southern Kurdufan in 1988, but postponed this because of the spread of civil war. Several other foreign companies indicated an interest in petroleum exploration in 1988, following the completion of a three-year World Bank study of Sudan's hydrocarbon potential. The minister of energy and mining had announced in May 1987 that Sudan's confirmed oil reserves totaled 2 billion barrels, with an estimated 500 million barrels recoverable.

TRANSPORTATION AND COMMUNICATIONS

Sudan's transport infrastructure in 1990 included an extensive railroad system that served the more important populated areas except in the far south, a meager road network (very little of which consisted of all-weather roads), a natural inland waterway--the Nile River and its tributaries--and a national airline that provided both international and domestic service. Complementing this infrastructure was Port Sudan, a major deep-water port on the Red Sea, and a small but modern national merchant marine. Additionally, a pipeline transporting petroleum products extended from the port to Khartoum.

Only minimal efforts had been expended through the early 1980s to improve existing and, according to both Sudanese and foreign observers, largely inefficiently operated transport facilities. Increasing emphasis on economic development placed a growing strain on the system, and beginning in the mid-1970s a substantial proportion of public investment funds was allocated for transport sector development. Some progress toward meeting equipment goals had been reported by the beginning of the 1980s, but substantial further modernization and adequately trained personnel were still required. Until these were in place, inadequate transportation was expected to constitute a major obstacle to economic development.

RAILROADS

The country had two railroads. The main system, Sudan Railways, which was operated by the government-owned Sudan Railways Corporation, provided services to most of the country's production and consumption centers. The other railroad, the Gezira Light Railway, was owned by the Sudan Gezira Board and served the Gezira Scheme and its Managil Extension. Railroads dominated commercial transport, although competition from the highways has been increasing rapidly. The preeminence of the railroad system was based on historical developments that led to its construction as an adjunct to military operations, although the first line, built in the mid-1870s from Wadi Halfa to a point about fifty-four kilometers upstream on the Nile River, was initially a commercial undertaking. This line, which had not proved viable commercially, was extended in the mid-1880s and again in the mid-1890s to support the Anglo-Egyptian military campaigns against the Mahdiyah. Of little other use, it was abandoned in 1905.

The first segment of the present-day Sudan Railways, from Wadi Halfa to Abu Hamad, was also a military undertaking; it was built by the British for use in General Herbert Kitchener's drive against the Mahdiyah in the late 1890s. The line was pushed to Atbarah during the campaign and after the defeat of the Mahdiyah in 1898 was continued to Khartoum, which it reached on the last day of 1899. The line was built to 1.067-meter-gauge track specifications, the result apparently of Kitchener's pragmatic use of the rolling stock and rails of that gauge from the old line. This gauge was used in all later Sudanese mainline construction.

The line opened a trade route from central Sudan through Egypt to the Merranean and beyond. It became uneconomical, however, because of the distance and the need for transshipment via the Nile, and in 1904 construction of a new line from Atbarah to the Red Sea was undertaken. In 1906 the new line reached recently built Port Sudan to provide a direct connection between Khartoum and ocean-going transport.

During the same decade, a line was also built from Khartoum southward to Sannar, the heart of the cotton-growing region of Al Jazirah. A westward continuation reached Al Ubayyid, then the country's second largest city and center of gum arabic production, in 1911. In the north, a branch line was built from near Abu Hamad to Kuraymah that tied the navigable stretch of the Nile between the fourth and third cataracts into the transport system. Traffic in this case, however, was largely inbound to towns along the river, a situation that still prevailed in 1990.

In the mid- and late 1920s, a spur of the railroad was built from Taqatu Hayya, a point on the main line 200 kilometers southwest of Port Sudan, southward to the cotton-producing area near Kassala, then on to the grain region of Al Qadarif, and finally to a junction with the main line at Sannar. Much of the area's traffic, which formerly had passed through Khartoum, has since moved over this line directly to Port Sudan.

The final spurt of railroad construction began in the 1950s. It included extension of the western line to Nyala (1959) in Darfur Province and of a southwesterly branch to Waw (1961), southern Sudan's second largest city, located in Bahr al Ghazal Province. This essentially completed the Sudan Railways network, which in 1990 totaled about 4,800 route kilometers.

Conversion of Sudan Railways to diesel fuel started in the late 1950s, but a few mainline steam locomotives continued in use in 1990, serving lines having lighter weight rails. Through the 1960s, the railroads essentially had a monopoly on transportation of export and import trade, and operations were profitable. In the early 1970s, losses were experienced, and, although the addition of new diesel equipment in 1976 was followed by a return to profitability, another downturn had occurred by the end of the decade. The losses were attributed in part to inflationary factors, the lack of spare parts, and the continuation of certain lines characterized by only light traffic, but retained for economic development needs and for social reasons.

The chief cause of the downturn appeared to have been loss of operational efficiency. Worker productivity had declined. For example, repair of locomotives was so slow that only about half of the total number were usually operational. Freight car turnaround time had lengthened considerably, and the reported slowness of management to meet growing competition from road transport was also a major factor. The road system, although generally more expensive, was used increasingly for low-volume, high-value goods because it could deliver more rapidly--two or three days from Port Sudan to Khartoum, compared with seven or eight days for express rail freight and up to two weeks for ordinary freight. At the end of the 1980s, moreover, only 1 to 2 percent of freight trains arrived on time. The gradual erosion of freight traffic was evident in the drop from more than 3 million tons carried annually at the beginning of the 1970s to about 2 million tons at the end of the decade. The 1980s also saw a steady erosion of tonnage as a result of a combination of inefficient management, union intransigence, the failure of agricultural projects to meet production goals, the dearth of spare parts, and the continuing civil war.

Despite the rapidly growing use of roads, the railroads have remained of paramount importance because of their ability to move at lower cost the large volume of agricultural exports and to transport inland the increasing imports of heavy capital equipment and construction materials for development, such as requirements for oil exploration and drilling operations. Efforts to improve the rail system reported in the late 1970s and the 1980s included laying heavier rails, repairing locomotives, purchasing new locomotives, modernizing signaling equipment, expanding training facilities, and improving locomotive and rolling-stock repair facilities. One project would double-track the line from Port Sudan to the junction of the branch route to Sannar, thus in effect doubling the Port Sudan-Khartoum rail line. Substantial assistance has been furnished for these and other stock and track improvement projects by foreign governments and organizations, including the European Development Fund, the Development Finance Company, the AFESD, the International Development Association, Britain, France, and Japan. Implementation of much of this work has been hampered by political instability in the 1980s, debt, the dearth of hard currency, the shortage of spare parts, and import controls. Railroads were estimated in mid-1989 to be operating at less than 20 percent of capacity.

The Gezira Light Railway, one of the largest light railroads in Africa, evolved from tracks laid in the 1920s' construction of the canals for the Gezira Scheme. At the time, the railroad had about 135 route kilometers of 1.6096-meter-gauge track. As the size of the project area increased, the railroad was extended and by the mid-1960s consisted of a complex system totaling 716 route kilometers. Its primary purpose has been to serve the farm area by carrying cotton to ginneries and fertilizers, fuel, food, and other supplies to the villages in the area. Operations usually have been suspended during the rainy season.

ROADS

In 1990 Sudan's road system totaled between 20,000 and 25,000 kilometers, comprising an extremely sparse network for the size of the country. Asphalted all-weather roads, excluding paved streets in cities and towns, amounted to roughly 3,000 to 3,500 kilometers, of which the Khartoum-Port Sudan road accounted for almost 1,200 kilometers.

There were between 3,000 and 4,000 kilometers of gravel roads located mostly in the southern region where lateritic road-building materials were abundant. In general, these roads were usable all year round, although travel might be interrupted at times during the rainy season. Most of the gravel roads in southern Sudan have become unusable after being heavily mined by the insurgent southern forces of the Sudanese People's Liberation Army (SPLA).

The remaining roads were little more than fair-weather earth and sand tracks. Those in the clayey soil of eastern Sudan, a region of great economic importance, were impassable for several months during the rains. Even in the dry season, earthen roads in the sandy soils found in various parts of the country were generally usable only by motor vehicles equipped with special tires.

Until the early 1970s, the government had favored the railroads, believing they better met the country's requirements for transportation and that the primary purpose of roads was to act as feeders to the rail system. The railroads were also a profitable government operation, and road competition was not viewed as desirable. In the mid-1930s, a legislative attempt had been made to prevent through-road transport between Khartoum and Port Sudan. The law had little effect, but the government's failure to build roads hindered the development of road transportation. The only major stretch of road that had been paved by 1970 was between Khartoum and Wad Madani. This road had been started under a United States aid program in 1962, but work had stopped in 1967 when Sudanese-United States relations were broken over the June 1967 Arab-Israeli War. United States equipment was not removed, however, and was used by government workers to complete the road in 1970.

Disillusionment with railroad performance led to a new emphasis on roads in a readjustment of the Five-Year Plan in 1973--the so-called Interim Action Program--and a decision to encourage competition between rail and road transport as the best way to improve services. Paving of the dry-weather road between Khartoum and Port Sudan via Al Qadarif and Kassala was the most significant immediate step; this included upgrading of the existing paved Khartoum-Wad Madani section. From Wad Madani to Port Sudan, the road was constructed in four separate sections, each by different foreign financing, and in the case of the Wad Madani-Al Qadarif section, by direct participation of the Chinese. Other section contractors included companies from Italy, West Germany, and Yugoslavia. The last section opened in late 1980.

Other important road-paving projects of the early 1980s included a road from Wad Madani to Sannar and an extension from Sannar to Kusti on the White Nile completed in 1984. Since then the paved road has been extended to Umm Ruwabah with the intention to complete an all-weather road to Al Ubayyid. Paradoxically, most truckers in 1990 continued to pass from Omdurman to Al Ubayyid through the Sahelian scrub and the *qoz* to avoid the taxes levied to use the faster and less damaging paved road from Khartoum via Kusti.

A number of main gravel roads radiating from Juba were also improved. These included roads to the towns southwest of Juba and a road to the Ugandan border. In addition, the government built a gravel all-weather road east of Juba that reaches the Kenyan border. There it joined an all-weather road to Lodwar in Kenya connecting it with the Kenyan road system. All these improvements radiating from Juba, however, have been vitiated by the civil war, in which the roads have been extensively mined by the SPLA and the bridges destroyed, and because roads have not been maintained, they have seriously deteriorated.

Small private companies, chiefly owner-operated trucks, furnished most road transport. The government has encouraged private enterprise in this industry, especially in the central and eastern parts of the country, and the construction of allweather roads has reportedly led to rapid increases in the number of hauling businesses. The Sudanese-Kuwaiti Transport Company, a large government enterprise financed largely by Kuwait, began operations in 1975 with 100 large trucks and trailers. Most of its traffic was between Khartoum and Port Sudan. Use of road transport and bus services is likely to increase as paved roads are completed south of Khartoum in the country's main agricultural areas.

INLAND WATERWAYS

The Nile River, traversing Sudan from south to north, provides an important inland transportation route. Its overall usefulness, however, has been limited by natural features, including a number of cataracts in the main Nile between Khartoum and the Egyptian border. The White Nile to the south of Khartoum has shallow stretches that restrict the carrying capacities of barges, especially during the period of low water, and the river has sharp bends. Most of these southern impediments have been eliminated by Chevron, who as part of their oil exploration and development program dredged the White Nile shoals and established navigational beacons from Kusti to Bentiu.

A greater impediment has been the spread of the water hyacinth, which impedes traffic. Man-made features have also introduced restrictions, the most important of which was a dam constructed in the 1930s on the White Nile about forty kilometers upriver from Khartoum. This dam has locks, but they have not always operated well, and the river has been little used from Khartoum to the port of Kusti, a railroad crossing 319 kilometers upstream. The Sennar and Roseires dams on the Blue Nile are without locks and restrict traffic on that river.

In 1983 only two sections of the Nile had regular commercial transport services. The more important was the 1,436-kilometer stretch of the White Nile from Kusti to Juba (known as the Southern Reach), which provided the only generally usable transport connection between the central and southern parts of the country. Virtually all traffic, and certainly scheduled traffic, ended in 1984, when the SPLA consistently sank the exposed steamers from sanctuaries along the river banks. River traffic south of Kusti had not resumed in mid- 1991 except for a few heavily armed and escorted convoys.

At one time, transport services also were provided on tributaries of the White Nile (the Bahr al Ghazal and the Jur River) to the west of Malakal. These services went as far as Waw but were seasonal, depending on water levels. They were finally discontinued during the 1970s because vegetation blocked waterways, particularly the fast-growing water hyacinth. On the main Nile, a 287-kilometer stretch from Kuraymah to Dunqulah, situated between the fourth and third cataracts and known as the Dunqulah Reach, also had regular service, although this was restricted during the low-water period in February and March. Transport facilities on both reaches were operated after 1973 by the parastatal (mixed government and privately owned company) River Transport Corporation (RTC). Before that they had been run by the SRC, essentially as feeders to the rail line. River cargo and passenger traffic have varied from year to year, depending in large part on the availability and capacity of transport vessels. During the 1970s, roughly 100,000 tons of cargo and 250,000 passengers were carried annually. By 1984, before the Southern Reach was closed, the number of passengers had declined to less than 60,000 per year and the tonnage to less than 150,000. Although no statistics were available, the closing of the Southern Reach had by 1990 made river traffic insignificant.

Foreign economists have characterized the RTC's operations as inefficient, a result both of shortages of qualified staff and of barge capacity. The corporation had a virtual monopoly over river transport, although the southern regional government had established river feeder transport operations, and private river transport services were reported to be increasing until the resumption of the civil war. Despite its favored position, the RTC and its predecessor (SRC) experienced regular losses that had to be covered by government appropriations. In the late 1970s, the corporation procured new barges, pusher-tugboats, and other equipment in an effort to improve services, but this attempt proved useless because of the warfare that had continued from 1983.

MARINE PORTS AND SHIPPING

In 1993 Sudan had only one operational deep-water harbor, Port Sudan, situated on an inlet of the Red Sea. The port had been built from scratch, beginning in 1905, to complement the railroad line from Khartoum to the Red Sea by serving as the entry and exit point for the foreign trade the rail line was to carry. It operated as a department of SRC until 1974 when it was transferred to the Sea Ports Corporation, a newly established public enterprise set up to manage Sudan's marine ports. Facilities at the port eventually included fifteen cargo berths, sheds, warehouses, and storage tanks for edible oils, molasses, and petroleum products. Equipment included quay, mobile, and other cranes, and some forklift trucks, but much of the handling of cargo was manual. There were also a number of tugboats, which were used to berth ships in the narrow inlet.

During the early 1970s, port traffic averaged about 3 million tons a year, compared with an overall capacity of about 3.8 million tons. Exports were somewhat more than 1 million tons and imports about 2 million tons; about half of the latter was petroleum and petroleum products. By the mid-1970s, stepped up economic development had raised traffic to capacity levels. In 1985, however, largely as a result of the civil war, exports were down to 663 thousand tons (down 51 percent from the previous year) and imports were 2.3 million tons (down 25 percent from the previous year). Physical expansion of the harbor and adjacent areas was generally precluded by natural features and the proximity of the city of Port Sudan. However, surveys showed that use could be increased considerably by modernization and improvement of existing facilities and the addition of further cargo-handling equipment.

In 1978, with the assistance of a loan from the IDA, work began on adding deep-water berths and providing roll-on-roll-off container facilities. A loan to purchase equipment was made by a West Germany body. The first phase was completed in 1982, and the second phase began in 1983, aided by a US$25-million World Bank cr. One of the major improvements has been to make the port more readily usable by road vehicles. Developed almost entirely as a rail-serviced facility, the port had large areas of interlacing railroad tracks that were mostly not flush with surrounding surfaces, thereby greatly restricting vehicular movement. Many of these tracks have been removed and new access roads constructed. Much of the cleared area has become available for additional storage facilities.

In the early 1980s, the Nimeiri government announced a plan to construct a new deep-water port at Sawakin, about twenty kilometers south of Port Sudan. Construction of a new port had long been under consideration in response to the projected growth of port traffic in the latter part of the twentieth century. A detailed study for the proposed port was made by a West German firm in the mid-1970s, and plans were drawn up for three general cargo berths, including roll-on-roll-off container facilities, and an oil terminal. Major funding for the port, known as Sawakin, was offered in 1985 by West Germany's development agency Kranstalt für Wiederaufbau and the DFC. After the Nimeiri government repeatedly postponed work on the port, the German government allocated the funds instead for purchase of agricultural inputs. Once work resumed, however, Sawakin port opened in January 1991, and was capable of handling an estimated 1.5 million tons of cargo a year.

A national merchant marine, Sudan Shipping Line, was established in 1962 as a joint venture between the government and Yugoslavia. In 1967 it became wholly government owned. From the initial two Yugoslav-built cargo vessels, the line had grown by the mid-1970s to seven ships, totaling about 52,340 deadweight tons. During 1979 and early 1980, eight more ships were added, including six built in Yugoslavia and two in Denmark. In 1990 the merchant marine consisted of ten ships of 122,200 deadweight tons. The Yugoslav vessels were all multipurpose and included container transport features. The Danish ships were equipped with roll-on-roll-off facilities. Sailings, which had been mainly between Red Sea ports and northern Europe, were expanded in the late 1980s to several Merranean ports.

COMMUNICATIONS

Domestic telecommunications in Sudan were sparse, and the system suffered from poor maintenance. In 1994 the country had only 73,000 telephones, two-thirds of which were in the Khartoum area. Telex was available in the capital. A domestic satellite system with fourteen ground stations, supplemented by coaxial cable and a microwave network, linked telephone exchanges and broadcast facilities within the country. Eleven cities had amplitude modulation (AM) radio stations, and Khartoum, Atbarah, and Wad Madani had television stations with broadcasts in Arabic seven hours nightly.

The country had an estimated 6 million radio receivers and 250,000 television sets in 1994. International telecommunications were modern and provided high-quality links to the rest of the world. A satellite ground station near the capital working with the International Telecommunications Satellite Corporation's (Intelsat) Atlantic Ocean satellite permitted direct dialing of telephone calls between Sudan and Europe, North America, and parts of Africa. In addition, a second satellite ground station was linked to the Arab Satellite Communications Organization's (Arabsat) pan-Arab communications network. The Arabsat network was used for live television broadcasts, news exchanges, and educational programming among the members of the League of Arab States (Arab League).

INVESTMENT SYSTEM IN THE SUDAN

With its large size and varied climatic zones stretching from the lush vegetation of the equatorial south to the arid deserts of the north, Sudan is endowed with huge natural as well as human resources as follows:

1. Extensive stretches of cultivable land estimated at 200 million fertile feddans.

2. A huge livestock wealth, among the top largest in Africa and estimated to be over 116 million head of camels, cattle, sheep and goats. There are also more than 200 million feddans of forest, bushes and natural pastureland.

3. Great water-supply reserves in forms of rain waters, rivers, surface and underground water reservoirs.

4. Huge deposits of mineral wealth which have not yet been fully explored, exploited or utilized, such as gold, silver, chromium, asbestos, manganese, gypsum, mica, iron, lead, uranium, zinc, copper, cobalt, granite, marble, in addition to petroleum and natural gas.

5. Sudan is now an oil-producing country. The first shipment of Sudanese oil sailed to the international market on 30th August, 1999. Investment in the oil and energy sectors is a top priority in the country.

6. In Sudan, there is a surfeit of qualified manpower in the agricultural, industrial and economic services sectors. There are specialized research centres in food industries, leather and tanneries, weaving industry, oceanography and marine science, administrative sciences besides numerous institutes for banking, accountancy and computer studies, constituting a solid basis for successful interaction with the latest developments in science and technology.

Present Investment Climate in Sudan

The government is making serious efforts to create conditions to attract foreign investment to Sudan. Some of the important steps taken by it in this direction are as follows:

1. A three-year economic salvation programme (1990-1993) was formulated whereby several reforms were introduced, including abrogation of state monopoly of agricultural and industrial products, the economic services sector and marketing. The state has also withdrawn from some public sector corporations and institutions.

2. Radical changes in Investment Acts and Laws that regulated all economic activities has lifted all the curbs on private sector participation.

3. Economic, trade and financial policies supportive of the country's move towards a market-driven economy have also been adopted. These include:

i) Lifting of major consumer-goods subsidies.
ii) Freeing the Sudanese Dinar vis-a-vis other international currencies.
iii) Removing control on the prices of agricultural and industrial commodities to provide incentives to producers and encourage growth.
iv) Abrogation of the former import license system, except with the defrayal and preferential trade countries.
v) Abrogation of the mandatory declaration of hard currencies carried by travellers, who are now

allowed to carry any amount of hard currencies in whatever form.
vi) Lifting of all restrictions on the movement of hard currency accounts. Now the client is allowed to feed such accounts by all possible methods of payment.

4. Promulgation of a new Investment Encouragement Act, 2000, the older 1990 Act and the ammended one of 1988.

The Investment Act consolidates the legal base for investment and while aiming at promoting and encouraging investment activities, endeavours to ease, unify and simplify procedures for foreign investors.

Salient Features of the Investment Encouragement Act, 1999
1. The Act encourages investment in the following sectors: agricultural (animal and crop), industrial, energy, mining, transport, warehousing, tourism, marine resources, information technology, health, education, electricity, roads, ports, water, communication, environment, storage, housing, contracting, basic infrastructure, economic services, etc.

2. It encourages investment in projects that endeavour to evolve alternatives for the country's main imports and projects that depend, to a large extent, on local raw materials for their inputs.

3. It grants the following incentives to investors:
i) Exemption from business profit taxes for not less than 10 years effective from the year that follows commercial production or commencement of activities.

ii) Total exemption from taxes and custom duties, and any other fees, as may be levied on imports during the period of exemption of the project.

iii) Total or partial exemption from customs and excise or any other duties pertaining to imports related to the project's requirements.

iv) Production and consumption tax cuts.

v) Foreign capital investors may transfer their profits and initial financing costs or debts provided that all the legally binding commitments pertaining to the project are met and settled. The transfer shall be in the original currency or currencies the capital was transacted in.

vi) Import of raw materials for project in whatever quantities without being restricted by the procedures of importers/ exporters registrars.

vii) Freedom of movement, residence or transfer of the project's expatriate employees is guaranteed in accordance with the prevailing laws.

4. Some of the most significant guarantees of the investment Act are:
i) The investor's project shall not be liable to nationalization or confiscation, whether totally or partially.

ii) The project's funds shall not be distrained, seized, freezed, confiscated, provisionally seized or sequestrated.

iii) Remittance of invested capital in its currency or currencies of origin in case the project has not started, or in case the project got liquidated or disposed off wholly or partially, provided that all legally binding commitments are met.

iv) Sudan is one of the signatories to several international and regional bodies concerned with investment disputes. The Act also stipulates ways and means and procedures for the settlement of any legal dispute that might arise.

5. Projects shall be granted licenses and/or privileges, facilities, guarantees as set in the Act, unless after submission of a technical and economic feasibility study of the project and a preliminary approval is obtained.

The Investment Authority

The Ministry of Investment has been established as the ministry responsible for setting up, advertising and publicizing for investments in Sudan.

It is also responsible for the creation of an ideal investment climate that attracts national and foreign capital in Sudan and removal of all obstacles to capital inflows. It is the body that draws encouraging investment policies, simplifies procedures for investors, issues licenses of investment projects and the relevant facilities and guarantees, follows up the actual execution of the proposed projects, prepares investment maps and saves the investors the trouble of data collecting by providing them with all the necessary information and data. The ministry shall also follow up all procedures of the investment licensing with relevant government circles on behalf of the investor.

The Investment Ministry enjoys close relations with local, regional and international corporations and organizations concerned with investment such as the Arab Organization for Investment Guarantee, the International Investment Guarantee Agency, the United Nations Industrial Development Organization (UNIDO) and other regional and international grouping and institutions of which Sudan is a part.

Privatization

Some of the major economic policies pertain to freeing the Sudanese economy from bureaucratic control and ensure let it be a market-driven entity. Besides, more open policies towards the private sector are recommended and implemented.

Under the aforesaid guidelines, the state monopoly over agriculture, industry, economic services, internal and external marketing sectors have already been abrogated, and the government has actually begun to pull out from many public sector corporations, establishments and companies operating in these fields.

The government has made radical amendments in all acts and lifted restrictions on investments and economic activities so as to encourage greater private sector participation in all sectors.

The government has also placed some state assets and public sector companies on the block for sale, partnership or transfer. Some of these units operate in the agricultural and industrial sectors (spinning and weaving, ready-made clothes, food industries and tanneries), others are in the services sector (hotel keeping, transportation, communication and telecommunication services) and some are trading and marketing corporations.

Certain guidelines are strictly observed throughout the privatization processes such as competitive bidding, prior publicity for sale, transparency so as to ensure justice and fair play.

Licensing and Facilitation Procedures for Investment:
1. The investor shall submit an economic "feasibility study of the project.

2. The investor shall file applications for licensing, privileges or facilities for an investment project against payment of prescribed fees. The form shall be issued by the investor's services section in the ministry.

3. The Investment Ministry shall review the application form and consult the competent technical organs if necessary.

4. Upon receipt of the provisional approval from the Ministry of Investment regarding the particular project, the investor shall then register a business name or company whose activities shall be limited to its specific field of licensing only.

5. Upon approval of the business name of company, the investor shall submit all the relevant documents to the Ministry in order to obtain the license covering the facilities granted and location of the plot where the premises of the project in question shall be sited.

6. Upon completion of all licensing procedures and issuance of the license, the investor may then import the project's requirements in accordance with "an itemized requisition list" which the Ministry must consent to in advance.

7. The Ministry shall then contact the customs authorities upon clearance of the project's imported items through the custom's co-ordinator in the Ministry.

8. The Ministry shall also contact the taxation authorities to exempt the project from tax duties in accordance with the granted privileges.

It is to be reiterated again that the Ministry follows up all procedures with the relevant government bodies on behalf of the investors.

INVESTMENT, LEGAL AND BUSINESS CLIMATE

Currently, the trade and investment environment in Sudan is not favorable for American firms. Endemic corruption, minimal ground and air transportation links, very limited banking services, high unemployment, multiple exchange rates, government misrule, and internal conflicts undermine trade and investment efforts. There is no American Chamber of Commerce in Sudan, although a U.S.-Sudan Business Council (USSBC) was formed in late 2014 to promote bilateral trade. In addition, the potential American investor must be aware of the comprehensive U.S. and international sanctions regime placed on Sudan. General licenses from the Department of Treasury exempt U.S. exports of agricultural equipment and inputs, food, medicines and medical supplies, certain educational activities and exchanges, and information and communications technology products and services from the sanctions regime. Opportunities thus exist in these areas. Sudan has recently emerged as an attractive market for U.S.-manufactured agricultural machinery such as tractors, combines, and pivot irrigation systems, and Sudan's major dairies began buying thousands of American-breed dairy cattle in the past year. Financial transactions with Sudan are difficult to execute, even for legal and permitted activities. Since mid-2014, correspondent banks have closed accounts of clients in Sudan and have in many cases refused to conduct financial transactions if Sudanese individuals, businesses, or institutions were involved – including ones with licenses issued by the Treasury Department's Office of Foreign Assets Control (OFAC). Banks and financial institutions abroad have declined to do business with clients who have any connection to Sudan.

OPENNESS TO, AND RESTRICTIONS UPON, FOREIGN INVESTMENT

Attitude toward Foreign Direct Investment

There are limited possibilities for American investors and export-import firms to conduct business in Sudan. U.S. and other economic sanctions, high taxes and frequent changes to the investment code are all factors discouraging foreign direct investment. To date, gum Arabic is the only Sudan-originated product that is permitted to enter the American market, and U.S. purchasers of Sudanese gum Arabic must obtain an import license from the Treasury Department's Office of Foreign Assets Control (OFAC). Additionally, U.S. sanctions prohibit Americans from engaging in any business transaction involving the Government of Sudan, including state-owned companies. At present the Bank of Khartoum is the only Sudanese bank not designated under OFAC sanctions.

Other Investment Policy Reviews

Potential investors should bear in mind that U.S. sanctions generally prohibit U.S. persons from importing or exporting goods, services, or technology from or to Sudan, and generally prohibit U.S. persons from engaging in financial transactions with the Sudanese government, among other prohibitions. Certain types of transactions, specified by economic sector or geographic regions within Sudan, are generally licensed, such as the export of certain agricultural commodities, medicines, and medical devices to certain areas of Sudan. In mid-February 2015, the Treasury Department issued a General License D on information and communications technology (ICT), including handheld mobile devices and U.S.-manufactured computers, laptops, and notebooks. This license exempts ICT from U.S. sanctions.

In addition, otherwise-prohibited transactions may qualify for OFAC licenses. American investors interested in business opportunities in Sudan are strongly encouraged to review the Code of Federal Regulations chapter on "Sudanese Sanctions Regulations," Chapter 31 C.F.R. Section 538. Information on how to apply for an OFAC license is found at http://www.treasury.gov/resource-enter/sanctions/Pages/licensing.aspx.

OFAC's page on Sudan is found at http://www.treasury.gov/resource-center/sanctions/Programs/pages/sudan.aspx.

Investors should be aware that even when operating pursuant to an OFAC license, many U.S. businesses face difficulties in transferring money to Sudan, as international financial institutions exercise extreme caution in processing transactions related to Sudan. Since mid-2014, correspondent banks have been closing the accounts of clients in Sudan and refusing to conduct financial transactions if Sudanese individuals, businesses, or institutions were involved – including ones with OFAC licenses.

For companies operating with appropriate licenses, Sudan offers a huge potential market for agricultural equipment and irrigation systems. Sudanese farmers represent a significant source of demand for seed, including GMO cotton seed, sourced from the United States. Exports of commercial agricultural equipment require a specific license, though seeds are covered by a general license for agricultural exports to specified areas in Sudan, such as Darfur and the Two Areas (South Kordofan and Blue Nile States). Currently, about 16.8 million hectares are under cultivation in Sudan; however, 84 million hectares are suitable for agriculture. Rain-fed traditional practices continue to dominate, but large-scale mechanized farming is growing, especially along the Nile and its tributaries. There is a robust market for American-manufactured pivot irrigation systems, water pumps, and well drilling equipment. Sudan's major dairies began buying thousands of American-breed dairy cattle in the past year.

Sudan has a formal private sector, led by the Sudanese Businessmen and Employers Association and the Gum Arabic Board of Sudan. The private sector is dominated by numerous large, often family-owned industrial, agricultural and consumer products conglomerates. Many Sudanese corporate leaders have studied in the West and are fluent in English. While there is no U.S. Chamber of Commerce in Sudan, in late 2014 a number of Sudanese business leaders formed the U.S.-Sudan Business Council to promote bilateral trade.

Sudan presents one of the most challenging business environments in the world to the would-be investor. Sudan ranks 160 out of 189 countries on the June 2014 World Bank-International Financial Corporation's "Doing Business Report – Ease of Doing Business," down from position 149 in 2013. It is ranked 173 of 175 countries on Transparency International's 2014 Corruptions Perception Index, ahead of only North Korea and Somalia. On the 2014 UN Human Development Index, Sudan is ranked 166 out of 187 countries. An estimated 47 percent of Sudan's population lives on less than USD 2 per day. According to the PRS (Political Risk Service) Group, Sudan is listed 137 out of 140 countries with respect to political risk. The central government is involved in two internal conflicts: in Darfur and in the "Two Areas" of South Kordofan and Blue Nile States. Sudan and South Sudan have yet to demarcate their common border and continue to dispute the sovereignty of the territory of Abyei. Armed UN peacekeeping missions (UNAMID and UNISFA) are located in Darfur and Abyei.

International air service to Khartoum is limited. Egypt Air, Ethiopia Airlines, Kenyan Airways, Turkish Airways, Bahrain's Gulf Airways, and several Emirati-based carriers (Etihad, Emirates, Fly Dubai, and Air Arabia) are among the carriers that serve Khartoum; no American carrier is permitted to fly to Sudan. Two private domestic airlines service Port Sudan, other regional Sudanese cities, and Juba, South Sudan.

LAWS/REGULATIONS OF FOREIGN DIRECT INVESTMENT

In January 2013, the Economic Development Sector of the Council of Ministers passed the National Investment Encouragement Act of 2013 that was subsequently adopted by the National Assembly. This act ensures that foreign investors enjoy the same protections as Sudanese nationals. Foreign investors, however, do complain that they are often asked for bribes to establish businesses or undertake economic projects in Sudan. There is often a difference between treatment provided by law and treatment received in practice.

Industrial Promotion

In response to the loss of oil production and revenue following the secession of South Sudan in 2011, Sudanese officials are attempting to recover revenue by expanding existing oil and gas production, increasing mining operations (particularly gold mining), and reviving the agricultural and livestock sectors that had been the mainstay of the Sudanese economy prior to the advent of crude oil exports in 2000. These efforts are made more difficult by the international sanctions regime.

Sudan emphasizes its desire for more foreign direct investment. Sudan has introduced two significant investment reforms in the last three years: lowering the corporate tax rate and capital gains tax and improving the timeliness of customs clearances.

Trade missions, mainly from Saudi Arabia, Qatar, Kuwait, and the United Arab Emirates, visit Khartoum on a regular basis, often accompanied by public announcements of signed agreements and purported deals. Most foreign investment to date has been related to natural resources, particularly in petroleum and gas exploration and extraction, and agriculture. China, Malaysia, Brazil, and India have made major investments in the oil sector, and Arab Gulf states and Brazil have made major investments in Sudan's agricultural sector. Other countries, including Indonesia, Turkey, Iran, Italy, Spain, and South Africa have also shown interest in expanding existing commercial relations with Sudan.

Limits on Foreign Control

Despite the legal protections guaranteed under the National Investment Encouragement Act of 2013, there are foreign investment restrictions in the transportation sector, specifically in railway freight transportation, inland waterways barge service, and airport operations. Most telecommunications and media, including television broadcasting and newspaper publishing, are closed to foreign capital participation. Foreign ownership is also restricted in the electrical power generation and financial services sectors. In addition to those overt statutory ownership restrictions, a comparatively large number of sectors are dominated by government monopolies, including, but not limited to, those mentioned above. Such monopolies, together with a high perceived difficulty of obtaining required operating licenses, make it more difficult for foreign companies to invest.

PRIVATIZATION PROGRAM

In the last two decades, the government of Sudan has privatized many state-owned firms in the aviation, telecommunications, transportation, textiles, and agriculture sectors. However, there is very poor transparency on privatization deals. Formerly government owned businesses are frequently sold to businessmen loyal to the regime or security services. There is no public bidding process. Some foreign firms have purchased formerly government owned assets, but they typically must do so as part of a joint venture with a Sudanese firm.

Screening of FDI

Sudan does screen FDI, and all potential foreign investments must receive approval from the Ministry of Investment. Due to onerous bureaucratic processes, obtaining approval can sometimes be a lengthy process. Foreign investments are prohibited or restricted in some areas, mostly due to security concerns.

Competition Law

The Ministry of Justice regulates competition, both domestic and foreign, through the Public Corporations Act, which was amended in 2015.

Investment Trends

Due to US and international sanctions, the poor investment and regulatory climate, corruption, and ongoing conflicts, foreign investment in Sudan remains weak. Nevertheless, investments have grown in some areas of the economy, particularly in gold mining, agricultural cash crops, and beef production.

Table 1

Measure	Year	Index or Rank	Website Address
TI Corruption Perceptions	2014	173 of 175	transparency.org/cpi2014/results

index			
World Bank's Doing Business Report "Ease of Doing Business"	2015	149 of 189	doingbusiness.org/rankings
Global Innovation Index	2014	143 of 143	globalinnovationindex.org/content.aspx?page=data-analysis
World Bank GNI per capita	2013	3230.00	data.worldbank.org/indicator/NY.GNP.PCAP.CD

Millennium Challenge Corporation Country Scorecard

The Millennium Challenge Corporation, a U.S. Government entity charged with delivering development grants to countries that have demonstrated a commitment to reform, produced scorecards for countries with a per capita gross national income (GNI) or USD 4,125 or less. A list of countries/economies with MCC scorecards and links to those scorecards is available here: http://www.mcc.gov/pages/selection/scorecards. Details on each of the MCC's indicators and a guide to reading the scorecards are available here: http://www.mcc.gov/pages/docs/doc/report-guide-to-the-indicators-and-the-selection-process-fy-2015.

CONVERSION AND TRANSFER POLICIES

Foreign Exchange

The presence of four official exchange rates and the large gap between them and the black market rate add to the difficulty and complexity of repatriating profits and foreign exchange. While Sudanese and foreigners are permitted to hold foreign currency accounts in private commercial banks, access to the currency can be delayed and/or limited without prior notification. Individuals and businesses often resort to obtaining hard currency on the black market. Local businesses may avoid holding significant cash in domestic deposit accounts all together. Sudanese authorities periodically crack down on dealers involved in unlicensed foreign exchange transactions.

Remittance Policies

The government can introduce changes to policies governing currency access, conversion, and capital repatriation without warning, and such changes generally become effective immediately upon announcement. High inflation, which reached 36.9 percent in 2014, and exchange rate instability are major disincentives to foreign direct investment in Sudan. Additionally, the Central Bank is expected to further devalue the Sudanese pound (SDG) against the U.S. dollar in 2015, in line with an IMF recommendation under the March 2014 Staff Monitored Program that Sudan takes steps to move toward a managed float. (Note: The official exchange rate is 5.9 Sudanese pounds to the U.S. dollar, while the parallel black market rate has hovered around 9 SDGs to the dollar for the past year.) Numerous international companies, notably foreign airlines operating in Khartoum, have been unable to repatriate their capital from Sudan for several years, mostly due to Central Bank of Sudan hard currency shortages.

The Sudanese Financial Information Unit (part of the Central Bank) has cooperated extensively with the Middle East and North Africa Financial Action Task Force (MENAFATF), in particular by fine-tuning its legislation to be in accordance with international standards. After several amendments, MENAFATF officially approved of Sudan's recent anti-money laundering legislation.

EXPROPRIATION AND COMPENSATION

Sudanese investment law states that "just compensation" must be offered in the case of nationalization or confiscation of all or part of any investment for "the public interest." No mechanism exists for determining compensation or defining what are specific public interests. The U.S. government is unaware of any outstanding cases involving the expropriation of property belonging to a U.S. citizen or corporation.

DISPUTE SETTLEMENT

Legal System, Specialized Courts, Judicial Independence, Judgments of Foreign Courts

The legal system in Sudan is a mix between a British common law system and Islamic sharia codes. While laws are often robust, the judicial system is widely regarded as controlled by the executive branch. Courts cannot be relied upon to deliver objective rulings, especially in sensitive or high-level cases. Judgements of foreign courts are not regularly respected.

Bankruptcy

Bankruptcy in Sudan is criminalized. Frequently creditors and debtors settle commercial disputes through special courts for commercial claims. If a settlement cannot be reached, debtors are imprisoned until they are able to pay back claims.

Investment Disputes

US persons are legally prohibited from investing in Sudan. However, foreigners investing in Sudan have frequently found themselves in disputes with both government entities and private firms. Dispute resolution is lengthy, complex, and often informal, given the poor rule of law and lack of impartiality in the judicial system.

International Arbitration

Despite mandates in the 2013 Investment Encouragement Act promising compliance with international norms and regulations, Sudan does not regularly cooperate with foreign arbitration efforts.

ICSID Convention and New York Convention

Sudan's investment law does provide for international arbitration. Sudan is a party to the Convention on the Settlement of Investment Disputes between States and Nationals of Other States (ICSID Convention). However, Sudan has not signed the 1958 New York Convention. Sudan's Arbitration Act of 2005 governs all arbitration matters, to include foreign investments.

Duration of Dispute Resolution

According to the World Bank's publication "Doing Business 2014," enforcement of a commercial contract in Sudan takes an average of 53 procedures and 810 days at a cost of almost 20 percent of the claim. These figures are unchanged for the last seven years. The World Bank reports that it takes 25 weeks to enforce an arbitration award rendered in Sudan (assuming no appeal) and 19 weeks for a foreign award.

PERFORMANCE REQUIREMENTS AND INVESTMENT INCENTIVES

WTO/TRIMS

Sudan is an observer of the WTO. However, according to a Sudanese official who worked on WTO ascension efforts, Sudanese customs, IPR, and taxation laws may be inconsistent with TRIMS requirements.

Investment Incentives

The government of Sudan frequently grants investment incentives, including land grants and tax credits, to foreign investors. However, these incentives are offered on a case-by-case basis, and the terms of most investment incentives are opaque.

Research and Development

Due to US sanctions, American firms do not participate in government financed research and development partners. However, some foreign firms do engage in joint ventures with government of Sudan entities, typically as part of broader investment efforts.

Performance Requirements

The government of Sudan does mandate local employment, though rules and regulations are not standardized or enforced evenly. Especially for foreign firms, obtaining visas, work permits, or similar requests are extremely onerous, lengthy, and costly procedures. Standards are not applied evenly. Many domestic firms with connections to political leadership receive preferential treatment from the government.

Data Storage

The National Telecommunication Corporation (NTC) sets regulations for and coordinates with foreign IT providers, but claims that the only censoring or surveillance that it mandates is to block pornographic and other "indecent" websites. However, many Sudanese suspect that IT departments of the National Intelligence and Security Service (NISS) surveil the internet regularly, though it is unknown whether foreign IT providers comply directly with NISS. The NTC does not mandate data storage within Sudan, nor does it require foreign investors to use domestic technology content.

RIGHT TO PRIVATE OWNERSHIP AND ESTABLISHMENT

Foreign and domestic private businesses may register as a sole trader, partnership, limited liability company (private or public), special concession, or branch of a foreign registered company.

However, restrictions on foreign equity ownership apply in many sectors, particularly in service industries. Businesses involved in railway and inland waterway freight transportation, airport operations, television and radio broadcasting and newspaper publishing are closed to foreign participation. The government used this restriction to shut down newspapers owned wholly or in part by South Sudanese investors after the secession of South Sudan in July 2011. In addition, foreign participation is limited in the telecommunications and financial services sectors. The Investment Act of 2013 allows non-Sudanese participation in the communications and financial services sectors provided that they have received prior approval from the National Telecommunications Service and the Central Bank of Sudan.

Sudanese law does allow for the foreign purchase of privately or publically held land in Sudan, but instances of such sales are rare. The government has provided land without transferring ownership to foreign companies as an investment inducement. Land may be leased in Sudan without restrictions on the amount or the duration. The lease may not be transferred without permission.

PROTECTION OF PROPERTY RIGHTS

Real Property

According to the World Bank, securing rights to property takes an average of six procedures over nine days and costs, on average, three percent of the property value. This has not changed in three years. However, protecting property rights can be problematic. Security and civil authorities do not follow due process at times. The judiciary is influenced by other branches of government, exercises little independence, and is widely perceived as corrupt.

Intellectual Property Rights

The legislative framework on intellectual property rights (IPR) is adequate, but enforcement is uneven. There have been instances of the authorities conducting raids on shops selling counterfeit pharmaceuticals and animal dips, but no nationwide campaign to enforce IPR. Most, if not all, grocery and hardware stores display American and British name brands shipped from Dubai, Cairo, and Abu Dhabi, and many consumer goods from Egypt, South Africa, and South Korea are also on store shelves. The Sudanese Consumers Protection Society, the only consumer protection society in Sudan, has held seminars and issued warnings about counterfeit goods/pharmaceuticals that threaten public health and safety. The Sudanese Businessmen and Employers Association has also complained about IPR violations.

For additional information about treaty obligations and points of contact at local IP offices, please see WIPO's country profiles at http://www.wipo.int/directory/en/.

Resources for Rights Holders

Embassy point of contact on IPR concerns is Aysa Miller, MillerAM@state.gov.

TRANSPARENCY OF THE REGULATORY SYSTEM

The World Bank June 2014 "Doing Business" annual report ranked Sudan 160 out of 189 countries in terms of the process of starting a business. The report states that there are 10 procedures required to start a business, procedures which can take upwards of one month to complete, higher than the average for Sub-Saharan Africa. Additionally, the report measured the ease with which information about the regulatory process can be obtained. While information about fee schedules for starting a business is available upon request, it is generally difficult to obtain and not published in laws or decrees. There are no informational brochures, boards or public notices on the topic in government offices, and this information is not available online, but it can be obtained from High Investment Council on request.

EFFICIENT CAPITAL MARKETS AND PORTFOLIO INVESTMENT

Sudan's financial system is relatively small by regional standards. The banking sector is comprised of 32 banks, including five foreign and four state-owned banks. The government has an ownership stake in many of the remaining domestic banks. Sudan remains under-banked, with banking and other financial institutions concentrated around Khartoum. The rate of non-performing loans is high.

Money and Banking System, Hostile Takeovers

Sudan's banking industry is largely cut off from the international financial system due to US and international sanctions. American, European, and Gulf Arab banks have in the last year severed relationships with Sudanese banks for compliance purposes. Still, several of the largest banks in the country control several hundred million USD in assets.

Sudan has a central banking system dominated by the Central Bank of Sudan (CBOS), which controls monetary policy and maintains a degree of independence from the rest of the government. The CBOS also maintains the fixed exchange rate of the Sudanese Pound (SDG) and sets interest rates for commercial bank lending.

COMPETITION FROM STATE-OWNED ENTERPRISES

According to a 2009 World Bank report, "the state indirectly owns enterprises through government officials and political parties in addition to direct ownership of enterprises by all levels of government. The broad range of activities in which the State participates as direct or indirect owner of enterprises distorts competition in those markets, as the presence of state firms provides a strong disincentive to private entry. This undermines policies...to allow greater entry of the private sector." Despite the government announcing a mass privatization campaign to begin in 2011, it actually has privatized few enterprises or corporations. On January 19, 2013, President Omer El-Bashir issued a presidential decree privatizing 13 government agencies and liquidating five companies owned by the government. A Kuwaiti fund company sold back its share of the national airway, Sudan Air, to the government.

OECD Guidelines on Corporate Governance of SOEs

Many state-owned enterprises, such as the national cellular carrier Sudatel, are owned in whole or part by ruling National Congress Party (NCP), military, police, and National Intelligence and Security Services (NISS) officials. In addition, many of these same government and party officials own and operate private businesses that receive favorable treatment by the government, including favorable exchange rates and awarding of contracts. Major government contracts are often awarded first to a firm controlled by one of these officials and then subcontracted to a firm or firms that will actually perform the work.

Sovereign Wealth Funds

There is minimal transparency or accountability in state business decisions or operations. Post is not aware of any sovereign wealth funds (SWF) in Sudan.

CORPORATE SOCIAL RESPONSIBILITY

Both American and international activist organizations and advocacy groups for corporate social responsibility (CSR) and peace and justice in Darfur target multinational corporations with economic interests in Sudan for protest and economic boycott. As a result, many institutional investors have divested their share holdings of companies that do business in Sudan. The Chinese government and the state-owned China National Petroleum Corporation have come under international criticism for their involvement in the Sudanese petroleum sector.

A number of large Sudanese-owned corporations have active and full CSR programs that compare favorably with what one would see in the U.S. The results have been positive, and foreign investors should consider an active CSR program to build goodwill among local communities, their employees and the national, state and local governments.

OECD Guidelines for Multinational Enterprises

Many state-owned enterprises, such as the national cellular carrier Sudatel, are owned in whole or part by ruling National Congress Party (NCP), military, police, and National Intelligence and Security Services (NISS) officials. In addition, many of these same government and party officials own and operate private businesses that receive favorable treatment by the government, including favorable exchange rates and awarding of contracts. Major government contracts are often awarded first to a firm controlled by one of these officials and then subcontracted to a firm or firms that will actually perform the work.

POLITICAL VIOLENCE

While Sudanese authorities have taken some steps to limit the activities of terrorist groups, Sudan remains on the U.S. State Sponsors of Terrorism list. The terrorist threat level throughout Sudan and particularly in the Darfur region remains critical, and the U.S. Embassy has implemented enhanced security measures to protect U.S. government personnel assigned to Sudan. The embassy itself was attacked on September 14, 2012.

The threat of violent crime, including kidnappings, armed robberies, home invasions, and carjackings, is particularly high in the Darfur region of Sudan, as the Government of Sudan (GoS) has limited capacity to deter crime in that region. Some observers assert that the GoS encourages instability and criminal activity through its support of militias. In addition, militia and armed rebel groups are known to have carried out criminal attacks against foreigners, and a number of other foreign nationals have been abducted and held for ransom by criminal groups in Darfur. There have been attacks on foreign business operations in the conflict-torn southern and western states, such as on road building operations.

Violent flare-ups occur between various armed militia groups and Sudanese military forces with little notice, particularly in the Darfur region, along the border between Chad and Sudan, and in areas on the border with South Sudan. Clashes between Sudanese forces and armed opposition groups in Blue Nile and South Kordofan States, including the disputed area of Abyei, are real and immediate dangers to travelers and business operators. In addition, U.S. citizens found in these areas without permission from the Government of Sudan face the possibility of detention by government security forces. Violent anti-government demonstrations occur periodically, mostly in Khartoum.

Travelers can get updates by checking the U.S. Embassy website at http://sudan.usembassy.gov/.

CORRUPTION

Sudan's public sector is perceived as one of the most corrupt in the world, ranking 173 out of 175 nations in the 2014 Transparency International (TI) Corruption Perceptions Index. According to TI, Sudan is ahead of only North Korea and Somalia in terms of government transparency.

Over the past two years, the government has taken limited steps to combat official corruption.

Sudan signed the UN Anticorruption Convention in 2005 and ratified it in September 2014. Sudan also signed the African Union Convention on Preventing and Combating Corruption, but has yet to ratify it.

In April 2014, a Sudan chapter of Transparency International was formed. It has already begun presenting evidence of official corruption to the semi-independent "Financial Information Unit" (FIU – formerly the Central Bank of Sudan's Financial Intelligence Unit) for investigation. The FIU is empowered to present its findings to the Ministry of Justice for adjudication.

UN Anticorruption Convention, OECD Convention on Combatting Bribery

On September 5, 2014, Sudan ratified the United Nations Convention against Corruption (UNCAC).

Resources to Report Corruption
George Aldridge
Senior Economics/Commercial Specialist
Department of State
AldridgeGW@state.gov
Sudanese Transparency Organization
El-Tayeb Mukhtar, President
www.transparencysudan.org.sd
tayibm@hotmail.com
+249912300021

BILATERAL INVESTMENT AGREEMENTS

Bilateral Taxation Treaties

Sudan does not have a bilateral investment agreement with the United States. Sudan has bilateral investment agreements with Germany, Netherlands, Switzerland, Egypt, France, Romania, China, Indonesia, Malaysia, Qatar, Islamic Republic of Iran, Morocco, Oman, Turkey, Yemen, Bahrain, Ethiopia, Jordan, Syrian Arab Republic, United Arab Emirates, Libya, Tunisia, Algeria, Kuwait, Lebanon, Chad, Republic of Djibouti, India, Vietnam, Bulgaria, and Italy. Sudan has bilateral taxation treaties with Egypt, United Kingdom, Malaysia, South Africa, Turkey, and Syria.

Bilateral Taxation Treaties

Sudan does not have a bilateral taxation treaty with the United States.

OPIC AND OTHER INVESTMENT INSURANCE PROGRAMS

Sudan is no eligible for Overseas Private Investment Corporation (OPIC) programs because of comprehensive U.S. economic sanctions. Sudan has been a member of the Multilateral

Investment Guarantee Agency (MIGA) since November 7, 1991. MIGA is not currently active in Sudan.

16. Labor

Sudan has ratified seven of ILO eight core conventions protecting workers rights but has not yet ratified Convention 87 on Freedom of Association and the Right to Organize, and falls short in law and practice of international standards.

Complete statistics reflecting the demographic situation in Sudan after the July 2011 secession of the South are not yet available. Sudan's labor force was estimated at 12.2 million in 2010, with a participation rate of 51.4 percent for those aged 15-64. The government of Sudan claimed that the unemployment rate was 17 percent after the secession of South Sudan. Most observers believe it to be closer to 20 percent. Underemployment is also a significant social problem, as the economy is not creating sufficient jobs for graduating university students. Accordingly, Sudan is witnessing a severe loss of educated professionals that includes medical doctors, engineers, and IT professionals, who routinely emigrate to the Arab Gulf states, Europe, and the United States seeking better job prospects.

Sudan's minimum wage is 420 Sudanese pounds per month (approximately 70 U.S. dollars at the official exchange rate). The work week extends from Sunday to Thursday and is 8 hours per day and 40 hours per week. Per capita income is estimated at USD 1,450 per annum.

Foreign workers must have valid residency and work permits or face imprisonment and deportation. In practice, the majority of unskilled labor positions are filled by day workers, who are not reported or taxed.

There are no clear procedures for obtaining residency permits for South Sudanese who wish to remain in Sudan, unlike other foreigners. As part of the September 2012 cooperation agreements between Sudan and South Sudan, Sudan agreed to grant liberal labor, residency and education rights to Southern Sudanese. While there was finally some movement towards establishing committees to implement the agreements in April 2013, there has been little progress since. A "Four Freedoms" preferential labor agreement exists with Egypt, and Sudan enforces the freedoms in general for Egyptians.

Among Sudan's 37.2 million people, the adult literacy rate is 69 percent. Gross school enrollment rate in Sudan in 2009 was 71 percent. However, only one in five children completed primary school in 2010.

FOREIGN TRADE ZONES/FREE PORTS/TRADE FACILITATION

Sudan has established two free trade zones: Suakin on the Red Sea near Port Sudan and Aljaily near Khartoum. According to the Free Zones and Free Markets Law of 1994, industrial, commercial or service investments which are licensed in the free zones enjoy the following advantages:

Exemption of the projects from tax on profits for 15 years, renewable for an extra period depending on the decision made by the concerned minister;

Salaries of expatriates working in projects within the free zones are exempted from personal income tax;

Products imported into the free zone or exported abroad are exempted from all customs fees and taxes except service fees and any other fee imposed by the board of the Sudan Free Zones Company;

Real estate inside the free zones area is exempted from all taxes and fees;

Invested capital and profits are transferable from Sudan to abroad through any bank licensed to operate in the free zone;

Money invested in the free zones may not be frozen or confiscated.

Sudan has been in the process of creating a free trade zone in Kosti, near South Sudan, but the mid-December 2013 outbreak of internal strife in South Sudan has dramatically slowed trade between the two countries.

FOREIGN DIRECT INVESTMENT AND FOREIGN PORTFOLIO INVESTMENT STATISTICS

Table 2: Key Macroeconomic Data, U.S. FDI in Host Country/Economy

	Host Country Statistical source*		USG or international statistical source		USG or International Source of Data: BEA; IMF; Eurostat; UNCTAD, Other
Economic Data	Year	Amount	Year	Amount	
Host Country Gross Domestic Product (GDP) ($B USD)	2013	75.6	2013	66.57	www.worldbank.org/en/country
Foreign Direct Investment	Host Country Statistical source*		USG or international statistical source		USG or international Source of data: BEA; IMF; Eurostat; UNCTAD, Other
U.S. FDI in partner country ($M USD, stock positions)	N/A		N/A	0	http://bea.gov/international/factsheet/factsheet.cfm?Area=441
Host country's FDI in the United States ($M USD, stock positions)	N/A		N/A	0	http://bea.gov/international/factsheet/factsheet.cfm?Area=441
Total	N/A		2013	3.3%	www.worldbank.org/en/country

inbound stock of FDI as % host GDP					

*Central Bank of Sudan statistics

SUDAN LAWYERS

Mahmoud Elsheikh Omer & Associates - Advocates
Khartoum, Sudan www.mahmoudelsheikh.com
Business & Investment Law Firm in Khartoum, Sudan

Phone+249 183 772270
Mahmoud Elsheikh Omer & Associates - Advocates, is a professional law firm that has been dwelling in the legal arena in Khartoum-Sudan since 1968, serving a wide variety of clients, Sudanese and non-Sudanese, ranging from families and individuals to corporations and offering a broad range of legal services....

Ali Gailoub & Samia EL Hashmi
Ali Gailoub & Samia EL Hashmi
Khartoum, Sudan www.gailoub-elhashmi.com
Full-Service Law Firm in Khartoum, Sudan

Phone+249 (183) 778018
Ali Gailoub and Samia El Hashmi in Khartoum, Sudan, to help companies conduct business in Sudan. The firm handles corporate law cases, litigation and other business transactions. Since 1987, the practice has helped clients establish a presence in Sudan and address their corporate problems.

Talal Abu-Ghazaleh Legal (TAGLegal)
Talal Abu-Ghazaleh Legal (TAGLegal)
Khartoum, Sudan
Global Legal Services Law Firm

Phone(+249 1) 83765771
Founded in 1998, Talal Abu-Ghazaleh Legal (TAGLegal) added yet another professional firm to TAGorg's wide group of internationally acknowledged firms, which are recognized as the largest group of professional service providers in the Middle East.
TAGlegal is currently a global business law firm...

Abdalla A. Abuzeid & Associates
Khartoum, Sudan
Full-Service Law Office in Khartoum, Sudan
Phone +249 83 787890
Abdalla A. Abozaid & Associates is a business law law firm. Our practices include but not limited to Business Law, Corporate Law, Banking Law, IP, Debt collection and Litigation.
Abdelazim Hassan & Associates
Khartoum, Sudan

IP ATTORNEYS

Phone 249 11 789 154

Allied IP Attorneys is a professional partnership registered under the laws of United Arab Emirates, with branches in most of the Arab and African countries.
Our firm specializes in the prosecution, maintenance and enforcement of patents, designs, trademarks, copyrights, domain names, trade...

Abdullah A. Abozaid & Associates
Khartoum, Sudan
Full-Service Law Firm in Sudan
Phone +249 83787890

Abdullah A. Abozaid & Associates is a Full-Services Law Office located in Khartoum and licensed to practice throughout the Sudan. Since its founding by attorney Abdullah A. Abozaid in 1995, our Office has provided the highest quality legal representation to individuals and institutions through our...
Abu-Ghazaleh Intellectual Property (AGIP)
Khartoum, Sudan
Trademark, Patent, Design and Copyright Registration
Phone (00 249-1) 8376 5771

Abu-Ghazaleh Intellectual Property (AGIP) was established in Kuwait in 1972, under the name of T.M.P Agents in a time when Intellectual Property (IP) protection was still in its early stages of development in the Arab region. However, since our launch, AGIP has consistently been at the forefront of...

Adelhag & Partners
Khartoum, Sudan
Civil Litigation, Arbitration, Consultation, Business Law , Intellectuall Property
Phone +249 91 2251286
our office rendering all legal services except family laws and as consultant by retainer Agreement we serve corporates and investors to form companies and entitled the right to establish project under encourge of investment Act. we also register trademarks .

Ahmed Osman Mohamed El-Mubarak Associates
Khartoum, Sudan
Joint Venture, Incorporation, Intellectual Property, Business and Employment Law
101 1st Floor, Al-Muhajir Tower
Street 15th. Al-Amarat Phone +249 91 1600041
Aziza Ismat Hassanien & Associates
Khartoum, Sudan
Full Service Law Firm
Khartoum South, Plot No. 3, Squire. No. 1/KH
East Piyoyo Kwan St. - North of Taxation Office Phone +294-183- 483344-
Aztan Legal Consultancy
Khartoum, Sudan
Full-Service Law Firm in Sudan
Phone +249 183769107
Since our establishment in 1989, we have earned a solid reputation for providing highest quality of legal services in a wide range of substantive fields.
Our pragmatism, our aggressive use of technology and our distinguished law firm as we take innovative approaches to meet our clients needs,...
Cross Regional Law Firm
Khartoum, Sudan
Business and Private Law Attorneys in Khartoum, Sudan
Phone +249 9 12831336

"CRLF" Law Firm was found in 1994 by Mr. Sami Abdel-halim Saeed (LL.D). Services are rendered in both Arabic and English languages translation of documents (ArabicEnglish) is part of the firm's services. The"CRLF" is committed to a partner led personal service supported by properly qualified...

Dirdeiry & Associates
Khartoum, Sudan
Corporate & Business Law Firm in Sudan
Phone +249 183741779
Dirdeiry & Associates is a leading law firm to reckon with in Sudan commercial law practice and consultancy. Currently, the services of the firm are retained by international banks, international airliners, leading regional and national companies, TV and Radio stations, and reputable funds and...
Dr. Adam & Associates
Khartoum, Sudan
Intellectual Property Law Firm in Sudan
Phone +249 9 12828540

Dr. Adam & Associates recognizes that intellectual property is one of the company's most valuable assets. We are living in a knowledge driven economy where commercialized high technology is taking the lead. In the present commercial environment corporate intangible assets are considered much more...

Dr. Adam & Associates LLPArticles
Khartoum, Sudan
Business & Commercial Law Services in Sudan
Phone +249 155139184
Dr. Adam & Associates LLP is a full service law firm located in Sudan. We offer a full range of legal services to meet the diverse and rapidly evolving needs of our clients of national and international standing. We provide quality services to a diverse clientele including individuals, small...

Egaimi & Nassar
Khartoum, Sudan
Full Service Law Firm
Khartoum sigairoun building second floor
Bo Box 1184 Phone +249 12 2142245
El Karib and Medani Advocates
Khartoum, Sudan
Business Law Firm in Khartoum, Sudan
Phone +249 183 779998
El Karib and Medani Advocates was established in 1972. Since then, the firm had helped oil companies and major industrial projects in Sudan regarding their legal needs.

Eshraga Fadlalla & Associates
Khartoum, Sudan
Plot# 2 Block 2H Al Amlak Khartoum North Phone +249912214736
Faisal El-Faki Legal Consultant & Advocate
Omdurman, Sudan
Arbitration, Civil Litigation, Commercial and Contract Attorneys in Omdurman, Sudan
Shake Idress Building, Flat 2 Phone +249 187 559227

Hamo Legal Office
Khartoum, Sudan

Domestic and International Criminal, Civil & Business Law
Al Takamul
P.O. Box 6285 Phone +249 91 2216971

House of Legal Consultancies & Services Ltd
Khartoum, Sudan
Full Range Corporate and Commercial Law Firm
Phone +249 83 785704
House of Legal Consultancies & Services Ltd. is a major Khartoum based law firm founded in 2002 by a Merge of three well reputed law offices; Dr. Abdulwahab M. Elhassan Attiat-Allah Law Office, Omer Abusham Law Office and Mekki Osman & Partners Law Firm.
We provide a full range of...

Law Office of Omer Abdel Ati
Khartoum, Sudan
baraka Tower, Suite 1007 P.O. Box 2298
Khartoum, Sudan Phone +249 83 776 400

Law Office of Safwan Mohamed
Khartoum, Sudan
Investment, Civil, Commercial Law & Litigation
Gamhoria Ave
P.O. Box 2392 Phone +249 91 2166549

Law Office of Safwan Shorra
Khartoum, Sudan
Corporate, Banking, Civil Litigation, International Business Law Firm
AlBaraka Tower Khartoum - P.O. Box 2392 Phone +249 121277150
Mustafa & Associates
Khartoum, Sudan
Full-Service Legal Firm
Katarina Street - Khartoum 3 Phone +249 12 2142245

Omer & Omer Advocates & Legal Consultants
Khartoum, Sudan
Al Huriya Street
Al Redha Bldg. Phone +249 183 277 314

Samir El-Haj Law Firm
Khartoum, Sudan
Businesses & Financial Matters, Investment law, Real Estate, Islamic Finance
3rd Floor, Horya Tower
Horya Street Phone +249(183)785869

Shami Advocates & Legal Consultants
Khartoum, Sudan
Corporate, Finance and Business Law Firm in Sudan
Phone 249 183 777464
Shami Advocates & Legal Consultants is a Sudan premier law firm providing legal services as transactional, advisory and litigation counsels. The firm has a long experience in representing and advising big companies whether local or international. We advised in ground breaking transactions in Sudan....

Sudan Global Law Firm
Khartoum, Sudan
GLF, Corporate Finance & Business Law Office. Corporations & Individuals Immigration Attorneys
Phone +249-9-11600041
Sudan GLF is a Sudanese law firm with correspondent offices in Malysia, Egypt and United Arab Emirates. As a Sudanese firm, we can offer particular value to our clients through our ability to serve them on Sudanese law from both the Khartoum and correspondence office. In addition to serving our...

Sudanese Commercial Law Office
Khartoum, Sudan
Full-Service Law Firm in Khartoum, Sudan
Phone +249 (922) 530-704
Sudanese Commercial Law Office serves the international business community with the support and representation of a team of expert lawyers and advisers, each committed to the growth and success of client endeavors in Sudan. The firm's reputation for professional and rapid service has earned the...
Wanni & Wanni
Khartoum, Sudan
PO Box 1460
Khartoum Phone + (249)(11)777517

ECONOMY AND INVESTMENTS REGULATIONS

FOREIGN DIRECT INVESTMENT

Investment in Sudan has witnessed remarkable progress in terms of efficiency, performance and investment laws. Investment laws are in continuos improvement and amendment since first Investment Encouragement Act of 1956 till the new Act of 1999.

Efforts has gone far to streamline and simplify project approval and procedures and by identifying projects by providing preliminary feasibility and final feasibility studies.

- Free Zone areas were created in Suakin (600 square km) in the Red Sea coast, and in Khartoum North.

- Bonded warehouses were allowed in all parts of the country.

EIGHTEEN STRATEGIC REASONS FOR INVESTMENT IN SUDAN:

1. Cheap labour.
2. Availability of raw materials, land, water.
3. Liberalisation of market, removing price controls, currency floating.
4. Big market (ten countries neighbouring) + 29 million Sudanese.
5. Member of COMESA (Common Market for East & South Africa) with tax reductions and preference, ACP groups, new grand Arabs free trade area under progress & LDC member with preferences in EU and world markets.
6. Skilled labour, 22 universities research institutions (Agriculture, Animal Resource, Industrial Research & Consultant food research centre, health research & training ... etc.)
7. Continental Climate: from 3c to 48c, (Desert, Merranean, Savannah,Equatoria).

8. Investment law: gives all incentives without discrimination between foreigners & nationals in joint venture, partnership, complete ownership with guarantee against any form of nationalisation or confiscation.
9. As LDC in WTO Sudan will benefit from the preference hi Access to markets without barrier and reduced taxes for its products and benefit from rise in food prices due to elimination of subsidies in other countries.
10. Infrastructure : 7000 Km of rail, asphalt roads connecting most regional capitals and production areas to Khartoum, and sea ports, 6 international airports and 22 regional airports, 2000 km of river steamers service.
11. Telecommunication: advanced telephone & fax service through privatisation of sector.
12. Baking service: 32 commercial & specialized Banks with 800 branches.
13. Twelve insurance companies and reinsurance companies.
14. Stock market with 30 registered joint stock companies out of 140 in the country.
15. Organized business sector ready for Joint venture.
16. Success Projects of foreign investment like Kenana Sugar, Eriab gold (French) Daewoo (Korea) and Many investing in oil may be incentive for others to invest in Sudan.
17. Peace Agreements to end the civil war which started in 1995 with many
18. fighting groups and negotiation with SPLA under IGAD.

Economic reforms stressing on development of infrastructure

- Privitzation
- Export oriented policies
- Encouragement of micro, small and medium scale enterprises
- Encouragement of women to enter business by forming and supporting organizations of business women.

A. INVESTMENT IN AGRICULTURE:

Total arable land is about 200 million feddan (4200 sqm) and only 30 million feddan is cultivated.

Investment needed welcomed in :

1. wheat production.
2. Sorghum (Dura).
3. Oil seeds (sesame, groundnut, sunflower).
4. Fruits (mango, banana, Juava, lemon, strawberry, pineapple (ananas), grapefruit.
5. Vegetables (tomato, through out the year and 9 months ill the central regions, greenbeans, okra, cucumber, potatoes, onion, garlic, spices, legumes, lentils.
6. Beekeeping to produce honey .
7. Organic fruits and vegetables (alluvial soil along the Nile Banks and deltas of wadi-Toker, El Gash etc.), makes the soil fertility very high and makes very big potentiality for production of organic fruits and vegetables to meet the rapid growing demand which will reach 10 % of European food consumption within the coming 10 years.

LIVESTOCK

50 million feddan of pasture land ill addition to crop residue and oil cakes make cost of feeding very cheap. 106 million heads of cattle, sheep, goats and carriers producing only 3 million tons of milk and less than one million ton of meat. Also Sudan is very rich in wild life and there are investment opportunities for modem farms for ostriches, antelopes, crocodiles etc.

Investment is welcomed in:

1. Modern farms to fatten and produce meat, milk, wool etc.
2. Slaughter houses to export meat.
3. Milk factories, to provide fresh milk, milk products for local and export.
4. Investment in transport facilities for life animal and refrigerated means for meat and milk products.
5. Fisheries (Nile perch) in the Nile, lake Nubia, Red Sea Poultry.
6. Animal fodder.
7. Drugs and vaccines.
8. Improvement of quality of the natural herds by introducing new breeds crossbreeding to improve milk and meat production.

MINING

Potentiality:

Sudan has vast mineral deposits that have not been exploited, mineral deposits which are discovered in different parts of the country are waiting for local and foreign investors which include;

1. Gold (now exported by joint French/Sudanese Eriab company-8 tons per annum.
2. Silver, iron ore, chromate, mica, silica, gypsum, granite, marble, chinaclay, manganese, asbestos, trauna (costic soda), talc and lime stone, copper, zink, lead, cement (production 500.000 toils and tons, and consumption above 1.5 million tons).
3. Small quantities of mica, chromate, asbestos and marble are exported ill addition to gold.

d. Energy

Potentiality:

One of the bottlenecks in Sudan is shortage of energy as fuel for all uses and electricity. River Nile with many cataracts and waterfalls, strong winds, agricultural by -products, sun, forests covering 200 million feddans, all these sources give excellent opportunity for investment in those areas:

1. Petrol and gas production.
2. Hydro-electric projects (micro, small and big)
3. Solar energy for lighting, heating, irrigation wind power for irrigation
4. Wind power for irrigation
5. Water turbines for irrigation from the Nile.
6. Biomass.
7. Charcoal from agricultural by-products.
8. Coal.

FIELDS FOR INVESTMENT IN INDUSTRY

The biggest investments in Sudan was in edible oil with capacity of 600 thousand tons, soap, textile and sugar industry and the share of industry is 16% in GDP (1994/1995).

1. Joint venture **in** rehabilitation of (edible oil mills, leather industry, textile etc..).
2. New sugar factories.
3. Oil productions (petrol and gas).
4. petrochemical.
5. Fertilizers: urea (demand 500.000 tons).
6. Tomato paste & syrup (9 months tomato season).
7. Fruit juice & concentrates, dried fruits : mango, juava, lemon, grapes, papaya, dates, strawberry, and pineapples.
8. Yeast (from sugar by products, dates).
9. Leather products.
10. Dehulling of sesame seed.
11. Spray dry for gum Arabic and guar gum.
12. Packing industry: cardboard, plastic, glass and sacks for grains.
13. paper industry: from dates tree, agricultural by products and forests.
14. compressed earth brick machines.
15. pharmaceutical products and medical equipments.

Sudan Oil Production : self sufficiency & export in 1999

Oil exploration started in Sudan in late fifties and in seventies oil was discovered in Sudan. After the withdrawal of Chevron Overseas many other international companies started oil exploration in Sudan specially after 1992. Now there are many companies working in exploration and productions and construction of pipe lines.

Oil deposits till now is estimated by two billion barrels.

Companies working in oil development:

1. The Canadian Arakis Energy Corporation, and International Petroleum of Canada (I PC).
2. Malaysian Petronas Oil company.
3. China National Petroleum.
4. Qatar National Petroleum.
5. Sudanese National Petroleum.
6. Chinese company to construct 1100 km of pipe line.
7. German company to construct 500 km of pipe line.
8. Some other companies in preparation and development from Russia, Iran.. etc.
9. Now oil production due to limitation of transport and refineries is around 17 thousand barrels per day after the construction of the pipe line and refineries oil exportation will start in 1999.

What Oil Production Means to Sudan?

The Oil importation bill is above 400 million US Dollar taking 66 % of export earnings and by oil production this amount will be released for development. Oil means production of electricity, asphalt for roads, fertilizer for agriculture, packing industry for export, fuel for irrigation pupms, for transport. 011 production will push Sudan economy upward by increasing production iii all sectors in addition to providing capital goods, spare parts ... etc. to economy which was mainly hampered by energy shortage and by of hard currency.

Giant consortium of 1.2 billion us signed:

In March 1997, the group of companies working in Sudan come to an agreement on setting up against partnership to extract Sudan's oil reserve for commercial use. The consortium which s16,.iied a 25 years long agreement is pooling together u$ 1.2 billion to pump out 150,000 BPD of oil by 1999 with exploration continuing for new discoveries.

Gas Discovered:

Huge gas deposits was also discovered in the Red Sea Coast Waiting investment for production.

SUDAN EXPORTS

Sudan export many products mainly agricultural and agricultural processed goods:

- Cotton, Cotton yarns, Cotton Waste,
- Gum Arabic raw and semi processed - guar gum, lubban.
- Sesame seed, groundnuts, sunflower,
- Edible oils, oil cakes and meal, sorghum (Dura)
- Livestock, meat semi-processed leather,
- Gold, mica, marble, asbestos, chromium, fruits (mango, grapes,
- guava, lemon, banana, dates, Galia melon etc.)
- Vegetables (onion, garlic, beans, spices),
- Fresh vegetables (green beans),
- Medical herbs (senna pods, henna... etc.),
- Hibiscus flowers, melon seeds,
- Sugar & molasses ... etc.

INVESTMENT LAWS AND REGULATIONS

SUDAN COMPANY LAW

PART I EXPLANATION

In this Act unless the context otherwise requires: -

"Official recognition" means recognition of who gets in front of the judge in the manner provided for in the Evidence Act of 1994 or in any other applicable provisions on the admissibility of statements.

"Statement" means any statement, notice or leaflet or advertisement or any proceedings.Offering to the public subscription in the shares of any company or bonds or purchase of those shares or bonds.

"Support" includes a bond (Stoke).

"Shares" means shares in the company's capital includes equity group (Stoke) paid-up value except in the case of explicit or implicit distinction between the stock and the equity group paid its value.

"Company" means a company formed and registered under the provisions of this Act and defined the responsibility of its members as much as it did not pay the value of the shares - if any - carried by each of them.

"Insurance company" means a company that engaged in insurance business alone or with work or other work .

"Private company" means: -

(A) company that provides its own rules on the following: -

(I) restrict the right to transfer its shares.

(Ii) determine the number of its members fifty members (not included in the calculation of this number of people employed by the company or who have previously been in service and they were members during their service and remained its membership after the end of their service mentioned).

(Iii) The prohibition of the public claim to subscribe to any of the shares or bonds.

(B) a company that continues to follow the above-mentioned restriction and identifying and blocking.However, in cases where that has two or more persons in common with each one share or more of the shares in any company of such persons is one member within the meaning of this definition.

"Board member" includes any person holding center board member, whatever name you call it,

"The Company" means the Company as originally set or as amended pursuant to the provisions of this law,

"Editor" includes paper summons and advertising matter and any legal action and records,

"Court" means the competent court under the provisions of this law,

"Director" includes any person holding center director of the company whatever name called and whether the use of contract or otherwise,

"Registrar" means the Registrar or Deputy Registrar who proceed under the provisions of this law, the company registration process,

"Decision" is intended for the provisions of Chapter atheist th of this law decides what the rules issued by the Committee on Rules and in relation to all other provisions of this law, as determined by the Minister of Justice,

"Employee" includes any board member or manager or secretary but does not include only references in articles 226 227 228,

"The Company" means the Company as originally set or as amended pursuant to a special resolution, including the drop-down menu in the menu number (a) of Schedule I of this Act to the extent to which those Regulations apply in the company.

The competent court.

3 - General Court is the competent court under the provisions of this law.

PART II THE COMPANY

A recipe for the company with legal personality.

4 - may be for seven or more persons (or two or more persons if the company you want to configure a private company) are involved to achieve the purpose of the legitimate purposes. To be a company with legal personality and limited liability. In the sense that its members have limited liability under the Memorandum of Association. To the extent not paid from the stock - if any) - carried by each of them by signing their names to such persons the Company and do otherwise than required by this Act regarding the registration.

The Company.

5 - (1) must include the Company the following data: -

(A) The name of the company plus at the end the word "limited" as in the case of any bank based in Sudan, and includes its name registered the word "bank" or the word "bank" may - if he wants - that omits the word "limited" to his name registrar Although the responsibility of its members are in fact limited liability.

(B) the place where the registered office of the company.

(C) the purposes of the company.

(D) provide that the limited liability company members.

(E) the amount of capital that you want to register the company and the division of capital into shares of the said specific value.

(2) shall not one of the signatories of the Company to subscribe for less than one share.

(3) Any person who signs his name to write for the number of shares subscribed.

The signing of the memorandum of association.

6 - must be signed by each subscriber to the Company in the presence of one witness at least testifies to the authenticity of the signature.

Restrictions on the Amendment to the Company.

7 - The company may not modify the conditions listed in the Memorandum of Association except in the circumstances and in the manner and to the extent expressly provided for in this law.

Company name and change it.

8 - (1) shall not register a company with the same name you use Aasim by any company or home business or association exists in Sudan and operates it - whether that company or home business or association is registered under the provisions of this Act or is registered - and the name is similar with that name similar close calls to deceive the public. Only if the House or that company or business in the role of the Assembly resolved to accept this designation in the manner required by the Registrar.

(2) The Company may change its name if approved by the Registrar was due to omissions or other had registered in the name is enrolled in. prejudice to the provisions of subsection (1).

(3) may not be registered on behalf of the company includes the words that express explicitly or implicitly a statement from the Government of the Republic of Sudan or the approval or sponsorship of or in the name includes the words of the Registrar deems it intended to suggest or imply the existence of

Some connection to any government or any other local authority. Unless approved by the Council of Ministers issued a decision on the use of such words as part of the name of the company .

(3 a) may not be registered on behalf of the company includes the word chamber of commerce. Without the consent of the Minister of Justice .

(4) The Company may change its name special resolution subject to the approval of the Minister of Justice in writing and signed by him .

(5) if the company changed its name must be registered to include the new name in the record instead of the former name and shall issue a certificate establishing the company modified. As required by the situation in each issue. The name change has been the issuance of this certificate.

(6) does not affect the name change on the Company's rights or obligations or disadvantage of any legal action taken against the company or all legal proceedings that could have been continued or commenced against the company and its former name may continue or begin the new name of the company .

Amendment to the Company.

9 - (1) Subject to the provisions of this law. The Company may amend the provisions of a special resolution relating to articles of incorporation its purposes to the extent necessary to enable the following: -

(A) operate in a more economical and efficient, or,

(B) means of achieving the primary purpose of new or better or,

(C) extend or change the Service or its local operations,

(D) engage in some business that can in the circumstances then annexed to the company's business in a manner appropriate or useful, or,

(E) Restricting or leave any purpose set forth in the Memorandum of Association or,

(F) the sale of all or some of the company and its projects, disposition or,

(G) merger in any company or other body of persons,

(2) the amendment is not effective. Unless endorsed by the Court, upon application to it.Amendment does not enter except to the extent supported by the Court.

(3) required by the support of the amendment that the court is convinced of the following: -

(A) that this amendment has been declared a sufficient declaration of support for each holder of bonds of each company and the range of a person or persons the Court considers that the amendment affects their interests.

(B) that all the Court considers that the creditor has the right to object to the amendment and expressed his objection in the manner ordered by the court had been obtained to accept the amendment or that his religion or his claim may have passed or carried out or ensured satisfactory, including the court.That the court may dispense with the declaration required by this Article if it considers that for special reasons in the case of any person or a range of people.

(C) The Minister of Justice. Behalf of the government. Sees no reason to make the proposed amendments .

The authority of the court, when the support of the amendment.

10 - The Court may make an order in support of the amendment to the Company an amendment in whole or in part in accordance with the terms and provisions of which Tstsoppea. It may make the order as it deems appropriate with regard to expenses.

However, the Justice Minister. Behalf of the government. Notify the court that if the Registrar to the Company adjusted the proposed change as a contract to set up a new company under the provisions of item (2) of Article 19. The Council of Ministers will reject the establishment of the company, the Court must accept this statement from the Minister of Justice without force him to establish a proof of it or to give details or explanation about it. They then refuse to support the amendment .

Court use its discretion.

11 - the Court must when using its discretion under the provisions of Articles 9 and 10 into account the rights and interests of the members of the Company or any variety of them and the rights and interests of creditors and may - if Astsopt it - to postpone action so as to facilitate the work of an agreement it pleases on the purchase of interests of members of opposition. It may be issued as it deems appropriate instructions and orders to facilitate or to effect any of the above agreement. Shall not be paid any part of the capital of the company in the procurement process mentioned above.

Procedure to be followed when you support the amendment.

12 - (1) the company must be deposited with the Registrar within fifteen days from the date of the order of the support of the amendment certified copy of this and a printed copy of the Company as amended and must be registered on the register mentioned and attested to by the Baamadaúh. The certificate is conclusive evidence of the fulfillment of all requirements of this Act with regard to the amendment and his support. It's that time of incorporation be amended contract is a contract establishing the company.

(2) The court may by an order issued at any time to extend the deadline filing documents with the Registrar under the provisions of this Article until such time as it deems appropriate.

The impact of non-registration of the amendment.

13 - may not work the above-mentioned amendment only after its registration on the face properly and in accordance with the provisions of Article 12. If they are not recording during the fifteen days following the date of the order of the court to support the amendment, or within any longer period authorized by the Court in accordance with the provisions of Article 12 and passed any appointment of these two Almiaadin, as the case has become of that amendment and it and all actions associated with them invalid deemed absolutely null and does not affect them.

That the court may, upon application to it within thirty days to renew the order if the support of the amendment have shown sufficient reasons for it.

Company registration system

14 - (1) shall be registered with the Company, signed by the Company who signed the Memorandum of Association and set it on the list of the company.

Application menu (a).

(2) may be included in the Company of all or parts of the Regulation on the list (a) of the first table.

15 - If the record company or the system did not record. Along the extent to which this does not rule out the system or amending regulation listed (a) of the first table. These regulations - to the extent to which it applies - be the list of the company and the same manner and to the same extent as if they were properly included in the Company's Registrar.

The Company's form and sign it

16 - must be the Company: -

(A) printed. And

(B) divided into paragraphs, consecutive serial numbers. And

(C) signed by each person who signed the memorandum of association in the presence of at least witness testifies to the authenticity of the signature and adds it to his profession and address.

Amend the Company's special decision.

17 - Subject to the provisions of this law and the conditions listed in the Company may be the company's special resolution to amend or add to its other provisions. Any amendment or addition is in this manner is as valid as if it had been originally included in the Company subject to be modified in the same manner and under the special resolution.

(3) The Registrar upon receipt of a license the Minister of Justice to register the company doing the following:

(A) to retain the records of the Company and its system - if any -.

(B) to publish the Company or its summary in the Official Gazette at the expense of the company.

(4) If the Minister of Justice that it is not the public interest to continue in the exercise of any company operating in Sudan may after obtaining the approval of the Council of Ministers to issue guidance in writing that the registrar cancels the registration of such company .

(5) The Registrar shall issue guidance as soon as it is handed over cancellation is considered in terms of its effect and impact of a liquidation order issued by the Court in accordance with the provisions of this law.

The impact to the registry.

20 - (1) The registrar must register at the Company sign a certificate that the company was founded and it is limited.

(2) from the date of incorporation mentioned in the certificate of incorporation become signatories to the Company and other persons who become from time to time members of the company. Body corporate known by name set out in the Memorandum of Association and have a civil immediately all acts of joint stock company and the authority have the funds and have the status of permanent sequential and the Seal of the year. But with the commitment of members that contribute to the company's assets in case of liquidation, as shown by this law.

Authentic certificate of incorporation

21 - (1) certificate of incorporation given by the Registrar is for any company under Registration argument conclusive to meet all the requirements of the provisions of this law with regard to registration and matters of the former upon branching from it and that it may become one of the companies that licenses recorded and it is recorded properly recorded under the provisions of this the law.

(2) must be filed with the Registrar statutory declaration from a lawyer he worked in the formation of the company or person named in the Company's capacity as a member of the board of directors or manager or secretary of the Company fulfilling all or any of the requirements mentioned above and the Registrar may accept this decision as sufficient evidence of met.

Give a copy of the Memorandum of Association of the Company

22 - (1) Each company must be sent to each member a copy of the Memorandum of Association and the Company, if any, at his request when payment thousand dinars, or a lesser amount determined by the company.

(2) If the company defaulted on the implementation of the provisions of subsection (1) who may judge by a fine determined by the court for each violation.

22 A - If the court is satisfied at the request of the Minister of Justice that the members of the board of directors of any company engaged in or is likely to Izawloa work in any way beyond the purposes of the company as set out in the Memorandum of Association must issue an order barring the company from engaging in such acts

PART III SHARES

(2) distinguishes each share sector.

Certificate of shares or equity group

25 - The certificate sealed stamp of the company and year indicated by the number of shares or equity group (Stoke) owned by a primary structure on the eligibility of a Member of the shares or equity-driven value set forth therein.

User definition.

26 - (1) The signatories to the establishment of the company and they agreed to become members and must register at the company to include their names in the Register of Members.

(2) be a member in the company of each other person who consents to become a member of the company and his name was included in the register of its members.

Register of members.

27 - (1) Every company must keep in the book and record one or more of its members, which shall include the following information: -

(A) the names and addresses of members and their professions - if any - and to clarify the number of shares held by each member with distinction, each share of which Bno.h private as well as the amount paid or agreed to be driven by consideration for shares of each member. And

(B) the date on which registered a membership of any person. And

(C) the date on which it ended the membership of any person.

(2) If the company defaulted on the implementation of the provisions of subsection (1) who may judge by a fine determined by the court for each day the violation continues is governed by the same punishment for each employee authorized by the company or intentionally allow the occurrence of the offense with the knowledge of [14] .

Annual list of members and summary.

28 - (1) Every company should prepare at least once each year a list of all members of the company in the day, which is held the first public meeting in the year, or which is held the general meeting of the average per year and the names of the outgoing of the last report. Since the founding of the company or if the report is the first report of the work.

(2) must be mentioned in the list of all members past and present addresses and occupations - if any - and the number of shares held by each of the members present at the date of that report with a statement of shares that has moved since the last report or since the founding of the company (if this report is the first Report of the work) and people who are still members of the company and persons who completed their terms of office of each individual and the dates of registration transfers must also include the list on the summary distinguishes it among the shares issued to pay the value of cash and shares issued as the value of all or part of it driven punk money. Remember, when in particular the following data: -

(A) Amount of capital and number of shares divided the capital in question.

(B) the number of shares that were issued since the founding of the company to the date of the report.

(C) the amount requested for each share.

(D) Total amount of applications received.

(E) total orders that have not paid.

(F) Total amount paid as commission for any shares or debentures or allowed by way of discount for any bonds since the last report.

(g) the total number of shares that fell right in it.

(H) The total amount of stock or equity group (Stoke), which did not issue the instruments contributed to the reporting date.

(I) The total amount of equity instruments issued and returned since the last report.

(J) the number of shares or the amount of equity group (Stoke) included in each instrument of stock

(K) the names and addresses of members of the Board of Directors of the Company and the names and addresses of its directors - if any - in the history of the report .

(L) total amount of debt owed by the company's peer-mortgages and privileges to be registered with the Registrar under the provisions of this law.

(3) must be included the list and summary past mentioned in a separate part of the register of members must be done within twenty-one days after the day which is held the first public meeting in the year, or which is held the general meeting of the average per year and the company must then be deposited with the Registrar a copy signed by the members of a board of directors or secretary or manager of the company accompanied by a certificate of that member or manager or secretary that include those mentioned in the list and summary of the facts is correct, as occurred in the session on the above-mentioned.

(4) Every private company to send with the list of members and annual summary to be sent out under the provisions of this Article a certificate signed by a Board of Directors or the secretary certifying that since the date of the last report or since the date of establishment of the company (if that report is the first report of the work) has not made the company any invitation to the public to subscribe to any shares or securities of the company and must be in the cases of apparent from the list of members that the number of members of the company more than fifty members to send a company is also a certificate signed by the person above-mentioned that the excessive number consists of the whole of people who do not walk in the calculation of the number of members according to the session the company's own definition contained in article 2.

(5) If the company defaulted on the implementation of the requirements of this article who may judge by a fine determined by the court for each day the violation continues is governed by the same punishment for each employee authorized by the company or intentionally allow the occurrence of the violation with the knowledge . [15]

Inadmissibility under the credit in the record.

29 - The Registrar shall not be registered in the record or accept any credit reference in respect of any express or implied or constructive.

Registration of transport at the request of the carrier.

30 - the company must be recorded in the Register of Members at the request of transmission of any share or interest in the company name of the transferee in the same and taking into account how the same conditions as if the transferee is the one who requested restriction.

Transport of those who act on behalf of the deceased on behalf of law.

31 - Transportation of the representative who is legally responsible for deceased members of the company's shares to that member in the company or other interest which he has had to be true as if it were a member of the company's deputy at the conclusion of the transport document, even if you do not personally a member of the company.

See the register of members.

32 - (1) the company must keep at its registered office a register of its members from the date of registration, with the exception of the cases closed by the Bureau under the provisions of this law must be a record before it during working hours in order to make it Member for free and share it with non-member by paying the amount of one thousand dinars, or less than the amount determined by the Company for each view. Taking into account the constraints imposed by the company sealed in its General Assembly. So that not less than the time allowed in which familiarized themselves with the record for two hours every day.

(2) Any member or other person may request a copy of the record or part thereof or copy of the list and the summary required under the provisions of this Act or of part of them by paying the amount of fifty dinars for every hundred words or break them asked to copy [16] .

(3) If the company declined to request access, or give a copy required under clauses (1) and (2) who may judge them for each refusal a fine is bordered by the court and additional fine determined by the court for each day of continuing rejection and sentenced to the death penalty to each employee the company authorize or permit such rejection with the knowledge that the court may make an order forcing the company to immediately view the log to see [17] .

The authority of the Record Date.

33 - A company may publish an advertisement in a newspaper published in the body that is located where its registered office for lock register of members for any period or periods not exceeding in the aggregate thirty days in the year.

Court's power to correct the record.

34 - (1) if: -

(A) included in the register of members of the company or deletes from the name of any person in a fraud or without sufficient reason, or

(B) the record did not include the fact the end of the membership of any person or happened in this incident include undue delay, it is permissible for the person who suffers from it or the company or any member thereof may request the court to correct the record.

(2) The Court may either refuse a request for correction or amendment of the register to order and compel the company to pay compensation for the damage to the Palmtdharr, and may make an order as it deems appropriate on expense of its discretion.

(3) The Court may, when lifted to a request under the provisions of this Article shall rule on any dispute concerning the eligibility of any person who is a party to demand the inclusion of his name in the record or delete it, whether such dispute had arisen between the members or persons claiming to be members of the part of the company On the other hand, the court may decide in general in any matter necessary or appropriate to adjudicate in order to correct the record.

Declaration of registrar to correct the record

35 - when the Court must order the correct one record companies that this Act requires the deposit of a register of its members with the Registrar, to decide the matter should be deposited with the Registrar announcement correction.

Considered the record evidence

36 - is evidence of a primary register of members on any matters determined by that law or authorized the inclusion in it.

The authority of the company in keeping a record of sub-outside Sudan

37 - (1) may be authorized if the company has its own rules so that you keep a record of a sub out of Sudan for its members there.

(2) the company shall be deposited with the Registrar within three months from the date of the establishment of any sub-record declaration of place of office, which maintains the record in question, if the change in the office or place of work did not continue in it, it must be deposited with the Registrar within three months from the date of the change or not declaration to continue to do so.

(3) If the company defaulted on the implementation of this Article may determine appropriate, by a fine determined by the court for each day the violation continues. [18]

Regulations on the sub-register.

38 - (1) is a sub-record part of the record company members named in this article the original record.

(2) the sub-register must be kept in the same manner required by this law to maintain the original record, except that the declaration before the closure of the sub-registry must be published in a newspaper issued in the body that maintains the registry subkey.

(3) the company must be sent to its registered office in Sudan receive a copy of the record under sub as soon as possible after registration and must be maintained in that office were scored by replica of the sub-restriction updated from time to time. This is the image in the application of the provisions of this law is part of the original record.

(4) Subject to the provisions of this article on the mirror image of the record, must be distinguished in the original record of registered shares in the sub-record may not be recorded in the register of any other transaction relating to any shares registered in the sub as long as such registration exists.

(5) The Company may terminate a sub to keep any record, and must in this case the transfer of all Alacodat the registry subkey to the original record.

(6) Subject to the provisions of this law, any company may, in its place that they consider appropriate in the regulations would keep a record of a sub.

39 - The Company may, if authorized to do so under its own rules to issue shares paid value of the entire or a set of shares (stock) instruments sealed Boukhatmha year entitlement holder of the instrument in equities or equity group (Stoke) set out therein, and may decide in a manner coupons or other pay worth of shares in the future or to a group shares (stock) set forth in those instruments of the shares in profits and in this instrument is called the law an instrument of the shares.

The implications of the equity instrument.

40 - authorizes the instrument to the holder the right to shares in stocks or equity group (Stoke) set out therein, and may transfer shares or equity group (Stoke) to hand over the instrument.

Registered holder of shares of the instrument.

41 - be the holder of the instrument shares when delivery of the instrument for the company to cancel the right to be included in the Register of Members as a member and taking into account the system company, the company responsible for any loss incurred by any person if included in the record name holder of the instrument for the shares or equity group (Stoke) set out therein, without the instrument was handed to them and canceled.

Center of the instrument holder.

42 - may be if the text of the Company that as a bearer instrument shares a member of the company within the meaning of this Act, whether considered a member of all the faces, or for specific purposes in the Company except that the stock or equity group (Stoke) in the instrument does not qualify him to be a member the Board of Directors of the company or its directors, in which case the system requires the company to be a member of the Governing Council or the Director of these qualifications.

Limitation due to take place in the record when issuing equity instruments.

43 - (1) must be on the company when the share issue be removed from the register of members User Name restricted then in the record as a carrier of the shares or equity group (Stoke) set forth in the instrument as if the membership has expired and must be recorded in the record the following data: -

(A) and the reality version of the instrument.

(B) A statement of equity or equity group (Stoke) set forth in the instrument and distinguish each share Bno.h sector.

(C) the date of issuance of the instrument.

(2) If the company defaulted on the implementation of appropriate provisions of this article who may judge by a fine determined by the court for each day the violation continues is governed by the same penalty to each employee or the company continues to intentionally allow this violation with the knowledge of [19]

Re-stock instrument.

44 - The data of the above data that it requires that the law recorded in the register of members to be re-instrument shares and when the instrument restricts the date of return as if it ended with the date on which the membership of the person.

The authority of the company in making arrangements on the amounts paid for various stocks.

45 - The Company may, if authorized so that the system has conducted pursuant to one or more of the following acts is that: -

(A) arrangements are made when issuing shares on the difference between the shareholders in the amount and timing of payment of installments of stock,

(B) who agrees to accept members from all or some of what did not pay for the rest of the amount carried by any shares although not has been demanded to pay a portion of this amount,

(C) pay the share of profits by the amount paid for each share in cases where the pay for some of the stocks which pay a higher amount for some of the shares.

The authority of the company limited by shares to amend the capital.

46 - (1) may be authorized if the company has amended its rules so that the conditions of its Memorandum as follows namely that: -

(A) increase its capital by issuing new shares, the value that it deems appropriate,

(B) consolidate all or part of its capital and divide it into shares of the largest value of the shares present,

(C) shift all or some of its stock value fully paid shares to a group (Stoke) and re-conversion of this group of stocks (Stoke) to any type of equity value paid in full,

(D) sufficient shares or some of them into shares of less value than the value specified in the Memorandum and must obtain the retail so that the ratio between the amount paid and unpaid - if any - for the stock reduced equal to the ratio that existed in the stock, which resulted from the stock reducer,

(E) cancel shares which have not taken or not taken in accordance to any person until the date of the decision of the cancellation and that reduces the amount of capital by the shares canceled in this manner.

(2) must be exercised stock split powers conferred under the provisions of this Article shall be a special resolution.

(3) if received under the provisions of this Article any changes in the Company must be both a copy of the memorandum issued after the date of change is identical to that change.

(4) If the company defaulted on the implementation of the provisions of Article (3) who may judge by a fine determined by the court for each copy is located off for it, and governs the same punishment for each employee authorized by the company or deliberately allowed this violation with the knowledge of [20] .

(5) is not considered cancellation of shares under the provisions of this Article a reduction of capital within the meaning of this law.

Declaration of the registered capital and the consolidation of transfer of shares to a group shares (stock) ... Etc..

47 - (1) If the limited company's capital and apportioned to the shares of the largest value of the shares present or turned something of its shares to a group shares (Stoke) or re-transfer of shares (stock) into shares, it must be deposited with the Registrar within thirty days from the Date

of consolidation, division, conversion or re-conversion, including a declaration mentioned, and found a stock that united and divided, or stocks that have turned to a group shares (stock) or a group of stocks (Stoke), which was converted.

(2) If the company defaulted on the implementation of the provisions of subsection (1) who may judge by a fine determined by the court for each day the violation continues is governed by the same punishment for each employee authorized by the company or intentionally allow the occurrence of the offense with the knowledge of [21] .

The impact of the transfer of shares to a group shares (Stoke)

48 - If you turned the company something of its shares to a group shares (Stoke) and deposited with the Registrar a declaration that stopped the entry into force of the provisions of this law, only private equity on the amount of the shift from capital to the equity group (Stoke) and must be indicated in the register of members of the company and the list of members to be Aadallma with the Registrar the amount of equity group (Stoke) carried by each member instead of the amount of data on stocks and shares provided for in the foregoing of this law.

Declaration of the capital increase.

49 - (1) the company must when increased capital of the registered capital, whether transformed or not transferred their shares to a group shares (Stoke), to deposit with the Registrar within thirty days after the decision authorized an increase or later support this decision in the case of a declaration of a special resolution to increase the capital and the Registrar shall record the increase.

(2) If the company defaulted on the implementation of the provisions of subsection (1) who may judge by a fine determined by the court for each day the violation continues. Governed by the same punishment for each employee authorized by the company or intentionally allow the occurrence of the offense with the knowledge of [22] .

Reorganization of capital

50 - (1) The Company may, by virtue of a special resolution supported by order of the Court shall modify the conditions listed in the contract established by an amendment to re-organize its capital stock, whether the consolidation of different species or divide its shares into shares of different types.

It shall not prejudice any preference or special features related to any type of equity only by a decision issued by the regular majority of the shareholders of this type having a three-quarters of the capital of the kind that supports this decision at a meeting a campaign of this type of stock the same how Ataad by a special resolution of the company and all the decision issued in this manner shall be binding upon all shareholders of this kind.

(2) If the order was issued under the provisions of subsection (1) must be deposited at a certified copy of it recorded during the twenty-one days from the date of issue or within any longer time limit allowed by the court does not have this resolution shall take effect until this copy shall be deposited in the manner mentioned above.

53 - from the support of the company's decision to reduce capital or to submit the petition to the court a request to support the reduction, if this reduction does not include the reduction commitment for capital that did not pay all or does not include pay anything for one of the

shareholders of any capital paid value shares must be fully on the company to add to the stock phrase "reduced" to be this phrase is the last part of its name and remain until the date on which the phrase determined by the court and is part of the name of the company the said date.

However, if the reduction does not include a commitment to reduce the capital they did not pay all or was not in pay anything to a shareholder of any share capital fully paid shares of the Court may decide to dispense with the addition of those words that it deems appropriate.

Objection of creditors to cut and prepare a list of creditors objecting.

54 - (1) in circumstances which includes the required reduction of capital. Commitment to reduce the capital they did not pay the entire amount or pay anything for one of the shareholders of any capital paid the full value of his shares in any other situation designated by the Court. Each creditor of the company's right to object to reduction if he has on the date specified by the Court the right to any religion or any claim which may make it against the company if that date is the date of commencement of the liquidation of the company.

(2) is the court a list of creditors who have the right to object to reduction and to this end the Court must be met as much as possible of the names of those creditors and the nature and amounts of their debts and their demands without assigning one of them to apply it and the court may publish a declaration specifying the day or days that must be where the creditors who have not been included in the list of objectors to request the inclusion of their names and where only fell right to object to the reduction.

Authority to dispense with the consent of the creditor when providing a guarantee of his religion.

55 - Should not the creditor named in the list of creditors, which did not diminish his faith or his claim, or have not been met them on the reduction may be to the court if Astsopt that dispense with his consent when the company introduced a guarantee to meet the debt or claim as to allocate it as the court shall order the amount as follows: -

(A) the amount of debt or claim in full if the company is recognizing all of the debt or claim, if she agrees to allocate the other hand to meet them, even if not recognizing them.

(B) the amount determined by the Court after conducting an investigation and render a decision as if it holds the liquidation of the company and in the case of non-recognition of the company the full amount of the debt or claim or disagreement on the allocation of charge to meet the full debt or claim or if the amount of debt or claim is an investigator or fixed.

This pro-cut.

56 - If the court is satisfied that each creditor of the creditors of the company who have under the provisions of this law, the right to object to the reduction, may before the reduction or that the claim or debt has been paid or has passed or provided for security, it may issue an order supporting the reduction conditions and in accordance with the provisions of which Tstsoppea.

Registration is the reduction and the minutes of the meeting.

57 - (1) when presented the registered order issued by the court the support of reducing the capital of the company and deposited to have a certified copy of this Order and the record of the meeting approved by the court, explaining it to the company's capital, as amended by decree the amount of capital and the number of shares that divides them and the value of each share and

the amount of which is driven by the per share at the date of registration - if any - should be recorded on the recording and record it.

(2) No decision shall be issued to reduce capital pro thing recorded in the manner above-mentioned take effect only registration and not before.

(3) Declaration of Registration shall be published in the manner ordered by the court.

(4) The Registrar must witness and sign the registration of the matter and the record and his testimony is conclusive evidence of the fulfillment of all this is required by law with regard to reducing capital and that the capital of the company is in the manner specified in the record.

The record considered as part of the Memorandum of Association.

58 - (1) the record is when you recorded it a substitute for the corresponding part in the Company is true and subject to adjustment as if the asset has been included in this contract and should be integrated in every copy of the memorandum issued after registration.

(2) If the company defaulted on the implementation of the provisions of subsection (1) who may judge by a fine determined by the court for each copy is located off for her and judged the same punishment for each employee authorized by the company or intentionally allow the occurrence of the offense with the knowledge of [23] .

Liability of members in respect of the shares reduced

59 - (1) does not abide by the company's current or previous with respect to any shares of any claim or contribution in any amount in excess of the difference - if any - between the value paid or the value is reduced - if any - which shall be deemed to have paid for the stock, as the case and the value per share as determined in the record.

However, if the creditor who has the right to object to capital reduction because of religion or claim is restricted in the list of creditors because of his ignorance of procedures for the reduction or what it is or its impact on the demand and the company was unable to after reduction for the payment of the value of his religion or his claim within the meaning of the provisions of this law Private companies liquidated by court order in this case: -

(A) every person who was a member of the company at the date of registration of order reduction and the record is committed to pay in settlement of that debt or claim an amount no more than what was committed to pay if the liquidation of the company started the day before the registration, and

(B) If the liquidated company, the Court may at the request of any creditor eg a above-mentioned, having to submit evidence of lack of knowledge as the above statement, that is, if desirable, the list of persons who are required to contribute to the payment and asking them and ordering them to pay and to implement this claim and orders against them as if they were obliged to pay at ordinary liquidation.

(2) Nothing in the provisions of subsection (1) shall affect the rights bound to pay among them.

Hide the name of the creditor of the death

60 - If concealed a staff of the company intentionally the name of any creditor the right to object to the reduction or gave deliberately statement is incorrect for the type or amount of debt or claim of any creditor or instigated the concealment or administration of the data is correct punishable by imprisonment for a term not exceeding one year or fine or both.

Publish the reasons for the reduction.

61 - The Court may, in any case reduces the capital. That cost the company as ordered by the Court justified the deployment of the reduction or publication as it deems appropriate court of the other information related to reduction of the public stand on the correct information and may request deployment of the reasons that led to a reduction if Astsopt it.

PART III COMPANY'S LIMITED LIABILITY

Decision issued by the company's limited liability and makes the board members is limited.

64 - (1) shall be for a company with limited liability under the amended resolution on the amendment of the Articles of Association would make the responsibility of the members of its Board of Directors or one of them is limited if its authorized her that.

(2) When this decision was upheld its provisions shall be valid as if it were originally included in the articles of incorporation and each copy of the memorandum issued after the support of the resolution must be included or attached to a copy of the resolution.

(3) If the company defaulted on the implementation of appropriate provisions of this Article by a fine judge designated by the Court for each copy is located off for her and judged the same punishment for each employee authorized by the company or intentionally allow the occurrence of the offense with the knowledge of [25] .

PART IV COMPANY NAME AND ITS CAPITAL

The company's office of the Registrar.

65 - (1) must be for each company registered office in Sudan are sent to which all correspondence and advertising.

(2) must be filed with the Registrar a written declaration at the registered office of the company and get all the change which must be registered shall be noted.

(3) if practiced without the company of its work be carried out as required by this article who may judge by a fine determined by the court for each day engaged in the work [26] .

The company to publish her name.

66 - Every company that: -

(A) Skip or affixed in a conspicuous place outside every office or place of business you conduct a banner bearing her name in letters easy to read and to maintain the survival manuscript or a sticker.

(B) The embossed seal of the company's name on the letters read.

(C) put her name in letters Read all bills printed papers Mkatebadtha and their notifications and declarations, and other publications of official and in all bills of exchange and promissory notes and transfers, checks and orders to pay money or request merchandise featuring the signature of the company or to sign on its behalf and in all bills of parcels, invoices, receipts and letters of dependence of the company.

Announcement of the limited liability of the bank.

A 66 - Every bank based in the Sudan: -

(A) does not include his name registered the word "limited", and

(B) shall be the responsibility of its members in fact limited, to announce this Limited Liability her statement letters Read in each statement issued by the invitation for subscription and in all bills printed papers correspondence and advertisements, and other bulletins of official and stick it at a conspicuous place in letters Mqrauh outside each office or engaged in the work place.

Penalty omission publish the name or the announcement of limited liability.

67 - (1) If Skip the company or affixed its name and maintain its survival manuscript or a poster of how readable under the provisions of this law, who may judge by a fine determined by the court for lack of a line or paste the name and on every day does not remain where this Name manuscripts or sticker is governed by the same penalty Every employee authorized by the company or intentionally allows the occurrence of the violation with knowledge of them. [27]

(2) If I use one of the staff of the company or any person on its behalf or authorized the use of the Seal of the company without having her name engraved upon as already explained, issue or authorized the issuance of an invoice or a sheet of paper correspondence or declaration or any publication other official of the company or signed or authorized sign on behalf of the company any bill of exchange or promissory note, transfer, check or money order to pay or request goods or letter of credit to the company without the company name mentioned as already explained it. Judgeth him a fine determined by the court and shall be in addition to that responsible person before the recipient of the bill of exchange or promissory note or check or money order to pay for goods or request the value of that company unless you pay [28] .

(3) If any bank omitted to apply the provisions of Article 66 a into account any of the provisions of that article. Punishable by a bank and each employee or agent has intentionally engaged in acts of omission that a fine determined by the court or in the case of continuing offense a fine of five dinars for each day the violation continues [29] .

68 - (1) If you included any ad or any publication other official of the company for a statement about the value of capital authorized must also include the announcement or bulletin other authorization by the subscribed capital in and how much they pay him and that this statement, the second in a I like the status apparent statement and letters are clear and legible like him.

(2) If the company defaulted on the implementation of the provisions of subsection (1) who may judge by a fine determined by the court and judge with the same punishment for all the company employees involved in the offense with the knowledge of [30] .

Meetings and procedures

Annual General Meeting

69 - (1) Every company must hold a public meeting at least once each year. Shall not delay the convening of this meeting more than fifteen months after the last session of the meeting of the year. If no meeting is held on the dates judgeth the company and every employee has a part in the offense, knowing the fine set by the Court[31] .

(2) If not held a general meeting of the company, in accordance with the provisions of subsection (1) The Court may at the request of any member of the Company to call general meeting of the company to convene or order directing the call for this session.

Founding meeting of the company.

70 - (1) Every company must hold a public meeting of its members within six months from the date on which have the right to begin its work and called this meeting, "the founding meeting."

(2) The Governing Council shall be sent in advance of that meeting at least ten days a report (called in this law, "the report Constituent") to each member of the company and to each person shall be entitled to receive this report under the provisions of this law.

(3) The report must be approved by the founding of at least two members of the board of directors of the company or from a member of the Board of Directors only if the members less than two. The report must indicate: -

(A) The total number of shares that were distributed with the discrimination of which are distributed as the value paid in whole or in part without the money and how much they pay for all of the shares paid part of it and the amount of the corresponding distributed in its counterpart in both cases.

(B) the total of what you acquired the company in cash for all shares that were distributed with the above-mentioned discrimination.

(C) a summary of the company's revenues, whether from capital or from bonds, and exchange of such revenues until the date preceding the date of the report to one and twenty days are shown in this summary under separate headings the company's revenues from stocks, bonds and other resources and expenditures that has been spent, including the details of the balance Fund and the rest in an account or estimate of the initial expenses of the company.

(D) the names and addresses of the recipes board members and auditors - if any - and managers - if any - and the company secretary.

(E) details of any contract to be modified in view of the meeting for adoption with the amendment or clarification on the proposed amendment.

(4) must be witnessed by the company auditors - if any - on the accuracy of the Founding Act on the report as it relates to shares allocated by the company and the money collected for these shares and the income and expenditure of the company's capital account.

(5) The Governing Council shall send the report as soon as the founding members of the company to be filed with the Registrar a copy of said report, relying on the face that required by this Article.

(6) Each member of the Board of Directors authorized or permitted intentionally not to implement the provisions of item (2) or item (5) knowingly liable to a fine determined by the court for each day the violation is located where that [32] .

(7) The Governing Council to submit at the start of the meeting a list of the members of the company and the profession of them all and address and the number of shares owned. And should be kept up for this list view and accessible to every member of the company during the meeting.

(8) The members of the company present at the meeting to discuss any matter relating to the composition of the company or arising from the report whether the founding previously or not previously announced on this issue, but may issue a decision in question was not announced in accordance with the company.

(9) may adjourn the meeting from time to time. And may at any meeting of the meeting postponed making any decision previously announced in accordance with the company either before or after the previous session. The meetings will be deferred for the same authorities prescribed for the original meeting.

(10) If the court request in the manner provided for in Part V to the liquidation of the company for not filing the report constituent or not to hold a founding meeting is permissible for the court rather than to order the liquidation of the company to order the deposit of the report founding or the holding of the meeting or to be issued, which it deems fair.

(11) does not apply the provisions of this Article to private companies.

To convene a general meeting Extraordinary at the request of the shareholders.

71 - (1) Notwithstanding what is contained in the Company should the Board of Directors to take immediate steps to convene a general meeting Extraordinary of the company as soon as the requested number of shareholders holding at least one-tenth of the issued share capital of the company and who paid the value of all premiums and other amounts due thereon.

(2) must be indicated in the request to convene a meeting of its intended purposes and sign seekers convened at the request and filed in the Office of the Registrar, the company may be a demand from several images, each image on the site, including one student or more.

(3) If you do not take the Board of Directors within twenty-one days from the date of filing this application procedures for the call to convene may seekers convene or to possess them to stock the most valuable to direct their own call to convene, but must in any of these cases that the meeting be held within three months from the date of filing the application.

(4) if issued by the said meeting a decision requires the support of another meeting should the Board of Directors shall promptly call a meeting in extraordinary to consider the resolution and support as a decision particularly if he saw fit, if does not have a Board of Directors within seven days from the date of issuance of the first procedures call for the meeting may be convened for asylum or to possess them on the most valuable stock. themselves to direct the call to convene.

(5) any meeting of the call to him under the provisions of this Article of the applicants must be convened an invitation to him in a manner as close as possible to the way in which the Board of Directors in the invitation to the session.

Provisions for meetings and voting.

72 - except if the Company from the text or if it finds the text should follow the text, taking into account the following: -

(1) may be invited to the meeting of the company convened by a written declaration of fourteen days and to direct advertising to each member in the manner used in the ads under the Report menu.

(A) of Schedule I,

(B) may be invited to the meeting of five members,

(C) shall preside over the meeting of any person elected by the members present,

(D) Each member shall have one vote.

Represent the company at the meeting to be held by another company is a member.

73 - The Company may, to be a member of another company, the scarring of a decision of the Board of Directors One of its employees or any other person to be represented at any meeting of that other company and be the person delegated to represent the company the right to be used on its behalf with the authorities that have, as if The shareholders of the company that scar to attend the meeting.

Extraordinary decision and the decision.

74 - (1) shall be considered a decision is not normal if approved by a majority of not less than three quarters of the members who have the right to vote and present in person or agents for them (if allowed by proxy) at a public meeting announced by the declaration is true and stated in the Declaration's intention to submit a proposal that the decision is a decision unusual.

(2) shall be considered a special resolution: -

(A) When issued in the manner established by a resolution is not normal, and

(B) if endorsed by a majority of members who have the right to vote and present in person or agents for them 0 if allowed by proxy) at a general meeting later announced a declaration is true and took place after a period of not less than fourteen days and not exceeding one month from the date of the first meeting.

(3) if presented to any meeting pass a resolution or an unusual version of a special resolution or support. The declaration of the President. After taking in a show of hands vote that the meeting approved the decision is a conclusive argument for approval without the need to prove the number or proportion of the votes were in favor of or against the decision only if the request for voting on the resolution.

(4) If you view any meeting a resolution is not normal or the issuance of a special resolution or support may be any person having the right to vote in accordance with the Company, the resolution requests except as required by the Company to be asked the ballot of a number of

such persons shall not exceed any If the five in this case must be demand from the number designated by the system.

(5) If the system allows the company in the circumstances under which the ballot, that gets in the manner approved by the Chairman of the meeting, may make the ballot in the same session in which he requested that when the President decides.

(6) If the ballot request in accordance with the provisions of this article should count when the majority of voters to calculate the number of votes each member shall have the right to build on the decision of the Company.

(7) In applying the provisions of this article is that the announcement of the meeting had been properly and that the meeting was held true when he announced the meeting was held in the manner set forth in the Company.

Registration and Business Photos decisions and resolutions unusual.

75 - (1) must within thirty days from the date the support of all special resolution or the date of issuance of each decision is unusual as the case may be written on a typewriter or printed copy of this resolution and is deposited with the Registrar who must write it down.

(2) In cases where the Company's registered must ensure that all or cause a copy of the order issued after the date of any special resolution is effective as a copy of the resolution.

(3) In cases where the system did not record the company must send a printed or written on a typewriter of each special resolution to each member if requested by the payment of one thousand dinars, or any amount determined by the company[33] .

(4) If the company failed to deposit a copy of the decision or the decision of the extraordinary with the Registrar who may judge by a fine determined by the court for each day the offense continues it [34] .

(5) If the company failed to include or appended. A copy of the resolution on the basis of its rules or to send printed or written on a typewriter of the resolution to the member who requested under the provisions of this article who may judge by a fine determined by the court for each image is located off for them [35] .

(6) Each employee authorized by the company or intentionally allow the occurrence of a breach of the company in implementing the requirements of this article with a knowledge of it. Judged by the same penalty. Under the provisions of this article to the Company for such breach.

Minutes of meetings of public meetings and meetings of members of the Board of Directors.

76 - (1) Every company must keep books recorded in the minutes of all meetings of public meetings and meetings of its Board of Directors.

(2) Minutes of all such records in a visible signature of the President of the meeting, obtained by the action or the head of the next meeting it is proof for these procedures.

(3) each holding a general meeting of the company or a meeting of the Board of Directors has prepared special procedures by the lecturer in the manner previously considered that a meeting

took place on the face properly and at the invitation of correct and that all actions on it has been properly and that all appointments of members of the board of directors or liquidators is correct and that that the evidence to the contrary.

Limitations of the appointment of members of the Board of Directors or the announcement of their names.

77 - (1) shall not appoint a person a member of the Board of Directors of the company under its own rules and be called a board member or a member of a candidate for the Board of Directors in any statement issued by the Company or issued on its behalf or for any company to be created or in any report issued instead of statement and file it with the company or is filed on its behalf unless that person himself or his agent authorized in writing before registration and that the Company or publish the statement or the deposit of that report, as the case may implement the following: -

(A) agrees in writing to work as a member of the Board of Directors and signed on this approval and deposited with the Registrar, and

(B) be signed and filed with the Registrar recognition of a written pledge in which to take the company a number of shares not less than the number that qualifies for membership - if any - and pay their value, and that is what has not signed a contract establishing the company that he has had all of these shares.

(2) Upon application for registration of the Company and its system should the applicant be filed with the Registrar a list of persons who have accepted to be members of the Board of Directors If listed on a person's name did not accept this membership who may judge the student a fine determined by the Court [36] .

(3) does not apply the provisions of this Article to private companies or on the statement issued by the Company or to be issued on behalf of one year after the date on which it is entitled to direct their work.

Board member qualifications.

78 - (1) Without prejudice to the restrictions imposed under the provisions of Article 77 must be a member of the Governing Council, which requires it by the Company to be the owner of a certain number of shares qualify for this position had not happened after this number of shares to get the shares listed during the two months after the date of his appointment or within a period specified by the Company less.

(2) is a member of the Board of Directors is free if you do not get that member within two months from the date of his appointment or within the period stipulated by the Company, if shorter. The required number of shares which qualify for the job, or if no longer the owner of this number at any time after the expiration of a period of months or duration shorter ones, may not be appointed by the member without office under the provisions of this article again in the Governing Council only after obtaining the required number of the shares.

(3) If the person remains who does not have the required number of shares standing to work as a member of the board of directors after the expiration of a period of months or the time at least the above-mentioned, it is punishable by a fine determined by the court for each day that lies between the expiration of a period of months or the time at least and the last day which proved to be where he worked as a member of the board of directors [37] .

Health behavior of members of the Board of Directors.

79 - the acts carried out by the Member of the Board appeared valid, even if later a defect in his appointment or qualifications. That nothing in this Article shall correct the behavior by the member of the Board of Directors after the appearance that his appointment is not true.

Send a list of board members to the Registrar ..

80 - (1) must retain each company in its registered office a register containing the names of the members of its Board of Directors and address of each of them and his profession and to deposit with the Registrar a copy of this record and get notification of any change between the board members or managers.

(2) if the company failed to implement appropriate provisions of this article who may judge by a fine determined by the court for each day the violation continues is governed by the same penalty to each employee or authorized by the company allows this violation with the knowledge of [38] .

PART V CONTRACTS

Form of the contract

81 - (1) may enter into contracts on behalf of the Company as follows: -

(A) each contract entered into between individuals and the imperative to be in writing and signed by the parties bound by it may be concluded on behalf of the company in writing and signed by any person authorized by the company that explicitly or implicitly, as may be amended or repealed in the same way,

(B) Each contract entered into between individuals and be true according to the law, even if orally on behalf of the Company from any person authorized in that of which explicitly or implicitly, as may be amended or repealed in the same way.

(2) All contracts concluded in accordance with the provisions of subsection (1) be legally effective and binding on the company and its successors and all other parties and their heirs or their representatives, as the case law.

Bills of exchange and promissory notes.

82 - The bill of exchange or promissory note or an editor or withdrawn or acceptable appearance on behalf of the company if he edited or withdrawn, acceptance or endorsement of the company or on its behalf or on behalf of or on behalf of any person employed by the mediation of the delegation of authority, whether explicit or implicit.

Documented and signed contracts abroad.

83 - The Company may under a written sealed Boukhatmha General to authorize any person specifically authorized in the specific issues to be an agent by entering into contracts documented and so on its behalf in any place outside the Sudan and all the contract signed by an agent on behalf of the company and Echtmh seal in the circumstances so warrant. Company is required and shall have the same implications as if the year stamped stamp of the company.

The authority of the company in possession of an official seal for use abroad.

84 - (1) The Company may that require or include purposes the business outside the borders of Sudan to have a ring official for use in any territory or area or place in the outside Sudan when the system allows for that and this should be ring mirror image of the seal of the year plus the name of the region, area, where you want to use it.

(2) The Company may, once had a ring official delegate under a written sealed Boukhatmha year, any person designated for that purpose in any territory or area or place not in Sudan to end this ring any contract notary or other document which the Company is a party in that region or that region or that place.

(3) continue the authority of this agent throughout a period mentioned in the authorization for the transactions that occur between the company and the person dealing with the agent, if not designated document the authorization period remained mandate exists to declare the person who is dealing with the agent to cancel the authority or end of it.

(4) The person who stamped the seal of the company's official on any documented contract or other document that attests to the health history and where you got the personal seal signed by him in that contract or other document binder.

(5) Each contract or other document notarized sealed the company's official seal of the company's needs as if it were stamped Boukhatmha year.

(3) The Registrar shall not register unless the statement was dated and signed by the image of him in the manner required by this Article.

(4) must be mentioned in each statement was issued that he had deposited him a picture of the registration as required by this Article.

(5) If the statement was issued without a copy thereof shall be deposited as mentioned earlier. Vtaaqb the company and every person involved in the release with his knowledge by a fine determined by the court on each day of the date of issue to be deposited a copy of it [40] .

Special requirements in the details of the statement

86 - (1) each statement issued by the Company shall issue or issued by or on behalf of any person who configures the company has worked in the composition or has an interest in composition or issued on behalf of that person must remember the following details: -

(A) The content of the Memorandum of Association and the names of the signatories and their attributes and their addresses and the number of shares subscribed in each of them and the number of shares allocated to the founders or management or shares with deferred profits - if any of this type of stock - and the type and extent of the rights of shareholders in company funds and profits, and

(B) the number of shares - if any - determined by the Company as a minimum for membership of the Board of Directors and provided for by the Company on remuneration of board members, and

(C) the names and addresses of the qualities and the Board of Directors or candidates for membership, directors or managers of the functions of the candidates - if any -, and

(D) oversubscribed minimum that may be beyond the members of the Board of Directors direct the allocation of shares and the value payable on each share at the request of stocks and their allocation should be in the circumstances that displays the stock offer second or subsequent statement of the amount that opened for subscription in each allocation previously obtained during the previous two years and the amount of What of the shares already allocated and the value paid for the shares were distributed - if any, and

(e) The number and value of shares and bonds issued during the two years preceding the issuance as stock and bond value paid all or some of them without money and in the latter case, little prompting from their value as mentioned in both cases the amount of contrast that issued these shares, bonds or agreed to issued by, and

(F) the names and addresses of any money bought the company, or owned or wish to have and want to meet the value of all or part of the proceeds of shares and bonds offered for subscription in the statement, and money which has not yet been purchased or owned at the date of issuance of the statement and the amount paid out of its value in cash or its name bonds or the seller if there is more than one vendor independent of each other and the company was sub-buyer must pay the stated amount for each vendor, that if independent vendors, and

(G) The amount paid or payable in cash or shares or bonds, the price of money that the foregoing with the appointment of what pays for the name of goodwill, and

(H) how much they pay, if any, during the previous two years or to be paid as commission to subscribe or undertaking to subscribe or for or promise to obtain IPO shares or pads of the company or group the percentage of that commission that it is not necessary to said commission paid to the subscribers of sections , and

(I) the amount of expenses or the initial estimated value, and

(J) the amount paid during the previous two years or which is intended to pay for any founder of the company and return to be paid that amount Venzirh, and

(K) The dates of all public contracts and the names of contractors and the time and place to see the possibility that those contracts or a picture of them. That this text does not apply to contracts concluded during the regular work, which she exercises the company or not you want to Mbacherth to contracts entered into prior to issuance of the statement more than two years,

(L) the names and addresses of the Board of the company - if any -, and

(M) adequate data on the type and extent to which each member of the Board of Directors of an interest in the establishment of the company or the money you want to own the company. If the interest of that member as a partner in the house of another business you should clarify the type and the interest of that house commercial the other with an indication of all amounts paid or promised to pay any person for the partner in question or of the house of trade, whether in cash or shares or otherwise to induce him to accept the Center Board Member or rehabilitation of his or other services which may be carried out by the member or the house of trade in connection with the establishment of the company or its composition, and

(N) if the company had more than one type of stock should be a statement right to vote in company meetings, which grants him all kind of different types of stocks.

(2) If the statement mentioned in this article as a declaration published in the newspapers do not need to remember that the inclusions in the Declaration of Association or by the undersigned and the number of shares subscribed by each of them.

(3) does not apply the provisions of this article on the publication or announcement of the company invited members of the current holders of its bonds or to subscribe to shares or bonds and giving them or not

giving them the right to be waived in the interest of others.

(4) do not apply to the requirements of the provisions of this Article in the case of the Memorandum and qualifications, remuneration and the interests of the members of the Board of Directors and the names of recipes and addresses of board members or candidates for membership of the Board of Directors and the amount of expenses preliminary or estimated value in cases where a later statement after more than a year from the date on which Company has the right to begin practicing their work.

(5) Nothing in this Article limits or reduces the obligation borne by any person under the provisions of general law or the provisions of this law.

Seller is meant in Article 86

87 - in the application of the provisions of Article 86 is a salesman every person who is a party to any contract, whether delivering the contract or commenting on the condition on the sale, purchase or option to purchase the company's acquisition of money you want, in any case of the following cases if:

(A) has not paid the entire price at the date of issuance of the statement or,

(B) the price paid or Cioffi all or part of the proceeds of shares or bonds offered for subscription in the statement or,

(C) the validity of the contract or its implementation dependent on the result of the issuance of those shares or bonds.

The application of Article 86 on the status of funds rented

88 - If the company wants to take the money you want the path of acquisition of lease shall apply the provisions of Article 86 on the grounds that the word "seller" includes the lessor and the word "price" for rent and include the words "sub-purchaser" includes sub-tenant.

The invalidity of certain conditions concerning the waiver or advertising

89 - a null requirement obliging each student shares or bonds that give up a stick as required by the provisions of Article 86 Belzamh declare any contract or document, or anything not mentioned on the face of the appointment in the statement .

Exception of certain cases when you do not implement the provisions of Article 86

90 - If you do not implement something than required by Article 86 not be a board member or other person responsible for the statement is responsible for the lack of implementation if it is proved the following:

(A) it was not a world in anything or omitted the statement said.

(B) non-performance resulting from the error of fact it was issued in good faith.

However, in cases where that has not been implemented as required by paragraph (m) of subsection (1) of Article 86, not be a board member or other person responsible unless it is proved that he was a world of issues omitted.

The company's obligations in the absence of a statement

91 - (1) No company may not issue a statement when the composition or on it to distribute some of its shares or bonds are not deposited with the Registrar before the first distribution of shares or bonds, a report instead of the statement signed by each person whose name appears on it being a member of the Board of Directors company or a candidate for the job or his authorized agent in writing that the report shall be as set out in Schedule II and including the data contained therein.

(2) do not apply the provisions of this Article to private companies.

Under the amendment provisions contained in the statement or in the report instead of him

92 - The company may not be amended at any time the provisions of contract referred to in the statement or report them instead of the statement only after the approval of the company in general meeting.

Responsibility for the statements contained in the statement

93 - (1) if it contains the statement inviting the public to subscribe to shares or bonds Everyone who is a member of the Board of Directors at the time of issuance of this statement and any person authorized to be called as a member of the Board of Directors and named as well as already in the statement or agreed to be a member of the Board management, either immediately or after a period of time and all the founder of the company and every person who authorized the issuance of that statement will be obliged to pay for all of the subscribed shares or bonds, trust them, including the statement as compensation for all damage to them from loss or damage by reason of any statement is misleading or abuse of the truth contained in the statement or in a report or memorandum of the statement was issued or because of any reference or included in the statement issued with it unless it is proved the following:

(A) for the statement is misleading or contrary to the fact that apparently he did not act on the expert opinion or on a document or official permission in must prove that he had reasonable grounds afford to believe and that he still believed at the time of the distribution of shares or bonds, as the case that the statement question applies to the reality of it is true or or.

(B) for the statement is misleading or contrary to the fact that seems to be a statement from one of the experts or who is included in an apparent image, or extract from a report or a statement one of the experts must be proved that that statement is identical to a statement by an expert or as a true and correct to the extract taken from the report or permit expert, however, Member of the Board of Directors or the person who called the description instead of the Board of Directors or the founder or the person who authorized the issuance of the statement is liable to pay compensation mentioned above if it is proved that he were not to have reasonable grounds to believe that the person who has done this permit or appreciation of the report or the specialist or his work.

(C) for the statement is misleading or contrary to fact which seems to be issued by a public official or who is included in an apparent image, or extract from an official document in must prove that the statement is true and is identical to permit the employee, or an image document or extracted from it unless it is proved:

First, that after acceptance of the person to be a member of the board of directors for the company came back this acceptance before the issuance of the statement and that it was issued without his permission or acceptance, or

Second: that the statement was issued without his or his satisfaction and that his knowledge after its issuance initiated reasonable action announcement that the statement was issued without his knowledge or satisfaction,

Third, when he learned that after the issuance of the statement and prior to the allocation whereby it includes any misleading statement contrary to fact or has withdrawn his satisfaction for its release announced the declaration of the drawing of reasonable and its causes.

(2) If the statement included the name of the person being a member of the Board of Directors of the company or in which he stated that before a board member with the fact that he did not accept the withdrawal of acceptance prior to the issuance of the statement is not permissible for its issuance was not satisfied by all members of the Board of Directors - except for the statement was issued without his knowledge or satisfaction - and every person authorized the issuance of the statement required to compensate the person named in the statement on the face Advanced all fall ill from damage and bear expenses and expenses due to involve his name in the statement or because of his defense in any case or legal proceedings are carried out or take him on that

(3) Every person committed under the provisions of this article shall pay the amount due being a Member of the Board or by the so called, or be a member of the board of directors authorized the issuance of the statement or he may recover what he paid - as is the case in the decades - from any other person who was committed to pay if the charges filed against him only if issued independent of the person who committed fraud with intent to defraud to pay There was no other person of such fraud.

(4) In applying the provisions of this Article:

(A) the word "founder" means a person who participated in the preparation of the statement or the part of the statement, which included a misleading statement or variant of the truth but does not include a person who acts as the technical people who sought in the formation of the company.

(B) the word "expert" includes engineer and appraiser and an accountant and all of his career gives a compelling force worked by the reports.

(10) does not apply to item 8 on the private companies.

The impact of privatization is against the law

95 - (1) If the allocated company shares to any applicant, bucked that the provisions of items (1) to (8) of Article 94, the allocation voidable at the request of the student within one month after the

formal meeting, not after this period and the allocation voidable in the face of the company in this manner, even if a company is in liquidation.

(2) if it goes against one of the members of the Board of Directors of the Company or allowed or authorized the violation of any provision of Article 94 with regard to privatization, with the knowledge that was bound to indemnify the Company or persons allocated to them what caused their share of losses or damages or expenses because of this as a procedures may not directly claim such loss or damage or expenses after the expiration of two years from the date of allocation.

Restrictions on the entry in the company operate

96 - (1) The company may not begin practicing any of the acts or conduct of any authority in borrowing but the following conditions are that:

(A) The shares provided conveyers Hazha pay all cash value has allocated an amount not less in the sentence at the minimum subscription, and

(B) Each member of the board of directors may pay the company for each share taken or promised to take him than it is obliged to pay its value in cash as part equal to the portion to be paid on demand and allocation of shares offered to the public for subscription or she shares due performance of their value in cash in the case of a company that not issued a statement inviting the public to subscribe to its shares, or

(C) The secretary of a company or members of its Board of Directors has filed with the Registrar as a formal acknowledgment that the conditions set above have been implemented, and

(D) may be filed with the Registrar a report instead of the statement and in the case of a company that does not issue a statement inviting the public to subscribe in its shares.

(2) Upon the deposit of official recognition in accordance with the provisions of this Article must be registered free certificate that the company has the right to begin to engage in their work and are considered the certificate conclusive evidence to prove the right of the company at that However, in the case of a company that does not issue a statement inviting the public to subscribe in its shares. The Registrar may not give such a certificate, unless the report was filed instead of the statement.

(3) Each contract entered into before the date on which the company have the right to commence operate temporarily be under no obligation by the company until that date and shall be binding from the date mentioned.

(4) Nothing in this Article shall prevent that from happening at the same time display of stocks and bonds for subscription or allocation or receipt of cash to be performed at the request of documents.

(5) If the company started to operate or exercise its borrowing in violation of the provisions of this Article shall be punished every person responsible for such violation by a fine determined by the court for each day the offense continues it without prejudice to any liability consequences of the violation. [42]

(6) do not apply the provisions of this Article to private companies.

Report customizations

97 - (1) must be conducted on the company whenever the allocation of shares may, within a

Month to make the allocation as follows:

(A) shall be deposited with the Registrar a report on the allocation set out the number of shares covered by the privatization and the nominal value and those shares allocated to them and their addresses and their attributes and found that the amount per share paid or payable and be paid for each share, and

(B) for shares allocated as the value driven by the total number of shares taken to the day .... Of the month of .... Years ....

Written proof right person in the shares allocated to him with this contract any contract for the sale or any contract that provides the services that shows the corresponding allocated shares in the counterpart in order to inform the Registrar of such contracts and examine them and the company must also be deposited with the Registrar of these contracts are all photographs certified as an account of the decision and indicating the number of shares allocated and the nominal value and the extent to which it will be treated as a value that is paid in full and on the other hand, who has a counterpart.

(2) If none of the contracts mentioned above must be written on the company to deposit with the Registrar within sixty days after the allocation provided for the details of this contract.

(3) if the company omitted to implement the requirements of this Article punishable where every employee participated in it with his knowledge by a fine determined by the court for each day of continuing non-implementation that if the non-implementation document for the deposit of documents to be filed with the Registrar under the provisions of this Article within sixty days after the allocation is permissible for a company or any other person responsible for that to ask the court to be excused from the penalty if the court is satisfied that the failure to deposit the document was accidental or due to forgetfulness or if she sees other reasons that justice and equity require waiver of the penalty it may order the to extend the deadline to deposit at their discretion. [43]

Commission and discount

Authority to pay certain commissions and prohibition of payment of all commissions and other liabilities ... Etc.

98 - (1) The Company may pay commission to any person for Akttabh or pledge to subscribe to any shares of the company IPOs accomplishing or commenting on the condition or for receiving or his pledge to obtain subscriptions to any shares of the company whether it is accomplishing or commenting on the condition that if the payment authorized by the commission in the Company and the commission paid or agreed to pay no more than the price or amount authorized and the amount of commission paid or agreed to pay the price or the percentage is:

(A) is described in the statement of the company and in the case of shares offered to the public for subscription.

(B) is described in the report which was released instead of the statement in the case of shares that have not been to the public for subscription or described in any report, other issues as decision and signed by the same way she signs on that report and filed with the Registrar or described in the publication or announcement of the invitation the public to subscribe to shares.

(2) with the exception of the above company may not be used as something of its shares or capital money - either directly or indirectly - in payment of any commission or make a discount or pay a premium to any person for Akttabh or pledge to subscribe to something of its stock IPOs accomplishing or commenting on the condition or for receiving or his pledge to obtain subscriptions in something of the shares of the company whether it is accomplishing or commenting on the condition and whether the added stock or cash used in the manner above-mentioned to the price that haunted the company of money or the value of what works for her works under a contract or money of the price paid nominal or par value or said otherwise.

(3) Nothing in this Article shall not the right company to pay the commission reasonable traditionally been paid by everyone who sold something to the company and all the founder of her and everyone else received the money or shares of the Company may and shall have the right always to use any part of cash or stock Astmlha in which payment of any commission is paid legally under the provisions of this Article if paid by the company directly.

Said the commission, the discount in the company's budget

99 - If the company has to pay any amounts for the commission of any shares or debentures or allowed any sums for discount on any bond must be stated in each budget total amounts paid or allowed or unless the write off of them, to be written off all of these amounts.

101 - (1) Each company within three months from the date of the allocation of any of its shares or bonds or a bond (Stoke bonds) during the three months after registration to convert any of the above to be completed and prepared for delivery of certificates of all shares and bonds and a bond (Stoke bonds) allocated or transferred unless the conditions provided for the issuance of stocks or bonds or a bond (Stoke bonds) otherwise.

(2) If not implemented the requirements of this article Vtaaqb company where every employee participated in the non-implementation with the knowledge that a fine determined by the court for each day the violation continues. [44]

PARTY VI INDEX RECORD MORTGAGES, GUARANTEES AND PRIVILEGES

106 - The Registrar must be kept Pfhurst sorted by dates and in a form with details to be prescribed for mortgages and privileges he has recorded under the provisions of this law.

Certificate of Registration

107 - Registrar shall give a certificate under the signature of any registered mortgage or lien recorded under the provisions of Article 102 and that the amount mentioned in the certificate or privilege secured by the mortgage and the certificate is conclusive evidence to meet the requirements of the provisions of Articles 102 to 105 inclusive on the registry.

Writing on the certificate of registration

Apparent authority and the apparent

Certificate of the portfolio

(Stoke bonds)

108 - must be based on the company's endorsement copy of every certificate of registration certificates given under the provisions of Article 107 on the apparent meaning of all of the issued bonds or certificates of the portfolio (Stoke bonds) have met or privilege secured by mortgage registered as progress.

That it shall not be construed as a provision of this article required the company's endorsement of a certificate of registration of any mortgage or lien on the apparent meaning of the issued bonds or certificates of the portfolio (Stoke bonds) before the establishment of such a lien or privilege.

109 - (1) the company must be deposited with the Registrar of the registration details of assessments for each mortgage or lien established by the Company and the issuance of bonds series, which requires registration under the provisions of Article 102 may, however, with the registration of the mortgage or privilege at the request of any person who has an interest in the registry.

(2) If there is registration at the request of a person other than the company was right for that person to recover from the company have been paid to the Registrar of the fees required for registration.

Retained in the company's office of the Registrar of the instrument creating the mortgage or privilege

110 - Every company must keep at its registered office with a copy of each instrument created by the subject or a privilege which must be registered under the provisions of Article 102 provides that in the case of serial bonds similar enough to keep one copy of one of these bonds.

Appointment of a record company funds

111 - (1) If there is any person is appointed guardian or manager of money for a company or has is to appoint a guardian or manager under any competent authority with any instrument he must be filed with the Registrar a declaration of that fact within fifteen days from the date of the order or from the date of appointment, conducted by virtue of the authority contained in the instrument and the Registrar shall record the incident in the register of mortgages and privileges once paid him a fee of fifty dinars . [46]

(2) Every person who fails to implement the provisions of subsection (1) shall be punished by a fine determined by the court for each day the default continues.[47]

Guardian of the deposit accounts

112 - (1) Every keeper or manager of money for the company appointed under the authority provided in any instrument and put his hand on the money that is filed with the Registrar in every half year during the period he placed his hand as well as at the end of his work as a guard or director of a summary as scheduled on revenue and expenses in the period covered by the summary and it must also at the end of his work as guardian or manager that is filed with the Registrar a declaration to that effect and the Registrar shall be recorded in the register of mortgages advertising and concessions.

(2) Every keeper or manager fails to implement the provisions of subsection (1) shall be punished by a fine determined by the court. [48]

Correct record mortgages

113 - If the court is satisfied that the omission of recording the mortgage or privilege within the period specified in Article 102 or that the omission of any details or details are incorrect relating to that lien or privilege It was accidental or due to omissions or for some other reason enough or that it is not the kind that hurt the status of the creditors of the company or its shareholders or that, based on the court at the request of the Company or any other person who has an interest to order the extended deadline to register or correct the omission or error by other reasons it is justice and equity exemption from the penalty may condition, and this terms and conditions as it deems fair and appropriate It may also be issued which sees fit on the expenses of the application.

Is to meet debt

114 - If presented convincing evidence to the Registrar to meet the established religion of the mortgage or privilege for which he may be ordered to register the memorandum in the Register obtaining this meeting and give the company a copy of this note if requested.

Sanctions

115 - (1) If the Company did not deposit the following details mentioned with the Registrar for registration, namely:

(A) details of any mortgage or lien created by the company or,

(B) the details of the issuance of serial bonds or bonds that should have been Tsgeleta with the Registrar under the foregoing provisions of this Act. Vtaaqb Company and upon conviction shall be punished where each employee or other person who participated in default with his knowledge by a fine determined by the court for each day the default continues, unless the registration has been at the request of another person. [49]

(2) Subject to the above, if the failed company in the implementation of something of this law on the record established by the mortgage or privilege with the Registrar Vtaaqb company upon conviction is punishable by each employee in which the permission or permitted intentionally to this omission with knowledge of its fine determined by the court and without prejudice any other liability.[50]

(3) If any authorized person or intentionally allowed to hand over any bond or any certificate group bonds (Stoke bonds), which must be registered with the Registrar under the foregoing provisions of this Act without a certificate of registration to be written on the apparent meaning of the bond or certificate is punishable with the knowledge that when conviction by a fine determined by the court, without prejudice to any other liability. [51]

Record your mortgage company

116 - (1) Every company to retain its special register of mortgages and restrict where all mortgages and privileges which particularly affect the company's funds and must be stated in each case a brief description of the funds pledged or the lien and the amount of the mortgage or privilege and the names of hostages and the privileged except in the case of guarantees due to its holder.

(2) shall be punished by a fine determined by the court any member of the Board of Directors of the Company or any director or employee of an authorized or permitted under any intentional omission must be conducted under the provisions of this article with the knowledge to do so. [52]

The right to see the images the constituent instruments of mortgages and privileges and to record your mortgage company

117 - (1) Photos constituent instruments of mortgages or liens which must be registered at the Registrar under the provisions of this law and keep it in the office of the company registered pursuant to the provisions of Article 110 as well as record mortgage saved pursuant to the provisions of Article 116 must be shown at all reasonable times for the information of any creditor of the company or a member of it, without fee, and must also be a record for mortgages before seen by any other person if payment of the fee prescribed by the company to not more than one thousand dinars for each view. [53]

(2) if the company refused to allow access to the log and pictures above-mentioned Vtaaqb a fine determined by the court and additional fine determined by the court for each day of continuing rejection and shall be punished in the same sentence every employee of the Company authorize or permit such knowing it, and the court may in addition to the sentence above the male may make an order immediately to see pictures and record Jabra for the company. [54]

The right to review the record holders of bonds and obtain copies of the credit

118 - (1) Except for cases in which close the record holders of bonds the company in accordance with its period or periods not exceeding in the aggregate thirty days in each year as shown in the Company should be the record before it in order to make it carrier bond registered his name and any shareholder in the company and taking into account reasonable limits imposed by the Company in General Meeting, so as to determine for a period of not less than two hours each day and may each holder of bonds who they said to take a copy of the record or part of it if you pay fifty dinars for every hundred words or fractions of a cent request a picture of them. [55]

(2) must send a copy of each document credit to guarantee the issuance of bonds to each holder of a campaign of such bonds if so requested and the payment in the case of a document credit printed amount of fifty dinars or any amount less than that determined by the company or the amount of ten dinars for every hundred words or fractions of a cent request a copy if you do not print the contract. [56]

(3) If the company refused to allow access or to give or send the image Vtaaqb a fine determined by the court and additional fine determined by the court for each day of continuing rejection and shall be punished in the same sentence every employee of the Company authorize or permit such rejection knowing him and the court may issue an order allowing access Jabra immediately on the record about the company. [57]

Bonds and floating privileges

Floating bonds

119 - the condition contained in any bonds or in any document to ensure that any bond is not void merely because these bonds are non-refundable only when there is not an investigator to fall no matter how it happens away or at the expiration of any time no matter how long.

Authority to issue bonds recovered in certain cases

120 - (1) If recovered Company any bonds previously Asaddaraha shall be entitled to retain the bonds valid for re-released This is a right entitled to her always, unless the text of its rules or stipulated conditions for issuing bonds expressly stated otherwise or if the bonds had recovered at the company's commitment to recover (and this commitment is not the commitment that can be implemented only mediated by the person who issued a bond refunds or brokered on their bonds), if used by the company this right had the right to reissue the bonds either issued is itself again, or to issue other bonds instead This is a right which has always existed and when it was re-version to the right holder in the bonds the same rights and priority as if it were not such bonds have been issued and these rights are considered and the priority it had at all times.

(2) If the ownership of securities transferred to a person appointed by the company and the purpose of the transfer of ownership retention bond valid for re-issuance of the transfer of that is for the purpose of applying the provisions of this article as a re-released.

(3) If you deposited the company a thing of the bond guarantee of self that you get from time to time on current account or on the other there is this bond that it had recovered just because the company no longer Medina during the time that remained where deposited for this purpose.

(4) reissue the bond or another bond is issued instead. Virtue of the authority vested in the company or that are conferred upon it under the provisions of this article shall be regarded as a new bond is issued on stamp duty, but it is not considered as a new bond is issued on any text or number determines the amount of bonds to be issued.

(5) Nothing in this article shall not affect the following:

(A) the application of any rule or order of a court of competent jurisdiction prior to the issuance of this law among those who were party to the proceedings that gave the judgment or order and separated by any appeal made for any judgment or such order as if this law has not yet issued, or

(B) any authority empowered under the company's bonds or guarantees these bonds in the bond issue bonds in lieu of any paid or been met or passed through without payment.

Implementation of contracts in-kind subscription to the bonds.

121 - the contract with the company to take any of the bonds and the payment amount may be carried out by virtue of serving implemented in kind.

Payment of some debt from assets subject to floating lien priority to the claims under the concession

122 - (1) if appointed guardian on behalf of the holders of bonds secured the company or as a floating lien holders of these bonds put their hands or placing other hand on their behalf on any funds covered by the floating privilege or be subject to the said his company was not then in liquidation, the debt be in each filter is payable way of preference, must be paid immediately of any assets up to the keeper or other person to the author of the hand as the path of progress and that has priority over any claim arising out of bonds.

(2) calculated by the dates specified in the provisions of Chapter V of the above from the date of appointment of guardian or from the date of the seizure of money, as the case.

(3) all amounts paid under the provisions of this Article shall be recovered as much as possible, the company's assets allocated to pay the debts of ordinary creditors.

The annual budget.

124 - (1) Every company that you balance the accounts and prepare a budget at least once each year at intervals of not more than fifteen months.

(2) references the company must review the budget in the manner to be later and accompanied by his or puts at the end of a reference to his report and recited in front of the company in general meeting and must be seen to before it by members of the company,

(3) Each company is private companies to send a copy of the budget which was revised to every member of the company through its title recorded before the meeting, which will be presented the budget to the members at least seven days, and the company must deposit a copy in the office of the company's registered for a period not less than seven days before the meeting, for the information of the members of the company.

(4) If the company failed to implement the requirements of this article Vtaaqb a fine determined by the court and judge with the same punishment for each employee in the company willfully authorizes or permits the default so knowing it. [ii]

Inclusions of the budget.

125 - (1) must include a summary of the budget funds for the company and Mgodadtha and capital and commitments, with details that show the general nature of these obligations, assets and manner as was done in the evaluation of fixed assets.

(2) operating budget depending on the model (c) in Schedule III or nearly form as allowed by the circumstances of the case.

Adoption of the budget

126 - (1) Except as provided in subparagraph (2) The adoption of the budget as follows:

(A) if the company's corporate banking must be signed on the budget of the Secretary or the Director, if any, in the case of more than three members of the Board of Directors of the company, it must be the signature of at least three members, if there is no more than three members shall be signed them all,

(B) In the case of other companies must sign the budget two members of the board of directors if the number of members less than that to be the signature of the sole member of the Board of Directors and the Secretary or the Director, if any.

(2) if the total number of members of the Board of Directors who are in Sudan, less than the required number signed under the provisions of subsection (1) must then sign the budget of all board members present in Sudan, if located in Sudan, a member of only one, it must sign the budget, but in this case must be attached to the budget memorandum signed by the members of the Board of Directors or Board Member to clarify the above-mentioned reason for not implementing the provisions of subsection (1).

(3) if exported from the budget picture is signed by the required signatures under the provisions of this article or this picture published or circulated hands Vtaaqb company where every employee participated in the violation with knowledge of the fine determined by the Court [iii] .

Send a copy of the budget and the auditor's report to the Registrar

127 - (1) must be on the company after the budget presentation at the public meeting to be deposited with the Council a copy thereof signed by the Director or the Secretary, in the same time, which is deposited a copy of the annual list of members and summary prepared by and in accordance with the provisions of Article 28.

(2) If you do not reconcile the general meeting on the budget when you view it, it must be accompanied by a note to this effect causes of non-approval, and must be attached to the memorandum and the reasons are budgeted to be deposited with the Registrar.

(3) does not apply the provisions of this Article to private companies.

(4) If the company failed to implement the requirements of this Article shall be punished Vtaaqb and every employee of an authorized or allowed to willfully failing to knowing the same penalty provided for in the provisions of Article 28.

Right member of the company to take a picture of the budget and the auditor's report

128 - Except as provided in the provisions of this law on succession, each member of the company the right to be given a copy of the budget and the auditor's report if you paid a fee not exceeding fifty Dinars for every hundred words or break them [iv] .

Report, which is committed to publishing companies, insurance

(4) If the company failed to implement the requirements of this article Vtaaqb a fine determined by the court on each day of continuing non-implementation is governed by the same punishment for each employee authorized by the company or intentionally allow the non-implementation with the knowledge that[vi] .

PART VII EXAMINATION OF THE RECORDED DOCUMENTS

Authority of the Registrar to request

Information and explanations

130 - (1) If the Registrar when informed of any document from the corporate documents to be submitted under the provisions of this law, the need to obtain any other information to complete the details adequate to the subject to which the that document, it may be issued to the company that comes before him this written document is required to provide him with the writing what he wants from the information or explanations, within the period designated in the command.

(2) Upon the arrival of the order issued by the Registrar under the provisions of subsection (1) must be on the staff of the company and the employees have to do the maximum it can to provide the Registrar with information or explanations required.

(3) If the refusal of any such persons or neglected to provide information or clarification required, it is punishable by a fine determined by the court for each violation committed by [vii] .

(4) "canceled."

(5) The provisions of this article on companies that set up outside the Sudan and operates in Sudan.

Inspection and audit

Examination of the company at the request of members.

131 - (1) The Registrar may, at the request submitted by the hundred at least one member or members have ten per cent less than the number of shares issued for any of the companies to appoint one or more inspectors qualified to inspect the company's business and report the way that designated by the Registrar.

(2) must be supported by the evidence that the application requested by the Registrar for the purpose of proving that the applicants have reasonable grounds to demand the examination.

Examination of the company in other cases

132 - Without prejudice to the powers of the Registrar under the provisions of Article 131:

(A) he must appoint one or more competent inspectors to examine the work of the companies and to report thereon in the manner specified by the declared if:

(I) a special resolution of the company, or

(Ii) by order of the court, that the company should be examined by an inspector appointed by the Registrar,

(B) may take such action:

(I) If the information and explanations required to be submitted to him under the provisions of Article 130 within the period specified or where the Registrar after reading that the document referred to in that article reveals is not satisfactory in the affairs of the company or it does not appear an explanation adequate and acceptable for the matter to which the , or

(Ii) If it appears to the Registrar that there are circumstances suggesting that:

- the company's business is managed or were managed structure of cheating creditors or members or any other person or for the purpose of fraud or for an unlawful purpose, or in a manner prejudicial to any group of members of the company, or that the company had been established for the purpose of fraud or for an unlawful purpose, or

- people who have created or linked to the management of the Company had been convicted in relation to that configuration or management fraud or deviation in their behavior or convicted of disgraceful behavior towards the company or to its members, or

- members of the company are not getting them acquainted with all the information relating to the work the company, which was reasonable to expect getting them acquainted with them.

Provide documents and evidence in the case of examination

133 - (1) must be on all the staff of Ocla company that scans its work in accordance with the provisions of sections 131 and 132 to maintain all books and documents that are in the possession or under their authority, which belong to or relating to the company and to give the inspectors or to attend to them, if asked to do so and that make them all the assistance necessary for the examination when possible.

(2) An Inspector may cross-examine the company's employees and agents under oath and is thus to ask them under oath.

(3) If the refusal of any employee the company or agent of its agents to make any book or document to the inspectors, which have a duty was submitted under the provisions of this article, or refused to appear before the inspector personally when asked to do so or refused to answer any question raised by the inspectors with regard to the work of the company, it is punishable by imprisonment for not exceeding three months or with fine which is bordered by the court or both a fine and also the other determined by the court for each day during which the offense continues after the first day [viii]

(4) Any reference in this Article, the employees or agents, including employees, agents, past and present, as the case, and include the word "agents" bankers and advisors to the company's legal and any persons appointed by the company serve as reviewers, whether these people staff the company or otherwise.

Report of the Inspector.

134 - An Inspector may make interim reports to the Registrar and shall be submitted and duty if asked Registrar, in the end of the examination must submit a final report to the Registrar.

Claims arising from the inspector's report.

135 - If it appears to the Registrar of any report submitted in accordance with the provisions of Article 134:

(A) that any person has committed a crime which makes him criminally responsible for it for the company, the registrar may, to sue that person for that crime,

(B) it should be to achieve the public interest that any company covered in the report to take legal action to claim compensation for any fraud or deviation in the behavior or conduct disgraceful for the establishment of the company, and create and manage its affairs or to recover any property of the company misused or detained illegally Jazz The Registrar shall himself take such action on behalf of the company and on its behalf and the Company shall bear any fees or expenses arising out of them .

The costs of screening

135 A - (1) The following expenses mentioned Baafa emergency arising from the examination conducted by the Inspector [ix] :

(A) Applicants request for examination in the case of the appointment of the Inspector under the provisions of Article 131 (1).

(B) the company in the case of the appointment of the Inspector under the provisions of Article 132 (1)

(C) Members of the Board of Directors of the company personally in the case of the appointment of the Inspector under the provisions of Article 132 (b), but if convicted of any person in proceedings brought under the provisions of section 135 (a) or order was issued against him to pay compensation or restitution of any property in proceedings brought under the provisions of section 135 (b) may issue an order against him in the same case to pay the expenses in question, the amount determined by the court that his conviction, or ordered to pay compensation or restitution of the property, as the case, and this person is responsible for the border to meet Applicants request for examination or for the company or the directors, as the case.

(2) The Registrar must, before his appointment to the inspector, may request of the applicants request for examination or from the company or the directors, as the case may provide a financial guarantee to the extent that it deems sufficient in those circumstances and to meet the costs of the examination.

(3) the recorded amount of estimated expenses and emergency arising from the inspection and ratified by the Minister of Justice and charged to the person to be honoring him, as if it were a fine imposed by the court, may not be followed by any court of this estimate [x] .

(4) The court may order the company Baafa to afford applicants request examination or borne by managers, as the case, when the amounts to be levied under the provisions of subsection (1) less than the expenses listed when the court is satisfied, based on the report, which was under the provisions of Article 134, that the applicants were right in the screening examination or request that none of the members of the Board of Directors was not guilty of any breach in the performance of his duties.

Broad liquidation of the company.

135 B - if it appears to the Registrar of the facts of any report submitted in accordance with the provisions of Article 134 in the case of any company that is subject to liquidation under the provisions of Article 155 that it is appropriate to achieve the public interest that the liquidation of the company, he may:

- What were not described by the company may petition the court to lift the liquidation basis of the requirements of justice and equity.

Accept the inspectors' report as evidence.

136 - a report prepared by the Inspectors concerned under the provisions of this law and notary seal of the company that its examination of these inspectors be admissible in any legal action on the opinion of the inspectors as evidence in any matter included in the report.

Qualifications and appointment of auditors.

137 - (1) shall not appoint any person auditor for any company unless it holds a certificate from the Minister of Finance and National Economy, enables him work as auditor of companies, as the Council of Ministers may by order published in the Official Gazette to draw to be members of any institution or body or body mentioned in this matter the right to appoint and work serve as reviewers for companies in all parts of Sudan.

(2) Council of Ministers may by order published in the Official Gazette to develop rules that provide for giving certificates entitle their holders the right to work serve as reviewers for companies, and may be provided in these rules to the conditions and restrictions to be observed

in granting these certificates, and have a certificate holder mentioned the right to work as references for companies in all parts of Sudan unless restricted or certificate identified the use of this right.

(3) Each company must be appointed at the Annual General Meeting an auditor or auditors to carry out the review to take place the next annual meeting.

(4) If you do not designate references at the Annual General Meeting, the court may at the request of any member of the company, to appoint an auditor of the company for the current year and to determine the remuneration paid to him for his services.

(5) shall not be appointed auditor of the company any of the following persons:

(A) members of the Board of Directors of the Company or its employees, and

(B) partners, members of the board of directors or partners of their employees, and

(C) Any person who is in the service of a Board of Directors or the staff of the company.

(6) shall not be appointed to the annual general meeting a person as auditor of the company's auditor, who retired only if one of the members of the company shall notify the Company prior to the Annual General Meeting fourteen days at least his desire to nominate that person for a job reference and the company must send a copy of the such notification to the Auditor who retired and to notify its members that the path of the declaration or in any other way permitted by the Company prior to the Annual General Meeting at least seven days.

However, if, after notice to the company's desire, a member of the nomination of references that called for Annual General Meeting to convene after the date of notification of fourteen days or less, the provisions of this article is updated for the duration of advertising, the company may instead send or make the declaration required of them in the promised scheduled The provisions of this article may be sent or declaration issued at the same time announcing the holding of annual general meeting.

(7) The Board may appoint the first auditors of the company prior to the founding meeting, if appointed auditors in this way remained in their jobs to be held the founding meeting, unless cut off by a decision issued by the members of the company in general meeting and in this case shall such members be appointed reviewers in this meeting.

(8) Board of Directors may fill any function of the auditors without an offer, but shall be vacant during the function that is doing the auditors or the organizers of the remaining work or rest, or reference-based work.

(9) define the company in general meeting fees of auditors, but the Board of Directors may, determine the fees of the auditors concerned prior to the founding meeting or when filling a job references that without an offer.

Powers and duties of auditors.

138 - (1) Any references to the right to have access to books and accounts and bills the company at any time and the right to request the Board of Directors of the company and its employees the information and explanations necessary for the performance of his duties as auditor.

(2) must produce a report on the auditors to the members of the company's accounts that they have examined and for each budget submitted to the Company in general meeting, and during their term of their jobs and must be mentioned in this report are the following:

(A) whether they had received all the information and explanations requested by them, and

(B) What if they think that the budget referred to in the report have developed a conformity to the law, and

(C) whether the budget was the financial situation of the company offer a real and true, according to the information and explanations given to them according to what is shown in the books of the company.

(3) If the company's corporate banking and had a sub-banks outside the borders of Sudan, it is sufficient to be placed to inform the auditor have been sent to the main center for the company in Sudan copies and extracts from the books and accounts of the branch.

The right of holders of preferred stock, etc. .. to receive reports and examined.

139 - (1) The holders of shares and documents to be excellent with the right to holders of ordinary shares in the delivery of the budget of the company and auditors' reports and other reports and examined.

(2) do not apply the provisions of this Article to private companies.

The company to conduct its business without the

The legal minimum of members

Liability arising from doing business with a number of Members at least seven or at least two in the case of private companies

140 - If you lack, at any time, the number of members of the company for two in the case of private companies, or seven, in the case of any other companies, and practiced its business for more than six months with the existence of this deficiency Each member shall be in the company during the period that practiced the work after a period of six months mentioned, and he knows it is engaged in business less than two or seven, as the case is committed to pay all debts of the private company that contracted during this period, and may be prosecuted on them, without the

PART VIII DOCUMENTS ANNOUNCEMENT OF THE COMPANY

141 - Declaration may be leaving them the documents in the Office of the Registrar or the company, send them to that office by registered mail.

Declaration documents to the Registrar.

142 - may be declared the documents to the Registrar by sending it by post or handed over to the Registrar by leaving him in his office.

Documentation of the documents.

143 - Documents or procedures that need to be documented from the company may be signed by a member of the board of directors or secretary or any other officer authorized in that company does not need to stamp stamp-General of the company

Lists, forms and rules on matters prescribed

Application and modify menus, forms, and the authority of the rules of the issues assessed.

144 - (1) use the models shown in Table III models, or close to it as much as circumstances permit in all matters to which the models.

(2) Council of Ministers may amend any list or any model in the table the first amendment does not increase the amount of the fees to be paid to the Registrar in that table may also modify the forms in Schedule III or add to.

(3) must be published in the Official Gazette all adjusted from the menus, forms, and when the post was should have effect as if they had been issued under the provisions of this law, but not the amendment is conducted by the Council of Ministers in the list (a) of Schedule I of any impact any company registered before the amendment or repeal any part of that list.

(4) in addition to any authorized authorities as provided under the provisions of this Article, the Minister of Justice may establish rules providing for all or some of the issues that the law requires him to report the order [xi] .

(5) These rules must be published in the Official Gazette is published and when it must act as if they had been issued under the provisions of this law.

PART IX CONVERT PRIVATE COMPANY INTO A PUBLIC COMPANY

147 - (1) The company may own, subject to any text included in the Memorandum of Association or in its system, to become a public company under the special resolution, and must be deposited with the Registrar a copy of this resolution and to deposit also has a report instead of the statement was must deposit with the Registrar if it were a public company before the allocation of shares or any of the documents and must also be deposited with the Registrar a statement confirming it properly than it should have checked before starting to operate if it were a public company.

(2) When filed documents described in clause (1) The Registrar must be recorded in its books relating to the change in the company.

Liquidation

Obliged to pay

The responsibility of the members of the company's current, former and as obliged to pay.

149 - Subject to the provisions of this Article is committed m each member of the company's current and former that contributes to the company's assets in case of liquidation of an amount sufficient to meet the debts and liabilities and liquidation expenses, costs and expenses and to settle the rights bound to pay for them, and that the following conditions:

(A) No former member is required to contribute to the payment if the membership is over before starting the liquidation a year or more,

(B) No former member is required to contribute to the payment of company debts or obligations that arose after the end of its membership,

(C) No former member is required to contribute only if the court finds that the current members can not fulfill the contribution committed to pay under the provisions of this Act,

(D) Except as provided in Article 150 shall not be required of any member of the company to pay more than the amount of the shares did not pay - if any - which promises to pay them as a member of a current or former,

(E) Nothing in this Act shall invalidate any provision included in any insurance policy or a contract setting out the responsibility of Members, in relation to the document or contract, or fallen short of that responsibility on the company's funds alone,

(F) is not the amount owed to any member of the company, as a member of the shares or profits or other our company is committed to pay for this member in the case of overcrowding between him and any other creditor not a member of the company, but it may be that this amount is subject to consideration of the settlement The final payment for the rights bound with each other.

Responsibility of board members if their responsibility is limited

150 - in the case of liquidation of the company is committed to every member of a former or current members of the Board of Directors or all of the former or current director who is their responsibility under the provisions of this law, liability is limited also to pay in addition to his commitment to pay - if any - in his capacity as an ordinary member, other amounts as if it were to start filtering its commitment to pay under the provisions of Article 149 subject to the conditions contained in paragraph (d) of the said article with this:

(A) does not comply with Council member or former director to contribute to the payment of such additional amounts if the cut to hold office before starting liquidation a year or more,

(B) does not comply with Board Member or former director to contribute to the payment of any additional amount for any debt or obligation of the company grew after an interval to hold office,

(C) Subject to the systems the company does not comply with Board Member or Director to contribute to the payment of any additional amount, unless the court, that that contribution is necessary to meet the company's debts and obligations and expenses, costs and expenses of liquidation.

The meaning of binding to pay.

151 - The term "binding payment" Everyone is committed to pay the money to the company's assets in case of liquidation and in all measures taken to appoint persons to be considered obligated to pay and all procedures prior to the appointment of a nomination for good, and include the phrase everyone prosecutor that he is obliged to pay.

Bound nature of the liability to pay.

152 - (1) result in binding responsibility to pay the emergence of a debt by the time it begins its responsibility, but it is not the duty of performance only in the time when claims for the implementation of responsibility.

(2) consider the case based on the binding responsibility to pay before the General Court only.

Obliged to pay upon the death of the member.

153 - (1) If you died to pay the binding before inserting his name in the list bound to pay or thereafter, committed to his legal representative and his successors to pay to the company's assets, while managing to meet the amount of the debts he owes and consider therefore obliged to pay.

(2) If no heirs of the deceased or his legal representative to pay the amounts ordered to be paid, it may then be asked to take action to manage the funds to pay the binding of the deceased or of movable property, or both, and the payment of amounts due from such funds Jabra.

Obliged to pay in case of bankruptcy of member.

154 - if pay-binding bankrupt before inserting his name in the list of mandated payment then or thereafter:

(A) acting on its behalf in all purposes of the liquidation secretary in bankruptcy is that the Secretary build that binding payment may be requested to confront any evidence provided against the assets of the bankrupt or to accept to pay, according to the law, of the assets of any amounts owed by the bankrupt in a match his commitment to pay for the company's assets ,

(B) may establish a proof against the assets of the bankrupt the estimated value of the amounts for the binding to the next and previous claims.

(A) If any creditor of the company the amount of their debts over a million dinars, whether a creditor in a transfer or other solution Deadline entitlement to his religion to declare the company a request signed by him to leave in its registered office and requesting the payment of the amount owed and neglected the company met for three weeks after that request or neglected to provide guarantee to fulfill it, or where the conciliation reasonably acceptable to the creditor, or [xiii]

(B) If the action has been taken enforcement or any other actions, based on the judgment or order of the Court, for the benefit of any creditor of the company and returned it without judgment or to carry out all or part of, or

(C) If the court found convincing evidence that the company is unable to meet their debts, and must be on the court when deciding whether the company was unable to meet their debts, to enter into account the company's debt and contingent debts that will arise in the future.

Special provisions applied filter.

157 - Subject to the provisions of this Article have requested the liquidation petition submitted to the Court or from the company and any creditor or creditors, including holders of debt or contingent which arise in the future will believe in the binding or bound to pay or all of these or one of them collectively or individually as :

(A) is not obliged to pay for the right to petition for the liquidation of the company, except in one of the following two cases:

(I) If a shortage of members of two in the case of private company or in the case of seven members of other companies, or

(Ii) if the shares that promises to pay for them or some of these shares were allocated in origin, was in possession in the original and registered in his name for a period not less than six months during the eighteen months prior to the start of liquidation or had fallen to him by the death of former holder,

(B) No petition may be filed for the liquidation of the company for not filing the report or not to hold the founding meeting of a constituent, but shareholders may not be provided before the lapse of fourteen days after the last day that I had to hold the meeting.

(C) the Court is considering a petition for the liquidation of the company's introduction of the probabilistic religion or religion will arise in the future only after submission of security as the court deems reasonable for the expenses of liquidation and after the court is satisfied that the issue of the existence of an initial order of liquidation.

Impact on the order of liquidation.

158 - carried out the order to liquidate the company, for the benefit of all creditors and all bound to pay to the company, as if it was issued at the request of a creditor and a payment bound together.

Start of the liquidation by the court.

159 - The liquidation of the company by the court that they had started a petition at the time of liquidation.

Court's power to discontinue proceedings against the company

160 - The Court may at any time after the submission of a broad liquidation of the company under the provisions of this Act and prior to ordering the liquidation of the company to prevent any actions or continuing in any case or action against the company if the company asked it or request one of the creditors of the company or one bound to pay them and be This prohibition conditions Tstsoppea court.

Authority of the court's consideration of the request filter.

161 - (1) The court may upon consideration of the submission be rejected with the provision of expenses or otherwise, and may postpone its consideration of the condition or without condition, and may also issue an interim order or any other matter in accordance with justice, but may not refuse to issue an order liquidation of assets just because the company has mortgaged for an amount equivalent to those assets or increase them, or just because he is not the company's assets.

(2) If the liquidation petition presented on the basis of non-deposit of the report or not to hold the founding meeting of the founding, is permissible. The court to rule on the expenses of people who see them are responsible for such violation.

Off issues when an order of liquidation.

162 - When was ordered to liquidate the company may not walk in any case or any other legal action or initiated against the company, except with the permission of the court and the conditions determined by the.

Upload a picture of an order of liquidation with the Registrar.

163 - (1) the company must be deposited with the Registrar a copy of the liquidation order issued upon a petition submitted to the filter that also filed a copy of the Ordinance.

(2) must be deposited when the Registrar has ordered the liquidation of a record in the books of the company and the minutes of the deposit must be advertising in the Official Gazette for the issuance of this order.

(3) the above command is tantamount to a declaration for users of the company removed them from service only if it continues the company's business.

Court's power to stop the liquidation.

164 - The Court may at any time after the command liquidation may make an order to stop all of those liquidation proceedings Aaagafa at all or for a limited period conditions and in accordance with the provisions of which Tstsoppea if requested by any creditor, is obliged to pay, and proved to have the evidence convinces her and should stop all of those procedures.

Authority of the court to take into account the wishes of the creditors, who are required to pay.

165 - in all matters related to liquidation the court may take into account the wishes of creditors or who are required to pay to prove that her evidence must convince her to stop all of those procedures.

Submission of the report to the Court for the affairs of the company.

165 A - (1) If the Court issued an order liquidation or appointed liquidator formally temporarily must work report on the affairs of the company as scheduled and submitted to the Court in favor of the adoption of accompanying oath, unless the Court otherwise and issue an order as you see, and must make it clear in this report details the company's assets The debts, obligations, and the names and residences of the creditors and their professions and guarantees that each of them and the dates that these guarantees were given for each of them and other information determined by the court or requested.

(2) must submit this report to be certified by one or more of those who were on the scheduled date members of the Board and who was on the said date as secretary or a senior official in the company or of persons mentioned later in this item who are sponsored by the liquidator the official submission of the report and support taking into account the order of the court and these people are:

(A) Members of the Board of Directors of the Company or its employees or those who were board members or staff,

(B) persons who participated in the formation of the company at any time within one year prior to the date of the decision,

(C) Persons employed by the company or were in service during the year mentioned, the Court considers that they can give the required information,

(D) employees or employees who were mentioned during the year and those who have served or are serving this year in the company of the companies used or were used in the company to which the report during the year in question.

(3) The report must be submitted within fourteen days of the date in a date or the corresponding longer appointed by the liquidator or the official appointed by the court for special reasons.

(4) allows any person who is doing the report and acknowledged as supplemented oath required under the provisions of this article or for those who help in the work request from the liquidator the official expenses and expenses incurred in the preparation of the work of the report and acknowledged as supplemented by his right hand, and related, which sees the liquidator the official as an expense and reasonable expenses and pay the official liquidator of the assets of these funds to the company that the report is subject to appeal before the Court of Appeal the road.

(5) Any person who fails to implement the requirements of this article without an acceptable excuse, a fine determined by the court for each day the default continues [xiv].

(6) per person, claiming in writing that a creditor of the company or is obliged to pay them, the right to see for himself or agent about the report submitted under the provisions of this article shall at all reasonable times and after paying the prescribed fee, and may obtain a copy or extract of the report mentioned.

(7) Every person, falsely claims that the creditor, is obliged to pay, shall be guilty of offense and liable to a fine determined by the Court [xv].

(8) The term "due date" in this article date of appointment of provisional liquidator the official if there is such appointment shall be, if not get the words intended date of the order of liquidation.

The report of the official liquidator.

165 b (1) If an order is liquidation the liquidator should be the official, after the delivery of the report to be submitted under the provisions of Article (156 a) or in the case ordered by the Court after the submission of any report, to hasten as much as possible to report the primary court, including the following:

(A) the amount of capital issued and subscribed, and paid him and the estimated value of assets and liabilities,

(B) the reasons for the failure of the company if they have failed, and

(C) whether he could see that it is desirable to carry out further investigation in any matter relating to establishment of the company or its composition or its failure or course of business.

(2) the liquidator may, if desirable, the work of an additional report or additional reports stating the method of composition of the company and whether it was of the opinion that any person has committed a fraud in the establishment of the company or its composition or that fraud has occurred from one of the members of the Board of Directors or any employee last of its employees with the company since its formation Ptalq and any other matters of opinion is desirable to inform the court on it.

(3) If the liquidator mentioned in any report of the above-mentioned additional reports that he felt that the fraud of the above has occurred shall be the court the right to exercise other powers provided for in Article (187).

The official liquidator

Appointment of official liquidator.

166 - (1) The court may appoint a person or persons who called the official liquidators directly to the liquidation procedures of the company and do the duties imposed by the Court of liquidation and the appointment of liquidators of these ends all the powers of the members of the Board of Directors of the company.

(2) The court may make the appointment of a liquidator provisionally at any time after the submission of a petition of liquidation and prior to ordering the liquidation.

(3) If the court appointed liquidator of the more formal it must decide whether to delegate the work of this law on the official liquidator to do or his authorized representative in carrying out the intimate all official liquidators appointed or Apasharham one or more of one of them.

(4) The court may decide whether to provide a guarantee that the liquidator on his appointment, with a statement that the warranty.

(5) the actions of the official liquidator valid, even if later emerged that his appointment was flawed,

That nothing in this heading is corrected for any acts carried out by the official liquidator after his appointment he had to be incorrect.

Resignation of the official liquidator, isolated and fill his job and pay him compensation.

167 - (1) the official liquidator may resign from his job and may be isolated with the court explaining the reasons therefore unjustified.

(2) If no official liquidator and the function designated by the court, the court and fill the job.

(3) pay the salary of the official liquidator or pay a percentage or as otherwise ordered by the court if the court has appointed more than one liquidator is distributed to them this wage rates to be determined by the court.

The official liquidator

168 - known as the official title of the liquidator liquidator of the company appointed the official liquidator has in his own name.

Sequestration on the funds of the company.

169 - (1) puts the official liquidator under the custody or supervision of all company assets and belongings safe and Daawiyeha of litigation, which the company is right or it appears to have a really in it.

(2) considers all the company's funds in the custody of the court if the company does not appoint a liquidator or official if they are free and the function of liquidator.

The authority of the official liquidator.

170 - the official liquidator for the permission of the court the authority to direct the following acts:

(A) litigation and direct legal action was a civil or criminal, defense and other in the name of the company and on its behalf,

(B) engage in the business to the extent necessary for the liquidation of rewarding,

(C) sale of company assets, including real estate and movable in a public tender or private contract has the power to transfer their entirety to any person, company or sell it piecemeal,

(D) all work directly on behalf of the company and on its behalf and to conclude all contracts and other documents are documented and given vouchers to use and has the seal of the company if necessary.

(E) enter into adversaries and claim any outstanding balance of the assets of the bankruptcy of any obligation to pay and to demonstrate that the balance has to receive shares in the distribution of bankruptcy in a match like that balance in debt owed by the bankrupt independent rate of this debt to the rest of the debt,

(F) withdraw and accept, edit and endorse any bill of exchange or document promissory note on behalf of the company and on its behalf shall have to do this effect for the responsibility of the company as if it happened clouds, acceptance, and editing or endorsement of the company itself or on its behalf in the course of its regular work,

(G) management of cash necessary to ensure the company's assets,

(H) to get its official name on the orders of management legacy of any obligation to pay may have died and may initiate its official name any other act necessary for any amounts and money owed by binding to pay or to his estate, which is not possible to work on behalf of the company, and in all these cases is this as if the amounts owed to the liquidator himself to be able to get the orders mentioned the estate management to meet those amounts, that nothing in these authorities delegated to the official liquidator shall affect the rights of the Director of the byproducts of the official or his duties and prerogatives.

(I) do other acts necessary for the liquidation of the company and distributing its assets.

The discretion of the liquidator.

171 - The court may provide that any order issued provided that the liquidator the official directly any of the authorities mentioned above without the permission of the court, with or without

intervention and may in the circumstances which they are appointed liquidator, the official temporary basis to determine the powers and compliance with the order of appointment.

Providing legal assistance to official liquidator.

172 - the official liquidator may with the permission of the court to appoint a lawyer to help him fulfill his duties, that if the official liquidator is himself a lawyer - he can not appoint his partner in his office, unless before the latter can be done without pay.

The duty of the liquidator to retain the books in formal liquidation

173 - the liquidator shall official of the company which will exercise the Court filter that retains the manner prescribed books regularly recorded by the restrictions and the minutes of proceedings at meetings and decided the other issues may be of any creditor, is obliged to pay to get out on these books by himself or agent, taking into account the control of the court.

Direct the liquidator power and control.

174 - (1) Without prejudice to the provisions of this law must be the liquidator of the company official that the court take into account the liquidation in the management of the company's assets distributed among creditors in the instructions contained in the decisions issued by the creditors or who are required to pay in any public meeting.

(2) the liquidator may official call on all creditors or who are required to pay to hold a public meeting to verify that their desires should be to convene meetings on the dates specified by the creditors or obliged to pay the decisions issued them, or when requested to do so in writing the owners are held by ten (10 / 1) of the creditors or who are required to pay, depending on the circumstances.

(3) The official liquidator in the manner prescribed may request guidance from the Court with respect to any particular issue arising from the liquidation.

(4) Without prejudice to the provisions of this law, the liquidator shall be used his discretion in the management of the company's assets and distribute to creditors.

00 - (1) must be the liquidator appointed by the company in voluntary liquidation be sent within seven days of his appointment a declaration by mail to all who need it that they are creditors of the company informing them when a meeting of creditors of the company in the history of not less than twenty-one days and not more than month of his appointment, time and place set forth in the Declaration and must also publish an announcement of this meeting, once in the Official Gazette and at least once in a newspaper - if any - are issued in the fact by the Office of Company Registrar or the shop's main business.

(2) must be on the creditors to decide at the meeting to be held under the provisions of subsection (1) whether it is necessary to provide the company or the appointment of a liquidator last with him, then decided to creditors making such a request, may be submitted to the court at any time not exceeding fourteen days after date of the meeting by any creditor for this purpose at the meeting, as the Court may be issued, at any time, is to extend the deadline to apply under the provisions of the item to the time that it deems appropriate.

(3) The Court may upon application to be ordered either by isolating the liquidator appointed by the company and the appointment of a liquidator other or the appointment of a liquidator jointly

with the liquidator appointed by the Company or to issue any other order it deems just taking into account the interests of creditors of the company and who are required to pay them.

(4) the court must make the order as it deems appropriate regarding the expenses of the application if it considers it is based on reasonable grounds taking into account in this estimate may be ordered to pay expenses of the application of assets of the company turned down the request, even if separated or when otherwise not in accordance with his request is submitted demand.

Authority to fill the position of liquidator.

201 - (1) if they are free function liquidator appointed by the company in voluntary liquidation because of the filling of this post in a public meeting convened by taking into account any agreement with its creditors.

(2) may be invited to the General meeting convened for the purpose for which the above-mentioned payment of a bound or liquidators of a rest if he had had to filter more than one liquidator.

(3) general meeting held in the manner set forth in the Company or in the manner determined by the court at the request of the binding or the liquidators to pay those who work the filter.

Authorization in the power to appoint liquidators.

202 - (1) The Company may on the verge of voluntary liquidation or in the role of these filters to delegate to its creditors or any committee of them under the decision of an extraordinary power to appoint liquidators or one of them and fill devoid of the functions of liquidators and the Agreement on the authorities intimate liquidators and direct way this authorities.

(2) The work done by the creditors, based on any authority delegated to the aforesaid manner, the same effect as if issued by the company.

Situations where the agreement binding on the creditors.

203 - (1) Subject to the right of appeal provided for in item (2) The agreement between the company and its creditors when the company is about to voluntary liquidation or in the role of this filter binding on the company if sanctioned by the decision of an unusual and binding on the creditors if accepted by three-quarters of the creditors of in number and value.

(2) Any creditor or obliged to pay to raise an appeal to the Court for such an agreement within three weeks of completing it and the court may in this case modify the said agreement or change or support as it deems consistent with justice.

The authority of the liquidators to accept shares of ... Etc. as opposed to sale of company funds.

204 - (1) in circumstances which meant the liquidation of the company the whole filter is optional, or where already in the role of this filter and I want to transfer or sale of all or some of its or their money to another company (called in this article the company transferee) may be the liquidator of the company's first (called in this article the company transferred) under a special resolution of the company, authorized by a mandate years or a mandate to conclude a special agreement, to receive in compensation or part compensation for the transfer or sale of shares or insurance policies or similar rights in the company transferee for distribution to members of the company

transferred may also be entered into any other agreement allows the company members to participate in the profits of the company transferee or to get them to any other privileges instead of or in addition to receiving cash or taking shares or insurance policies or other rights of the like that.

(2) any sale or agreement to the provisions of this Article shall be binding upon the members of the converted company.

(3) If you do not vote for a member of the company transferred for the benefit of the decision at a meeting held for the issuance of that decision or his support and expressed his violation of the decision letter sent to the liquidator and leaving him in the center of the company's registrar within seven days from the support of the resolution, it is permissible for this member to request the liquidator either to abstain on the implementation of the resolution and to either buy his interest in the company a price determined by agreement or by arbitration in the manner set forth hereinafter.

(4) If the liquidator chose to buy this member's interest in the company he must pay the price to be resolved before the company and he has to Edberh the way that the decision had to be special.

(5) is not the decision is incorrect in applying the provisions of this article because of its release before or with the decision to liquidate the company or the decision to appoint liquidators, but if issued during the year from the date of the order to liquidate the company by the court or under its supervision shall not be of this resolution is true only if passed by the court.

Method for determining the price.

205 - the price to be paid for the purchase of the interest of the offending Member of the resolution may be determined by agreement, if signed between the parties dispute thereon shall decide the dispute through arbitration.

Authority to raise the matter to court.

206 - (1) If a company in the role of voluntary liquidation may be the liquidator or any obligation to pay or any creditor may request the court to adjudicate any dispute is in liquidation or to proceed with regard to the implementation of the claims or other matters of all or one of the authorities which may if they are conducted, which holds the filter itself.

(2) If the court is satisfied the fairness and usefulness of the chapter in the conflict or power required to directly conducted all or part of the conditions Tstsoppea and may be issued regarding this request is consistent with the last you see of justice.

The authority of the liquidator to call for a general meeting

207 - (1) If a company in the role of voluntary liquidation the liquidator may be called from time to time to convene a general meeting of the company whose purpose is to obtain approval from the company under a special resolution or decision of an unusual or for any other purpose it deems appropriate.

(2) If the continued liquidation of the company for more than a year should be the liquidator be invited to hold a general meeting of the company at the end of the first year of the start of the filter and in the end of each year following her or whenever possible, be convened after that and he

must be presented to the meeting a report form to be inclusive of the details of assessments in respect of the liquidation procedures and condition.

General Meeting of the final resolution of the company.

208 - (1) In every case of voluntary liquidation the liquidator shall as soon as the liquidation of the company's full liquidation to prepare an account of the liquidation showing the manner in which initiate the liquidation and how he got the disposition of the company's funds and must then be calling for a general meeting of the company to offer him This account provides for the clarification.

(2) be invited to the meeting announcement illustrates the path of the time and venue and purpose and must be performed before the date of publication convene at least one month and in the manner set out in Article 197.

(3) the liquidator shall be filed with the Registrar within one week after the meeting a report on the meeting date, and if does not have done so, who may judge by a fine determined by the court for each day the violation continues [xix].

(4) must be recorded when filed the report referred to that recorded immediately and the company is dissolved at the expiry of three months from the registration report, that the court may at the request of the liquidator or request of any other person that the court has an interest in the subject, may make an order postpone the effective date of dissolution of the company to term as the court deems appropriate.

(5) The person who issued the court order under the provisions of subsection (4) at his request be filed with the Registrar during the twenty-first days following the issuance of the order a certified copy of the Ordinance, if not carried out that judgeth him a fine determined by the court for each day of continuing the violation. [Xx]

The cost of voluntary liquidation.

209 - All amounts are spent properly in the expenses, costs and expenses of voluntary liquidation including the remuneration of the liquidator should be performed on the assets of the company priority all other claims existing at the date of liquidation.

The right of creditors and who are required to pay in the request for liquidation by the court

210 - liquidation of the company voluntary liquidation do not fall the right of any creditor or any obligation to pay to be in liquidation by the court if the court held at the request of the creditor or binding payment that their rights adversely affected by liquidation optional.

Court's power to follow the procedures for voluntary liquidation.

211 - If a company is in the role of the voluntary liquidation and the liquidation was ordered by the court is permissible for the court to decide the matter in question or in any subsequent Order for him to work all the voluntary liquidation proceedings or to each other and if it deems it appropriate.

Invalidity and other transfers after the start of liquidation.

218 - (1) In the case of voluntary liquidation be null and void all transfer of shares except that prevents them or with the consent of the refinery, as well as any amendment shall be void in case of members of the company receives after starting the filter.

(2) In the case of liquidation by the court or under its supervision shall be void in the disposal of all funds of the company (including the cases suitable for litigation) and all transfer of shares or changes in the case of members occurs after the initiation of liquidation unless the court ordered otherwise.

Must prove the debt of all kinds

219 - in each filter (taking into account the application of the provisions of the Bankruptcy Code of 1929 to insolvent companies in accordance with the provisions of this Act) shall be proof of all debts outstanding to pay on the order probabilistic and all claims against the company, whether state or a future possibility or likelihood of working estimate is true as far as possible from the the value of those debts or claims pending on the order probabilistic or that do not have a specific value for another reason.

Application of the rules in the bankruptcy liquidation of the company.

220 - The rules in force in the bankruptcy law of 1929 for the assets of persons who-month bankruptcy to liquidate the insolvent company and follow the rules regarding the rights of creditors secured debts and unsecured debts as well as regarding the debt midwife to demonstrate and assess the value of the amounts paid annually, claims or future probability and may all people of their right to any such case proof of receipt of the shares of the company's assets in liquidation to enter and submit claims against the company that may be provided to them under the provisions of this Article.

Payments the path of preference.

221 - (1) must be paid upon liquidation path priority over all other debts, the following amounts:

(A) non-trade debt owed to the Government or to any interest from the interests of the Government or any local authority is authorized to receive government money

(B) All salaries and wages that do not exceed one million dinars and due to the clerks or servants for services that they have done for the company during the six months preceding the date mentioned below,

(C) all wages that do not exceed one million dinars, and payable to any worker or maker for services performed by the company during the six months preceding the date mentioned below whether those wages paid for a period of time or calculates the piece,

(D) all amounts owed to the lessor peer-fare of homes and land leased to the company for a period not exceeding six months prior to the date mentioned for the houses and land occupied by the Company on the said date,

(E) all amounts not exceeding in any individual case and the amount of two million dinars owed to the company match compensation under the provisions of any law of the workers' compensation be in force and be the responsibility under which originated before the said date. Compensation under the provisions of any law of the workers' compensation be in force and be the responsibility under which originated before the said date. [Xxi]

(2) The solvency previous mentioned as follows:

(A) shall be equal among themselves in the place and gets fulfilled only if the entire assets of the company are not enough to satisfy them shall be reduced in equal proportions,

(B) have an amount sufficient to meet the debts of ordinary creditors of the company's assets are available for this purpose priority to requests for holders of bonds under the lien created by floating the company and therefore pay from any funds covered by the franchise floating or be subject to him,

(3) pay the debt immediately prior to the extent that sufficient assets to meet them after booking the necessary funds for the expenses and expenses of liquidation.

(4) In cases in which takes in or have been taken by the owner or any other person the path of implementation of goods or baggage of the company during the three months immediately preceding the order filters have a debt that has priority under the provisions of this Article the right of lien on such goods, baggage, return on their sale.

To be the owner or other person for any amount may be paid under any lien which stated that the priority of the rights of the person who paid him the amount.

(5) the date referred to earlier in this article is:

(A) the date of the liquidation order for the company, which was ordered liquidated by Jabra has never initiate liquidation newsletter,

(B) the date of initiation of liquidation in other cases.

Preference by fraud.

222 - (1) Any transfer or mortgage or delivery of goods or the payment or execution or other actions relating to money, which is the arrangement of the advantage by fraud, even if Pashrh one individual or signed against him in Tfelicth is also for the creditors of the company's arrangement to advantage by fraud and then falls void if the company initiated it or against it Mbacherth got a role in the liquidation.

(2) In applying the provisions of this article is to apply the filter in the event of liquidation by the court or under its supervision and the decision as an act of voluntary liquidation of the incident from a bankruptcy of individuals.

(3) Any transfer shall be void or get a waiver from the company of the Trustees for all funds for the benefit of all creditors.

Invalidity of the seizure and execution ... Etc. certain cases.

223 - (1) shall be void of any attachment or execution happens without the permission of the court against the company's money or belongings after the initiation of the filter when the company was in liquidation by the court or under its supervision.

(2) do not apply the provisions of subsection (1) the actions undertaken by the government.

The impact of the floating privilege.

224 - Privilege floating that arises on the commitments the company and its funds within three months from the initiation of liquidation shall be void when the company was in liquidation unless it is proved that the company was solvent after the establishment of franchise floating directly, but shall not be void as much as it pays for the company in cash or after the establishment of that right and in his stead.

May be the year the project was approved for liquidation.

225 - (1) the liquidator may, with the permission of the Court, if the liquidation of the company by the court or under its supervision pursuant to Resolution of unusual from the company if the optional filter to proceed the following acts or some of them:

(A) pay any debts of the entire range of creditors,

(B) There will be no reconciliation or compromise with creditors or of claiming to be creditors, or that they may have or claim that they have a present or future claims may adhere to the company,

(C) reconcile all claims, liabilities claims and debts and obligations that become debts and all claims present or future realized presence, social, and existing or anticipated doing between the Company and any obligation to pay or any person claiming that he is obliged to pay or a debtor or other person expects his commitment to the company and to reconcile in all disputes relating to any form of assets or liquidation of the company or that affect them and that the conditions agreed upon and takes no guarantee of Tkhals in any claim or debt or obligation and gives full clearance to the above required.

(2) initiate the liquidator powers under the provisions of subsection (1) under the control of the court and shall be binding on any creditor or to raise the pay of the Court on an appeal directly to the authority of any of these authorities, or concerning what is intended Mbacherth them.

Court's power to impose damages on the fault of the board members or others.

226 - (1) If it appears, during the liquidation of the company, the person who co-founded, or in its composition, or that none of the members of the board of directors or managers or liquidators or former employees or current where the abuse of any money or funds of the company or held her or become bound by or responsible for it or abuse of position or has committed a breach of the Secretariat for the company the Court may, at the request of the liquidator or any creditor, is obliged to pay, to examine the actions of the founder or board member or manager or liquidator or officer and to force him to return or restitution of money or funds or any part thereof or to force him to pay the amount of the assets of the company as the court deems appropriate as a matter of compensation for the abuse, detention, or breach of trust.

(2) The provisions of this Article if the offense took place of which the accused asked him a criminal.

(3) shall apply the Civil Transactions Act of 1974 to the request made under the provisions of this article as if that was the issue of demand.

Fraud penalty notebooks.

227 - if the damaged member of the board of directors or a director or employee or pay any binding company liquidation or distorted, or replaced or concealed in a false or fraudulent any books or papers, warranties, or falsely made or under any fraud in any record or book of accounts or document of the company or was a party to the action that restriction intending thereby to cheat or deceive any person, punishable by imprisonment for a term not exceeding seven years and a fine may be punished as well.

Trial at fault of the board members and others.

228 - (1) If the court finds during the liquidation of the company by the court or under its supervision that none of the members of the board of directors or managers or employees or members of the company present them or the former has been committed to the company a criminal offense is permissible for the court on its own initiative or at the request One of those concerned in the liquidation order that the official liquidator or the liquidator, depending on the circumstances, to take proceedings for that offense and may order the payment of costs and expenses of the company's assets.

(2) If it appears to the liquidator during the voluntary liquidation that none of the members of the board of directors or managers or employees or members of the company present them or the former has been committed to the company a criminal offense may be the liquidator, with the prior authorization of the court, to take action to prosecute the accused and pay all expenses necessary to spent by the liquidator in the case of company assets priority over all other debts.

Penalty of perjury.

229 - all the result of intentionally false testimony when questioned under oath under the provisions of this Act or any acknowledgment or certificate accompanying oath or official confirmation of the liquidation of any company or on the liquidation under the provisions of this law or other matters arising under the provisions of this law, or which shall be punished by imprisonment for a term not exceeding seven years and a fine may be punished as well.

Meetings to ascertain the wishes of creditors or who are required to pay.

230 - (1) in circumstances permitted by the law of the Court for liquidation into account the wishes of creditors or who are required to pay to prove to the court sufficient evidence may, if Astsopt to ascertain from those wishes, order invited to the meetings of creditors or who are required to pay and the complexity of these meetings and be walk the manner determined by the court and may appoint a person to the presidency of any of these meetings and report to the outcome of the meeting.

(2) must in the case of creditors into account the value of the debt each creditor.

(3) in the case must be bound to pay into account the number of votes decided by the Company for each of them.

Company documents as evidence

231 - If in the case of liquidation of all documents shall be considered as evidence documents the liquidators among elementary bound to pay the health of all the issues mentioned in the documents mentioned.

Access to documents.

250 - (1) Each company shall apply under this section should be prepared in each calendar year budget according to the form and containing the same details and included with the documents that the company is obliged prepared in the manner described under the provisions of this Act as if they were subject to him and must be submitted to the company in general meeting and that the receipt of a copy of this budget to the Registrar for registration.

(2) If the budget were not mentioned by the former editor of the Arabic language must be accompanied by a translation certified to it.

Commitment with the name of the company and whether they are limited and the country which was founded

251 - Every company under this section shall apply to the following:

(A) be stated in the statement calling for the subscription to the shares or bonds in Sudan Country name, which was established in it.

(B) are displayed in a conspicuous place in each place of work engaged in the Sudan's name and the name of the country which was founded,

(C) to mention in all printed bills and papers Mkatebadtha and in all advertising and other publications from the official name and the name of the country which was founded in letters legible,

(D) If a limited liability company members must be declared in writing letters in Read each statement said they were driven in all printed bills and papers Mkatebadtha and declarations and other official publications in the Sudan and everywhere you conduct business.

Declaration of court orders for the company to which it applies Part VIII

252 - judicial orders or declarations required declaration to the company that applies under this section shall be deemed announced the declaration sufficient if you send the title of any person who was named delivered to the Registrar under this Part and left or sent through the post office at the address delivered to the Registrar also stated that:

(A) if the company had not been delivered to the Registrar the name and address of the person who lives in Sudan and the Commissioner of acceptance of declarations of judicial proceedings or ads or other ads on behalf of the company. Or,

(B) If at any time of his death all persons who recognized the names and addresses of as male or dropped out of the residence in Sudan or refused to accept advertising on behalf of the company or can not be their ad for any reason, may announce it legal for the company by leaving at any place of shops work created by the company in Sudan, or send an email to the store.

Office, which is deposited documents

253 - (1) must be delivered to the Registrar all documents required to be delivered from the company to which it applies this door and be recognized in the Registration Office in Khartoum.

(2) If the company is no longer applicable to them by this section place of business in Sudan, it must declare the registered do so immediately and expire from the date on which it gets this advertising company's commitment to deliver any document to the Registrar.

Sanctions

254 - If you do not the company that applies under this section the implementation of any of its provisions Vtaaqb the above-mentioned company where every employee or agent by a fine determined by the court or a fine determined by the court for each day the violation continues if the violation of the violations continued. [X]

Interpretations to Part VIII

255 - For the purposes of this section:

(A) Certified that means the prescribed manner that is identical to the original or a correct translation.

(B) The term "board member" in relation to the company any person accustomed to the members of the Board of Directors to act according to his orders or instructions.

(C) The term "workplace" Office of transfer of shares or registered office.

(D) the word "statement" of its intended meaning when used in respect of a corporation organized under the provisions of this law.

Organization of public sector companies

General Provisions

Application

256 - (1) This section applies and the law of the financial procedures and accounting for the year 1977 and the regulations issued thereunder to the public sector companies established before or after the issuance of this law.

(2) on all public sector companies adjust their positions according to the provisions of this section in a period not exceeding thirty-atheist of the month of March 1997. [Xi]

INVESTMENT ENCOURAGEMENT ACT 1996

In accordance with the 13th Constitutional Decree for 1995, the National Assembly has passed the Act below with the approval of the President of the Republic.

Chapter (1)

Preliminary Provisions The Title of the Act and Date of Enactment:

1- This act may be cited at the Investment Encouragement Act for 1996 and is valid from the date of signing (May 14, 1996).

Cancellation and Exemption:

2- This Act cancels the investment Act for 1995, provided that all rules and orders issued and procedures taken in accordance with it remain valid unless they are canceled or ammended in pursuance of its provisions.

Predomination of Provisions:

3- The provisions of this law shall predominate over any other rules of law in case of conflict in a way that amends the conflict between them.

Application of the Provisions of the Act:

4- The provisions of this acts shall be applied on the existing projects which were established in accordance with the Investment Encouragement Act for 1990 (cancelled) or any private deal in a way that serves the ends of this act and that preferences, facilities and guarantees granted in pursuance of its provisions should not be less than that which stipulated by the repealed act or the deal.

interpretation :

5- In this act, unless the context otherwise requires: The invested money means:

a. The local money paid by the investor to establish, operate, rehabilitate or expand a project. b- The foreign currency which is transferred through one of the banks registered by the Bank of Sudan for the establishment, operation, rehabilitation and expansion of a project. c - The capital in kind, machinery, equipment, set, materials, requirements and imported or locally made means of transport significant for the establishment, operation, modernisation, reconstruction and expansion of a project. d- The judicial rights applied on the project with condition that these rights should be registered in pursuance of the rules of the law which is owned or authorised for the investor. e- The profits 'generated by the project including profits transferable abroad if used to complete the capital of the project or added or invested in any other project.

The investor means the person who invests his money in accordance with the rules of this act whether he is a Sudanese national or non-Sudanese.

The project means any economic activity established at the federal or state level and included the domains stipulated by this Act or any project that aims at rehabilitating,

reopening, expanding existing project and raising its production.

The public administration for promotion means the public administration in charge with the promotion of investment and which has been established in accordance with Article 22 The minister means the finance and economic development minister. - The authorised minister means any federal minister involved in any field of investment. The concerned minister means the finance and economic development minister in the respective state. Investment unit means any investment unit established in the states in compliance with Article 26 (1) and the investment directorates at the federal concerned ministries which were established in accordance with Article 29.

Chapter (2) Encouragement of Investment, Fields of Investment:

6-a: This Act encourages investment in the agricultural, animal, industrial, energy and mining, transport, tourism, storage, housing contracts, basic services, infrastructure, and economic services fields or any other field determined by the Council of Ministers. b- This act encourages investment initiative by the Sudanese and non-Sudanese private sector, co-operative, mixed, and public sectors. c- Regarding Clause (a), basic services include education, health, culture, and information services.

Goals of Investment Encouragement :

7-This act aims at encouraging investment in any of the fields provided for by Article (6), and expanding and modernizing the existing project with the objective of raising their productivity and exploiting its resources properly. The projects are that which realize one of the following: a- Efficiently contribute to increasing the national income, broadening the base of the national economy, diversifying aspects of the economic activities, and increasing the added values to the production. b- Realize food, housing, clothing, and medicine security. c- Boost infrastructure, water, energy, communications and land reclamation projects. d- Boost the country's export capability. e- Help realize self-sufficiency. f - Contribute to boosting rural development and developing traditional technology of the different sectors and small-scale industries. g - Provide services fundamental for boosting development plans and removing problems impeding the country's development process. h- Transfer and help apply modem technology adequate for the country. i- Attract savings of the Sudanese expatriates. J- Create investment opportunities utilize domestic resources and develop natural resources and provide hard currencies. k- Produce or help produce equipment and use the technologies of new and renewable energies instead of the traditional energy. I- Create work opportunities for the citizens and help promote technical, professional and administrative capabilities. m- Support environmental balance. n- Realize great social benefit. o- Create cooperation and integration among Islamic , Arab African and friendly nations.

Non-Segregation Between Projects :

8-1- For the purpose of this Act, the invested capital should not be segregated because of whether being local, Arab foreign or public, private, co-operative, mixed sectors.

2- Similar projects should not be excluded form privileges, facilities and guarantees.

Chapter (3)

PRIVILEGES, FACILITIES AND GUARANTEES SECTION ONE PRIVILEGES

TAXES & DUTIES EXEMPTIONS:

9-1- The authorized minister may grant the national, inter-state, foreign or mixed investment project the following privileges:

a- Exemption from taxes and any other duties entirely or partially put on the project by a federal decree during the term provided for by the paragraph (b) . b - Exemption from the profit taxes for a duration not exceeding five years begins from the first year that follows the start of the commercial production, resumption of the activity or a year after the operation of the reconstruction projects and that if any loss takes place during the exemption term, the loss is regarded as if it is occurring during the last year of the set term provided that the project shall not be exempted from the business profit tax except for the benefit for the national economy and not for the benefit of another state and that the minister at a recommendation by the authorized minister may prolong the term mentioned in this paragraph. c - Exemption no exceeding 70% of the consumption taxes or the determined customs duties or any tax or duty on the following imports: I- Machinery, equipment and sets. 2- Framework, ready made building, electricity generators and handling means of transport. 3 - Spare-parts, elementary and secondary production inputs. d- In During the tax exemption period mentioned in paragraph (b) taxes should be reduced to not more than 70% to include the following : I-Taxes and export fees on the manufactured and semi-manufactured commodities produced by the project. 2-Any tax or other duties to be put later on the project. 3-Consumption and production fees. e- Allocation of land for the project with approval of the concerned authorities at encouraging price. f- Accounting the depreciation of assets in accordance with the alternate values decided by the regulations and circles of work and operational age.

2- The concerned minister may grant the investment project established in the states the following facilities:

a- Exemption from taxes and duties which are completely or partially imposed by the state during the term provided for by clause (1), (B) and that the minister with the approval of the state government may prolong the taxes exemption terms for projects determined by the investment administration unit provided for by Article 29. b- Reduction during the tax exemption term stipulated by clause 1 (b) of: First- Local and state taxes and duties. Second- Any taxes or duties to be imposed later on the project. c- Assigning of the land required for the project at encouraging price in co-ordination with the concerned authorities.

3- The concerned minister, with the approval of the minister, may grant the privileges and exemptions stipulated by the clause (1), (b),(d). 4- Any state, province or a locality has no right to impose any tax or statal or local duties on any investment project at the federal level during the tax relief term stipulated by the paragraph (1), (b)

Preferential Privileges :

10-1- The authorised minister or the concerned minister with the minister's approval may offer preferencial privileges for projects characterized by any of the following:

a- Direct investment to underdeveloped areas. b- Realize food, housing clothing or medical security. e- Contribute in developing the country's export capabilities. d- Contribute in realizing integrated rural development. e- Boost equal distribution of wealth, incomes and create new work opportunities. f- Provide local alternatives for the country's basic imports. g- Depend on local raw materials. h- Operate in the mining field. i- Reinvest its profits.

2- For the purpose of clause (1), the privileges means any of the privileges provided for by article (9) regarding their magnitude, scope and period as determined by the rules.

ECONOMY AND COMMERCE SECTOR

SECTION (2) FACILITIES

Facilities Granting:

1 1 -The authorised minister or the concerned minister with the approval of the minister may offer the projects the following facilities:

a - Transfer profits and finance cost of the foreign capital or loans in the currency in which the capital and loans were brought in to begin from the date of liability after the settlement of the legal dues on the project. b - Assigning appropriate percentage of the exports revenues if the project operates in field of exportation to meet the provision of production inputs and settlement of dues. For the purpose of this clause, (assigning) means keeping part of the project's export revenues aside in special account for the use to meet the project's requirements with the approval of the minister. c- Allowing the project to export part of its production if it is producing for local marketing to settle its foreign dues and import its needs. d-Importation of raw material required by the project and export its products after having being registered to in the importers and exporters register. e - Transfer saving of foreign employees of the project in accordance with the prevailing laws. f - Guaranteeing freedom of movement of the persons employed by the project and their residence in accordance with prevailing laws. g - Facilitate employment of foreign experiences which are not available in the country in accordance with the prevailing laws. h- Allowing payment land value in installments.

SECTION (3) GUARANTEES

Guarantees against Nationalization, Confiscation and Expropriation :

12- The investor enjoys the following guarantees:

a- Guarantee against nationalization and confiscation. b - Guarantee against attachment, confiscation or freeze of the capital of his project, except in case of judicial warrant. c - Guarantee against expropriation of the project's real estates, except in case of public interest according to law and in return of a fair compensation on the bases of the market price of the estates at the time of payment of the compensation. d- Transference of the invested capital in case of non-implementation of the project in the currency in which it had been imported, provided that all legal obligations on it are met. And in case of the non-implementation of the project, machinery, equipment, means of transport, other supplies and petroleum products, which have been imported for the purpose of the project, may be re-exported after meeting all the said obligations. Protection of The Project's Products:

13-1- The project's products enjoy the following protections:

a - Increase the customs duties levied on the imported commodities competing the project's products or their alternatives. b - Impose restrictions entirely or partially on the importation of products competing the project's products. c - The duties levied on the products of the project whether they are customs duties or production taxes should equally be imposed on the competing imported commodities. d- Give preferential treatment to the project's products with regard to the government's purchases.

2- The minister should be responsible for offering protection with the approval of the authorised minister. 3- The protection provided for by clause (1) shall be adopted for projects which realise abundancy and high quality at a reasonable price in accordance with criteria set by the regulations.

CHAPTER (4) INVESTMENT REGULATIONS

Authorizing An Investment Project:

14-1- Notwithstanding the provisions of article (4), no one is allowed to establish a project in the Sudan or contribute in it unless he has obtained a license from the authorised minister or the concerned minister. 2- Notwithstanding the provisions of clause (1), the foreign investment licenses shall not be issued by the states. 3- Federal ministries are in charge with offering licences for foreign investment in accordance with the rules of this law. Presentation of Feasibility Study :

15- Any project shall not be licensed, granted any privileges, facilities or guarantees provided for by this Act unless a technical and economic feasibility study has been presented-

Application for Licencing, Privileges, and Facilities:

16- An application for licencing of any project or request for privileges and facilities which are provided for by this Act shall be submitted before the authorised minister or the concerned minister in a special form set for this purpose.

Licencing Procedures :

17-1- The authorised minister or the concerned minister shall decide on the licencing application within a duration not exceeding one month begins from the date of reception of application meeting the conditions. 2- Applicants have the right to complain to the Council of Ministers or the state government to decide the applicant's complain within a reasonable period beginning from the reception of the application.

Investment Maps :

18- Notwithstanding Article 8 (2) of the 12th Constitutional Decree, the General Administration for the Promotion of Investment shall prepare, in accordance with the polices and the directives of the National Council for Economic Planing, the national investment map provided that it includes specific proportion of the federal projects in the states and to be submitted to the Council of Ministers for approval and that the investment map should include sectors' investment maps which are prepared by the investment administration provided for by the Article 29. The Delivery of the Project's Land: 19- The concerned federal or statal authority shall hand over the land assigned for the project which is determined by the investment map within a duration not exceeding two months from date authorization.

Conditions of Validity of Authorization, Privileges and Facilities :

20-1- The investor shall not adopt any of the procedures below during the term of applicability of the license, privileges and granted facilities

according to rules of this act without obtaining a written approval from the minister with recommendation of the authorised minister of the concerned minister:

a- Ammending or changing the size of the project or the goal for which the license is awarded, or transferring the project from its location stipulated by the authorization to another place. b- Dispose of the project or its equipment, machinery, raw materials entirely or partially through either donation, selling or partnership. c- Using any of the equipment, machinery, resources and spare-parts for which the privileges and facilities are awarded for any other purpose. d- Changing the purpose of the land assigned for the project or selling, mortgaging or leasing it entirely or partially.

ECONOMY AND COMMERCE SECTOR

2 -The investor shall: a- Start executing his project within a duration not exceeding 12 month begining from the authorization date unless it is prolonged by the authorised minister or concerned minister. b- Submit a regular report every three months to the authorised minister or the concerned minister during the privileges and facilities validity term on the progress of the execution of the project up to the start of production and resumption of activity. c-Keep regular registering and records showing assets exempted from the customs duties and also the exempted imported materials. d- Submit a copy of the project annual accounts certified by an auditor during the validity of privileges and facilities term to the authorised minister or the concerned ministers.

The Investor's Infringement of the Provisions of this Act:

21-1- The investor is considered committing a violation of the provisions of this act if he:

a- Breaches provisions of Articles 14,20. b- Gives false or misleading information or uses illegal means for obtaining any kind of benefits for himself or other person according to the rules of this law. c- Halts the project without an adequate reason. d- Breaches the country's laws in a way that threatens its security and stability.

2- Notwithstanding any penalty stipulated by any law, the authorised minister or the concerned minister may, when the investor commits one of the contravention stipulated by Article (1) of this Act, inflict one of the following penalties according to the magnitude of the violation, the circumstances of its committing and the degree of the harm it causes to the national economy. The penalties include:

a- The investor shall be warned to remove the reasons of the contravention if it is possible within the duration he determines. h- Shortening the duration or reducing the magnitude of any privileges granted to the project. c- Ale depriving from any of the privileges, facilities and guarantees stipulated by the provisions of this law. d- Cancellation of license, privileges and facilities completely or partially a matter which leads to the expropriation of the land allocated for the project in accordance with this law and that the investor shall be obliged to return the values of the material benefit he gained consequent of obtaining any of the previous privileges or facilities if the gaining of the benefit is resulting from the reason which led to the issuance of the cancellation decision.

3- The investor against whom the decision is taken in accordance with clause (2) may complain to the Council of Ministers or the state government according to the circumstance within one month from the date of the issuance of the decision. Although the decision in this case is considered as a final judgement, it shall not prevent the investor from resorting to courts.

Chapter (5) Investment Organs

General Administration for Investment Pro-motion :

22-1- In compliance with the minister's decision, an administration called the General Administration for Investment Promotion' shall be formed under the chairmanship of a general Director aided by a group of members who are experienced in investment. 2- The headquarters of the General Administration for Investment Promotion shall be located in Khartoum State. 3- The General Administration shall be under the supervision of the minister.

23- The General Administration for Investment Promotion has the following powers:

a - Promotion of investment in the Republic of Sudan and briefing on its various fields and available investment projects. b - Collection of information from the federal and state ministries with the aim of providing them to the circles desiring to enter into investment domain.

CHAPTER

c- Study of laws, regulations , decisions and policies associated with the encouragement and improvement of investment atmosphere and making appropriate proposals in this regard. d- Promulgation of internal regulations. e- Any other powers entrusted to it by the minister.

Appointment of the General Director and his Powers:

24-1- The General Administration for Investment Promotion shall have a general Director appointed by the Council of Ministers at a recommendation from the minister. The decision shall also decide the general director's terms of service. 2- The general director's powers shall be determined by the regulations.

Powers of Federal Ministries :

25- The federal ministries concerned with investment are responsible for deciding investment priorities and policies and preparing sector's investment maps which are endorsed by the Council of Ministers, issuing licenses, and awarding exemptions and facilities in accordance with the rules of this law in the following fields:

a- Investment in national energy projects which includes oil, gas, and inter-state electricity. b- Major mining projects (iron, gold and strategic minerals). c- Military sector projects. d- Basic services, national economic and industrial projects, inter-state highways and telecommunications. e-Major, national and inter-state agricultural and irrigation projects provided for by the law. f- Projects executed according to international agreements.

Establishment and Supervision of Investment unit :

26-1- An investment unit shall be established in every state under the chairmanship of a general director along with a number of workers who are appointed by the concerned minister.

2- The investment unit shall be under the concerned minister's supervision. 3- Local resources assigned for the investment unit shall be determined by a decision issued by the concerned minister and that the unit shall submit an annual elaborate report on its financial and administrative performance.

Powers of the Investment Unit:

27- The investment unit shall have the following powers:

a- Promote investment in the state and explain its various fields in addition to the investment projects in the state. b- Collect information from the state ministries with the aim of providing them to the circles desiring to enter into investment projects. c- Studying of laws, regulations, decisions, and policies regarding encouragement of investment and improving its atmosphere and presentation of possible suggestions. d- Promulgation of internal regulations that arrange its meetings. e- Promulgation of any other regulations entrusted to it by the concerned minister.

Licencing of State Projects :

28-1- Notwithstanding the provisions of Article 14(2), the concerned minister has the authorities to license the state projects. 2- The state's investment projects are abided by Article (20) of this law.

Investment Administrations at the Federal Concerned Ministries An investment administration shall be established at any federal concerned ministry and that the unit's responsibilities shall be decided in pursuance of a decision by the concerned minister.

CHAPTER (6) FINAL PROVISIONS

Investment Dispute Settlement :

30-1- If any legal investment dispute arise, excluding disputes which are governed by the

provisions of agreements stipulated by Clause (2), it shall be submitted for reconciliation or arbitration and that the government shall be committed to provide all facilities required by the procedures. The provisions of the unified agreement on investment of the Arab capitals of 1980, the Investment Settlement Dispute Agreement among the Arab states of 1974, the Agreement on settlement of investment disputes between countries and national of other states for 1965, the General Agreement for Economic, Technical and Commercial Co-operation among the member states of the Organization of the Islamic Conference (OIC) of 1977 or any other agreement in this regard in which the Sudan is a member shall govern any dispute to arise directly from these agreements.

Power of Regulations Promulgation:

31-1- The Council of Ministers at a recommendation from the minister may issue regulations adequate for the execution of the rules of this law. Notwithstanding any of the above mentioned, the regulations may include the following:

a- Determine type and magnitude of the project which is granted preferential privileges. b- Set regulations for protection and linking it with production and banning of monopoly. c- Map out regulations to prevent contradiction in the Federal, State and Local investments. d- National Sectoral and inter-state projects. e- Procedures of license, privileges, and facilities application and determine its kind and magnitude. f- Determine services fees. g- Regulations and principles related to supervision and follow-up of the projects licenced in accordance to the rules of this law.

2- The concerned minister with investment unit's authorities in the State may issue the regulations adequate for the execution of the provisions of this Act.

PROVISIONAL DECREE THE TRADE (ORGANIZATION) ACT, 1994

In accordance with the provisions of Article 27 of the 5th. Constitutional Decree, The President of the Republic hereby makes the following Provisional Decree:-

CHAPTER IPRELIMINARY PROVISIONS

Title and commencement

1. This Provisional Decree may be cited as the, "Trade (Organization) Act, 1994", and shall come into force, as from the date of signature.

Repeal

2. The Goods Control Act, 1978 shall be repealed; provided that all the regulations and orders made under the provisions thereof shall remain in force, until revoked or amended, in accordance with the provisions of this Act.

Interpretation

3. In this Act, unless the context otherwise requires, : -
"Commodities", include all goods in which trade exchange is made;
"Concealment", means the possession of any commodity under such circumstances, as may warrant the existence of a reasonable doubt that the possessor or proprietor thereof refrains from selling the same to the public;
"Court", means the competent court under section 23;
"Governor", means the Governor of the state provided for in the 4th. Constitutional Decree, 1991;
"Minister", means the Minister of Industry and Trade;
"Ministry", means the Federal Ministry of Industry and Trade;
"Monopoly", means obtaining and control of a certain commodity, or commodities, with a view to control the prices and distribution thereof;

"National factories", mean such factories, as may produce commodities distributed at all the country level, and do not include such factories, as the production of which is consumed locally, at the level of the state, wherein the factory is established, or the neighboring state, to the exclusion of the rest of the country, as the Minister may specify, upon the approval of the Council of Ministers;
"Smuggling", means the transport of any commodity outside the Sudan, for the purpose of exportation, on the introduction of any commodity, for the purpose of importation, with intent to evade any prohibition, restriction, fees, taxes or customs, on the exportation or importation thereof, and the same includes attempt to smuggle, or any other act connected with smuggling;
"State's Minister", means the minister responsible for industry and trade in the state;
"State's Ministry", means the ministry responsible for industry and trade in the state,
"Supply commodities", mean such commodities, as the Minister may specify under section 4(1)(a) hereof;
"Under-Secretary", means the First Under-Secretary, at the Federal Ministry of Industry and Trade.

CHAPTER IIORGANIZATION OF INTERNAL TRADE

Powers of the Minister

4. (1) The Minister, by an order to be made thereby, may : -
(a) specify the national supply commodities, at the federal level, upon the approval of the Council of Ministers;
(b) specify the prices of the national supply commodities;
(c) constitute a consultative council, to tender advice and consultation, to the competent bodies, to lay down the policies of pricing, distribution, supervision of markets, the movement of commodities and the stability of prices;
(d) specify prices for commodities : -
(i) upon delivery ex the national factories;
(ii) which are imported;
(e) require any data, or information, on the national supply commodities, or the commodities produced in the national factories .
(2) There shall be effective every order made under the provisions of sub-section (1), forthwith the publication thereof, by any of the ordinary means of publication .

Powers of the state's minister

5. (1) A state's minister, upon the approval of the Governor, may by an order made thereby : -
(a) take the procedure and measures necessary for the flow of the national supply commodities provided for in section 4(1)(a), by removing any such state's administrative, or financial procedure, as may impede the movement of commodities, between his state and the other states ;
(b) declare the prices of the national supply commodities, in his state, after addition of the prices of transport and other reasonable costs, as the Minister may approve .

CHAPTER III POWERS OF THE MINISTER IN FOREIGN TRADE

Export and import general directives

6. The Minister may, by an order to be made thereby, issue general directives, and safeguards, for the export and import trade .

Export and import trade organized

7. The Minister may, by an order to be made thereby, organize the export and import trade, by any such means, as he may deem fit, and does not affect free competition and the freedom of trade movement .

Exports movement organized

8. The Minister may, by an order to be made thereby, organize the Sudanese exports movement, by the known export methods, in accordance with the economic policy of the State .

The exports movement general directives specified

9. The Minister, in consultation with the Sudanese Union of Chambers of Commerce, and the Sudanese Union of Industrial Chambers, may by an order to be made thereby, issue any directives or indicators, for the movement of exports, as to the minimum prices, or the manner in which exportation may be made, or the quantities, or quotas of any commodities prepared for exportation, wherever he may deem necessity therefor .

Sudanese commodities promoted in international markets

10. The Minister, in co-ordination with the Sudanese Union of Chambers of Commerce, the Sudanese Union of Industrial Chambers and the Sudanese diplomatic missions abroad, shall promote the Sudanese commodities, in the international markets, by the appropriate methods .

Borders trade organized

11. The Minister, in consultation with the Governor and the state's minister, may lay down such policies and rules, as may help to organize and facilitate the borders trade, between the state concerned and the foreign states neighbouring the same; provided that the state's minister shall implement such policies .

CHAPTER IV GENERAL DUTIES IN TRADE

Restrictions upon movement of commodities prohibited

12. No restriction shall be imposed upon the freedom of movement of commodities, between the states, or the commodities directed towards the exportation exits and ports, save upon permission from the Minister .

Smuggling

13. There shall be deemed to have committed the offence of smuggling whoever smuggles any commodity outside, or inside the Sudan, by taking any method, or means or both together .

Artificial decrease or increase of prices
14. (1) No exporter shall artificially increase, or decrease the prices of the commodities he exports .
(2) No importer shall artificially increase, or decrease the prices of the commodities he imports .

Monopoly of commodities prohibited
15. No person shall monopolize any of the commodities .

Concealment of commodities prohibited
16. No concealment of any national supply commodity shall be made by any such way, as may warrant the deduction, or presumption that the possessor, or proprietor thereof conceals the same, from the public or refrains from the sale thereof .

Documents and deeds
17. (1) Every importer and wholesale trader shall keep such documents and accounts, as may show the quantity, or the price in which he has purchased any commodity, the date of sale and the price in which he has sold. All the documents shall be kept for a period not less than three years .
(2) Every importer, producer or wholesale trader shall sell every commodity by such an invoice, as may show exactly the quantity of the commodity, the price in which he has sold and the date thereof .
(3) Every retailer shall sell every commodity by an invoice, where the purchaser requires the same .

Card placed upon offered commodities
18. Every retail trader shall place a card of the price of the offered national commodity, at such a conspicuous place, as the purchaser may see the same without difficulty .

Harbouring
19. No person shall cause the concealment of any evidence of the commission of any contravention of the provisions of this Act, the orders and regulations made thereunder knowing, or having reason to believe that the same has occurred, or delivers any such statements, as he may believe that they are not true, intending thereby to protect the offender from the legal penalty, or to prevent his arrest .

Chapter V
Penalties

20. (1) Without prejudice to any penalties in any other law, there shall be punished with imprisonment for a term, not exceeding five years, or with fine, or with both, whoever contravenes the provisions of this Act, the regulations or orders made thereunder .
(2) Whoever contravens the provisions of section 13, shall be punished with imprisonment for a term, not exceeding twenty years, or with fine, or with both, without prejudice to any penalties in other laws .
(3) In addition to any other penalties : -
(a) the court may, upon conviction under section 13, the regulations or orders made thereunder, confiscate any commodity with respect to which the contravention has been committed ;
(b) the court may confiscate any means of transport, used, by the knowledge of its proprietor, in committing any contravention of the provisions of this Act, the orders or regulations made thereunder ;

(c) the court shall, upon conviction under the provisions of sub-section (1), enter onto the trade register or the trade licence, such notation as may show such trial .

CHAPTER VITHE COMPETENT COURT

21. (1) The court, which is designated by the Chief Justice, shall have competence to consider the contraventions of the provisions of this Act, or the provisions of any orders or regulations made thereunder .
(2) The Chief Justice may grant the powers of the competent court, under sub-section (1), to any magistrate, a public servant or any such other person as he may deem fit .
(3) The Chief Justice may make such regulations, as may be necessary for organizing the business of such courts .

CHAPTER VII THE PROCEDURE

The procedure of information and trial

22. Notwithstanding the provisions of the Criminal Procedure, Act, 1991, there shall be followed, in the information and trial of contraventions of the provisions of this Act, the following procedure :-
(a) a complainant shall present his information, in writing, to the competent prosecution attorneys bureau ;
(b) saving the contraventions occurring against the provisions of section 13, trials shall be conducted by a summary way, unless the magistrate is of opinion that the procedure, in such information, will not be fair .

Power of arrest and search
23. Any policeman, who has a reasonable suspicion that commodities are concealed, in any place, may by an order issued by the competent prosecution attorney, enter such place, for the purpose of searching the same and discovery of such commodities, placing them under seizure and arrest any person in respect of whom there is a reasonable suspicion that he has committed a contravention of the provisions of this Act, or the provisions of any order or regulations made thereunder; provided that there shall apply, in the execution of the order, the provisions of the Criminal Procedure Act, 1991 .

Power to make regulations
24. (1) The Minister may make such regulations and orders, as may be necessary for the implementation of this Act.
(2) The state's minister, upon the approval of the Governor, may make such regulations and orders, as may be necessary for the implementation of the provisions of this Act, within the limits of his state .

The power of the Minister or the state's minister to delegate
25. (1) The Minister may, by an order to be made thereby , as to such terms, as he may specify, delegate all, or part of his powers, to the State Minister, the Under-Secretary, or any such other responsible person, as he may deem fit .
(2) The state's minister may, by an order to be made thereby, as to such terms, as he may specify, delegate all, or part of his powers, to the director of the state's ministry, or any such responsible person, as he may deem fit .

Made , under my hand, on the 4th. of Jumada I, 1415 A.H., being the 9th., of October, 1994 A.D.

Lieutenant General (P.S.C.)

Omar Hassan Ahmad Al-Basheir
President of The Republic of The Sudan

THE PETROLEUM WEALTH ACT, 1998

(Signed by the President of the Republic on 11.8.1998)

INTRODUCTION :

1. This Act provides the prescribed legal framework and regulates Exploration and production of oil and / or Gas accumulations in Sudan both onshore and offshore.

Major amendments have been introduced in the Wealth Act which give the Minister of Energy and Mining, with the approval of the Board of Petroleum Affairs, the right to conclude agreements for the exploration and production of oil and / or gas in the Sudan.

All the Agreements signed by the Sudan Government with the international oil companies are Exploration and Production Sharing Agreements (EPSA).The EPSA embodies the entire rights and obligations of the Government and the Oil Company.

The Oil Company, under the EPSA, recovers its operations cost from an agreed and negotiable percentage of the total production. The profit oil is divided between the Government and the Oil Company according to certain percentage to be agreed upon by both parties.

Equipment of the Oil Company used in petroleum operations are exempted ftom custom duties.

The oil discovered and exported by the Oil Company is exempted from any export taxes.

Exchange rights are provided for in the EPSA and the Oil Company is given the right to sell its share of oil and / or gas and keep the proceeds outside Sudan.

Hereunder is the text of the Sudanese Petroleum Act, 1998:

In the Name of Allah, the Gracious the Merciful

Provisional Decree

The Petroleum Wealth Act, 1998

In accordance with the provisions of Article 90(1), of the Constitution of the Republic of the Sudan, 1998, the President of the Republic hereby makes the following Provisional Decree :-

CHAPTER I PRELIMINARY PROVISIONS

Title and commencement

1. This Provisional Decree may be cited as the , " Petroleum Wealth Act, 1998", and shall come into force as from the date of signature .

Repeal and saving

2. (1) There shall be repealed :-

(a) the Petroleum Act, 1931;

(b) the Petroleum Resources Act, 1972 .

(2) In the Geological Research Public Corporation Act, 1986 :-

(a) in section 7 :-

(i) paragraphs (b), (c) and (h) shall be repealed;

(ii) in paragraphs (g), (l) and (m) the words, " petroleum", and "petrolic", wherever they may occur, shall be omitted;

(b) in section 12(a), the phrase, "and petroleum", shall be omitted .

(3) Notwithstanding the repeal, set out in subsections (1) and (2) , all the regulations, orders, measures and licences, made or issued under such laws, shall remain in force, subject to the competent body and licinsing authority, until amended, or revoked .

Interpretation

3. In this Act, unless the context otherwise requires, :-

" Consolidated profits

and losses account", means the final account of the Institution, its subsidiary companies and shares in such companies and other institutions, as to which it may subscribe, for each financial year ;

"Council", means the Petroleum Affairs Council, established in accordance with the provisions of section 14 ;

"Depot", means any place licensed for the storage of, or dealing in petroleum, and includes, in addition to tanks and storage sheds and the contents thereof, all the means of transport of petroleum and distribution stations;

"Development", means all the petroleum operations and activities, as to such work programmes and budgets, as may be approved in every agreement, and includes the following :-

(a) the drilling, plugging, sidetracking and completing and equipping of wells for the purpose of production;

(b) the design, construction, installing, operating, servicing and maintenance of equipment, pipelines, road networks and otherwise of infrastructure, water and electricity and otherwise of networks, facilities and plants necessary to produce from such wells, and take the petroleum, save, treat, handle, store, flare, transport and deliver the same for export ,

"Drilling", means boring the surface of the earth, whether the drilling may be vertical, inclined or horizontal, and includes such operations, as may by nature, prevent the bore from collapsing;

"Exploration", means all the operations of prospecting for petroleum, for the purposes of discovery of the same, and includes geological, geophysical, geochemical surveys and research, and aereal surveys and tests, and also drilling and exploration and delination of fields for petroleum ;

"Exploration area", means such tract, as may be covered by the exploration licence, the area of which is specified in the production sharing agreement ;

"Exploration licence", means such licence, as may be granted by the Institution, for prospecting for petroleum, in accordance with the provisions of this Act ;

"Institution", means the Sudanese Petroleum Institution, established under the provisions of section 18 ;

"Land", means :-

(a) any land, within the territorial borders of the Sudan, including such land, as may be submerged by water, permanently, or intermittently ;

(b) the Sudan's continental shelf, and such territory, as may be adjacent to the sea, to such a distance, inside the sea, and such depth and area, as may be specified by the law ;

"Minister", means the Minister of Energy and Mining ; "Petroleum", means :-

(a) all hydrocarbons, in the natural state thereof , whether liquid of all densities, or natural gas, or gaseous substances, associated with oils and products capable of being extracted from the ground ;

(b) asphalt substances and solid hydrocarbons, capable of being extracted directly , or by dissolution in oil, or in gas;

(c) all hydrocarbons derived from the substanses referred to in (a) and (b) ;

"Petroleum agreement", means the agreement concluded between the Institution and the companies, in accordance with the provisions of section 6 ;

"Petroleum area", means the area, upon which rights for exploration and production of petroleum are granted , under a petroleum agreement, which is shown by longitudes and latitudes ;

"Petroleum field", means such area of land, as in which the presence of petroleum has been proved, in one stratum or several strata, in economic quantities;

"Petroleum operations", mean the operations of exploration, drilling, exploitation, development, production, specification of fields, refining, manufacture, storage, transport, distribution, importation and exportation of petroleum ;

"Pipeline", means a pipeline used for the transport of hydrocarbons, by way of such pipes, as may be designed, as to such specifications, as the Institution may set up, or approve, and the same includes specification of the route thereof ;

"Production", means extraction of petroleum, from any field, and handling the extracted petroleum, treating and transport of the same to tanks, or pipes, or a refinery laboratory, in the field, or near it;

"Reserve", means such reserve, as may be measured and calculated, after drilling and development, or production of the petroleum fields , and contain such part, as may be capable of extraction, of hydrocarbons, in pursuance of such economic terms and technologies, as may be prevalent, upon calculation of the same ;

"Secretary-

General", means the Secretary-General of the Institution, appointed in accordance with the provisions of section 21 .

CHAPTER II OWNERSHIP AND EXPLORATION OF PETROLEUM AND SAFEGUARDS OF LICENSING

OWNERSHIP BY THE STATE OF PETROLEUM

4. (1) Petroleum, found in its natural state, in the strata of the earth, or the continental shelf of the Republic of the Sudan, shall be deemed to be a national wealth, owned by the State, and operated by the Federal Government , through the Institution .

(2) The Institution shall supply the Federal Government with the net share thereof, of the produced petroleum, as the production sharing agreements may specify, as a share of the State, after deduction of all the expenditure and commissions , and such as may be allocated by the Council to the Institution, in accordance with the provisions of section 24(f) hereof .

(3) No person shall conduct any exploration, research, prospecting or extraction of petroleum, or any other petroleum operations, in any place, in the Republic of the Sudan, unless he has been licensed therefor, in accordance with the provisions of this Act .

PETROLEUM AGREEMENT AND EXPLORATION LICENCE TO BECOME EFFECTIVE

5. No petroleum agreement, or exploration licence, which is concluded by the Minister with the companies, in accordance with the provisions of this Act, shall become effective, save after being approved by the Council .

CONDITIONS TO BE SATISFIED BY COMPANIES

6. There shall be satisfied, upon concluding any petroleum agreement, or granting an exploration licence, to companies, to companies subsidiary thereto, or holding companies, the following conditions in such companies, namely :-

(a) technical capability and sufficient experience, during the previous activity thereof, in petroleum industry ;

(b) the financial ability to execute the contractual obligation thereof ;

(c) abidance thereof, by the general policies of the State, prescribed in the field of petroleum ;

(d) registeration of a branch thereof, in the Sudan ;

(e) acceptance , and satisfaction of any other conditions, as may be prescribed by the Council, from time to time .

Exploration licence applied for

7. (1) There shall be presented, to the Minister, the application for obtaining the exploration licence, upon the form prescribed in accordance with the provisions of this Act, and the regulations made thereunder .

(2) An exploration licence confers, upon the holder thereof, during its validity, the right of exploration of petroleum, and execution of the necessary works, for the purposes of the licence in the exploration area .

(3) Notwithstanding the provisions of sub-section (2), an exploration licence shall not confer, upon the holder thereof any right as to :-

(a) utilizing petroleum, or striving to produce the same, in the exploration area, unless he has been licensed therefor ;

(b) drilling any well, for the purpose of production, in the exploration area, unless he has been licensed therefor, under a petroleum agreement .

COMPANIES TO BE BOUND TO CONTINUE EXPLORATORY OPERATIONS

8. No company, which has contracted, under a petroleum agreement , or been granted an exploration licence, shall keep the licence areas, without conducting therein continuous exploration works, unless the Minister grants it a temporary exception for reasonable grounds. In all cases, every petroleum agreement, or exploration licence shall contain a system and forms of relinquishment, in such a way that these companies shall not keep areas, save the productive fields areas, or such areas, as in which exploration may be conducted, or as wherein the companies are bound to execute an exploratory or development programme .

TERM OF VALIDITY OF THE PETROLEUM AGREEMENT

9. (1) The term of validity of the petroleum agreement shall not exceed, as a maximum, twenty five years, for the purposes of development and production; provided that such period shall include exploratory terms, at such stages, as may not, in total, exceed six years .

(2) The term of validity of the exploration licence shall not exceed, as a maximum, three years, and shall be subject to renewal once only, for the same term .

(3) Notwithstanding the provisions of sub-section (2) , where the licencee satisfies all his obligations, in accordance with the terms of the licence, the Minister may, upon the application of the licencee and recommendation of the Secretary- General, extend the term of validity of the licence, for a term not exceeding two years, to complement any additional exploratory operations

PIPELINE

10. (1) No company contracting with the Institution shall establish, or operate a pipeline or transport, store and export of petroleum facilities, save after obtaining the approval by the Minister, of the same, as to such terms, as may be prescribed .

(2) All contracting companies, which have an excess capacity of transport of petroleum, by pipeline, or any other means, shall place under the disposal of the Institution , the excess capacity, and the Institution shall be entitled to dispose of the same, in such manner, as it may deem appropriate .

(3) All contracting companies, which have petroleum, which cannot be transported by pipeline, or any other means, shall place, under the disposal of the Institution, such petroleum , and the Institution shall be entitled to transport , or dispose of the same, in such manner, as it may deem appropriate .

EXCHANGE CONTROL

11. The companies contracting with the Institution shall be subject to the exchange law, and such regulations, orders and circulars, as may be made by the Bank of Sudan, for the management of foreign exchange resources, subject to the following :-

(a) the contracting company shall be entitled to keep abroad such amounts, as it may obtain out of the share thereof, in the proceeds of petroleum exports, in accordance with the petroleum agreement concluded thereby ; provided that it shall provide the information relating thereto, to the Bank of Sudan, through the Institution ;

(b) the contacting company shall have the freedom to procure hard currency, to perform the business and execute the obligations thereof, in accordance with the petroleum agreement concluded therewith ;

(c) the contracting company may obtain Sudanese currency , and keep the same, to execute the contractual obligations thereof, by way of sale of foreign currency , according to the prevalent rates, and through the official channels;

(d) the contracting company may repatriate, outside the Sudan, such amounts, as may exceed the requirements of the business thereof, in accordance with the petroleum agreement concluded therewith; provided that repatriation shall be made in the same currency, in which such amounts have been procured, or any such other currency, as may be capable of being transmitted, after conducting the auditing by the Institution ;

(e) the contracting companies shall register, with the Bank of Sudanthe capital thereof, in kind and in cash, in addition to such loans, as they may have obtained, for the execution of the contractual obligations thereof .

TECHNICAL DATA AND INFORMATION

12. The contracting company shall keep, inside the Sudan, the origin of all the data, information, analysis and samples, resulting from the petroleum operations conducted thereby, in the Sudan, and shall not export the same abroad, or dispose thereof in any other way, save after obtaining a prior written permit, from the Secretary-General ; provided that they shall be returned, in the original condition thereof, to the Sudan, once more, in case of exporting the same .

OBLIGATIONS OF THE CONTRACTING COMPANIES

13. (1) The contracting company shall be bound, in all the petroleum operations thereof, to follow such technical principles, as may be prevalent, in the petroleum industry, in accordance with the provisions of this Act, and the regulations made thereunder .

(2) No Contracting company shall conduct any work, in the lands, utilized as public utilities, or privately owned, save after obtaining a prior permit from the Secretary-General, in co-ordination with the competent authorities .

(3) The Contracting company shall conduct such prospecting , drilling or any other operation, as may affect public utilities, permanent buildings or any existing establishments, save after obtaining the approval of the Secretary-General .

(4) The contracting companies shall give due regard to environmental health, safety measures and take such measures, as may be necessary for prevention of pollution of the environment, as a result of performing any of the petroleum operations, in implementation of the agreements concluded therewith .

(5) The contracting companies shall be subject to such restrictions, as may be imposed by the State, upon production, exportation and internal distribution of petroleum .

CHAPTER III PETROLEUM ORGANS

BRANCH I THE PETROLEUM AFFAIRS COUNCIL

Establishment and constitution of the Council

14. (1) There shall be established a council , to be known as the, “Petroleum Affairs Council”, to assume the responsibility of petroleum, and all petroleum operations, and lay down the policy and directives relating to petroleum, and the Institution, and supervise the same .

(2) The Council shall be constituted, as follows :-

(a) the President of the Republic, Chairman ;

(b) the Minister of Energy and Mining, member and deputy Chairman;

(c) the Minister of Finance and National Economy, member ;

(d) the Minister of Investment and International Co-operation, member ;

(e) the Minister of Justice, member ;

(f) six members of competence, experience and interest n the petroleum affairs, to be appointed by the President of the Republic .

(3) The Secretary-General shall be the rapporteur of the Council .

FUNCTIONS AND POWERS OF THE COUNCIL

15. (1) The Council shall have the following functions and powers, to :-

(a) specify objects, lay down policies and approve the petroleum general plans and programmes;

(b) approve the budget of the Institution, and the consolidated profits and losses account, and final account thereof , for every financial year, and approve the profits transferred to the Government, and specify the reserve funds;

(c) approve petroleum contracts with companies,

(d) approve such plans, as the Institution may lay down, for the enhancement and development of the ways and methods of the work thereof ;

(e) grant customs exemptions, for the petroleum industry inputs, in accordance with the provisions of the concluded agreements ;

(f) grant tax exemptions, in accordance with the provisions of the concluded agreements;

(g) obtain periodical reports, on the progress of work, in the Institution, and may request any other reports;

(h) approve internal regulations, for the organization of the business and procedure of meetings thereof .

(2) The Council may delegate any of the powers thereof , as to such terms and safeguards, as they may deem appropriate .

MEETINGS OF THE COUNCIL

16. (1) The Council shall convene periodically once, at least, every three months, and may convene in an emeregent meeting, upon call by the Chairman thereof .

(2) Quorum for any meeting shall be constituted by the presence of six members; on condition that there shall be among them the Chairman and his deputy .

(3) Decisions shall be adopted by the majority of votes of the present members; and in case of equality of votes, the Chairman shall have a casting vote .

DISCLOSURE OF INTEREST

17. Every member of the Council, who has a direct, or indirect interest, in a matter submitted before the Council for consideration, shall disclose, to the Council, the nature of such interest, as may connect him with such matter; and he shall not participate in any deliberation, or decision taken by the Council, with respect to that matter .

BRANCH II THE INSTITUTION

ESTABLISHMENT, QUARTERS AND SUPERVISION OF THE INSTITUTION

18. (1) Notwithstanding the provisions of the Public Institutions Act, 1996, there shall be established a public institution, to be known as the , "Sudanese Petroleum Institution", and shall have an independent corporate personality .

(2) The headquarters of the Institution shall be in Khartoum, and it may, upon the approval of the Minister, establish branches, or offices, inside and outside the Sudan .

(3) The Institution shall be subject to the supervision of the Minister .

OBJECTS AND POWERS OF THE INSTITUTION

19. (1) Within the framework of such objects, plans and policies, as may be prescribed by the Council, the Institution shall have the following objects and powers, to :-

(a) develop petroleum wealth, and better the utilization thereof ;

(b) manage all the petroleum operations, in the country, control and supervise such operations, and shall be the sole concessionaire, in all petroleum operations ;

(c) be responsible for the provision of the requirements of the country of the various petroleum substances ;

(d) conduct, inside and outside the Sudan, the exploration, prospecting and production of petroleum, either by itself, through the companies owned thereby, or in participation with others ;

(e) distill and refine petroleum ;

(f) market and distribute petroleum substances, and the products thereof ;

(g) lay down pipelines, and establish storage depots and other petroleum establishments, and operate and maintain the same ;

(h) transport petroleum and the derivatives thereof, and market the same, inside and outside the Sudan, and perform all such operations, as may be necessary for achieving this object ;

(i) lay down specifications of petroleum products, revise, approve and control the quality of the same ;

(j) follow the best way to conserve the petroleum wealth;

(k) control all petroleum operations, and the persons conducting such operations, in such a way as may achieve the objects of this Act;

(l) lay down such programmes, as may be necessary for training and qualifying cadres, in order to execute the work, in the petroleum industry, and petroleum operations, either by itself, or in participation with any other body having competence ;

(m) establish, own , operate and maintain petroleum ports, in order to use the same for the purposes of exporting petroleum products, in co-ordination and agreement with the bodies having competence ;

(n) conduct research, and studies, for all petroleum operations;

(o) construct such estates, factories and establishments, as may be necessary for performing the duties thereof, and acquire and invest the same ;

(p) borrow funds, from any body inside and outside the Sudan, or lend the same, for the performance of the business, and financing the projects thereof, in pursuance of such terms, as may be laid down by the Minister, in consultation with the Bank of Sudan, and approved by the Council ;

(q) establish subsidiary companies, and acquire shares in any existing company ;

(r) conclude contracts and enter in any obligations, inside and outside the Sudan, for the performance of the business thereof ;

(s) conclude petroleum agreements, and grant exploration licences, as to such policies, as may be approved by the Council , and be responsible for follow-up of the implementation thereof ;

(f) any such other functions, as may be necessary for the performance of the business thereof .

(2) The Institution may license any body technically and financially capable, to practise any of the objects set out in subsection (1), wherever necessity requires the same .

Functions of the Minister

20. (1) The Minister shall be responsible for follow-up of implementing the general policies, laid down by the Council , and shall have competence to supervise the management of the Institution, and take such measures, as may be necessary to enable it, to achieve the objects thereof , upon sound technical and commercial bases .

(2) Without prejudice to the generality of the provisions of subsection (1), the Minister shall have competence, as to the following, to :-

(a) follow-up the implementation, by the Institution, of such policies, as may be prescribed by the Council, and ascertain that it exercises the functions and powers thereof, upon sound technical, commercial and economic bases;

(b) supervise the procedure and terms of inviting national and foreign petroleum companies, to participate in negotiations with the Institution, concerning concluding the production sharing agreements, or obtaining exploration licences;

(c) specify such total area, as may be allocated, to each company, or group of companies ;

(d) specify the ceilings of production of petroleum, and export policies ;

(e) approve the plans of the Institution, for the development of petroleum industry , in the various fields ;

(f) specify the pricing policies of exported and imported petroleum, and the derivatives thereof, in consultation with the Minister of Finance and National Economy;

(g) sign petroleum agreements and exploration licences, on behalf of the Institution, after approval thereof, by the Council;

(h) represent the Institution, in the international organizations;

(i) sign international agreements, in the field of petroleum, after approval of the Council ;

(j) submit the proposed organizational chart, and terms of service of the employees of the Institution, to the Council , to approve the same ;

(k) submit draft administrative and financial regulations, to the Council, to approve the same ;

(l) supervise the companies owned by the State, which work in the petroleum sector, and issue general directions relating to the policies and work plans thereof, and such companies shall abide by such directions;

(m) approve opening of accounts, in banks, in local and foreign currency, inside and outside the Sudan, in consultation with the Bank of Sudan ;

(n) appoint employees of the Institution, upon the recommendation of the Secretary-General, in accordance with the regulations of the Institution .

(3) The Minister may delegate any of his powers, set out in sub-section (2) , to the Secretary-General, or any other person, as to such terms and safeguards, as he may deem appropriate .

APPOINTMENT AND FUNCTIONS OF THE SECRETARY-GENERAL

21. (1) The Institution shall have a secretary-general, from persons of appropriate qualification and experience, to be appointed by the Minister, after approval of the Council .

(2) The Secretary-General shall be the first executive official, responsible, to the Minister, for the management of the Institution, in accordance with the policy and directions of the Council, and such policies and decisions, as may be issued by the Minister . In particular he shall be responsible for the good management of the funds and property, and support the organs thereof . Without prejudice to the generality of the foregoing, the Secretary-General shall have the following functions, to :-

(a) lay down the detailed programmes and plans for the development and promotion of the Institution, and submit the same to the Minister, for approval , and supervise the implementation thereof ;

(b) take any such measures, as he may deem necessary for the management, organization and daily operation of the Institution ;

(c) supervise all administrations of the Institution, and ascertain the accuracy and enhancement of performance, and co-ordinate between the various administrations, in such a way, as may achieve harmony in performance ;

(d) prepare the estimates of the annual budget and the development budget, and submit the same to the Minister ;

(e) spend the funds allocated for operation expenditure, in accordance with the approved budget;

(f) carry out the approved construction works;

(g) represent the Institution, and speak in its name, before legal bodies, and other bodies having a relation thereto, inside and outside the Sudan, and sign the contracts, otherwise than petroleum agreements and exploration licences ;

(h) prapare such recommendations, as may be relating to the terms of service of employees of the Institution, and submit the same to the Minister ;

(I) propose the organizational charter of the Institution, and submit the same, to the Minister ;

(j) any such other business, as may be necessary for the exercise thereby, of his functions .

(3) The Secretary-General shall not make any material alterations, in the organs of the Institution, without the approval of the Minister .

(4) The Secretary-General may delegate any of the functions, or powers thereof , to any of his assistants, as to such terms and safeguard , as he may deem appropriate .

Secrecy to be abided by

22. Members of the Council and all employees of the Institution shall abide by honesty, in all such confidential matters , as may be related to the Institution, in accordance with the regulations, decisions and rules .

CHAPTER IV FINANCIAL PROVISIONS

VESTING OF PROPERTY

23. (1) There shall vest, in the Institution, such immovable and movable assets pertaining to petroleum, as may be allocated thereto by the Council of Ministers . Without prejudice to the generality of the foregoing, the following shall vest in the institution :-

(a) all such apparatuses, laboratories and any other things, as may be owned by the State and have connection with petroleum, as may be prescribed by the Council of Ministers ;

(b) all such exploitation and extraction of Sudanese petroleum projects, as may be owned by the State ;

(c) shares of the Government, in such existing companies, as the vesting of which , in the Institution, may be prescribed by the Council of Ministers .

(2) Such property, rights, debts and obligations, as may vest in the Institution, under the provisions of sub-section (1) , shall be assessed, and there shall be entered, into the records thereof, an amount equal to the net value of the same .

FINANCIAL RESOURCES OF THE INSTITUTION

24. The financial resources of the Institution shall consist of :-

(a) such amount, as may be entered into the records thereof, in accordance with the provisions of section 23 ;

(b) such shares and dividends, as the Institution may subscribe with, to the companies owned totally, or partially thereby ;

(c) such net profits of the business thereof, and the net profits of the business of companies subsidiary thereto, or to which it subscribes, as may return to the same ;

(d) such as may return thereto, from the investment of the funds thereof ;

(e) such funds, as it may borrow ;

(f) such funds as may be allocated thereto by the Council ;

(g) such fees, rent of land, gifts and gratuities (bonuses), as may vest therein, from the exploration and production of petroleum agreements .

USE OF THE FINANCIAL RESOURCES OF THE INSTITUTION

25. (1) The financial resources of the Institution shall only be used to achieve the objects thereof .

(2) Without prejudice to the generality of the provisions of sub-section (1), the resources of the Institution shall be used in the following :-

(a) management and performance of the business of the Institution;

(b) payment of the financial obligations of the Institution ;

(c) expenditure, on all the operation expenses of the Institution, including the appropriation of an appropriate allocation for depreciation and renewal ;

(d) payment of the capital of such companies, as it may subscribe, for the establishment thereof and subscription in such companies, as it may contribute to the same ;

(e) payment of salaries, allowances, remuneration and post-service benefits of employees of the Institution, and the remuneration of members of the Council .

CHAPTER V MISCELLANEOUS PROVISIONS

Customs exemption

26. (1) Such companies, as may be a party to a petroleum agreement, or whoever they may employ of contractors and engineers, may import, upon the approval of the Council, in accordance with the provisions of the concluded petroleum agreements, with total or partial exemption, from customs duties :-

(a) such apparatuses, machinery and other materials, as may be specified for use in petroleum operations, upon a recommendation from the Institution ;

(b) such goods and commodities, as decisions from the Minister, upon a recommendation therefor, by the Institution, may be issued from time, to time, in accordance with the provisions of section 15(1)(e) hereof .

(2) The provisions of sub-section (1) shall not apply to such commodities and things, as may be purchased from the local market .

(3) Such apparatuses, machinery and equipment, as may be specified for petroleum operations, the goods and other things shall be subject to customs duties, in accordance with the provisions of the Customs Act, 1986, on the sale thereof, in the Sudan, upon the approval of the Institution . Every person, to whom the Institution has approved the sale of any of the things, mentioned in sub-section (1) , shall present, to the customs authorities, before sale or transfer of ownership, a declaration thereby , after obtaining the approval of the Institution, and pay, upon request, such import duties, as the customs authorities may assess, unless the sale or transfer of ownership is made to such other companies, as may be contracting with the Institution, and enjoy such exemptions .

(4) The petroleum and all types of its derivatives and such imported goods and things, as may be specified in sub-section (1), may be exported abroad, without export duties .

(5) The Institution shall , upon approval of the Council, be exempted from taxes and customs duties, with respect to such imported machinery, apparatuses , equipment, materials, cars and tools, as mabe necessary for the projects thereof, in the field of petroleum operations .

Companies owned by the Institution

27. Such companies, as may be totally owned by the Institution, subscribed or contributed to thereby, and working in the field of petroleum, shall be deemed as contracting companies, with respect to implementation of the provisions of this Act, in relation to similar activities .

Accounts and books of contracting companies and auditing

28. (1) The contracting company shall keep all the commercial and accountancy books and records, within the Sudan ; provided that they shall be subject, in the keeping thereof, to such accountancy system, as may be compatible with the general principles of accountancy internationally known in the petroleum industry .

(2) The accounts and records of contracting companies shall be audited by the Institution, for the purposes of applying the provisions of division of production agreements .

Account and books of the Institution and auditing

29. (1) The Institution shall notify the Council, through the Minister, upon opening accounts with banks, in accordance with the provisions of the Act .

(2) The Institution shall keep proper and comprehensive accounts of the revenues and expenditure, in accordance with sound accountancy bases .

(3) The budget of the Institution shall be prepared, upon sound accountany bases, and be submitted, together with the development budget, to the Council, for approval thereof .

(4) The Institution shall keep a general reserve fund, to be fed, from time to time, upon approval of the Council, out of the surplus of resources of the Institution .

(5) The Institution shall keep a proper register of immovable and movable assets, and such register shall annually be audited .

AUDITING

30. The Auditor-General , or any such other chartered auditor, as may be approved by the Auditor-General, under his supervision, shall annually audit the accounts of the Institution .

EMPLOYEES OF THE INSTITUTION TO CONTINUE

31. The employees in the petroleum sector, at the Ministry of Energy and Mining, shall continue in service, and be assimilated into the Institution, as the charter of posts thereof may avail, in accordance with the new job description .

PROVISIONS OF THE ACT TO PREVAIL

32. The provisions of this Act shall, in case of inconsistency with the provisions of any other law, prevail to the extent of removing such inconsistency .

OFFENCES AND PENALTIES

33. (1) There shall be deemed, to have committed an offence, every person, who :-

(a) conducts exploration, or prospecting for petroleum, without having a valid exploration licence, issued under the provisions of this Act, and shall be punished with imprisonment, for a term, not exceeding five years, or with fine, or with both. In case of the continued commission of the offence, he shall be punished with an additional fine for each day, in which the offence continues;

(b) produces or attempts to produce petroleum, without having a petroleum agreement, made under the provisions of this Act, and shall be punished with imprisonment, for term, not exceeding seven years, or with fine, or with both. In case of the continued commission of the offence, he shall be punished with an additional fine, for each day in which the offence continues ;

(c) practises any petroleum works, outside the licence area, thereby contravening the provisions .

(2) Any things obtained by the person, as a result of commission thereby, of an offence, under the provisions of paragraphs (a) and (b) of sub-section (1) shall be the property of the State, and it shall be entitled to restitute such things, or the value thereof, and the profits derived therefrom .

(3) Without prejudice to the provisions of sub-sections (1) and (2), or any such severer penalties, as may be provided for in any other law, whoever contravenes the provisions set out in Chapter II, hereof, and the regulations made thereunder shall be pnished with fine .

POWER OF THE INSTITUTION TO ISSUE DIRECTIONS TO RECTIFY CONDITIONS

34. Where the Institution deems that there is squandering of the petroleum resources, or there is such work, as may endanger the lives, or property of people, as a result of the current petroleum operations, the Institution shall notify those carrying out the same, to rectify the conditions, and reform the damage, within such reasonable period, as it may specify. Where such direction does not find any response from those carrying out the same, it shall be entitled to take the legal proceedings, concerning such contraventions, before the competent courts.

POWER TO MAKE REGULATIONS

35. (1) The Council shall approve such regulations, as may be necessary for the implementation of the provisions of this Act.

(2) Without prejudice to the generality of the provisions of sub-section (1), there may be provided, in such regulations, for the following matters :-

(a) the administrative, financial and technical rules relating to petroleum operations;

(b) the rules relating to exercise of the rights granted, under exploration licences, and contracts of lease;

(c) the manner of collecting such fees, royalties, taxes and percentages, pertaining to the Institution, as may be paid by the contracting company;

(d) the bases organizing the operations of transport of petroleum and gas, use of pipelines, and the rules and procedure of licensing the establishment of such lines, and the export and storage facilities, and the uses thereof;

(e) such rules and specifications, as may organize the operations of storage and distribution of petroleum products, and gas;

(f) the financial, administrative and technical rules relating to the petroleum industry and the rules of financial, administrative and techncal control of the contracting companies;

(g) the establishment and organization of specialized administrations of the Institution, within the organizational chart;

(h) organizing the relation with the companies owned by the Institution, and those in which it subscribes, subject to such laws in force, as may govern this field;

(i) organizing the technical information and records and the manner of preparing, keeping and storing the same;

(j) forming specialized technical committees, and specifying the functions thereof;

(k) the form and manner, in which the accounts and budget of the Institution are to be prepared, and the organization of stores and rules of purchase and contracting;

(l) guarantees of security and safety and preserving the Institution and petroleum operations;

(m) the terms of service of employees of the Institution .

Made, under my hand, on the 18th. of Rabie II, 1419 A.H., being the 11th. of August, 1998 A.D.

(Signed)

Lieutenant, General P.S.C. Omar Hassan Ahmed Al-Basheir - The President of the Republic

INVESTMENT REGULATIONS

1. These Regulations may be cited as the, " Investment Encouragement Regulations, 2000 " amended2003 , and shall come into force, as from the date of signature.

Revocation and saving

2. The Investment Encouragement Regulations, 1990 shall be revoked; provided that all the licences and measures, taken there under, shall remain in force, until revoked, or amended .

Interpretation

3. In these Regulations, :-

(a) the words and phrases, set out therein, and interpreted in the Investment Encouragement Act,1999 , shall have the same meanings assigned therein thereto ;

(b) unless the context otherwise requires, :-

"Act", means the Investment Encouragement Act,1999 ;

"Federal project", means every project, the site of the facilities of which extends for more than one state, a foreign investment, or joint with foreign parties, works under licences from foreign companies, or established, under a special agreement, with the Republic of the Sudan, or that the project is established on investment in the federal natural resources;

"State project", means, other than the federal project, such project, as the site of the facilities of which may be in the state, and works according to a licence granted, in accordance with the provisions of the Act, and these Regulations, in the state.

Objects of encouragement of investment

6. This Act targets encouragement of investment into such projects, as may achieve the objects of the development policy, and the investment initiatives, on the part of the Sudanese and non-Sudanese private sector, the co-operative, mixed and public sector. Without prejudice to the generality of the foregoing, it aims at encouragement of investment into the projects of any of the fields set out in section7 .

Fields of investment

7. This Act encourages investment, into the fields of agricultural, animal and industrial activities, energy and mining, transport, communication, tourism and environment, storage, housing, contracting, infrastructure, economic, administrative and consultative services, information technology, education, health, water and culture and information services and any such other field, as the Council of Ministers may specify.

Discrimination between projects prohibited

8.(1) For the purposes of this Act, no discrimination shall be made between invested money, by reason of its being local, Arab or alien, or by reason of its being public, private, co-operative or mixed sector.

(2) No discrimination shall be made between such similar projects, as may be specified by the regulations, with respect to granting privileges or guarantees.

Branch I

Strategic projects

9.(1) Investment, in the following fields, shall be deemed strategic investment, namely :-

(a) relating to infrastructure, roads, ports, electricity, dams, communications, energy, transport, contracting business, education, health and tourist and information technology services and water projects;

(b) relating to extraction of subterranean and deep seas wealth;

(c) agricultural, animal and industrial production;

(d) crossing more than one state;

(e) any such other fields, as the Council of Ministers may prescribe.

(2) The regulations shall specify the strategic projects in the fields provided for in sub-section (1).

Exemption from taxes

10.(1) Subject, to the provisions of section19 , and without affecting any privileges, as may have been granted to any of the investment projects, in accordance with such conditions and safeguards, as may be in use :-

(a) the strategic project, specified in the regulations, shall after its registration, in accordance with the organizing laws, enjoy exemption from the business profits tax for a period of ten years, the effect of which shall commence, as of the date of commercial production, or practice of activity;

(b) the Minister may grant the non-strategic project exemption from the business profits tax, for a period, not exceeding five years, the effect of which shall commence, as of the date of commencement of commercial production, or practice of activity .

(2) Notwithstanding the provisions of sub-section (1)(a), the Council of Ministers, upon a recommendation, from the Minister, may extend the exemption of strategic and non strategic projects, as to such conditions and safeguards, as the regulations may specify.

Exemption from customs duties

11.(1) Subject, to the provisions of section19 , each of such strategic and non-strategic projects, as may be spcified in the regulations, after registration thereof, in accordance with the laws organizing the same, shall enjoy such customs privileges, as the Council of Ministers may prescribe.

(2) Notwithstanding the provisions of sub-section (1), customs privileges shall, with respect to cars, salon cars, box cars and station wagons, be granted as the regulations may specify.

(3) The Council of Ministers may, upon the recommendation of the Minister, amend the prescribed customs privileges, as he may deem fit.

Project granted the privileges of allocation

of land and depreciation account

12. The Minister may grant such strategic and non-strategic projects, as may be specified in the regulations :-

(a) the land necessary for the strategic project free of charge, and at the encouragement price for the non-strategic project, in co-ordination with the bodies concerned, from such lands, as may have been planned by the competent bodies;

(b) the privilege of depreciation account of the assets, as to such renewal value, as may be specified by the regulations, and in accordance with the circuits of operation work;

(c) deeming any such loss, as may have occurred, during the period of exemption, provided for in sections10 , as if it is such loss, as may have occurred during the last year of such period.

Grant of privileges to State projects

13. The State Minister may grant such state project, as may be specified in the regulations, the following privileges :-

(a) total, or partial exemption, from such taxes and fees, as may be levied by a state, or local law, for a period not exceeding five years; provided that he may, upon the approval of the State Council of Ministers, extend such exemption for another similar period;

(b) any such other state taxes, or fees, as may subsequently be levied on the project;

(c) allocation of the land necessary for the state project, at the encouragement price , in co-ordination with the bodies concerned, from the lands allocated by the competent bodies.

State projects granted federal privileges

14.(1) The Minister, upon the recommendation of the State Minister, may grant a state project the privileges provided for in section11 .

(2) The State Minister, upon delegation by the Minister, may grant a state project the privileges, provided for in section11 , as to such conditions and safeguards, as the Minister may deem fit.

No taxes or fees levied on federal projects

15. No state, or locality shall levy any state, or local taxes, fees or rates, on any investment project federally licensed, during the period of the tax exemption, provided for in sections 10 and11 , save in consideration of such services, as may be of public nature, performed by the state, or the locality.

Preference privileges

16.(1) The Minister, upon the approval of the Minister of Finance, and in consultation with the Competent Minister may grant preference privileges to such projects, as may satisfy any of the following features :-

(a) direct investment towards the least developed areas;

(b) assist in the development of export capabilities of the country;

(c) contribute to achievement of integrated rural development;

(d) create great chances of work;

(e) strive to encourage charitable trust;

(f) strive to develop scientific and technological research;

(g) re-invest the profits thereof.

(2) For the purposes of sub-section (1), privileges mean any of the privileges provided for in section10 , or11 , with respect to the size, extent, or term thereof, as the regulations may specify.

Branch III

Guarantees

Investment guarantees

17.(1) An Investor shall enjoy the following guarantees :-

(a) the non-nationalization, or non-confiscation of his project, non- acquisition of all, or part of the estates of the project thereof, or his investments, for public interest, save by law and in consideration of just compensation;

(b) the non-attachment, non-confiscation, non-custody or non-sequestration of the property of his project;

(c) the re-remission of the invested money, in case of the non-execution of the project, at the outset, liquidation, or disposal of the same, in any of the ways of disposal totally, or partially, in the currency, in which it has been imported; on condition of satisfying all the obligations legally due thereon, and in the case of non- execution of the project, at the outset, machinery, equipment, apparatuses, means of conveyance and other requisites, which have been imported for the project, may be re-exported, whenever all the obligations, mentioned in this paragraph have been satisfied;

(d) the remission of the profits and the cost of financing for the foreign capital, or loans, in the currency in which the capital or loan has been imported, at the date of accrual, after payment of the obligations legally due on the project;

(e) the import of such raw materials, as the project may need, and the export of the products thereof, after the automatic registering , of the investment project, onto the Exporters and Importers Register.

(2) For the purposes of paragraph (c) of sub-section (1), the invested capital shall be specified in foreign currency ; and the elements of the capital in kind shall be evaluated by the customs authorities by the customs certificate of value (CCV) , or the import form (IM).

Privileges and guarantees of

the project protected

18. Notwithstanding the provisions of any other law, no administrative body shall refrain from implementing the Privileges and guarantees, granted under the provisions of this Act.

Investor licensed to establish a project

19.(1) Subject to the provisions of section4 , no person shall establish any project, in the Sudan, save after obtaining a licence therefor, from the Minister, or the State Minister, as the case may be, in accordance with the provisions of this Act.

(2) Subject to the provisions of sub-section (1) , no licence shall be granted, for mixed or foreign investments, by states, save after approval of the Minister.

Feasibility study of the project presented

20. No project shall be granted licence, nor shall it be granted any such privileges and guarantees, as may be set out in this Act, save after presenting a technical and economic feasibility study of the project.

Grant of licence and privileges requested

21. An application, for the grant of licence, for any project, or of any of the privileges provided for in this Act, shall be presented, on the prescribed form as follows :-

(a) strategic and non-strategic federal projects, to the Ministry;

(b) strategic and non-strategic state projects, to the State Minister.

Grant of licence

22.(1) The Ministry, or the State Ministry shall, upon receipt of a satisfied licence application, for any project, transfer the application to the federal Competent Minister, or the State Minister, as the case may be, within one week, to obtain the primary approval of establishing the project.

(2) The federal Competent Minister, or State Minister, as the case may be, shall determine the application for primary approval, and send the same, to the Ministry, or State Ministry, as the case may be, within seven days, of the date of receipt of such application.

(3) In case of not sending the primary approval, in the period provided for in sub-section (2), the Minister, or the State Minister, shall determine the application, after lapse of such period.

(4) In all cases, the Minister, or the State Minister, as the case may be, shall determine the licence application, within a period not exceeding thirty days , of the date of receipt of the satisfied application, from the Investor.

(5) Every applicant, for licence, shall be entitled to grievance, to the Federal, or State Council of Ministers, as the case may be, against the non-determination of his application, in accordance with the provisions of sub-section (1), to determine his grievance, within the period of one month, of the receipt of the satisfied grievance.

Land allocated for the project delivered

23. The Federal, or State Competent authority, shall deliver the land allocated for the project, within a maximum period of one month, of the date of granting the licence.

Conditions of the continued enjoyment

of the licence and privileges

24. No Investor shall take any of the following measures, during the period of validity of the licence and privileges, granted under the provisions of this Act, without obtaining a written approval , from the Minister, or the State Minister, as the case may be, the measures being to :-

(a) conduct any amendment, or alteration, of the size of the project, or the object for which the licence has been granted, or transfer the project, from the place thereof prescribed in the licence;

(b) use, or sell any of the equipment, machinery , apparatuses, materials or spare parts, with respect to which privileges have been granted, for any other purpose, other than the purpose, for which the licence has been granted;

(c) change the purpose of use of the land allocated for the project, sell, mortgage or hire the same totally, or partially.

Duties of the Investor

25. The Investor shall :-

(a) commence executing the project, within a maximum period of twelve months, of the date of receipt of the land, unless such period has been extended, on the part of the Minister, or the State Minister, for any such period, as he may deem fit;

(b) submit, to the Minister, the Competent Minister and the State Minister, periodical reports, every six months, during the period of validity of privileges, on the progress of the operation of executing the project, up to the date of commencement of production, or practice of activity;

(c) keep regular books, and maintain records, whereon shall be entered the assets of the project exempted from customs duties, and the exempted imported materials;

(d) present, to the Minister, the Competent Minister and the State Minister, annually, during the period of validity of the privileges, a copy of the annual accounts of the project, approved by a certified auditor;

The Investor contravening the

provisions of this Act

26.(1) An Investor shall be deemed to have committed a contravention of the provisions of this Act, where he :-

(a) contravenes the provisions of sections19 , 24 and25 ;

(b) delivers false, or misleading information , or uses such unlawful methods, as may result in obtaining any benefit, in accordance with the provisions of this Act, for himself, or any other person;

(c) suspends the project, without reasonable cause;

(d) contravenes the laws of the country, in such way, as may endanger the security and safety thereof.

(e) Contravenes licence condition.

(2) Without prejudice to any such penalty, as may be provided for in any other law, the Minister, or the State Minister, as the case may be, may in case of commission, by the Investor, of any of the contraventions, provided for in sub- section(1), impose any of the following sanctions, in accordance with the size of the contravention and the circumstances of commission thereof, and the extent of such damages, as may affect the national economy :-

(a) warning him, to remove the grounds of the contravention, if the same is required, within such period, as he may specify;

(b) decrease the period of any of the privileges granted to the project, or the size thereof;.

(c) not granting him any of the privileges and guarantees provided for in this Act;

(d) total, or partial revocation of the privileges, and the same shall result in binding the Investor to restitute the value of the material benefit gained thereby, from obtaining any previous privileges, where gaining such benefit results, from occurrence of the ground which led to the issue of the decision of revocation;

(e) revocation of the licence, and the same shall result in acquisition of the land granted to him under the provisions of this Act.

(3) An Investor in respect of whom a decision, under the provisions of sub-section (2), has been passed may submit his grievance, to the Federal, or State Council of Ministers, as the case may be, within one month, of the date of his being notified of the decision, and the decision, in this respect, shall be final; provided that this provision shall not prevent the Investor from access to courts.

The ministerial committee

27. The Council of Ministers, upon the recommendation of the Minister , may constitute a ministerial committee under the chairmanship of the Minister, and membership of the Minister of Finance and the Competent Minister, and the regulations shall specify the functions thereof.

Constitution of the committee

of commissioners

27A. The Minister shall constitute the committee of commissioners, from a chairman and a number of members, representing the competent bodies, having a relation to investment, from the ministries and competent government units; provided that the post of any of them shall not be less than the head of the unit, or whoever may deputize therefor, and shall fully be officially authorized, by the body which he represents, and the committee shall include representatives of the private sector.

Functions of the Committee

28.(1) The Committee of Commissioners shall have the following functions, to :-

(a) consider the extent of compatibility, by strategic projects, with the priorities of investment, in the strategic fields;

(b) consider the needs, by strategic projects, to infrastructure and basic services, needed by the project, and the extent of availability, or possibility of providing the same;

(c) consider the needs of the project, to manpower and the specialized one, procured from abroad, in accordance with the prevailing laws;

(d) achieve the sector investment plans, by the approved and proposed investment projects;

(e) co-ordinate, between the Ministry, and the Competent Ministries, and the states, in every such thing, as may concern investment projects, especially on the map of investment lands.

(2) The Committee may call any person, or body of competence, upon discussing any such subject, as may fall within the competence of such Committee, and he shall not be entitled to vote.

Functions of federal ministries

29. Federal ministries, having connection with investment, shall have competence, as to the following :-

(a) specify priorities, and lay down the investment policies, at their ministries;

(b) prepare sector investment maps;

(c) approve, on point of principle, the establishment of the project, upon such primary feasibility study, as may be transferred thereto, by the Ministry; provided that the final feasibility study of the project shall be presented to the Ministry ;

(d) follow-up the execution of the projects concerning the Competent Ministry, and submit periodical reports, as the Minister may require.

State Investment

30. An investment Act in the states shall be promulgated, by a state law, as to the form of Federal Investment Encouragement Act,1999 .

Among the efforts which aim at promoting foreign investment, the government has established free zones which include:

1 - Suakin Free Zone

2 - Aljaily Free Zone.

THE FREE ZONES AND FREE MARKETS LAW1994

This law represents the legislative framework for the establishment and operation of free zones and markets in Sudan. The rules resultant from this law represent the organizational framework for operating and managing free zones in Sudan.

Advantages of investment in free zones:

Industrial, commercial or service investments which are licensed to be established in the free zones enjoy the following advantages:

a- Exemption of the projects from profits tax for a period of 15 years, renewable for an extra period dependant on the decision made by the concerned minister commencing from the 1 year period of grace which follows the year of commencement of production.

b- Salaries of expatriates working in projects within the free zones will be exempted from the personal income tax

c- Exemption of products imported into the free zone or exported abroad from all customs fees and taxes except service fees and any other fee imposed by the board of the Sudan Free Zones Company.

d- Real estate establishment inside the free zones area are exempted from all taxes and fees

e- Invested capital and profits are transferable from Sudan to abroad through any bank licensed to operate in the free zone.

f- Exemption of products of industrial projects established in the free zones from customs fees; depending on materials used and local costs incurred in production, provided that the value be estimated by a committee assigned for this purpose by the board of the Sudanese Free Zones Company.

□ • **Guarantees (rule10)**

Money invested in the free zones may not be frozen, confiscated, or arrested

• **Transiting (rule15)**

With respect to agreements binding on the government of Sudan, goods transiting, waiting to be transferred to other countries may be stored in the free zones under the supervision of the customs police available at the inlets and outlets of the free zones.

• **Rent (rule16)**

The company has the right to rent its land and buildings according to the terms it agrees upon and without being bound by any other law

PROCEDURAL STEPS FOR INVESTMENT TRANSACTIONS :

APPLICATION FOR A NEW LICENSE

1 .Provide 2 copies of the technical and economic feasibility studies

2.A copy of the company registration and a certificate of establishment if the owner is a specified company

3.Fill in the form prepared for that purpose after paying an application fee of 15 , 800dinars (fifteen thousand eight hundred dinars)

4.Pay the application fee

5.The study is then transferred to the concerned ministry to obtain the technical agreement for establishment of the project

6.Issue a primary consent to the project

7.Register a name for the project with the Delegate Commercial Registrar in the Ministry of Investment

8.Issue a final license for the project acceding with followed rules

9.Please submit an agency agreement authorized by a lawyer if the project is to be supervised by someone other than the owner or in the case of companies

Application for Activity Change

Firstly: the conditions

1. the new activity must be an encouraged activity
2. no planning, environmental or health impediment should exist

Second: required documents

1. a copy of the license for the first activity
2. a copy of the business name
3. a valid ownership certificate or rental contract
4. application to the administration

Third: the procedures

1. payment of the application fees
2. the application is transferred to the specialized sector for analysis
3. after the consent is issued a new business name should be registered for the new activity at the Delegate Commercial Registrars department.
4. the license of the new activity is issued after payment of required legal fees

ADDITION OF A PRODUCTION LINE TO AN EXISTING PROJECT

First: the conditions

1. the main line must be readily executed and is working in an acceptable manner
2. the availability of a suitable area for the new line
3. the new should not oppose the old line in any technical or planning manner

Second: required documents

1. a copy of the license granted to the first line
2. a copy of the business name
3. an ownership certificate or rental contract

Third: procedures

1. payment of the application fees
2. obtain approval from the concerned technical party
3. transfer the application to the concerned sector for examination, issue consent and then transfer the consent to the Commercial Registrar to add a new line to the original business name
4. Issue a license or decision after payment of the required fees

TRANSFER OF OWNERSHIP

First: the conditions

1. execution of the project to a reasonable extent not less than60 % of the required structures
2. it is not possible to transfer empty land granted in accordance with the investment encouragement act

Second: required documents

1. submit a valid ownership certificate of the transferred project
2. a copy of the projects license
3. a copy of the business registration
4. a primary concession contract from a recognized legal body
5. an application to the ministry for acceptance of the concession

Third: procedures

1. payment of application fees
2. transfer of the application to the specialized sector for examination
3. a field visit to the project by the monitoring department and preparation of a report explaining the execution of the project
4. the application will be transferred to the ministry's legal consultant to ascertain the legality of the proceeding
5. consideration of the application in agreement or disagreement; incase of agreement the project is registered with the Delegate Commercial Registrar in the ministry
6. issue a final license to the owner and a new business name

FORMING OR ENDING A PARTNERSHIP

As long as the purpose of involving a new partner is fully executing the project then agreement to this will be issued after the following documents are submitted:

1. a copy of the business registration
2. a copy of the license
3. a valid ownership certificate
4. a partnership contract ratified by a legal body
5. an application to the administration requiring the transaction

MORTGAGING THE PROJECT FOR FINANCE

First: the conditions

1. the project must be executed to an extent allowing the mortgage of the buildings not the granted land
2. a letter from a bank clarifying the purpose of finance which must be for the operation or execution of the project

Second: required documents

1. a copy of the license
2. a copy of the business registration
3. a valid ownership certificate
4. a banks letter of finance

Third: procedures

1. payment of application fees
2. transfer the application to the concerned sector
3. a field visit is executed by the monitoring department and a report is prepared showing the extent of execution
4. the documents are revised by the ministry's legal counsel
5. consideration of the application and making the decision concerned

General rules

First: cars and other transport means are not allowed except after the capital equipment is imported

Second: the project is not granted a tax exemption for more than 10 years except after the project is proven a strategic one with a capital of 10 million dollars and a budget audited by a legal auditor

Third: capital equipment has become an automatic concession with 0 customs and does not need any exemption

Fourth: rehabilitating the industrial projects now enjoys a constant percentage for business profits which is10 % instead of30 %

IMPORTANT PRACTICAL INFORMATION FOR STARTING BUSINESS

COMPANY REGISTRATIONREGISTRATION

1	Submit application for preliminary approval to Registrar and reserve company name	3 days	SDG 120
2	Notarize memorandum and articles of association	2 days	SDG 350
3	Notify taxation chambers	1 day	SDG 55
4	Register with commercial registry	4 days	Stamp duty and other application/administrative fees (see comment)
5	Conduct site inspection	2 days	no charge
6	Apply for tax identification number	1-2 days	SDG 5
*7	Register for VAT	2 days (simultaneous with previous procedure)	no charge
8	Register with labor authorities	14 days	SDG 192
9	Enroll employees for social security	3-7 days	SDG .25
10	Make a company seal	2 days	SDG 40

* Takes place simultaneously with another procedure.

REGISTRATION REQUIREMENTS

Procedure 1.

Submit application for preliminary approval to Registrar and reserve company name

Time to complete:

3 days

Cost to complete:

SDG 120

Name of Agency:

Comment:

The application for the business name registration is filled stating the name of the owner/ owners whether a company or a natural person, and stating the nature of the Business Name. The memorandum and articles of association and three proposed names must be attached to the application. The application shall then be submitted to the business names registrar after attaching the required stamps, the Business Names Registrar will then study the application and make sure that there are no similar names and issue a Business Names Registration Certificate. The name approval and the preliminary approval for establishing a company must be granted in 3 days.

Procedure 2.

Notarize memorandum and articles of association

Time to complete:

2 days

Cost to complete:

SDG 350

Name of Agency:

Comment:

The memorandum and articles of association and Form C2, the declaration of compliance, must be notarized the preliminary approval at a lawyers' office. The notarized documents are then submitted to the registrar for final approval. Muslim companies must also obtain a Zakat clearance certificate before notarizing the documents at no cost.

Procedure 3.

Notify taxation chambers

Time to complete:

1 day

Cost to complete:

SDG 55

Name of Agency:

Comment:

Before applying for final approval and registration, the company must submit a preliminary approval to the Taxation Chamber with the memorandum and articles of association, which should be stamped by the Chamber in acknowledgement of the notification.

Procedure 4.

Register with commercial registry

Time to complete:

4 days

Cost to complete:

Stamp duty and other application/administrative fees (see comment)

Name of Agency:

Comment:

Fee schedule for stamp duties:
SDG 55 for workers' association stamp duty.
SDG 4 for lawyers' association stamp duty.
SDG 425 for registry fees (0.25% of the nominal Capital for registration fees).
SDG 28 Certificate stamp

Procedure 5.

Conduct site inspection

Time to complete:

2 days

Cost to complete:

no charge

Name of Agency:

Comment:

As of 2005, a Companies' Registry representative must visit the proposed place of business to confirm its existence. therefore, before delivering the certificate of incorporation, a registry representative may visit the registered office to confirm its existence. It is now also mandatory for the company to obtain and post a signboard outside its place of business.

Procedure 6.

Apply for tax identification number

Time to complete:

1-2 days

Cost to complete:

SDG 5

Name of Agency:

Comment:

The following documents are required to apply for a tax identification number:
- Shareholder information.
- Memorandum and articles of association (notarized).
- Certificate of incorporation (two copies).
- Completed registration forms.

Procedure 7.

Register for VAT

Time to complete:

2 days (simultaneous with previous procedure)

Cost to complete:

no charge

Name of Agency:

Comment:

The company registers for VAT in the same building but at a separate department. It is not mandatory to register at the same time.

Procedure 8.

Register with labor authorities

Time to complete:

14 days

Cost to complete:

SDG 192

Name of Agency:

Comment:

The company must deposit the basic work and penalties regulations with the competent labor office.

Procedure 9.

Enroll employees for social security

Time to complete:

3-7 days

Cost to complete:

SDG .25

Name of Agency:

Comment:

The company must resister itself before the Social Insurance Fund. the required documents for this procedure are:
- Copy of Company Certificate of Incorporation and Memorandum and Articles of Association.
- Completed registration form.

At the same time, the company registers its employees for the social Insurance, registration procedure is free of charge, and the required documents for this procedure are:
- List with employees names and salaries
- Completed registration form.

Procedure 10.

Make a company seal

Time to complete:

2 days

Cost to complete:

SDG 40

Name of Agency:

Comment:

The cost to make a company seal depends on the kind of material used. Costs vary and are as low as SDG 40.

DOING BUSINESS IN SUDAN

ANNUAL INDICATORS

	2003	2004	2005	2006	2007	2008	2009 (est)
GDP at market prices (US $ bn)	17.6	21.5	27.5	36.7	50.7		
Real GDP growth (%)	5.1	5.2	9	11.8	10.2	6.5	3

Consumer price inflation (%)	6.5	8.3	8.5	7.2	8	18	10
Population (mn)	33.6	34.5	37	39	40	40	40
GDP per capita US$ PPP	499	590	720	1,000	1,250	2,200	
Exports of goods fob (US$ bn)	2.57	3.77	4.82	5.96	8.88	11.67	
Imports of goods cif (US$ bn)	2.53	3.58	5.94	8.07	8.3	9.35	
Current-account balance (US$ bn)	-0.955	-0.871	-3.013	-5.109	-3.812	-2.1	
Reserves excl gold (US$ bn) year end	0.529	1.338	1.869	1.660	1.4		
Total external debt (US$ bn)	24.2	26.3	27.7	28.2	29	34	35
Exchange rate (av) Sudanese Pound: US$	2.6	2.6	2.4	2.2	2.05	2.20	2.40

Net international reserves in mid-2009 were less than one month of imports.

Main exports: Crude oil, sesame, livestock, cotton, gum arabic

Main imports: Machinery and Equipment, manufactures, transport equipment, chemicals, cereals

2008 GDP = Agriculture (31%, Industry 35%, Services 34%)

Sudan's main sources of imports in 2008 were China, India, Saudi Arabia, Egypt, Japan, France, Italy, UK.

Despite its substantial natural resources (including 200 million acres of arable land of which only a fifth is presently exploited) Sudan is still classified as a Least Developed Country (LDC).

Doing business with Sudan is exciting, rewarding and uncertain. Most major projects need some kind of financing (preferably concessional). However, we advise commercial prudence and Indian exporters and investors should stay in touch with the Embassy.

Exports should be ONLY against full advance payment or letters of credit confirmed by first class international banks.

The 2008 Corruption Perceptions Index of Transparency International ranks Sudan as one of the most corrupt countries in the world – 173/180 (at the same level as Afghanistan and below Zimbabwe) while the World Bank ranks Sudan at 151/155 countries in its 2008 "Ease of Doing Business" Report.

Notwithstanding the negative perceptions, we encourage Indian companies to explore commercial possibilities in Sudan.

As this country develops, there will be opportunities for Indian companies in railways, roads, automobiles, power generation, telecommunications, water treatment, human resource development, agriculture, pharmaceuticals and IT. Import demand is surging as reconstruction moves into high gear.

PATTERN OF BILATERAL TRADE

(In US$ million)

YEAR	INDIA'S EXPORTS	INDIA'S IMPORTS	TRADE BALANCE
1998	63.36	26.51	(+) 36.85
1999	63.81	5.46	(+) 57.44
2000	77.54	5.46	(+) 72.08
2001	87.72	9.24	(+) 78.48
2002	104.62	5.93	(+) 98.69
2003	115.96	33.17	(+) 82.79
2004	197.10	27.90	(+) 169.20
2005	317.84 (+61%)	30.77	(+) 287.07
2006	599.04	20.00	(+) 579.04
2007	546.50	16.43	(+) 530.07
2008	886	182.3	(+) 703.70
2009	624.50	194.78	(+) 429.72

The Mission's target for 2009 is a 50% increase in India's exports

To give a sustained focus to India-Sudan trade relations, the Mission's commercial policy since October 2005 is a non-exclusive ***five-plus-one*** *policy. The five priority sectors in which India can respond to Sudan's developmental requirements are infrastructure, agriculture, human resource development, information & communications technologies, and small & medium industries. The "plus-one" is commercially viable investment in the energy sector (oil, electricity, gas). To achieve this, the Embassy has a Target and Introduce Programme (TIP) from January 2006 under which one new Indian export is introduced into Sudan every semester.*

TARIFF AND NON-TARIFF ISSUES

In 1992, Sudan abolished most export and import licensing requirements. It has also eliminated most export taxes although some have been reintroduced from May 2009 (especially in raw materials) following the country's poor economic situation.

Importers must present an import declaration, commercial invoice certificate of origin, quarantine license (where necessary), Sudanese Standards and Metrology organization (SSMO) requirements or other documents for specific type of goods, and completion of bank formalities. Importers must pay the required duties, taxes and fees and receive an official release for the goods.

SETTING UP OF OFFICES/FIRMS/COMPANIES FOR TRADE AND MANUFACTURING PURPOSES

A request is made to the Union of Chambers of Commerce and the Ministry of Foreign Trade conveying the intent to establish offices or firms/companies, etc. There are no special rules for renting office spaces or residential accommodation or hiring of local staff.

WTO

Sudan applied to join the WTO in 1994 and had completed the basic fact-finding stage of negotiations but is unlikely to be given entry to WTO while US sanctions are in place.

FORMS OF DOING BUSINESS IN SUDAN

A business may be a sole trader, partnership, registered limited liability company (private or public), or branch in the Sudan of a foreign registered company. The significant advantage of forming a local company is limited liability status.

A company can have 100% foreign shareholding if it does not engage in commerce (import and export).**To trade, it must have majority Sudanese shareholding.**

Tax concessions under the Investment Encouragement Act are being phased out under IMF pressure.

FOREIGN EXCHANGE REGULATIONS

The draconian "Dealing in Foreign Exchange Control Act", 1979 (introduced when Sudan had no reserves) has given way to a system free of restrictions on payments and transfers for current international transactions. However, intensified US sanctions since 2007 inhibit dollar denominated transactions at present.

Visitors can bring in any amount of foreign currency. Private financial transfer firms such as UAE Exchange can presently remit up to US$ 3,000 per transaction.

In practice, repatriation of foreign capital and profits (dividends) requires the approval of the Central Bank and tax clearance certificates.

IMPORT REGULATIONS

The importer should be registered with the Ministry of Foreign Trade.

Permission may be granted for temporary import of machinery and plant without customs duty against a letter of guarantee to the Customs Department. At the time of re-export, the difference in value of the goods at the time of import and subsequent re-export is calculated and custom tariff levied.

Sudan is founding member of the 20 member COMESA (Common Market for Eastern and Southern Africa) and all imports from and exports to member countries are exempt from customs duties.

ENCOURAGEMENT OF INVESTMENT ACT 1999 (AMENDED IN 2001, 2002, 2003, 2006, 2008)

The Act provides for specific additional benefits to encourage investment and classifies investment into strategic and non-strategic. Significant features include:

- Ø 1-3 year profit tax holiday
- Ø No discrimination for being of local, Arab or foreign origin in the public or private sector
- Ø Level playing field for analogous projects in terms of privileges and guarantees
- Ø Permission to expatriate staff to remit their post-tax savings
- Ø Carry forward of losses incurred during the exemption period
- Ø Customs exemption for strategic projects
- Ø Land free (strategic projects) or at concessional rates (non-strategic projects)
- Ø Transfer of profits and the cost of finance in the currency of import
- Ø No need for a local partner

INVESTMENT GUARANTEES

In theory, there are several investment guarantees:

- Ø Real estate (property) shall not be nationalized, expropriated or confiscated
- Ø Moneys shall not be seized, impounded, frozen or sequestered
- Ø Invested funds are remittable
- Ø Profits and import costs arising from the invested capital are remittable
- Ø Machineries, equipments, instruments, transport means etc can be re-exported

A social insurance scheme requires contributions from both employees and employers. Expatriate staff, if they receive part or whole of their salaries in the country (irrespective of whether they enjoy tax exemption) are also subject to social insurance.

BANKING

While North Sudan conforms to shariat banking laws, the South follows conventional banking norms.

FREE ZONES

There are two free zones: Suakin on the Red Sea near Port Sudan and Garri near Khartoum. The 1994 Free Zones and Markets Act permits fill possession for foreign investors, exemption from income tax for non-nationals working in the free zones, tax exemption for companies, free capital and profits transfer, no restrictions on entry and residence visas.

PREFERRED SECTORS FOR PRIVATE INVESTMENT

a) Meat processing

b) Jam, juice and tomato-paste concentrates

c) River and rail transport

d) Food processing

e) Grain silos

f) Water bottling plants

g) Refrigerated warehouses

h) Gum Arabic cultivation

i) Poultry farming

j) Animal husbandry

k) River transport

l) Roads and bridges

m) Sugar

n) Meat and fish processing

o) Wood industries

p) Rice cultivation

q) Forest development

r) Apiculture

s) Telecom services

t) Hotels and resorts

u) Airports

TAXATION

Sudan has direct and indirect taxation. The direct tax system comprises personal income tax, business profit tax, land tax, and capital gains tax. Indirect taxation includes value added tax, development tax and customs duties.

The Government of Sudan has double taxation avoidance agreements with various countries including India.

SOUTH SUDAN

The semi-autonomous region of Southern Sudan offers huge opportunities for the intrepid businessperson and risk taker. After over four decades of civil war, it needs everything. India became the first Asian country to open a Consulate General in Juba (capital of South Sudan) in October 2007.

The January 2005 Comprehensive Peace Agreement offers South Sudan a self-determination referendum in January 2011 with unity and secession as the options.

For further information contact the Embassy of India in Khartoum. We respond to all email commercial queries within eight working hours.

Address	61, Africa Road, Mailing Code 11111, P O Box 707, Khartoum II (Sudan)
Telephone	Country Code 249, Khartoum City Code 1 8357 4001, 8357 4002, 8357 4003, 8357 4004
Fax	8357 4050/1
Email	**ambassador@indembsdn.com** **commercial@indembsdn.com**
Website	www.indembsdn.com
Local Time	IST (-) 2 $^{1}/_{2}$ Hours
Working Hours	0830 to 1700 Hrs (Sunday through Thursday)

TRAVEL TO SUDAN

US STATE DEPARTMENT SUGGESTIONS

WARNING (Issued December 12, 2000): The Department of State warns U.S. citizens against all travel to Sudan because of the unstable security situation throughout the country. In addition to the ongoing civil war that affects both southern and eastern Sudan, the government of Sudan's control over its police and soldiers may be limited.

The government of Sudan continues to conduct a bombing campaign against rebel forces in southern Sudan. In addition, there has been rebel activity in and around Kassala, in eastern Sudan. Following a rebel incursion in Kassala in early November 2000, the government of Sudan authorities arrested an American relief worker in that area on suspicion of espionage and severely beat him. As a result of the rebel activity, the United Nations ordered all its personnel operating in Kassala to evacuate the area in and around the city. Other non-governmental organizations operating in Kassala evacuated their personnel as well.

The United States has no permanent diplomatic presence in Sudan because of concerns regarding the government of Sudan's ability to ensure adequately the safety of U.S. officials. While U.S. officials elsewhere in the region make periodic visits to Sudan, their ability to provide consular services, including emergency assistance, is severely limited.

U.S. citizens in Sudan are urged to consider their personal security situations in determining whether to remain in the country. Those who remain in Sudan should keep a low profile and stay alert to changing developments. Avoid large crowds and other situations in which anti-American sentiments may be expressed.

COUNTRY DESCRIPTION: Sudan is a large, developing country in northeastern Africa. Tourism facilities are minimal. The capital is Khartoum.

ENTRY REQUIREMENTS/REGISTRATION WITH LOCAL POLICE: A passport and visa are required. Americans citizens should apply for a Sudanese visa in a third country. Visas cannot be obtained in the United States, or at the Sudanese airport, or at the Sudanese border. Travelers must pay an airport departure tax in U.S. dollars or Saudi riyals or, if they have residence permits in Sudan, in Sudanese pounds. The Sudan Relief and Rehabilitation Association requires travelers to opposition-held areas of southern Sudan to obtain a travel permit at its office in Nairobi.

Travelers to Sudan are required to register with police headquarters within three days of arrival. Travelers must obtain police permission before moving to another location in Sudan and must register with police within 24 hours of arrival at the new location. These regulations are strictly enforced. Even with proper documentation, travelers in Sudan have been subjected to delays and detention by Sudan's security forces, especially when traveling outside Khartoum. Authorities expect roadblocks to be respected.

For further information on entry requirements and registration with local police, please contact the Embassy of the Republic of Sudan, 2210 Massachusetts Avenue, N.W., Washington, D.C. 20008; telephone (202) 338-8565 to 8570. Overseas, inquiries may be made at the nearest Sudanese embassy or consulate.

TRADE RESTRICTIONS: On November 4, 1997, President Clinton signed an Executive Order imposing comprehensive financial and commercial sanctions against Sudan, prohibiting U.S. transactions with Sudan. Travelers intending to visit Sudan, despite the Travel Warning, should contact the Department of the Treasury, Office of Foreign Assets Control (OFAC), Office of Compliance, regarding the effect of these sanctions; telephone 1-800-540-6322 or 202-622-2490; web site http://www.treas.gov/ofac/.

SAFETY AND SECURITY: Travel in all parts of Sudan, particularly outside Khartoum, is potentially hazardous. Civil war persists in the southern Sudan provinces of Upper Nile, Bahr El Ghazal, and Equatoria, and has spread to the eastern Sudan provinces of Blue Nile, Red Sea, and Kassala, along the Ethiopian and Eritrean borders. Banditry and incursions by southern Sudanese rebels are common in western Sudan, particularly in Darfur Province along the Chadian and Libyan borders, where a state of emergency exists. The land border with Egypt (ferry from Aswan to Wadi Halfa) has been reopened. Transportation between Eritrea and Sudan is currently halted. The Sudan People's Liberation Army controls all border crossings from Kenya and Uganda.

CURFEW: The curfew in Khartoum has been lifted. However, persons who are outside between midnight and 5:00 a.m. are subject to document searches at police checkpoints. Hotel officials and local police can inform visitors whether a curfew is in effect in other localities.

CRIME: Petty crime and thievery occur. Travelers should exercise caution at the airport, in markets and at public gatherings.

The loss or theft abroad of a U.S. passport should be reported immediately to local police and to the nearest U.S. embassy or consulate. The pamphlets, *A Safe Trip Abroad* and *Tips forTravelers to Sub-Saharan Africa*, provide useful information on personal security while traveling abroad and on travel in the region in general. Both are available from the Superintendent of Documents, U.S. Government Printing Office, Washington, D.C. 20402, via the Internet at http://www.access.gpo.gov/su_docs, or via the Bureau of Consular Affairs home page at http://travel.state.gov.

MEDICAL FACILITIES: Medical facilities in Sudan are extremely limited.

MEDICAL INSURANCE: U.S. medical insurance is not always valid outside the United States. U.S. Medicare and Medicaid programs do not provide payment for medical services outside the United States. Doctors and hospitals often expect immediate cash payment for health services. Uninsured travelers who require medical care overseas may face extreme difficulties.

Please check with your own insurance company to confirm whether your policy applies overseas, including provision for medical evacuation, and for adequacy of coverage. Serious medical problems requiring hospitalization and/or medical evacuation to the United States can cost tens of thousands of dollars. Please ascertain whether payment will be made to the overseas hospital or doctor or if you will be reimbursed later for expenses that you incur. Some insurance policies also include coverage for psychiatric treatment and for disposition of remains in the event of death.

Useful information on medical emergencies abroad, including overseas insurance programs, is provided in the Department of State's Bureau of Consular Affairs brochure, *Medical Information for Americans Traveling Abroad*, available via the Bureau of Consular Affairs home page or autofax: (202) 647-3000.

OTHER HEALTH INFORMATION: Information on vaccinations and other health precautions may be obtained from the Centers for Disease Control and Prevention's international travelers hotline at telephone 1-877-FYI-TRIP (1-877-394-8747), fax 1-888-CDC-FAXX (1-888-232-3299), or via the CDC's Internet site at http://www.cdc.gov.

TRAFFIC SAFETY AND ROAD CONDITIONS: While in a foreign country, U.S. citizens may encounter road conditions that differ significantly from those in the United States. The information below concerning Sudan is provided for general reference only and may not be totally accurate in a particular location or circumstance.

Safety of Public Transportation: Poor
Urban Road Conditions/Maintenance: Poor
Rural Road Conditions/Maintenance: Poor
Availability of Roadside Assistance: Poor

Road conditions are hazardous due to unpredictable local driving habits, pedestrians and animals in the roadway, and the lack of basic safety equipment on many vehicles. Roads are narrow and poorly maintained. Only some major highways are paved. Roads in southern Sudan may be impassable during the rainy season, while roads in the north can be quickly covered with shifting sand at anytime during the year. Nighttime driving throughout the country is dangerous and should be avoided if possible because vehicles often operate without lights or park in the road without warning. Ambulance and road emergency services are available in major urban areas, but the are extremely limited or unavailable elsewhere in the country.

Public transit is limited except in and between major urban areas. Passenger facilities are basic and crowded, especially during rush hours or seasonal travel. Schedules are unpublished and subject to change without notice. Vehicle maintenance does not meet the same standards as those in the United States or other Western countries. There is regular passenger train service from Khartoum to Wadi Halfa and Port Sudan. Inter-city bus service between major cities is regular and inexpensive. Intra-city bus service in the major urban areas is generally regular, but most buses and bus stops are unmarked. Taxis are available in the major cities at hotels, tourist sites and government offices. Public transit service to medium-size communities in the interior usually is limited to irregularly scheduled mini-buses. Most rural communities in the interior have no public transit.

U.S. citizens are subject to the laws of the country in which they are traveling. Traffic laws and custom in Sudan are substantially different from those in the United States. In Sudan, one drives on the right side of the road. There is no government agency specifically responsible for road safety, nor is there any regime to regularly inspect vehicle maintenance or safety. Seat belts and/or infant seats are not required. Many vehicles do not have seat belts or other safety equipment that is standard in the United States or other Western countries. Traffic on the right has the right of way. Right turns on a red light are prohibited. Speed limits are not posted. The legal speed limit for passenger cars on inter-city highways is 120 KPH (70 MPH), while in most urban areas it is 60 KPH (35 MPH). The speed limit in congested areas and school zones is 40 KPH (24 MPH).

All motor vehicle operators are required to purchase third-party liability insurance from the government. Nonetheless, many local drivers carry no insurance. Persons involved in an accident resulting in death or injury are required to report the incident to the nearest police station or official as soon as possible. Persons found at fault can expect fines, revocation of license, and jail sentences depending on the nature and extent of the accident. Penalties for persons convicted of driving under the influence of alcohol are strict, and convicted offenders may expect fines, jail sentences, and corporal punishment.

U.S. citizens may use their U.S. issued driver's licenses up to ninety days after arrival. After that, they must present either an "International Driving Permit" (IDP) or obtain a Sudanese driver's license. There are no restrictions on vehicle types, including motorcycles and motorized tricycles. Motorcycles, however, are relatively rare because of public perceptions that the highways are too dangerous for them.

The government of Sudan does not publish traffic statistics. The last reported instance of an American citizen injured in a traffic accident in Sudan was in 1996.

For additional general information about road safety, including links to foreign government sites, please see the Department of State, Bureau of Consular Affairs home page at http://travel.state.gov/road_safety.html. For specific information concerning Sudanese driving permits, vehicle inspection, road tax and mandatory insurance, please contact the Sudanese Embassy in Washington, D.C.

AIR TRAVEL: As there is no direct commercial air service by local carriers at present, nor economic authority to operate such service between the United States and Sudan, the U.S. Federal Aviation Administration (FAA) has not assessed the Sudan's Civil Aviation Authority for compliance with international aviation safety standards for oversight of Sudan's air carrier operations. For further information, travelers may contact the Department of Transportation within the U.S. at telephone 1-800-322-7873, or visit the FAA Internet home page at http://www.faa.gov/avr/iasa/. The U.S. Department of Defense (DOD) separately assesses some foreign air carriers for suitability as official providers of air services. For information regarding the DOD policy on specific carriers, travelers may contact the DOD at telephone (618) 229-4801.

Unforeseen circumstances such as sandstorms and electrical outages may cause flight delays. The Khartoum International Airport arrival and departure procedures are lengthy. Passengers on international flights should allow three hours for pre-departure security and other processing at the airport. Passengers for domestic flights should be at the airport at least two hours before flights. Domestic flights, including those to and from Port Sudan, Dongola and Juba, are subject to change or cancellation without notice.

CURRENCY REGULATIONS: A currency declaration statement is required upon arrival and departure from Sudan. Visitors who attempt to exchange money at unauthorized banking institutions or on the black market risk arrest and/or loss of funds. Please note restrictions on transactions with Sudan contained in the section on Trade Restrictions. Some visitors to Sudan have experienced difficulty exchanging U.S. dollar denomination instruments -- such as travelers' checks or cr cards -- due to U.S. economic sanctions.

PHOTOGRAPHY RESTRICTIONS: A permit is required before taking photographs anywhere in Khartoum, as well as in the interior of the country. Photographing military areas, bridges, drainage stations, broadcast stations, public utilities and slum areas or beggars is prohibited.

INFRASTRUCTURE: Disruptions of water and electricity are frequent. A new telecommunications system is in the process of being installed.

CRIMINAL PENALTIES: While in a foreign country, a U.S. citizen is subject to that country's laws and regulations, which sometimes differ significantly from those in the United States and may not afford the protections available under U.S law. Penalties for breaking the law can be more severe than in the United States for similar offenses. Persons violating Sudanese laws, even unknowingly, may be expelled, arrested, or imprisoned. Penalties for possession, use, or trafficking in illegal drugs in Sudan are strict, and convicted offenders can expect jail sentences and fines.

CHILDREN'S ISSUES: For information on international adoption of children, international parental child abduction, and international child support enforcement issues, please refer to our Internet site at http://travel.state.gov/children's_issues.html or telephone (202) 736-7000.

EMBASSY LOCATION/REGISTRATION: U.S. citizens traveling to Sudan, despite the Travel Warning, are encouraged to register with local employees at the U.S. Embassy in Khartoum located at Sharia Ali Abdul Latif, and to obtain updated information on travel and security in Sudan. The mailing address is P.O. Box 699, Khartoum; telephone (249)(11) 774-700 and 774-611; fax 774-137. The U.S. consular officer can be contacted via the Consular Section in Khartoum or directly at the U.S. Embassy in Cairo; telephone (20)(2) 795-7371; e-mail: consularcairo@state.gov. The workweek in Cairo and Khartoum is Sunday through Thursday. Information on services available for residents of Sudan may be found on the U.S. Embassy Cairo's web site: http://usembassy.egnet.net/sudan.htm.

IMPORTANT INFORMATION TO TRAVELLER TO SUDAN

VISAS & PERMITS

Entry visas are required by almost all nationalities, and are valid usually for one month.

Evidence of a previous visit to Israel will result in a visa refusal.

Permits are required by visitors wishing to travel anywhere outside Khartoum, and can take upto 2 days to obtain. Visitors arriving in any town or city in the Sudan must register with the police on their arrival, and show the necessary paperwork.

For those wishing to visit archaeological and/or historical sites, permits are again required. These are often fairly expensive, and can be obtained from the Department of Antiquities in Khartoum.

The Tourist Information Office in Khartoum will issue visitors with a photography permit. This is essential for anyone wishing to take photographs anywhere in the country, and is issued together with a list of items which may not be photographed.

CURFEW

A curfew operated in most large cities and towns from midnight until 4am.

HEALTH AND VACCINATIONS

As a result of the war, there is a severe shortage of medicines, trained doctors and hospital equipment in the Sudan. Many serious diseases are common, particularly malaria, hepatitis, dysentery, and bilharzia.

All visitors are strongly recommended to take out a good health insurance policy before travelling. Recommended vaccinations are yellow fever, cholera, typhoid, tetanus and meningitis. Malaria is rife, so preventative medication -- such as Paludrine -- should be taken before, during and after your trip. A mosquito net and repellent cream are both essential, especially if you are travelling south of Khartoum.

Water is rarely safe to drink straight from the tap, even in the larger cities. Boiling all water or the use of water purification tablets or boiled water is strongly recommended. Snakes and scorpions can present their own problems! Visitors should keep a watchful eye.

COMMUNICATIONS

Postal, telephone and telegraph services are administered by the government. In Khartoum, the post office is open from 8:30am to 1pm and from 5:30 to 6:30pm every day except Friday. International mail, both in and out, is often very slow.

International telephone calls are relativly easy to make from major cities from any of the telemunication stores.

PUBLIC HOLIDAYS

All regular Islamic holidays and festivals are kept, with the following additions:

- 1st January: Independence Day, commemorating the birth of the Sudanese Republic in 1956.
- 30th June: Salvation Day, Commemorating the Salvation Government takeover of government from civillian rule
- 25th December: Christmas Day

SHOPPING

Weaponry, such as daggers and swords in leather sheaths, can be unearthed in the markets of Sudanese towns. Some local men still wear these as part of everyday attire, but this is becoming an increasingly rare sight. As an exotic souvenir, however, these weapons are an interesting purchase.

Ebony carvings are for sale in the souqs at Omdurman and Khartoum, as well as gold jewellery. In the western region, in and around the town of Mellit, shoppers can find attractive carpets and some beautiful pottery.

Those interested in world wildlife and ecology will do best to avoid such purchases as ivory goods, stuffed crocodiles and purses made from crocodile skin. Animals are being massacred in large numbers to provide these goods, and they are -- unfortunately -- on sale throughout the Sudan and in other parts of Africa.

ENTERTAINMENT

Cultural events in the Sudan are few and far between. At the end of Ramadan, however, during the Eid Al-Fitr, it is possible to find Sudanese bands performing in the larger towns. As Sudanese music is an interesting blend of Arabian and African, listening can be a pleasant experience.

SUDAN: LOCAL TRANSPORTATION

Roads

There are about 50,000km (31,080 miles) of roads in the Sudan, but most are unsurfaced dirt tracks which may become completely impassable after heavy rain. Paved highways, runs between Khartoum - Port Sudan, Atbara, Dongola, Gedarif.

Buses run between Khartoum, Kassala, Port Sudan, Gedarif. These boast air-conditioning, comfortable seats and shock absorbers, but most buses are a far cry from this class of transport. The vast majority have wooden bench seats, no shock absorbers and are very crowded and uncomfortable.

Travel by lorry is probably even more unpleasant, as the rear section must be shared with all kinds of cargo and livestock. It is also open to the elements, and is hot and dusty in the extreme. Travel by both bus and lorry is extremely slow, due to the poor condition of the roads and the inevitable breakdowns en route.

A slightly faster way of getting about is by Toyota Hilux pick-ups, known to the locals as 'boxes' (boksi, plural bokasi). These cost a little more than lorries or buses and, although not a great deal more comfortable, they will certainly get you to your destination in a much shorter time. Boxes are mostly used as local transport between villages, but some longer routes are available, notably a trans-desert route from Dongola to Karima and Karima to Atbara.

Many of the locals travel by camel (western and northern Sudan) or donkey (country-wide). Bicycles are rarely seen, due to poor road conditions.

In the larger urban areas -- Khartoum, Omdurman, Kassala and Port Sudan -- taxis are available, but fares are erratic, and travellers need to bargain before starting their trip.

Rail

The railway system in the Sudan is extensive, with about 5,500km (3,420 miles) of track linking most of the major towns and cities. It is, however, in a poor state of repair and is currently operating at about one-fifth of its capacity. Most of the railway system dates from Kitchener's offensive against the Mahdi in the 1890s, and is a narrow gauge, single track line.

There are three classes of travel on the Sudanese railway. First-class compartments carry six passengers, while no limit seems to be fixed on the numbers in second and third classes, so these can be very crowded. Some passengers even ride for free on the carriage roofs. This practice is not recommended, however, as accidents have been known to occur.

Air

The national carrier is the government-owned Sudan Airways, Other airline companies operate on local routes.

SUDAN: PLACES OF INTEREST

Khartoum and Omdurman

Khartoum is one of three sister cities, built at the convergence of the Blue and White Niles: Omdurman to the north-west across the White Nile, North Khartoum, and Khartoum itself on the southern bank of the Blue Nile.

Khartoum has a relatively short history. It was first established as a military outpost in 1821, and is said to derive its name from the thin spit of land at the convergence of the rivers, which resembles an elephant's trunk (khurtum). Khartoum grew rapidly in prosperity during the boom years of the slave trade, between 1825 and 1880. In 1834 it became the capital of the Sudan, and many explorers from Europe used it as a base for their African expions.

Khartoum was sacked twice during the latter half of the 19th century -- once by the Mahdi and once by Kitchener when the Mahdi was ousted. In 1898, Kitchener began to rebuild the city, and designed the streets in the shape of the British flag, the Union Jack, which he hoped would make it easier to defend. On the opposite bank of the Nile, North Khartoum was developed as an industrial area at about the same time.

Today's Khartoum is a quiet, unremarkable city. It has peaceful, tree-lined streets, and in some ways still bears the unmistakable mark of an outpost of the British Empire. Its expansion to accommodate a rapidly-growing population, however, has added very little in terms of charm or atmosphere.

Places to visit in Khartoum

National Museum. This contains antiquities and artefacts from several periods of Sudanese history and pre-history, including glassware, pottery, statuary and figurines from the ancient kingdom of Cush. Ancient Nubia's Christian period is well-represented, with frescoes and murals from ruined churches, dating from the 8th to the 15th century. The Museum's garden contains two reconstructed temples, which have been salvaged from the Nubian land flooded by Lake Nasser. These Egyptian temples of Buhen and Semna were originally built by Queen Hatshepsut and Pharaoh Tuthmosis III respectively. The temples have corrugated iron covers built over them to protect them from humidity during the wet season. The original concept was to roll back these covers during the dry season, but whether this ever happened or not is unclear. The covers are rusted into place and are now permanent and immovable!

Ethnographical Museum. This is a small museum which contains an interesting collection of items relating to Sudanese village life. These include musical instruments, clothing, cooking and hunting implements.

Places to visit in Omdurman

Souq. This is the largest in the Sudan, and has an interesting variety of goods on display. Ivory and ebony candlesticks are carved by market craftsmen, goldsmiths and silversmiths fashion all kinds of jewellery in their shop-fronts, and the atmosphere is lively and bustling. The best time to visit is on Friday mornings.

Camel Market. This is situated about 2km north of Omdurman's main souq. Animals are mostly brought from eastern or western areas of the Sudan.

Tomb of the Mahdi. On the death of the Mahdi in 1885, his body was entombed in a silver-domed mosque in Omdurman. This was completely destroyed by Kitchener in 1898, when the Mahdi's body was burned and his ashes thrown into the river. In 1947 the Mahdi's son had the mosque and tomb rebuilt. Not surprisingly, it is closed to foreigners, but can be viewed from the outside.

Beit al-Khalifa. This is situated opposite the Mahdi's tomb. Once the home of the Mahdi's successor, the house was built of mud and brick in 1887, and is now a museum. It contains relics from Mahdiyya battles, including guns, war banners and suits of mail. An interesting collection of photographs depicts the city of Khartoum at the time of the Mahdi's revolt and its subsequent occupation by the British.

El-Obeid

This is the capital city of the Kordofan region in Western Sudan, and was once the Mahdi's capital and political centre. Situated in the middle of a vast stretch of barren desert, it has a population of 200,000 people and is an important centre for the production of gum arabic. This substance is used in the manufacture of food thickening, ink and medicinal products, and is obtained from acacia trees.

The city experiences problems with its supplies of both electric power and water. Electricity from the city's own generators is erratic and power cuts are the norm. In such an arid desert environment, water supplies often dwindle and have to be brought in by truck from other areas.

The two souqs in the city deal mostly in meat and vegetables. There are also some tailor's shops where fabric can be purchased and clothes made to order.

There is little to interest the visitor in El-Obeid, apart from a small museum, which displays exhibits relating to ancient Sudanese history. Its Catholic cathedral is impressive, however, and is said to be one of the largest in Africa.

Port Sudan

Port Sudan is a harbour city, established by the British in 1905 as a seaport. Once a thriving export centre handling the country's raw commodities such as sesame, cotton and sorghum, it has now fallen into decay as a result of the ongoing war.

Today's city is badly in need of care and repair, although it is still possible to see beautiful lattice woodwork on the window-screens of older buildings, which provide a glimpse into the city's more prestigious past.

It was once possible to travel by boat from Port Sudan to Jeddah in Saudi Arabia, but passenger traffic, like commercial activity, has dwindled to the merest trickle. As a result, passenger services from the port are no longer in existence.

For visitors interested in Red Sea diving, this is still quite a good place to use as a base, and local hotels and dive shops can make the necessary arrangements.

Kassala

Kassala is situated in Eastern Sudan and has a population of 150,000. The city is built on the Gash River and is the power centre of one of the Sudan's traditional families -- the Khatmiya Brotherhood, which opposed the Mahdi family in the last century.

On the outskirts of the city live the Rashaida tribe, mostly inhabiting goatskin tents. They are a nomadic people who breed camels and goats, and are closely related to the Saudi Arabian Bedouin, having migrated from the Arabian Peninsula about 150 years ago. It is the mysteriously-veiled Rashaida women who make a great deal of the silver jewellery sold in the Kassala souq.

The souq is said to be one of Sudan's best, and sells a wide variety of the fruit for which Kassala is renowned. Grapefruit, pomegranates, oranges, bananas and melons are all for sale here, as well as local handicrafts, fabrics and the aforementioned silver jewellery.

Several kilometres outside Kassala are the curiously-shaped 'sugar-loaf' hills, known as the jebels. They can be seen on the horizon from the city and are the habitat of a tribe of baboons, which come down from the hills at sunset to drink at a nearby village well.

Kassala is also a favourite retreat for Sudanese honeymoon couples, and in the nearby village of Khatmiya, the same village well is a traditional place for newly-wed couples to drink. Water from the well is said to bring good luck and a fertile married life.

Suakin Island

The island is situated 58km south of Port Sudan and was once a major trading centre, particularly in the 19th century, during the boom years of slavery. As far back as the 10th century BC, Suakin was used by Pharaoh Rameses III as a trading port, but declined in importance after the close of the 19th century AD, and in 1905 was superseded in importance by Port Sudan.

Its unique architecture is made of coral, but these once-beautiful buildings, although restored by the Mahdi in 1881, are now in the final stages of crumbling away.

The island is linked to the mainland by means of a causeway.

Dongola

Once an important centre of power in ancient Nubia, the remains of the old northern-Sudanese city are being excavated by a Polish-led team -- a project that has been in operation since 1964.

The town is now noteworthy for its palm groves and its September date harvest, when young boys climb the palm trunks, carrying sharp knives in their teeth, to cut the clusters of dates. The fruit and vegetable souq here is a colourful sight, occasionally dealing in camels, which the desert nomads bring in for sale.

The Cushite temple of Kawa is situated on the eastern bank of the river. The ruins of this temple can be visited by taking a ferry across the river from the main town.

Karima

This northern-Sudanese market town has a population of about 15,000. The town itself is of little interest, but there are several ancient sites nearby which are worth a visit.

Just 2km south of the town is the 100-metre high Jebel Barkal, a hill which was regarded as sacred by the Egyptians of the 18th Dynasty. From its summit, there is an excellent view of the Nile. At its foot lies the Temple of Amun, second only in length to the famous Temple of Karnak. This was once surrounded by about six smaller temples, and ruins of these, together with statuary and hieroglyphics, make this an interesting Cushite site.

Lying west of the temple are the Jebel Barkal Pyramids, similar in style to those at Meroe.

Atbara

Located at the conjunction of the Atbara tributary, flowing down from Ethiopia, and the River Nile, Atbara is on two main railway routes: from Atbara to Port Sudan, and from Khartoum to Wadi Halfa.

The city has a population of 75,000 people. In 1898 it was the site of a battle between the British and the Mahdists, when 2,000 of the latter were wiped out by Kitchener. After the battle, British officials settled here, building colonial-style houses, which are now used as government offices.

The ruins of the Royal City of Meroe are located about 100km south of Atbara. Residence of the kings of Meroe between 592BC and AD350, the city shows strong Egyptian architectural influence. The ruined Temple of Amun is still standing, together with the remains several palaces and a swimming pool.

In the desert, about 5km to the east, stand the royal pyramids, where the dead kings of Meroe are buried.

Jebel Marra Mountains

This western-Sudanese mountain range is dominated by the second-highest mountain in the Sudan, known as Jebel Marra. This is an extinct volcano which rises to a height of 3071 metres.

At the base of the mountain range lies the town of Nyala, and this town forms a good starting point for an exploration of the surrounding mountainous countryside. It is a beautiful region of hills, rivers and orchards, and is an interesting spot for walking enthusiasts. There is a waterfall near the village of Quaila and some hot springs near the crater of the volcano itself.

El-Fasher

In the 18th century, El-Fasher was the main centre of the Fur Sultanate. The sultan's palace can still be seen in this western-Sudanese town, and is now a museum.

The town was also famous as the starting point of one of the most important camel caravan routes in Africa. Known as the Darb al-Arba'een, or Forty Days Road, this route carried ebony, spices, rich cloth, ivory and slaves from all parts of Africa to the Egyptian bazaars of Aswan and Asyut.

MAJOR HOTELS IN THE KHARTOUM AREA

ACROPOLE HOTEL , Khartoum, Sudan
Single: USD 45, *Double:* USD 55
AMBASSADOR HOTEL , Khartoum, Sudan
Sorry no Price List
ARAAK HOTEL , Khartoum, Sudan
Sorry no Price List
FRIENDSHIP PALACE , Khartoum, Sudan
Single: USD 110, *Double:* USD 130
GRAND , Khartoum, Sudan
Sorry No Price List
***GREEN VILLAGE** , Khartoum, Sudan*
Sorry No Price List
***KHARTOUM HILTON** , Khartoum, Sudan*
Sorry No Price List
***LE MERIDIEN KHARTOUM** , Khartoum, Sudan*
Single: USD 130, Double: USD 160,
***SUDAN** , Khartoum, Sudan*
Single: USD 48

SUPPLEMENTS

STRATEGIC BUSINESS AND INDUSTRIAL CONTACTS

i) The Sudanese Businessmen & Employers Federation
Tel: 00-249-11-431279/431277/431278
Fax: 00-249-11-431281/431283
President: Mr. Izz Eldin Elsayed

ii) Sudanese Chambers of Industries Association
Tel: 00-249-11-471716/471717/471719
Fax: 00-249-11-471720
President: Mr. Saud El Berier

iii) Union Chambers of Commerce
Tel: 00-249-11-772346/776518/781886
Fax: 00-249-11-780748
e-mail: chamber@sudanchamber.org
Director General: Mr. Ibrahim Mohamed Osman Elnus

iv) Chambers of Small Industries Corporationbr> Tel: 00-249-11-331554
Fax: 00-249-11-331554

v) Businesswomen's Union
Tel: 00-249-11-797012
Fax: 00-249-11-797012

vi) Ministry of Industry & Investment Authority
P.O. Box 6286, Khartoum
Tel: 00-249-11-771063
Fax: 00-249-11-770156

DIRECTORY OF MEMBERS OF CHAMBER OF COMMERCE & INDUSTRY. LIST OF IMPORTANT BUSINESS HOUSES.

1. Hashimali Mohamed Kheir
General Manager
Wafi Foreign Trade & Investment
P.O.Box. 12136, Khartoum, Sudan
Tel: 00-249-11-787742/787750
Fax: 00-249-11-787749
2. Tariq Sir El Khatim
General Manager
Sidco Intl Co. For Import & Export
P.O. Box. 8142, Khartoum, Sudan
Tel: 00-249-11-477773
Fax: 00-249-11-464885
Mob: 00-24912304863
E-mail: sideoint@emirates.net.ae

3. Khalid Elhag Elhatir
Chairman

Mawafi Trading & Industrial co.
Al Barka tower, 3rd floor, office no. 609
P.O. Box: 13252, Khartoum, Sudan
Tel: 00-249-11-787384/789413
Fax: 00-249-11-787383
E-mail: nawafi@sudnet.net

4. Taha Elsayed Elroubi
President
Taha Elsayed Elroubu & Co
I.D.E. Place Ave P.O. Box: 467, Khartoum, Sudan
Tel: 00-249-13-334253
Fax: 00-249-13-334252
E-mail: TERCOSD@TERCOTEL.COM

5. Union Chambers of Commerce
P.O.Box: 81, Khartoum, Sudan
Tel: 00-249-11-772346/776518/781886
Fax: 00-249-11-780748
E-mail: chamber@sudanchamber.org
Web: http://www.sudanchamber.org

6. Sudanese Free Zones & Markets
Khartoum, Sudan
Tel: 00-249-11-272981
Fax: 00-249-11-272416/271485
E-mail: SFZ-FREEZONES@HOTMAIL.COM

7. Sudanese Businessmen & Employers Federation
Tel: 00-249-11-431276/431277/431278
Fax: 00-249-11-471220

8. Sudan Seaport Corporation
P.O.Box: 2534, Khartoum
Tel: 00-249-11-775859/779114

9. Sudan Shipping Line Corp.
P.O. Box: 1731, Khartoum, Sudan
Tel: 00-249-11-781675
Fax: 00-249-11-777902

10. the strategic Reserve Authority
P.O. Box 298, Khartoum
Tel: 00-249-11-779415/796227
Fax: 00-249-11-772595

11. Eng. Eltigani A. Farah
Giad For Automotive Industry Co. Ltd
P.O. Box: 444, Khartoum
Tel: 00-249-11-201290
Fax: 00-249-11-201373
E-mail: giadcars@suanmail.net
12. Khartoum Petrochemical Co. Ltd (KPC)
Gaili, Khartoum North, sudan

Tel: 00-249-13-350361
Fax: 00-249-13-350362

MINISTRIES COMMERCE, INDUSTRY, HEALTH, FOOD, OIL & GAS

i) Minsitry of Foreign Trade
Tel: 00-249-11-772793/772640
Fax: 00-249-11-773950/776359
Email: tic@sudanmail.net

ii) Ministry of Industry
P.O. Box: 6286, Khartoum
Tel: 00-249-11-771063
Fax: 00-249-11-770156

iii) Ministry of Health, Khartoum
Tel: 00-249-11-778704/772843/778704
Fax: 00-249-11-778704

iv) Ministry of Agriculture & Forestry
P.O. Box: 283, Khartoum
Tel: 00-249-11-770586

v) Ministry of Energy & Mining
Tel: 00-249-11-780478-77347-775428-773196
Fax: 00-249-11-777940-773663

4. Trade Point G. Director: AL-Fatih AL-Zein AL-Taib
For Trade Enquiries: trade@sudantradepoint.org
TPSudan@hotmail.com

For General Information: info@sudantradepoint.org
TPSudan@hotmail.com

Tel: 00249-11-762581, 00249-11-762583
Fax: 00249-11-788116
Mobile Phone: 00249-12141213. 00249-12140081

LEADING SUDAN COMPANIES

Company Name	PO Box	Phone 1	Fax	Mobile	Activity	Exp. Items	Imp. Items
Gedarif Oil Factory				+24912223886	Impex	Grains	Spare Parts
Niesser Pharmaceutical Co	44494	+24911787361	+24911787360	+24912305323	Importer		Medical Supplies
Ismaeil Opticals	6059	+24911788450	+24911788450		Importer		Glasses
Marawi Investment Co	2136	+24911779030			Serviceprovider		Toothpaste
Nur Al Huda Enterprises	2643	+24911785094	+24911775740		Impex	Meat	Chemicals

A\Moniem Industrial&Engineering Co.	2413	+24911777624	+24911773132	+24912304017	Impex	Meat	Chemicals
Trans Sudan Transportation Enterprise	720	+24911472210	+24911471636		Impex		Automobile
Elbarbary Motors Co. Ltd	760	+24911472209	+24911465625		Impex		Automobile
Hafez Elsayed Elbarbary Co. Ltd	760	+24911472208	+24911471636		Impex		Building Materials
Altawfig Warehousing Enterprise	27	+24931123859	+24931123895		Impex		Automobile
Almagboul Brothers Corporation Limited	1593	+24911776425	+24911770218		Impex		Agriculture Equip
Masa Contracting Co. Ltd		+24911226023	+24911225864	+24912349104	Importer		Automobile
Bashir Elnoor Elsafei		+24915590025		+24912368751	Importer		Food Stuff
Rikaz International Investment Co. Ltd		+24911785877	+24911785801	+24912307646	Importer		Cement
Modren Agriiculture Co.	825	+24911777166	+24911770139	+24912360995	Importer		Chemicals
Elrashideen For Investments Co. Ltd	11772	+25911779375	+24911779355	+24912391383	Importer		Medical Supplies
Chemimport Co. Ltd		+24911777166			Importer		Chemicals
Mina Talk Factory	1144	+24911776002	+24911782221		Importer		
Ayat For Trading&Investment Co. Ltd		+24911781998		+24912300571	Impex	Meat	Transport Products
Refrigeration House Ltd	2892	+24911771829	+24911772201		Importer		Spare Parts
Coldair Engineering Co. Ltd	804	+24913330482	+24913330975		Impex		Spare Parts
Golden Gate Co. Ltd	1111	+24911483865	+24911483865	+24912304824	Impex		Electrical Appliances
Kambal International Co.	10336	+24911779337	+24911775887	+2491235852	Impex		Medical Supplies
Almohandis Paint Factory	10008	+24915558317	+24915561255	+24912346612	Importer		Raw Material
Hagkol For Trading&Service Co.	5050	+24911472482	+24911467910	+24912358891	Importer		
Medco Co. Ltd		+24911798060	+24911798058	+24912394401	Impex		Cement
Aljadawel Althahabia For		+24911479982	+24911479983	+24912306477	Exporter	Dura	

Investment Co. Ltd							
M.M. Pharma&Chemical Co. Ltd	1449	+24911788833	+24911771393		Importer		Medical Supplies
M&S for Human Drugs&Veterinary Service Ltd	1449	+24911782640	+24911771398		Importer		Medical Supplies
Yarmouk United Co. Ltd	10665	+24911784881	+24911771405	+24912303120	Impex	Grains	Spare Parts
Emarets Metal Company		+24913325836		+24912391952	Importer		Raw Material
Al Turath Emarets Factory For Alluminum		+24913325836		+24912391952	Importer		
Elmozn Trading&Service Co. Ltd				+24912210669	Impex		Electrical Appliances
Mohamed Erbab Esmail		+24915591710			Impex	Grains	
Arcory International Eng Trade &Service Co	4291	+24911784383	+24911774337	+24912390932	Impex	Live Stock	Transport Products
Alpha Medical Ageneis Co. Ltd	3541	+24911797484	+24911782787		Importer		Medical Supplies
Alsabr For Import&Export Co. Ltd	5067	+24911473470	+24911475855	+24912301342	Importer		Building Materials
Ahbab Allah Foir Import&Export Co. Ltd	5067	+24911462497	+24911475855	+24912301342	Importer		Building Materials
Alnour Global Invest Co.	11715	+24911777334	+24911783635	+24912305560	Impex	Meat	Electrical Appliances
Saad Sweets Co. Ltd	603	+24911471583	+24911467179		Impex		Raw Material
Masang Kofa Co.	13186	+24913660980	+24911477642		Impex	Live Stock	
Seiseban Trading Co. Ltd	2276	+24911782652	+24911777245	+24912390164	Importer		
Fadoas Trading and Investment Co.		+24911792224	+24911792226	+24912300211	Impex	Live Stock	
Green Saloon	369	+24911772861		+24912344054	Importer		
Gebal Al sharag Investment		+24911797755	+24911797755	+24912309808	Impex	Grains	Food Stuff
Hadir International Co. Ltd	12637	+24911464328	+24911464328	+24912303858	Impex	Veg / Fruits	Medical Supplies
Avia Trans Air Transport Co. Ltd		+24911482786	+24911482787	+24912133472	Impex		Transport Products

Almahari International Co. Ltd		+24911792 490	+24911792 489		Impex	Meat	
Mahibbah Trans Contiinental J.V.Co.	11967	+24911794 266	+24911793 662		Impex		Electrical Appliances
The Misr Concretd Devolopment co.Sudan	290	+24911463 540	+24911473 025	+24912387924			Building Materials
Doctors Co. Ltd	6008		+24911797 817	+24912132728	Impex		Medical Supplies
Abu Nassier Trading&Service Co.	1470	+24911795 339	+24911788 854		Exporter	Live Stock	
Sky International Co. Ltd	2052	+24911777 694	+24911776 767	+24912229780	Impex	Grains	Electrical Appliances
Switch Co.for Trading&Egineering	6590	+24911489 166	+24911489 164	+24912208362	Impex	Grains	
Internet International Trade&Transport Co.	8185	+24911770 054	+24911778 753	+24912301851	Impex	Grains	Food Stuff
Azza for Food Processing&Packing	8185	+24911770 05	249117787 53	+2491230185	Impex	Grains	Food Stuff
Abdelmoneim Medical Industries Co. Ltd	355	+24911784 981	+24911779 578		Importer		Medical Supplies
African Poultry Co. Ltd	1913	+24911772 944	+24911772 944	+24912390437	Impex		
Engineering Automotive Co.	837	+24911460 892	+24915568 732	+24912304175	Importer		Automobile
Avico Drugs&Investment Co. Ltd	12015	+24911787 513	+24911773 571	+24912375744	Importer		Medical Supplies
Afrotan Co. Ltd	1103	+24911770 363	+24911772 673	+24912304643	Impex		Chemicals
El Nil Photo Studio	280	+24911770 363	+24911772 673	+24912304643	Impex		
Alomeria Trading & Investment co.	44914	+24911780 940	+24911776 262	+24912307220	Impex		Electrical Appliances
Kenana sugar Co. Ltd	3632	+24922470 3	+24911220 563	+24912357826	Impex	Sugar	
Therwat International Co. Ltd		+24911780 872	+24911773 094		Importer	Meat	
Ashraf Co. Ltd	3077			+24912380605	Impex	Grains	Food Stuff

Coral Co. Ltd	1899	+24911469250	+24911469248		Impex		Medical Supplies
Coral Hatcheries & feed Production Farms	1899	+24911469250	+24911469248				
Khartoum Spinning & Weaving Co. Ltd	193	+24913330073	+24913340726	+24912381332	Impex		
Integrated Solution Co. Ltd	912	+24911790901	+2449790703	+24912391045	Importer		
United Petroleum Co.	12964	+24911488796	+24911488797	+24912390152	Impex		
Cofftea Trading Co. Ltd	3561	+24911774530	+24911770687		Impex	Sessame	
Geogabe Trading Co. Ltd	1138	+24911770939	+24911770789	+24912346050	Exporter	Veg / Fruits	
Andrawos Commercial		+24911774720	+24911772584	+24912344803	Importer		
Abd Allah Elfadil Ebrahim		+24915590642	+24911466502	+24912300521	Impex	Veg / Fruits	
Sisoba for Exp & Imp. Co.		+24911777980			Importer		Medical Supplies
House Blasit Inserback				+2491230465	Importer		Packing Materials
Omdurman Medical Trading Agencies	13419	+24911783989	+24911785256	+24912392835	Impex		Chemicals
Ulisse Adventres Co. Ltd			+24911798887	+24915511371	Impex		
Tolia Industries Metal Equipment Co.		+24911486863	+24911486864	+24912364447	Importer		
El Hag Abbas El Hag Siddig	531	+24915552791			Impex	Grains	Home Appliences
Mohammed Abbas E l Hag Siddig	531	+24915554311			Impex	Hide/Skins	Home Appliences
Mirghni Abbas El Hag Siddig	531	+24915555024			Impex	Hide/Skins	Home Appliences
Salah El Gousi Co.	50	+24915555191			Impex	Grains	Chemicals
Kamal Al Gousi Co.	2028	+24915556044			Impex	Grains	Electrical Appliances
Abu Haraz Co. Ltd		+24915556062	+24915556052		Importer		Building Materials
A Safwa for Development & Animal Production	12957			+24912133195	Impex	Meat	Building Materials
Al Edahim		+24911573	+24915573	+24912360272	Impex		Building

Investment Co. Ltd		226	226				Materials
Abu Assabei For Transport & Investment Co.				+24912390427	Importer		Clothes
Srindra for Export & Import		+24913340036			Importer		
Maysa For Trading & contracting		+24911424813		+24912305790	Impex	Grains	Electrical Appliances
White Nile Plastic Co.	459	+24913312225	+24911780249		Importer		Spare Parts
Dali Lemousine	459	+24911781506	+24911780246		Importer		Automobile
Elshatrab Decoricatoraoil Mill	459	+24915570400	+24915570400		Impex		Spare Parts
Eldali & Elmazmoum National Co.	459	+24911781506	+24911780246		Impex	Grains	Food Stuff
Omeir International Commercial Co.	568	+24915556186	+24911234213	+24912301625	Importer		Food Stuff
Styrex Co.		24913339171		+24912304667	Importer		Raw Material
Sinan Trading & Contracting Co. Ltd		+24911796097	+24911796096	+24912280225	Serviceprovider		
Snnen for Agriculture & Investment Co. Ltd	1679	+249777254			Impex	Veg / Fruits	
Emdad for Investment Co. Ltd		+24913343133		+24912236038	Impex		Food Stuff
Fasco Co. Ltd	6314	+24911779030			Importer		Spare Parts
El Ismaili for Trading/Transport/Investment Co	4291	+24911784963	+24911785757	+24912393816	Impex	Grains	
Chemicals & Plastics Co. Ltd	1905	+24911778044	+24911778045	+24912301657	Impex		Chemicals
Elmedani Brothers Co .Ltd	5193	+24911467930	+24911471403	+24912303098	Importer		Spare Parts
Abou Haraz Co. Ltd		+24915556052	+24915556052	+24912348253	Exporter	Meat	
Bittar Engineering Ltd	1011	+24911771045	+24911780102	+24912300513	Impex		Electrical Appliances
Mona Sultan International Co.	305	+24911436198		+24912226930	Exporter	Veg / Fruits	
Umeish for Export & Import		+24915592385			Importer		
Tarig Commercial Co.	459	+24911781506	+24911780249		Importer		Transport Products

Sennar Agricultural Service Center	459	+24951140 751	+24951140 751		Importer		Transport Products
Eldali & Elmazmoum For Earth Moving&	459	+24911781 506	+24911780 246		Importer		
Gezera Trade Services Co.	1321	+24911783 358	+24911779 060		Impex		Transport Products
Al Mukhtar Enterprises	3715	+24911778 346	+24911771 478	+24912300492	Impex	Hide/Skins	Spare Parts
Astral Trading Co.	44310	+24911773 171	+24911783 255		Importer		Chemicals
Elmehad International Co. Ltd	3124	+24911772 152	+24911773 979	+24912308999	Importer		
El Sari Co. Ltd	3179	+24911783 004			Impex		

SELECTED COMPANIES

Saria Complex

It is one of the largest industrial complexes in Sudan that produces more .industrial technology different types of domestic products and household appliances Electronic Assembling 60than tory Plastic Factory Automotive Battery Factory Readymade Factory Electric Equipment Fac 11 470891 + :Sudan Tele -Khartoum North 5183 :Box.O.Clothes Packing Factory Shoe Factory P 249 11 477113 + :Fax 470895 /249
http://www.sariacomplex.com/
http://www.almasarra.htg-sdn.com/

Geological Research Authority of the Sudan GRAS

represents the State Geological Survey (GRAS)The Geological Research Authority of the Sudan continental shelf of rivers and the ,and is the guardian of all metals and minerals within the lands The 410Box .O .It comes under the umbrella of the Ministry of Energy and Mining P .the Sudan :Fax249 1 83777939 + :Sudan Tel 11111Geological Research Authority of The Sudan Khartoum 249 1 83776681+
http://www.gras-sd.com/

Sigma-Tau SUDAN Ltd
- .the plant was equipped initially to produce the following pharmaceuticals :Production facilities DRAY POWDERED - ,TABLETS This was shortly followed by -HARD GELATIN CAPSULES CREAMS AND OINTMENTS The plant ,PASTES -SYRUPS -SUSPENSIONS FOR ORAL Million per annum Tablets 100is Hard gelatin capsules (considering one shift per day)capacity Million per 3Million per annum suspension Syrups 4Million per annum Dry powder for oral 80 umann
http://www.betasudan.com/sigmatau.htm

Haggar Holding
a cigarette ,cultivation of Virginia tobacco in Southern Sudan (HHC)Limited .Haggar Holding Co &HAGGAR CIGARETTE)factory in the Yei District of Equatoria another factory in Khartoum was stalished for planting and (STCP)Coffee Plantations &Sudan Tea (RYTOBACCO FACTO processing both crops Acquired shoe manufacturing company LARCO Acquired bottling factories Established a company for developing solar energy resources in (FORAT)and (PASGIANOS)

Established HAGGAR PETROLEUM SERVICES COMPANY (SUDAN TECHNO SOLAR) Sudan ,Khartoum North 236Box .O.P 249 13 335940 +Fax 249 13 335193 +249 13 335937 +Tel Sudan

http://www.haggarholding.com/

Sudan Rotomouls Co
,flower pots RAD-traffic road barrier -traffic cone -tal crys-cubic -vertical -horizontal -Water tanks 576560 / 15-249 + :Fax 577995, 576550 / 15-249 + :Dorman industrial area Tel -SQR Um 11111code/ 11639:Box .O.P
http://www.sudanrotomould.com/

The Sudan Cotton Company

-Barlaman Street Khartoum 249 183 770703+ :Fax 249 183 775755 771567 779573 +: :Tel Sudan -Khartoum , 1672 :Box.O.Sudan P
http://www.sudancottonco.com/

Coldair Engineering Company CEC

CEC currently .is part of Haggar Holding Company (CEC) .Coldair Engineering Company Ltd water coolers and ,evaporative air coolers ,chest freezers ,manufactures domestic refrigerators door commercial refrigerators for supermarkets-glass

http://www.coldairengineering.com/

AHMED OSMAN ABDALSALAM GROUP
http://www.aoag.biz/

Alsalam Cement Production Company ACPC
Ahmed Osman Abdalsalam Group
http://www.alsalamcement.com/
موطرخلا : 00249183474685 ديرب قودنص: 00249183473944 سكاف 00249183474681 00249183474683 44058

http://www.smfsteel.com/

Molutech Aluminium

,o global customersMolutech Aluminium that provides consulting and professional services t Sudan -aluminium and development of custom applications Khartoum ,offering domain expertise 245 923 00249 187 245 922 00249 187:Tel
http://www.molutech.com/

Banan Plastics Factory -مصنع بنان للحبال ومنتجات البلاستيك
0024915251110:Tel
http://www.bananfactry.com/

IMPORTANT BUSINES CONTACTS

SUDAN BUSINESS SERVICES

- **Century GSE**
Qualtiy used ground support equipment and asset managment services.

Address: 5383 Hollister Ave. Suite 220
Phone: 805 637 9514
E-Mail: techinfo@centurygse.com

- **Salvo Grima (Freeport) Operations Ltd**

Salvo Grima Freeport Operations are fiscal representatives in Malta offering ...
Address: Ground Floor, Freeport Centre, Port of Kalafrana
Phone: +356 2220 7000 E-Mail: jperegin@salvogrima.com.mt

- **Web Desiging**

indiacraze Megrisoft Web Solution Provider offers Web Hosting, Web Promotion, ...
Address: #191713, Delhi
Phone: 011-2242413 E-Mail: nitinstar76@yahoo.com

- **spacemaker**

Spacemaker Self Storage provides business storage and domestic storage ...
E-Mail: space@cherryaid.co.uk

- **Kda Home Biz 4 U**

Learn how to build a home based business through network marketing to earn a ...
E-Mail: dion@kdahomebiz4u.com

- **Nationwide Self Storage**

Nationwide Self Storage provides business storage and domestic storage ...
E-Mail: nationwide@cherryaid.co.uk

- **Mosaic Services**

Offers Search engine optimization services, Latent Semantic Indexing (LSI) ...
Address: G-60, East of Kailash, New Delhi, India
E-Mail: sarika@ebrandz-online.com

- **Profit-Unlimited**

Work at Home Ideas and Opportunities, 5 Different Streams of Income All from ...
Address: 3842 W. Hatcher Rd.
Phone: 1-602-568-6456 E-Mail: mike@profit-unlimited.com

- **Reliant Marking Tools Manufacturer Birmingham UK**

Reliant Marking Tools UK: manufacturers of stencils, dies, marking tools, ...
Address: Unit 2 Benson Ind. EST. Benson Road Hockley
Phone: 0121 359-3366 E-Mail: webmaster@reliantmarkingtools.co.uk

- **Waterstore Trading Company**

Waterstore Trading Company is a phones superstore, we are the online electrical ...
Address: 19624 e montview dr

Phone: 13035749369 E-Mail: waterstore@usa.com

- **import/export**

Our company is called World Trade Hall. We are a private international services ...
Address: No#234,Pasdaran ave,11th floor
Phone: +98-21-22554000 E-Mail: marketing.division@gmail.com

- **RETAIL MANAGEMENT SOFTWARE**

WE ARE IN SOFTWARE DEVLOPEMENT & SALES. SOFTWARE LIKE PETROL PUMP MANAGEMENT ...
Address: B/215, Kailash Industrial Complex,Parksite, Vikhroli(West),Mumbai-400079.
Phone: +91(022)55551855 E-Mail: info@artrm.com

- **transaltionpro**

translation agency offers quality and efficiency french englsih spanish
Address: wolseley
Phone: 02078701068 E-Mail: info@translationpro.co.uk

- **curs valutar**

Provides currency exchange informations, currency statistics and related ...
Address: Lebedei no.5
E-Mail: mirceam321@yahoo.com

- **Sme telecom**

Sme Telecom - Providing UK Non Geographic Numbers and advanced call handling ...
Phone: 020 70 60 50 20 E-Mail: sudesh@smetelecom.com

- **GBS Freight Services**

We are a UK based freight forwarding & logistics organisation providing ...
Address: 25 Highfield Road
Phone: +44 (0) 1322-288061 E-Mail: steve@gbsfreight.co.uk

- **Business English UK c/o AREL**

Learn professional English in England. Business English UK offers links to high ...
Address: 56 Buckingham Gate
Phone: +44 207 802 9212 E-Mail: biseng@theenglishlanguage.org

- **DiscountSourcesDirect**

Discover Where To Get Top Brand Products At Knock-Down Clearance Prices.
Address: Arlington Road
Phone: $4 07768 018900 E-Mail: submission@sebiz.net

- **My Swag Bag Cashback and Rewards Service**

MySwagBag is a cashback and rewards website for members to get free cashback, ...

Address: 3rd Floor
Phone: 0035040335 E-Mail: submission@sebiz.net

- **Fabulous wooden doors**

Fabulous wood doors veneer, plywood, solid, molding doors.
Address: 12/234, ziang street 001#Linhu economic zone. Qidu town.wujiang.JS.
Phone: 008651263815408 E-Mail: cmanjunatha81@yahoo.com

- **Everest Metal Industries**

Manufactures and exports builders hardware, kitchen cabinet hardware, brass ...
Address: C-2/107, GIDC, Jamnagar - 361004
Phone: +91-288-2560827 E-Mail: sales@everestmetal.com

- **Venus Industries**

Manufacturer and exporter of brass hardware, door hardware, brass hinges, door ...
Address: 378/4, GIDC, Jamanagar - 361004
Phone: +91-288-2560596 E-Mail: mail@venus-ind.com

- **Welding machine**

Dear sir/madam, ...
Address: Room602,NO195,Fengxiyuan,Gangbei Street,Guangzhou,China
Phone: 86-020-36228308 E-Mail: dashengaw@gmail.com

- **Electrical Brass Components P Ltd**

makers of metal components of all types
Address: 14th Floor Nariman Point Bombay 400021
Phone: 91-9821074335 E-Mail: sales@electrical-brass-components.com

- **manufacturing**

I have a small company in Romania and I have a space good for manufacturing . I ...
Address: metalurgiei
Phone: 0040788411234 E-Mail: gabidanserv@rdslink.ro

- **Entreprendre en Roumanie / Invest in Romania**

I'm offering my help to people who want to come to Romania for business or just ...
E-Mail: alegria_peach@yahoo.com

- **Business English UK c/o AREL**

A free portal guide for English for business and professional language training ...
Address: 56 Buckingham Gate
Phone: +44 207 802 9212 E-Mail: biseng@theenglishlanguage.org

- **Printing,Packaging, Binding Machinery**

We are the largest manufacturer of Die Cutting Machine, Corrugated Box Plant, ...

Address: J-126B, Vishnu Garden ,
Phone: 011-25153953 E-Mail: friendsengg@friendsenggcorp.com

- **ukdir.biz**

Comprehensive UK business directory online for everything from small business ...
Phone: 234567 E-Mail: buylinks@gmail.com

- **Bracebridge Engineering Ltd UK**

Bracebridge an engineering company has been supplying quality presswork and ...

- **Graphcard Inc.**

Register with an online payment solution available to Internet shoppers ...
Address: 31 Olowu Street, Ikeja, Lagos, Nigeria
Phone: 234 803 326 8306 E-Mail: uofulue@yahoo.com

- **Mobile Phone Universe**

More Mobile Phone sites than you can find in a month of Sundays. Check them out ...
Address: 231 Rotherhithe Street
Phone: 020 7136 4963 E-Mail: mob-u@all-mobilephones-uk.com

- **Swedish Translator**

My name is Mattias Bergström and I translate all kinds of texts from English, ...
Address: Fredsgatan 11
Phone: § E-Mail: mattias@swedishtranslator.se

- **Emaze Holdings - Website Design**

Emaze Holdings creates professional websites, as well as logo creation, and ...
E-Mail: tsinfield@emazeholdings.com

- **Translation services lingo24**

Provides the translation services for most of the worlad languages.
Address: 18-20 Queen's Road
Phone: +44 (0) 870 765 4646 E-Mail: info@lingo24.com

- **Clear Answers Ltd.**

UK specialists in accident and personal injury claims, offering a unique ...
Address: Mallards House, Cottage Drive West
Phone: 0845 601 0303 E-Mail: claim@injury-compensation.org.uk

- **Premier ors**

Professional ing services providing high quality copywriting, copy ing ...
Phone: (905) 814 7928 E-Mail: president@premiertutoring.com

- **crgate.com**

Eliminate bad debt from your business forever! One Click to protect your ...

- **Dynamic Exim Corporation**

Indian merchant exporter of pharmaceutical machinery,mini tablet press machine, ...
Address: 242 Indraprasth, Near Nobat Press, Jamnagar Pin 361001
Phone: +91-288-2556844 E-Mail: mail@dynamiceximcorp.com

- **PRO CAR AUDIO INSTALLATIONS**

Installations services for your car audio systems, cd/mp3/dve players, ...
Address: 1 Ural Court, DANDENONG NORTH
Phone: 0422 227 110 E-Mail: imran.m@optusnet.com

- **Instant Publisher Platinum CDROM**

750 Books, Reports & Manuals You Can Reprint & Sell and Make a Fortune! How to ...
Address: 1200 Scotia Dr., #201
Phone: 561-582-1874 E-Mail: krismoor57@yahoo.co.in

- **Companiesmadesimple - Company Formation Services**

Same day company formations. Free online company name search. Start your ...
Address: 145-157 St John Street, London.
Phone: 02072537272 E-Mail: leonw@westbury.co.uk

- **Web Design and Software Programming**

Global Info Factory is a team of IT professionals providing IT services: Web ...
E-Mail: support@globalinfofactory.com

- **Jovial Enterprises**

We are importers, exporters and sourcing agents from india. Kindly contact us ...
Address: Pullichira Post, Kollam, Kerala, India. PIN-691304
Phone: + 91 9895254088 E-Mail: jovialent@rediffmail.com

- **DataWORKS Canada**

Canadian direct marketing company, specializing in business mailing lists, fax ...
Phone: 1-877-492-4200 E-Mail: sales@canadiandata.com

- **Tourism Milodon chile**

Milodon Tourism, a leading tour operator company in the Chilean Patagonia, ...
Address: urmeneta 729
Phone: 562-8562610 E-Mail: milodon.cl@gmail.com

- **Web Design and Software Programming**

Global Info Factory is a team of IT professionals providing IT services: Web ...

- **Electrical Brass Components P Ltd**
maker of Brass comonents and electrical fittings
Address: 1406 Dalamal towers Nariman Point Mumbai India
Phone: 91-22-56371096 E-Mail: sales@electrical-brass-components.com

- **Scientific & Audio Visual Instruments**
Manufacturers, & exporters of Scientific, medical and Audio visual products ...
Address: 171, Industrial Area, Ambala Cantt. India
Phone: 0171-2699712 E-Mail: jmt@sancharnet.in

- **Rajhans Impex Pvt Ltd**
Manufacturer of copper & brass ingots and billets, copper alloy extrusion, ...
Address: Plot No. 8, GIDC, Phase II, Dared, Jamnagar 361004. Gujarat. India
Phone: + 91 - 288 - 2730971 E-Mail: info@rajhansimpex.com

- **Best Plastic Processing Machinery**
High End Manufacturer & Exporter of plastic processing Machinery & spares
Address: kundanahalli
E-Mail: renukatan70@yahoo.com

- **Phoenix Telco**
UK based telephone call provider offers cheap international phone calls to the ...
Address: 5 Banbury Curt, Woodstock Avenue
Phone: 0208 5664826 E-Mail: phoenix@telecom-links.net

- **Document-Doctor**
Professional writing and ing service for all English language business ...
Phone: 44+ 7956874194 E-Mail: webmaster@document-doctor.co.uk

- **Scopulus Business Resources**
online Business resources, company formation, legal documents, accounting ...
Address: 39 Almer Road
E-Mail: craiy@scopulus.co.uk

- **Canada Pardons**
Canada Pardons is a leading Canadian firm specializing in helping people with ...
Address: 3442 Yonge Street.
Phone: 4164889000 E-Mail: submission@sebiz.net

PROFESSIONALS IN SUDAN

Simulation Services
Provides custom simulation models that improve energy, logistics, healthcare ...
Address: 0367 Oslo

Phone: - E-Mail: temp1@simulationservices.com

uttam consultants
we assist in getting you in india for higher studies we also provide you ...
Address: flat 12 shantha paradise 121 wheeler road cox town
Phone: 091 080 25485909 E-Mail: kiranku_2000@yahoo.com

Online Divorce Directory
Online-Divorce-Help.org is a web directory of Divorce related legal and other ...
Address: 231 Rotherhithe Street
Phone: 020 7136 4963 E-Mail: wt@online-divorce-help.org

Oxford College
$10 dental cleaning for children 5-16 years of age. $20 dental cleaning for ...
Address: 670 Progress Avenue
E-Mail: dentalhygiene@hotmail.com

Search Recruitment
List of Uk Industrial Manufacturing jobs are updated daily at Search ...
Address: 198 West George Street
Phone: 0141 272 7777 E-Mail: search@hire-exchange.com

Online Divorce Directory
Online-Divorce-Help.org is a web directory of Divorce related legal and other ...
Address: 231 Rotherhithe Street
Phone: 020 7136 4963 E-Mail: wt@divorce-uk.org

UK Industrial & Manufacturing Jobs at Search Consultancy
List of Uk Industrial Manufacturing jobs are updated daily at Search ...
Address: 198 West George Street
Phone: 0141 272 7777 E-Mail: search@hire-exchange.com

CARTER MORGAN
INTERNATIONAL MODELS REQUIRED. 18-26 ATTRACTIVE FEMALES REQUIRED FOR OVERSEAS ...
Address: park st
Phone: +44775 4126756 E-Mail: jameslouis1@yahoo.co.uk

International Personnel Consultants., Inc
Professional, Skilled, Non-skilled, Health Care, Technical, Construction, ...
Address: 1903 Jollibee Plaza Bldg., Emerald Ave., Ortigas Centre, Pasig City, Philippines
Phone: 0063-2-6872247 E-Mail: alex@ipc.com.ph

An Online UK Divorce Resource Directory
Find services and information related to divorces in the UK : Divorce-UK.org
Address: Flat 5, 1 Holmbush Rd
Phone: 0208 780 5493 E-Mail: info@divorce-uk.org

Web Design and Software Programming
Global Info Factory is a team of IT professionals providing IT services: Web ...

Omaya China Business Consultant Company
Business consulting, china consulting, China consultant, China Investigation, ...
Address: Fengtai District, Beijing, China
Phone: 86-10-83823755 E-Mail: 86-10-83822706

Emigrateforgood
EMIGRATE to NEW ZEALAND I'll deal with immigration papers, Expression of ...
E-Mail: draco2464@hotmail.com

SUDAN FINANCE COMPANIES

Financial Freedom Made Simple
Learn to take control of your financial distress with a free directory. The ...
Address: Nordjordkroken 8
Phone: +47.91-31-27-02 E-Mail: shiva2000@gmail.com

pikecpa
New Hampshire CPA Firm, located in the Seacoast NH and Portsmouth NH areas, ...
Phone: 12345678 E-Mail: devkumar123@gmail.com

1 Personal Finances - Information On Home Finance, Corporate
1 Personal Finances has information on Insurance, Loans, Cr Cards, ...
Address: 36 Walton St
Phone: 01226 231525 E-Mail: stefan@1-personal-finances.com

DebtFreeToday
Online debt consolidation services. Non profit debt consultations providing ...
Address: 4604 S Ironwood Ave
E-Mail: di_promote@yahoo.com

TRAVEL TO SUDAN

- **Cheap Airport Parking UK Gatwick, Heathrow, Stansted & Major**

Cheap Airport Parking - save up to 60% with cheap airport parking fees at major ...
Address: 15 Tunwell Greave, Sheffield S5 9GB
Phone: 0114 2467240 E-Mail: rpday@parkandsave.com

- **Cobico Travel & Tours Ltd**

Mauritius,a paradis island situated in the Indian Ocean. ...
Address: 89 Saint Jean Road Quatre Bornes
Phone: 4674084 E-Mail: kity@cobicogroup.com

- **Cobico Group**

Mauritius is a small paradis island situated in the Indian Ocean. ...
Address: 89 Saint Jean Rd Quatre Bornes Mauritius
Phone: 4674084 E-Mail: 4674052

- **Cruisestore**

Book cruise holidays to destinations across the world with TheCruiseStore.co.uk
Address: Holiday House, Sandbrook Park, Sandbrook Way
Phone: 01706 742 500 E-Mail: cruise@holiday-travel-flights.com

- **Travel agent**

My Qatar offers cheap flight from UK to Doha, Dubai, Muscat, Jeddah, Riyadh, ...
Address: 372-374
Phone: 2085181010 E-Mail: ajay@cityvacations.co.uk

- **Ibonia**

Votre billets d'avion charter avec Avion-charter.fr. Comparez votre billet ...
Address: 33 rue Ratsimilaho Antaninarenina
E-Mail: ibonia@avion.fr

- **PlaceClick Brisbane**

A general directory about Brisbane. Here you will find everything you need to ...

- **Map South Pacific**

South Pacific maps and travel guides to Tahiti, Fiji, Samoa, Vanuatu, Easter ...
Address: 1-5765 Turner Road
Phone: 1-250-756-0333 E-Mail: webmail@mapsouthpacific.com

- **Sofia Hotels on-line reservations**

On-line reservations at the best prices for all Sofia hotels

- **Expat Blog**

Expat-Blog.com is an open community dedicated to expatriates and their ...

- **DIY Travel Directory**

Accommodation and travel resources for independent travellers.

- **TRAVEL AGENCY**
Climbing,Horseriding,Roundtrips,Cruises,Ski,Rafting
Phone: 00359 32 653001 E-Mail: info@interjet-bg.com

- **Casas rurales, empresas de turismo activo y restaurantes**
Directorio de Casas rurales, hoteles con encanto, empresas de turismo activo y ...
Address: Julio A Roca 252 - Piso 1
Phone: 03546 461410 E-Mail: links@sleepinspain.com

- **discovering peru**
discover the unknown jungle and beautiful landscapes of the Andes in the ...
Address: lima
Phone: +5112427521 E-Mail: discoveringperuref@yahoo.com

- **Alessandro**
Low cost flight search engine and many tools that help you planning your ...

- **Thomas Cook**
Cheap holidays from Thomas Cook, book last minute deals online at ...
Address: Thomas Cook Business Park, Coningsby Road
Phone: 0870 750 5711 E-Mail: tc@holiday-travel-flights.com

- **Cheap Cruise**
Find more information out about cruises, mini cruises or chat in the forum and ...
E-Mail: forum@passionforcruising.com

- **111 Travel Directory**
Bed and breakfasts and lodging, including hostels and hotels. Searching for a ...

- **Athens Hotels**
Complete list of Athens hotels with detailed description photos and rates. ...
E-Mail: webmaster@travel-guide-greece.com

- **Globebookings**
Discount Hotel reservations with Globebookings in Cuba, Dubai, Singapore, Hong ...
Address: Vaclavske namesti 55
Phone: 420 245 005 631 E-Mail: info@globetravelgroup.com

- **Italy hotels reservations - Travel Mall**
Your personal online Mall for travel services reservation in Italy. Hotels and ...
E-Mail: info@travel-mall.net

- **Cheap City Breaks**

We offer bargain short breaks, cheap city breaks and cheap weekend getaways.

- **villasandbeds ltd**

providing a good range of vaction villas and apartments with private pools in ...
Address: 9 mill drive
Phone: 0044 1323491440 E-Mail: info@villasandbeds.com

- **UK Short Breaks**

Short weekend and midweek breaks in the UK, at luxurious hotels in beautiful ...
E-Mail: chris.hough@g-mapps.com

- **Lightfoot Travel**

Lightfoot Travel is your one stop shop for all your travel needs. Plus, click ...
E-Mail: BLitefoot@aol.com

- **City Portals**

City Portals - - accomodation, travel, tourism and business city information ...
E-Mail: ads@cityround.com

- **Discover China**

Information about independent travel in China, Hong Kong and Taiwan.

- **Electrobug Technologies**

Electrobug provides real-time, online pricing intelligence tools for making ...
Phone: +91-124-5034024/25 E-Mail: devrishi.arora@electrobug.com

- **1000 Tips 4 Trips: Travel Tips and Advice**

Over 1000 travel tips and hints submitted by users from around the world. ...

- **Sea& Desert Tours**

Incoming agent in Sudan , Libya and Egypt
Address: Khartum
Phone: 002 010 1380612

- **World-wide travel guide**

Travel guide to destinations, based on geographic region. ...

- **travel**

Travel portal offering flights, hotels, car hire, tailor-made and round the ...
E-Mail: neetu.chillar@tecnovate.co.in

- **Canuck Abroad**

A resource for expatriates and travellers backpacking in Europe or living ...

- **Thai-Experience.org**

Gain a deeper insight into Thai culture by volunteering in Thailand. Teach ...
Address: Km6 Udon-Nongkhai Highway
Phone: +66 42 411 079 E-Mail: sabine@thai-experience.org

- **tourism**

Welcome visitor's who'd like to visit Ukraine! (Kyiv). May 2005 year. ...
Phone: +380503213178 E-Mail: valera77@bigmir.net

- **1st Cruise Holidays**

Merranean Cruises, Caribbean Cruises, Mini Cruising Holidays with P&O, ...
Address: Flightline House, Westcliff, Essex, England.
Phone: 0800 316 5550 E-Mail: andy@flightline.co.uk

- **BestBuyAir**

Discount travel agent. Discount airfare, hotels, rental cars, cruises, vacation ...

- **TravelMake**

Travel for less. Save up to 65% on hotels, air tickets, cruises, rental cars ...

- **Xcape With us**

An online accommodation booking company.
Address: Gran via Asima
Phone: 0034 971 43 69 00 E-Mail: naomi.fryer@xcapewithus.com

- **Charmardon Consultants**

This one stop search shop offers search engines, news, travel, help & ...
E-Mail: info@trying2findu.com

- **Train Travel World**

TrainTravelWorld.com is a specialized directory of Train Travel web sites from ...
Address: Flat 5, 1 Holmbush Rd, Putney
Phone: 0208 780 5493

- **Secure Airport Parking at Birmingham**

Airport parking voucher available immediately online and via email wih full ...
Address:
Phone: E-Mail: submission@tridentindia.net

- **Car Parking at Manchester Airport**

Monitored car parking at Manchester airport. Easy online booking and instant ...
Address:
Phone: E-Mail: submission@tridentindia.net

- **Luton Airport Parking**

Luton airport parking in secure monitored parking compounds. We have car parks ...
Address:
Phone: E-Mail: submission@tridentindia.net

- **Airport Parking Heathrow**

Park your car safely at Heathrow airport whilst on holiday. Our online booking ...
Address:
Phone: E-Mail: submission@tridentindia.net

- **Compare hotel rates before you go!**

35.000 hotels at 5.300 cities of 110 different countries. HotelsFare.com is ...
E-Mail: cheap_flight@yahoo.com

- **Holiday Zone**

Holiday Accommodation directory australia wide.
E-Mail: info@holidayzone.com.au

- **Voyagenow**

Book a hotel for today or one year in advance. We cater for Business ...
Address: 1st floor 128 hindley street adelaide
Phone: 618 84155110 E-Mail: frank@e-channel.com.au

- **TravelRomp.com**

Hotels, Cars, Flights - We make the world your playground!

- **Golden Key**

Offering Vietnamese day courses (and longer) - learn essential words and ...
Address: 30 Hoa Ma
Phone: 04 9714880 E-Mail: info@goldenkey.edu.vn

- **Canuck Abroad**

A resource for expatriates and travellers backpacking in Europe or living ...

- **Trip-Savers.Com**

Discount Airfare, Hotel Reservations and Car Rentals worldwide. ...
Address: 9036 S. Knox Ave.
Phone: 7082299769 E-Mail: techsupport@trip-savers.com

SUDAN RECREATION AND LEISURE

•

- **Parish Chest**

The premier online family history and genealogy shop where you can buy just ...
Address: ancestors
Phone: 01872 - 864807 E-Mail: forefathers@btconnect.com

- **Beyond Retreats - Yoga and Sport Holidays**

Offers unique yoga breaks and yoga holidays at beautiful venues within the UK ...
Address: PO Box 46523
Phone: 0207 226 4044 E-Mail: br@holiday-travel-flights.com

- **Bedlam Weekends**

Online quotations, making it easier to plan your Stag, Hen or other event, with ...
Address: 28 Great King Street
Phone: 0131 558 19 19 E-Mail: info@bedlam.co.uk

- **Epeco Enterprises Ltd.**

Looking for a place to rest when you want to go for summer or winter. Our ...
Address: P.O. Box 68130-00200. Nairobi.Kenya
Phone: +254(0)722 255 311 E-Mail: epeco99@yahoo.com

- **Best Online Casino**

We review online casinos and help you find a honest online casino.

- **Langtry Manor Hotel**

The Langtry Manor offers some of the most stylish hotel accommodation in ...
Address: Derby Road
Phone: 01202 553 887 E-Mail: lillie@langtrymanor.com

- **A1 Online Slots**

Slot machine guide to online slots. How to play slots, tips, strategies, ...
Address: 55 Bluey Plaza
Phone: 012145 5 825 E-Mail: amuzemeats@hotmail.com

FOOD AND DRINK

Maad Food Ind.Co,L.L.C
We, Maad Food Ind. Co, L.L.C are happy to inform you that we are one of the ...
Address: 1km. up to police station of Tabriz - Mianeh road.
Phone: +98-411-6300463 E-Mail: sale@chocomaad.com

The Sweetmaster
Your favourite traditional old fashioned sweets, candy, and confectionery from ...

E-Mail: desousacosta@hotmail.com

CORNUCOPIA
Horn of Plenty provides a secure shopping experience that fulfills your needs, ...

CakeChannel.com
Find 1.000+ wedding cake pictures, designs and ideas
Address: 29 Carpenter St
Phone: 732-936-9336 E-Mail: enezok@yahoo.com

Wedding Cakes Channel
Wedding cakes: pictures, designs and ideas
Address: 29 Carpenter St
Phone: 732-936-9336 E-Mail: enezok@yahoo.com

Candocandy online Sweets and Candy
Traditional British Sweets, Chocolate, Toffee, Fudge and Gift Hampers. Find ...
Address:
Phone: E-Mail: sales@candocandy.com

Micro Diet
Micro diet
Address: Phoenix Az
E-Mail: info@classichits.com

AUTOMOTIVES IN SUDAN

- **ChipsAway Fareham**

Smart car repair in Fareham, Hampshire: Repair of alloy wheels, bumper scuffs, ...
Address: 20, Gudgeheath Lane
Phone: 01329 517576 E-Mail: webmaster_pioneer@yahoo.com

- **Firstcar**

Buy and sell new and used cars online specialising in young driver's ...E-Mail: firstcar@cherryaid.co.uk

- **Car Culture**

Car accessories for all motorists including lighting, gear knobs, alarms and ...

- **Electrical Brass Components**

makers of auto electrical components and cable lugs, battery terminals
Address: Alamal Towers Nariman POint Mumbai
Phone: 91-9821074335 E-Mail: sales@electrical-brass-components.com

- **Picknbuy24**

"Japan's No.1 used car dealer Network-Pick'nBuy24com.Car auction, car import, ...

- **M-BenzForum**

M-BenzForum is an online community for owners and enthusiasts of Mercedes Benz ...
E-Mail: andry_budiman2004@yahoo.com

- **Car Smart Online Automotive Auction**

Car Smart Online Automotive Auction - Buy and Sell everything and anything 100% ...
Address: 5 Linton Road
Phone: 01132664562 E-Mail: sales@car-smart.co.uk

- **Electrical Brass Components P Ltd**

makers of electrical parts and auto parts
Address: DalamAl Towers N. Point BOMBAY INDIA
Phone: 91-22-56371096 E-Mail: sales@electrical-brass-components.com

- **Goela engineers**

India tractor parts - producers and exporters of spare tractor part like ...
Phone: 0091-9810645100 E-Mail: agromachine@touchtelindia.net

- **Monu exports**

India's largest manufacturer, Exporter and Supplier, specialized in - ...
Phone: 91-11 -23913292 E-Mail: agromachine@touchtelindia.net

- **Pistonrings**

Piston rings by India piston-rings is one of the leading names in the industry ...
Phone: 91-11- 23966973 E-Mail: agromachine@touchtelindia.net

- **agromachine**

Used Tractors by AgroMachine. You've located the most powerful and complete ...
Phone: 32(0)52 55 31 28 E-Mail: agromachine@touchtelindia.net

- **Simeon George**

Seeking a joint venture cheap automobile manufacturer
Address: 9791 Westheimer road , Houston , Texas 77042
E-Mail: twinsint@yahoo.com

SUDAN INTERNET AND COMPUTERS

- **50000_CPUs_Harnessed**

Our group's goal is bring together 50000 CPUs for the purpose of forming a ...
Phone: 1-770-443-0115 E-Mail: sabarnett@yahoo.com

- **World Digital**

Offering digital media such as software, games, ebooks, audiobooks, mobile ...
E-Mail: inform@wdeonline.com

- **lizratechnologies**

Lizra Technologies is a specialist web, software development firm providing ...
E-Mail: jeena@lizratechnologies.com

- **LinkAssistant SEO Tool**
Increase your link popularity with LinkAssistant - powerful SEO software for ...
Address: Nezalezhnasti ave, 72a-86

- **Ambergreen Internet Marketing**
Search engine and internet marketing online traffic solutions through SEO, paid ...
Address: 111 George Street
Phone: 0131 225 7020 E-Mail: agim@all-web-design.com

- **esrmtech**
worldwide distribution of electronic components with emphasis on obsolete and ...
Address: D-325, Defence Colony 1st stage, Peenya Industrial estate
Phone: 91-11-24799792 E-Mail: hms_osa083@yahoo.com

- **GulfClick.NET Co**
GulfClick.Net is one of the leading web services provider located at KUWAIT ...
Address: hawally
Phone: 965-2650262 E-Mail: adib@newgulf.net

- **Adult Website Promotion Services**
Adult Website Promotion services sell porn - we offer free porn movies, free ...
Address: 101-New Street, New York, USa
Phone: 123-343-4545 E-Mail: harshseo@gmail.com

- **UK Webmaster World Link Exchange Directory exchange reciproc**
Add your website to uk webmaster world link exchange database free of charge ...
Address: Hereford
Phone: 8070 440 150 E-Mail: luqman@velnet-ngr.com

- **Wura - World - Internet Website Directory**
add your website to our internet website directory free of charge.
Address: Hereford
Phone: 80707 440 150 E-Mail: luqman@velnet-ngr.com

- **UK Web Directory**
UK Web Directory, Web Site Hosting Directory and web hosting resources UK
Address: Hereford
Phone: 08707 440 150 E-Mail: luqman@velnet-ngr.com

- **Cheap Web Hosting Directory, Web Design, Search Engine Promo**
Web Hosting Directory with cheap web hosting plans, domain registration, web ...
E-Mail: service@asterhost.com

- **Cut Price Ink 4U**
Cut Price Ink 4U offers inkjet cartridges, laser toners and printer accessories ...
Address: Victoria Market
Phone: 01453 543676 E-Mail: sales@cutpriceink4U.co.uk

- **Softafrik Arts Ltd**

Need a brilliant cost effective software solution for your enterprise? Big or ...
Address: Crescent Rd, Buruburu, Nairobi, Kenya
Phone: +254 (0)721991155 E-Mail: skmwenda@yahoo.com

- **SEO List Find search engine marketing companies**

SEOLIST.com is a List for SEOs Worldwide. You'll find everything you need for ...
Phone: 9815612193 E-Mail: seolist@gmail.com

- **Ambergreen Internet Marketing**

Boost your website traffic through SEO, paid listings and trusted feed.
Address: 111 George Street
Phone: 0131 225 7020 E-Mail: 0131 225 7030

- **UK Internet WebSites Directory**

UK Web Directory is collection of Internet web sites or web pages related to ...
Phone: 2627884 E-Mail: ukwebdirectory@gmail.com

- **iSys Group**

Worldwide manufacturer of high quality direct thermal printers, thermal inkjet ...
Address: 911 - 28 Street N.E., Calgary, AB, T2K0V6, Canada
Phone: 403.204.5200 E-Mail: customerservice@isys-media.com

- **Banner ad design**

Professional and affordable banner ad design including eye-catching flash ...
Phone: 07913520180

- **Net Explorers**

Net Explorers are providers of professional web hosting UK, web design and ...
Address: 22 Stainburn Crescent
Phone: +44 113 3683073 E-Mail: ne@cool-web-hosting.com

- **Webxperience! Directory**

Features a searchable, spam-free, human-ed directory of the Web. ...
Address: Bucharest
E-Mail: team@webxperience.org

- **HomeHighlight - Free for reprint home and family articles**

A virtual community offering free for reprint articles regarding home, family, ...
E-Mail: support@homehighlight.org

- **BusinessHighlight - Free for reprint business articles**

A virtual community offering free for reprint articles regarding ...
E-Mail: support@businesshighlight.org

- **Questlaunch - Web Search Portal**

Search the world wide web. Webmasters use the pay per click ...
Phone: 555-5555 E-Mail: admin@questlaunch.com

- **Bid Up**

Bid Up Online Auction - Buy and Sell everything and anything with no final ...
Address: 5 Linton Road
Phone: 01132664562 E-Mail: sales@bidup.org

- **Web Design and Software Programming**

Global Info Factory is a team of IT professionals providing IT services: Web ...
E-Mail: support@globalinfofactory.com

- **EmailAway.com**

Check any POP3 or IMAP4 email account from any computer, anytime, for free. ...

- **Sadikhov.com**

Free MCSE, CCNA, CCNP, A+, OCP and other certification resources for IT ...
Address: Bashir Safar Ogli
Phone: 994 50 2139190 E-Mail: admin@sadikhov.com

- **Web Design and Software Programming**

Global Info Factory is a team of IT professionals providing IT services: Web ...
E-Mail: support@globalinfofactory.com

- **Ink Cartridge Directory : TOPINK.com**

TOPINK is your online ink cartridge directory. Check out our top ink cartridge ...

- **Little Effort......More Earning**

Spare a few hours on your PC to earn more by posting Ads. Basic knowledge of ...
E-Mail: padma_sen@netambience.com

- **AssureYourPrivacy.com Privacy Protection Softwre**

Remove web tracks, computer tracks, sensitive information beyond recovery from ...

- **PromoteClick.Com**

Delivers targeted traffic at wholesale prices. Target your campaign by ...
E-Mail: vojin@net.yu

- **K Web Marketing**

K Web Marketing provides turnkey solutions for your web marketing needs. We do ...
E-Mail: jason@kwebmarketing.com

- **Stephen Hoods**
online resource directory
Address: d-47 new dekhi
Phone: 01825 723008 E-Mail: submit@online-global-directory.com

- **Ringtonescharts.com**
Style your Mobile with Ringtones Real Sounds and True Tones.
E-Mail: link@ringtonescharts.com

SUDAN BOOKS AND MEDIA

Miranda Book PUblishers
A source of classic books about the Knights of Malta, Maltese history, ...
E-Mail: gouldian@nextgen.net.mt

Best-Compare Limited
Find the best price for Books, CD - DVD. We search all the retailers in seconds ...
Address: 61 Victoria Road
Phone: 7654321 E-Mail: response@best-compare.com

Shriramsharma.com
Three free e-books on Indian Kundalini Yoga correlated to Neurosciences-ESP, ...
Address: Visnagar Road
E-Mail: ashokrawal@shriramsharma.com

CORNUCOPIA
Horn of Plenty provides a secure shopping experience that fulfills your needs, ...
E-Mail: llcrtr@yahoo.com

Instant Publisher Platinum CDROM
750 Books, Reports & Manuals You Can Reprint & Sell and Make a Fortune! How to ...
Address: 1200 Scotia Dr., #201
Phone: 561-582-1874 E-Mail: rranwarhussain56@yahoo.com

Magazine Subscriptions
MagazineSubscriptions.com is one of the larger magazine subscription sites. We ...
E-Mail: links@magazinesubscriptions.com

Police Test Prep
Police Test Prep essential study guide for all aptitude, pati, bpad, wct, ...
Address: 2 Stockman Crescent
Phone: 416 885 0258 E-Mail: cbedwell@policetestprep.com

MJ
I have books of all kinds for sale, old, religious, many different subjects. My ...
Address: 412 main street Salem WV
Phone: 304-782-3191 E-Mail: FoxNwsFan@aol.com

Mums Mag
Motherhood resources like articles, things to do, information about products & ...
Address: 14 Myro Drive, Glenmore, Durban, South Africa
Phone: +27 (0)31 261 6866 E-Mail: monique@mumsmag.co.za

SUDAN MERCHANDISE-STORES

- **Myjewelz Diamond Jewellery**

Online sellers of Diamond Jewellery
Address: 1406 Narman Point Mumbai India
Phone: 91-22-56371095 E-Mail: sales@myjewelz.com

- **Hand Tools & stationery**

We Are Exporting Brass Hand Tools, Stationery, Plastic Ware, Water Proofing ...
Address: Opp: Dreamland No.33Cinema ,Tribhuvan Road
Phone: 5182673 E-Mail: chandrashe81@yahoo.com

- **Custom Trading Cards | Schedule Cards**

Personalized, specialty trading and schedule cards for police and fire ...

- **Baby Boom 2000: Baby Nursery Store for Baby travel System, b**

BabyBoom 2000 specialize in Baby Travel Systems, Sleeping Bags, Rockers and ...
Address: 4 NEW POND PARADE,WEST END ROAD
Phone: 01895 675596 E-Mail: webmaster@babyboom2000.co.uk

- **Blue Nile TV**

Blue Nile TV Produces quality TV programmes and broadcast them to the Audiences ...
Address: Debreziet Road
Phone: +251 1 16 99 61 E-Mail: bluenileltv@yahoo.com

- **Gift Baskets Shipped Worldwide**

Unique gift baskets for all occasions. Featured on the NBC Today Show, with ...
Phone: 888-291-4039 E-Mail: April@WyomingImpressions.com

- **szjingfeng**

Fabulous wood doors veneer, plywood, solid, molding doors ...
Address: 12/234, ziang street 001#Linhu economic zone. Qidu town.wujiang.JS. china
Phone: 008651263815408 E-Mail: sureshdasani56@yahoo.com

- **Knife Country, USA**

Offers hunting, fishing, camping, pocket and kitchen knives. Specializing in ...

Address: 7111 Dixie hwy., 109
Phone: 877-399-1564 E-Mail: jterryah@knifecountryusa.com

- **Diamond Pendants India P Ltd**

makers of Diamond pendants in various shapes
Address: 1406 Dalamal Towers
Phone: 91-22-53555344 E-Mail: sales@diamond-pendants-india.com

- **High end Hydraulic Hose.**

Low cost high quality Manufactures of Hydraulic and stainless steel hose ...
Phone: 51170190/51272190 E-Mail: shilparud74@yahoo.com

- **Swimming Pools World**

All kind of swimming pools. Best swimming pool supplies.

- **dental equipments**

Manfacturer & Exporter for all dental Equipments.
Address: 368/3, MES Road, Jalahalli Industrial Area.
Phone: 28381345/2838443 E-Mail: abbrenian@yahoo.com

- **eMarksoft Inc.**

Offering server side graphing & charting & drawing components software for data ...
Address: Fl.9 Bond Building

- **Best Buys Online**

Online Shopping Mall. We offer quality gifts, jewelry, brand name electronics ...

- **Best Buys Online**

Online Shopping Mall. We offer quality gifts, jewelry, brand name electronics ...

- **2Guitar.com**

Learn How to Play the Guitar. We offer 6 comprehensive ebooks on mastering the ...
Address: 207 728 country hills road nw
Phone: 4035030177 E-Mail: support@pixelzen.com

- **Engagement Rings India P Ltd**

makers of engagement rings in diamond
Address: 1406 DalamAl Towers MumBai 21
Phone: 56371095 E-Mail: sales@engagement-rings-india.com

- **moneyprogram**

make money do nothing...only send out customised mails through official built ...
Address: box 4907 s/l

Phone: +234-8037139723 E-Mail: elisfid@yahoo.com

- **luminous network**

A seller company in the market of oil production is offering a ...
Address: 7 enitan road,surulere
Phone: +234-8037139723 E-Mail: elisfid@yahoo.com

- **luminous network**

A seller company in the market of oil production is offering a ...
Address: 7 enitan road,surulere
Phone: +234-8037139723 E-Mail: elisfid@yahoo.com

- **Engagement Rings India Ltd**

makers of diamond engagement rings and wedding rings
Address: 1406 Dalamal Towers Bombay 400021
Phone: 91-22-56371095 E-Mail: sales@engagement-rings-india.com

- **Diamond Engagement Rings India**

Makers of engagement rings in Diamonds
Address: 41, Yusuf Building Pudhonie Bombay 3 INdia
Phone: 91-22-56371095 E-Mail: sales@engagement-rings-india.com

- **Wyoming Impressions**

Top quality gift baskets for all occasions shipped worldwide from the U.S.
Phone: 888-291-4039 E-Mail: April@WyomingImpressions.com

REGISTRATION OF FOREIGN DRUG MANUFACTURING COMPANY

Name, address and type of the foreign company.

Name and address of local licensed local agent.

Copy of agency agreement certified by the Registrar of Companies

The manufacturing license (photocopy) for the company to manufacture pharmaceutical products for use in the country of origin issued by the health authority in the same country.

Valid Statement of Licensing Status of Pharmaceutical Products (SLSPP) conforming to the format recommended by the World Health Organization, issued by competent certifying authority in the country of origin authenticated, certified and stamped by Sudan Embassy in country of origin.

Valid GMP certificate issued by competent certifying authority in the country of origin authenticated, certified and stamped by Sudan Embassy in country of origin.

List of other divisions, subsidiaries□.etc. of the Mother Company and their full addresses.

Other countries where the company is registered confirmed by photocopies of the certificates of registration in those countries.

Full information and about the pharmaceutical plant including at least the following information :

Name and address of the drug manufacturing plant(s).

Date of establishment.

Name and address of both Chairman of Board of Directors and the Managing Director of the company.

Value in US $ of local sales of products manufactured in the plant during previous 12 months.

Value in US $ of exported products manufactured in the plant and names of importing countries during previous 12 months.

Products other than pharmaceuticals manufactured in that factory.

Layout plan of the factory, indicating location and floor area of all buildings and facilities.

List of all technical full-time staff of the factory, their posts and qualifications (name : post : qualifications).

List of lines and types of production.

List of major equipment.

Evidence of any internationally recognized awards or certifications of

Excellence or compliance with international standards, e.g. ISO 9000, 9001.

List of main research studies performed by the company during the last 5 to 10 years.

Pharmaceutical products released to the market based on that research.

Any other useful information about the company, its manufacturing plants and there products.

Fill in official forms if any are required.

Company Master file is required.

Dr. Salah edelin Abd Elrahman
Chairman, Committee
For registration of Pharmaceutical
Products for Human Use

GENERAL REQUIREMENTS FOR THE REGISTRATION OF PHARMACEUTICAL PRODUCTS

Introduction

According to the Pharmacy and Poisons Act it is an offence to manufacture, import, sell, offer for

sale any pharmaceutical product unless registered under the provisions of the Act, and regulations, and directives issued under the Act. So all applicants for registration of pharmaceutical products should be familiar with all such provisions and requirements issued by the Federal Board of Pharmacy. The Directorate General of Pharmacy in the Federal Ministry of Health is the executive arm of the Board.
Pharmaceutical products submitted for registration should be manufactured in a registered plant. The criteria for registration of a pharmaceutical product are :

Need (health or market need)
Efficacy.
Safety.
Quality.
Advantage over similar registered products.
Price.

General Rules to Applicants for Registration of Pharmaceutical Products

The applicant can receive application form for registration of a pharmaceutical product from the DGOP.

Applications for registration should be submitted to the DGOP according to the time schedule specified by the Directorate.

The applicant should be :

Holder of a valid wholesales pharmaceutical license and an agency agreement with the manufacturer.

A public sector establishment authorized by the Pharmacy and Poisons Act to deal with pharmaceutical products.

The applicant should fill two copies of the prescribed application form in typewriter and should not overlook any information required in any part of the form. The prescribed duty stamps should be fixed to the first copy of the form. The applicant should also pay the prescribed application and registration fees and attach the receipt to the application form.

The form certifying the accuracy of documentation and information submitted for registration should also be filled by type writing and signed by responsible person specified by the applicant.

The applicant should present with the application form, the specified documentation and samples (as shown in registration requirements). All documents should be in English and / or Arabic.

A general synopsis should be submitted with the application form and it should cover all aspects of the documentation with reference to the actual documents in a reference list. The general synopsis should provide a concise review of the information required by the Board about a pharmaceutical product to enable it to consider the application for registration. The general synopsis should be an accurate precise of the information in the manufacturer full data file. Claimed advantages over registered products should be shown.

Application for registration is accepted only for products produced in registered manufacturing plants.

Any incomplete or incorrect documents will not be accepted.

Any documents not properly arranged and filed will not be accepted.

Additional requirements for locally manufactured pharmaceutical products:

Special temporary pre-registration approval is required for locally manufactured products, which enables the manufacturer to start the production of new pharmaceutical product for final registration. The applicant should submit the following documentation.

Fully filled prescribed application forms in three copies and should not overlook any information required in any part of the form. The prescribed duty stamps should be fixed to the first copy of the form.

Composition formula showing amount and specification for each ingredient and purpose for its use.

Proposed method of manufacture.

Proposed method of analysis.

Specifications of the finished product.

Protocol for certificate of analysis.

Protocol for stability studies as required.

Method, type and material of packaging including pack sizes and description of the inner and outer package.

Draft of the product pack insert.

II. Registration Requirements:

The registration file submitted should include the following documents:

A Certificate of a Pharmaceutical Product (CPP)
Application for registration

Provide a WHO type Certificate of a Pharmaceutical Product (CPP) issued under WHO Certification Scheme on the Quality of Pharmaceutical Products moving in International Commerce.

The Certificate of the Pharmaceutical Product should be issued by the competent authority in the exporting country as notified to WHO, authenticated and stamped by Sudan Embassy in country of origin.

Date of introduction into the market in country of origin.

The composition formula in the Certificate of the Pharmaceutical Product should show the active and inactive ingredients.

The composition formula should be the same in country of origin.

Registration licensing or authorization in other countries

Provide a list of the countries in which this product has been granted a license for marketing, State for each.

The restrictions on sale or distribution

Container / closure system.

Photocopy of the certificate of registration in each of these countries.

Composition formula

Provide complete composition and quantitative formula of the product with justification and purpose of use of each ingredient with mentioning to reference book, which shows allowance for use of this ingredient for that purpose. This should show unit dose formula and batch formula.

Compatibility of active and inactive ingredients and their effects on the product physicochemical properties should be shown.

Properties of the Active Pharmaceutical Ingredients (API)

Provide at least the following information:

Active ingredient(s) by international non-proprietary names (INN), or generic or chemical name and their source (s).

Chemical data on the active ingredient(s) (chemical structure, solubility of active ingredient in water and other solvents such as ether, ethanol, acetone and buffers of different, pH, and other relevant physicochemical properties.

Structural formula (constitutional and empirical), molecular wt, copies of infrared, ultraviolet spectra.

Active ingredient present in the form of salts or hydrate should be described quantitatively by their total mass and by the mass of the active moiety of the molecules.

Information on the chemical stability of the active pharmaceutical ingredient and physicochemical stability if relevant.

Name and address of manufacturer of Active Pharmaceutical Ingredient(s) (API) including any alternative manufacturers. For each foreign site attach a GMP certificate issued by the drug control authority.

Specifications for the Active Pharmaceutical Ingredient (API)

Provide a list of tests and limits for results for the active pharmaceutical active ingredient (s),including test methods in sufficient .

Provide the results of the methods of the assay of the (API) and of impurities.

If the ingredient is tested on the basis of a monograph in pharmacopoeia, it is sufficient to provide a copy of the monograph, together with any test methods referenced but not duplicated in the monograph.

Provide of any specifications additional to those in the pharmacopoeia.

Specifications for inactive ingredients

Provide quality control specifications, certificate of analysis of starting materials.

Provide a list of tests and limits for results for each excipients (solvent, liquid to adjust pH, coating materials, capsule shell and ink imprinted on the dosage from) including test method.

If the ingredient is tested on the basis of a monograph in a pharmacopoeia, it is sufficient to provide a copy of the monograph together with any test methods referenced not in the monograph.

Provide of any specifications additional to those in the pharmacopoeia, including microbiological limits for materials of natural origin.

Manufacturing procedure for the finished product :

Provide a detailed method of manufacturing procedure for the finished product, including packaging and showing all materials used in the manufacturing process even if they do not appear in the final product.

In-process control procedures during manufacturing of the pharmaceutical product.

Description of the finished product:

Give a detailed visual description of the finished product and its packaging.

Specifications of the finished product :

If the Pharmaceutical product applied for registration is included in a Pharmacopoeia, its specification should be the same as that in the latest ion of that Pharmacopoeia.

Provide a list of tests and limits for results for the finished pharmaceutical product of test methods. If the ingredient is tested on the basis of a monograph in a pharmacopoeia, provide a copy of the monograph in that pharmacopoeia, together with any test methods referenced but not duplicated in the monograph.

Provide of any specifications additional to those in the pharmacopoeia. Provide both release and expiry limits for results.

Method of analysis of the finished product :

Provide a detailed method of analysis of the finished product to determine its compliance with quality specifications (identification of active ingredient(s) of the finished product, purity, uniformity, performance, etc□). Differences between the factory method and the latest pharmacopoeial method should be justified.

Provide the results of validation of the assay method for product formulation. For pharmacopoeial method provide data which demonstrate that the method is applicable to this formulation.

Containers/closure systems(s) and other packaging:

Give a detailed description of the container/closure system(s), including any liner or wading.

Provide of the composition of each component.

Describe other (e.g. outer) packaging, and state what material they are made from.

Provide the specifications for any part of the container / closure systems (s), which comes into contact with the product, or its protective, cover.

For parental products, packaging components that will at any stage come into contact with any part of the product must comply with requirements specified by the BP, USP, or EuP.

Provide information and data about the stability of the container and packaging materials to the product storage conditions.

12. Certificate of analysis of the finished product :

Provide original certificate of analysis of the same batch submitted for registration with batch number, manufacturing and expiry date signed and stamped by the quality control laboratory of the factory (on a headed paper).

13. Describe package size

Stability data (according to WHO protocol)

Provide the results of stability testing of the formulation in each of the proposed marketing pack. Results should include physical as well as chemical tests.

Data should also provided on the product's stability during any processing prior to use that may be recommended on the label or in product information, such as reconstitution of a powder, dilution of an injection, or dispersion of a tablet.

State the proposed shelf life with justification in terms of the results of stability testing, and the difference between release and expiry specifications.

State storage conditions for the finished product.

Stability indicating method should be used in testing and stability of the product.

Complete data and information about degradation products should be submitted.

With respect to both locally manufactured or imported products additional stability studies are required whenever major modifications are made to formulation, manufacturing process, packaging or method of preparation.

Conditions used for accelerated and ongoing stability studies will be as follows:

Type of stability	**Storage Temperature C**	**Relative humidity %**	**Duration of studies (months)**
accelerated stability studies	±2	±5	
ongoing stability studies	±2	±5	Minimum 24

15. Product package insert

15.1. the package insert must be written in clear and understandable terms for both prescriber and patient.

15.2. The package insert should be at least written in an English and/ or Arabic language(s).

15.3. Thirty copies of the product pack insert should also be submitted with the application forms.

15.4. Certificate authenticated, certified by competent authority confirming that all information in the insert should be the same as that in that country.

16. General information about the pharmaceutical product on package insert:

This should include at least the following:

16.1. Name of the pharmaceutical product, generic and scientific name.

16.2. different dosage forms and strength available for this pharmaceutical product.

16.3. Number of doses of the medicinal product in case of more than one pharmaceutical dosage form or strength.

16.4. Route of administration.

16.5. Pharmacology of the pharmaceutical product.

16.6. Main therapeutic group.

16.7. Indications and dosage regimen.

16.8. Contraindications, warnings, precautions and drug interactions.

16.9. Use in pregnancy and other special group of patients.

16.10. Adverse effects.

16.11. Overdose, signs, symptoms and treatment.

17. Sample and label:

17.1. Labeling of the outer pack should include at least the following information:

17.1.1. The name of the pharmaceutical product.

17.1.2. Name of active ingredient(s) showing the amount of each present in a dosage unit.

17.1.3. Specification of active ingredient(s)

17.1.4. Package size for retail sale (number of dosage units, volume or weight and description of unit).

17.1.5. Registration number of the pharmaceutical products in Sudan, (if registered)

17.1.6. Pharmaceutical dosage form.

17.1.7. Storage conditions and precautions.

17.1.8. Manufacturing and expiry date and batch number (expiry date should be in an uncoded form).

17.1.9. Warnings or precautions that may be necessary.

17.1.10. Others (measuring unit,□.).

17.1.11. The name, country and address of the manfucturer.

17.1.12. Legal status for distribution purposes (e.g. to be dispensed on prescription only)

17.1.13. Package insert

17.1.14. Method of administration and the route of administration, if not for oral use.

17.1.15. Name of excipients to be of a safety concern for some patients or known to have a recognized action or effect.

17.2 Labeling of the inner (primary) pack should include at least the following information:

17.2.1. The trade name of the pharmaceutical product and dosage form.

17.2.2. Name of active ingredient(s) showing the amount of each present in a dosage unit.

17.2.3. Specification of the active ingredient(s).

17.2.4. Manfuacturing and expiry date and batch number.

17.2.5. The name and country of the manufacturer.

17.2.6. Route of administration, (if not for oral use).

17.2.7. Package size for retail sale, (number of dosage units, e.g. volume or weight per pack) except for tablets, capsules, lozenges, powder for injection and suppositories (rectal and vaginal)

18. Price

Provide the following information:

18.1. Proposed C&F price for registration in Sudan. The specified port of entry should be indicated.

18.2. Whole sale and retail price in country of origin (certified, authenticated and stamped form the competent authority in country of origin).

18.3 Whole sale price in other countries including neigbouring countries to Sudan and African countries.

18.4 Proposed retail price for registration in Sudan.

19. Dispending category

19.1 Indicate dispending category (proposed method for dispending) in the country of origin with justification of that categorization, OTC (Over The Counter), pharmacy only, hospital only or prescription only.

20. Withdrawal of product from markets

20.1. Provide a list of all countries where the product has been withdrawn form the market or where the application for marketing has been rejected or withdrawn by the applicant, state the reason in each case.

21. Efficacy report:

21.1. For pharmaceutical specialists submit detailed report on all efficacy studies carried out on the product.

21.2. For generic product submit detailed documentations of equivalence studies on the product in accordance to WHO recommendations, stamped and authenticated from the competent certifying authority in country of origin. This is reguied only for attached list.

22. Claimed advantage:

21.1. Claimed advantage over the registered products should be shown and supported by reference to randomize, controlled, comparative trials. of these trials should be given in an appendix.

23. Samples of actual product and/or Reference Standard Substance:

23.1. The Registration Department will request only one sample of the actual products with document for approval. The remaining samples and Reference Standard will be requested after approval.

23.2. The number of samples required for each dosage form is shown on Table (1) and should be accompanied by the certificate of analysis.

23.3. A quantity of Reference Standard Substance, which is sufficient for testing at least TEN samples, should be submitted in an air tight, light resisting container and clearly labeled with the name, concentration, manufacturing date, and expiry date, batch number and storage conditions. An extra quantity should be supplied, if needed.

23.4. Samples of any other ingredient, that can be expected to be of importance in the quality control of the specialty, should also be submitted in sufficient akmount fo rtesting at least TEN samples.

Note: If special requirements must be imposed on the storage of samples of Reference Standard are needed, their storage conditions should be written on the label of the inner and outer container.

III. Special requirements for specific dosage forms

1/Tablets:
- appearance, colour, shape, friability, hardness, uniformity of weight with its specification, uniformity of thickness and diameter with pecilication, moisture and dissolution in full .

2/Capsules:
- appearance, moisture, colour, shape, brittleness, dissolution, description of appearance and the colour of the filled material, uniformity of weight with its specification.

3/Emulsions:
- appearance, colour, odour, pH, viscosity

It is recommended that a heating - cooling cycle to be employed between 4-45 C

4/Solutions:
- appearance, colour, odour, clarity of solution, pH

5/ Suspensions and powder for suspension
- appearance, precipitate and sedimentation rate, colour, odour, taste, cloudiness particle size, disperability, redispersibility, suspendibility, particle size, colouring matters, flavour used and pH.
- Strength through the recommended storage period before and after reconstitution for powder of suspension.

6/ Syrups and Elexirs:
- description of colour, odour, taste and appearance.. etc, pH with specifications, refractive index with its specification, specific gravity, viscosity with specification, couloring matters, flavour and preservatives used.

7/ Dry powder of external use:
- appearance, colour, odour, and moisture content.

8/ Ophthalmic, Otical and Nasal preparations:
- description, appearance, colour, clarity viscosity, uniformity of volume, particle size specification and pH.
- Preservative on label (for ophthalmic preparations).

9/ Injectable preparations
- type of container and sealing
- appearance, colour, clarity of solution, uniformity of weight, preservative (if applicable) and pH.
- Description of solution on reconstitution of powder for injection stability and strength through the recommended storage period before and after reconstitution of powder for injection.

10/ Suppositeries:
- appearance, shape, colour, uniformity of weight, disintegration time or melting time with specification.

11/ Ointment, Creams and Gels:
- appearance, colour, odour, consistency, viscosity, homogenecity, uniformity of weight, uniformity of content and water content determination.

12/ Antiseptic and Disinfectants:
- appearance, colour, clarity of solution and pH.
- The conscentration and recommended dilution for optimal action.
- Microbial spectrum
- Evaluation of bactericidal, fungicidal and bacteriostatic actions.

13/ Aerosol pharmaceutical:
- uniformity of content (with limitation).
- Propellant used.
- Active ingredient/ propellant ratio.
- Spray testing.
- Leaking testing.
- Pressure measurement.

IV. Additional requirements for pharmaceutical products containing new entities application

1- New entities should be registered in countries that have an advanced system for registration of new drug entities. Provide a list of these countries and photocopy of registration certificate in each of these countries.
2- Reprots on all pre-clinical and clinical studies should be submitted to the Registration Department; including:-

2.1. Toxicological data:
- single does toxicity, species used and route(s) of administration.
- Repeated dose toxicity, species, dose, duration, numbers and methods of evaluation.
- Reproduction toxicity, dose, species and numbers of animal used in studies of teratogenic and embryotoxic effects.
- Pharmacokinetic information to validate interspecies comparison of toxicity

2.2. Animal Pharmacology:
- Primary action relevant to the proposed therapeutic use.
- General pharmacology on vital body systems.
- Dose/concentration effect relationship of primary or general pharmacological action.
- Absorption, distribution, biotransformation and main routes of elimination.

2.3. Clinical documentation Synopsis:
2.3.1 Clinical pharmacological studies
- Pharmacological action(s) of the drug in man.
- Time course of effect of single and multiple doses.
- Dose-response relationship and concentration effect relationship.
- Absorption, route of biotransformation, (if of pharmacology of toxicological significance), routes of elimination.
- Systemic bioavailability of products intended to have a systemic effect.

2.3.2. Therapeutic efficacy:
- Controlled trials carried out to support each claimed indication.
- Dose range use, modification of dosage in special group, e.g. children, the elderly or malnourished individual, patients with renal or other irreversible effects.
- Interactions with other drugs like to be given concurrently.
- Interaction with specific foods.
- Evidence concerning dependency potential.
- Has the drug been used in pregnancy? Is it excreted in breast milk?
- Specific contraindications.
- Recommendations concerning treatment of overdose or intoxication (antidotes).

2.4. Any other relevant scientific informations.

VI. Table (1): Size of samples to be submitted for registration

No	Dosage Form	Number of sample (Unit) for QC lab	Number of sample (Unit) for committee
1	Tablets, capsules, lozenges, for dispensing in original pack to individual patient course of treatment.	100 tablets, capsules or lozenges in orginal packs	15 packs
2	Tablets, capsules, lozenges large pack (100 tablets, capsules or more)	100 tablets, capsules or lozenges + 3 empty packages	150 tablets, capsules or lozenges + 3 empty packages
3	Syrups, oral suspension, emulsions, elixir, aerosols	10 bottles	15 bottles
4	Dry powder or granules in sachets	20 sachets	15 sachets
5	Injectable ampoules and individual dose vial	50 ampoules+ 3 empty packages	15 ampoules + 3 empty packages
6	Multidose vials	50 vials + 3 empty packages	15 vials + 3 empty packages
7	Ointments, creams, eye drops (topical or ophthalmic)	10 tubes	15 tubes
8	Suppositories or vaginal tablets	100 suppositories or vaginal tablets	150 suppositories or vaginal tablets.

REQUIREMENT FOR REGISTRATION AND RE-REGISTRATION FOR MINOR CHANGES REGARDING COMPANIES AND THEIR DURGS

1. CHANGE OF THE PACK/ PACK SIZE AND / OR ADDITIONAL PACK

1- Request for minor change

2- Prescribed form should be filled correctly by type writing.

3- Five samples from each old and new pack

4- Photocopy of Certificate of Registration in Sudan.

5- Proposed price for the new pack (retail & whole) sale.

2. CHANGE IN THE INNER PACK

1. Request for minor change
2. Prescribed form should be filled correctly by type writing
3. Five samples from each old and new pack
4. Photocopy of Certificate of Registration in Sudan.
5. Stability Study for the pharaceutical product in the new pack
6. Approval from health authorities in the country of origin for the new pack
7. Batch Certificate of Analysis

8. Proposed price for the new pack

3. EXTENSION OR CHANGE OF SHELF LIFE OR STORAGE CONDITIONS

1- Request for changing shelf life or storage conditions.

2- Prescribed application form should be filled correctly by type writing.

3- New stability study confirming the new shelf life or storage conditions.

4- Five samples labeled with the new and old shelf life or storage conditions.

5- Batch Certificate of Analysis.

6- Approval of health authorities in the country of origin for the new shelf life.

4. CHANGE IN PACKAGE INSERT

1- Covering letter with explanations for changes in the information and supporting references.

2- 10 copies from old insert

3- 10 copies from new insert.

4- Approval of health authorities in the country of origin for the new package insert.

5. CHANGE OF SOURCE

1- Addition of new source(s) for the same pharmaceutical product is not allowed

2- New registration of new source and product is required

3- In addition to rigesteration form, the prescribed application form for change of source should be filled correctly by type writer.

6. CHANGE OF COMPOSITION (ACTIVE AND/OR INACTIVE INGREDIENTS)

1- New registration is required

7. CHANGE OF PHARMACEUTICAL TRADE NAME

1- Covering letter

2- Certificate of Pharmaceutical Product for the new pharmaceutical trade name issued by the health authorities in country of origin) as notified to WHO), certified by Ministry of Foreign Affairs, authenticated and stamped by Sudan Embassy in country of origin.

3- Five samples from each, old and new names, labeled.

4- Batch certificate of analysis

8. CHANGE OF COMPANY NAME

1- Covering letter with explanations

2- Approval of health authorities in the country of origin for the new company name authenticated and stamped by Sudan Embassy in country of origin.

3- New Certificate of Pharmaceutical Product for the new company name issued by the health authorities in country of origin (as notified to WHO), certified by Ministry of Foreign Affairs, authenticated and stamped by Sudan Embassy in country of origin.

4- Five samples from each, labeled with the new and old company name.

5- Batch Certificate of Analysis.

9. CHANGE OF PRICE OF PHARMACEUTICAL PRODUCT

1- Request for changing price.

2- Prescribed application form should be filled correctly by type writer

3- Justification for change of price should be explained.

4- Wholesale price in the country of origin and other countries as required.

5- Photocopy of certificate of rigesteration in Sodan.

10. CHANGE OF LOCAL AGENT OF A FOREIGN MANUFACTURER:

1- New agency agreement with the new local agent

2- Termination of the previous agency agreement.

11. RENEWAL OF REGISTRATION OF PHARMACEUTICAL PRODUCT

1- Specified application form should be filled correctly.

2- Payment of renewal fees

3- Photocopy of Certificate of Registration in Sudan

4- Photocopy of last Certificate of Renewal of Registration in Sodan

5- Valid Certificate of Pharmaceutical Product issued by the health authorities in country of origin (as notified to WHO), certified by Ministry of Foreign Affairs, authenticated and stamped by Sudan Embassy in country of origin.

6- Submition of application thirty days prior to expiration date of the Certificate of Registration on form (B)

N.B. If there is no Sudan Embassy in country of origin, the Registration Deparmtent will suggest an alternative.

Dr. Salah edelin Abd Elrahman
Chairman, Committee
For registration of Pharmaceutical
Prodcuts for Human Use

BASIC TITLES ON SUDAN

Title	ISBN
Sudan (North) Country Study Guide - Volume 1 Strategic Information and Developments	1438775644
Sudan (North): How to Invest, Start and Run Profitable Business in Sudan (North) Guide - Practical Information, Opportunities, Contacts	9781433084621
Sudan (South) Country Study Guide - Volume 1 Strategic Information and Developments	1438776004
Sudan (South): How to Invest, Start and Run Profitable Business in Sudan (South) Guide - Practical Information, Opportunities, Contacts	9781433084980
Sudan A "Spy" Guide - Strategic Information and Developments	1433047241
Sudan A Spy" Guide"	1438745974
Sudan Banking & Financial Market Handbook	1438745982
Sudan Banking & Financial Market Handbook	143304725X
Sudan Business and Investment Opportunities Yearbook	1433047268
Sudan Business and Investment Opportunities Yearbook	1438745990
Sudan Business and Investment Opportunities Yearbook Volume 1 Strategic Information and Opportunities	1438777973
Sudan Business Intelligence Report - Practical Information, Opportunities, Contacts	1438746008
Sudan Business Intelligence Report - Practical Information, Opportunities, Contacts	1433047276
Sudan Business Law Handbook Volume 1 Strategic Information and Basic Laws	1438746016
Sudan Business Law Handbook Volume 2 Investment and Trade Laws	143877110X
Sudan Business Law Handbook Volume 3 Mining Laws and Regulations	143877110X
Sudan Business Law Handbook Volume 4 Sharia and Islamic Laws	1433047284
Sudan Company Laws and Regulations Handbook	1433070650
Sudan Constitution and Citizenship Laws Handbook - Strategic Information and Basic Laws	1438779909
Sudan Country Study Guide - Strategic Information and Developments	1433047292
Sudan Customs, Trade Regulations and Procedures Handbook	1433047306
Sudan Customs, Trade Regulations and Procedures Handbook	1438746024
Sudan Diplomatic Handbook - Strategic Information and Developments	1433047314
Sudan Diplomatic Handbook - Strategic Information and Developments	1438746032
Sudan Ecology & Nature Protection Handbook	1433047322
Sudan Ecology & Nature Protection Handbook	1438746040
Sudan Ecology & Nature Protection Laws and Regulation Handbook	1433075008
Sudan Economic & Development Strategy Handbook	1438746059
Sudan Economic & Development Strategy Handbook	1433047330
Sudan Energy Policy, Laws and Regulation Handbook	1433072769
Sudan Energy Policy, Laws and Regulations Handbook	1438746067
Sudan Energy Policy, Laws and Regulations Handbook	1433047349
Sudan Export-Import Trade and Business Directory	1433047357
Sudan Export-Import Trade and Business Directory	1438746075
Sudan Foreign Policy and Government Guide	1433047365

Title	ISBN
Sudan Foreign Policy and Government Guide	1438746083
Sudan Healthcare Sector Organization, Management and Payment Systems Handbook - Strategic Information, Programs and Regulations	9781433085994
Sudan Immigration Laws and Regulations Handbook - Strategic Information and Basic Laws	1438783507
Sudan Industrial and Business Directory	1433047373
Sudan Industrial and Business Directory	1438746091
Sudan Internet and E-Commerce Investment and Business Guide - Strategic and Practical Information: Regulations and Opportunities	1433047381
Sudan Internet and E-Commerce Investment and Business Guide - Strategic and Practical Information: Regulations and Opportunities	1438746105
Sudan Investment and Business Guide - Strategic and Practical Information	1438768826
Sudan Investment and Business Guide - Strategic and Practical Information	143304739X
Sudan Investment and Business Guide - Strategic and Practical Information	1438746113
Sudan Investment and Business Guide - Strategic and Practical Information	1438768826
Sudan Investment and Trade Laws and Regulations Handbook	1433076667
Sudan Land Ownership and Agriculture Laws Handbook	1438760019
Sudan Mineral & Mining Sector Investment and Business Guide - Strategic and Practical Information	1433047403
Sudan Mineral & Mining Sector Investment and Business Guide - Strategic and Practical Information	1438746121
Sudan Mining Laws and Regulations Handbook	1433078252
Sudan Oil & Gas Sector Business & Investment Opportunities Yearbook	143874613X
Sudan Oil & Gas Sector Business & Investment Opportunities Yearbook	1433047411
Sudan Oil and Gas Exploration Laws and Regulation Handbook	143307897X
Sudan Recent Economic and Political Developments Yearbook	1433062623
Sudan Recent Economic and Political Developments Yearbook	1433062623
Sudan Recent Economic and Political Developments Yearbook	1433062623
Sudan South Business and Investment Opportunities Yearbook Volume 1 Strategic Information and Opportunities	1438777981
Sudan South Economic, Development Strategy and Programs Handbook	9781577515296
Sudan Starting Business (Incorporating) in....Guide	1433068303
Sudan Taxation Laws and Regulations Handbook	1433081040
Sudan Telecom Laws and Regulations Handbook	1433082489
Sudan Telecommunication Industry Business Opportunities Handbook	143304742X
Sudan Telecommunication Industry Business Opportunities Handbook	1438746148
Sudan Transportation Policy and Regulations Handbook	1433068311

TITLE
Cape Verde Business Law Handbook Volume 1 Strategic Information and Basic Laws
Cayman Islands Business Law Handbook Volume 1 Strategic Information and Basic Laws
Central African Republic Business Law Handbook Volume 1 Strategic Information and Basic Laws
Chad Business Law Handbook Volume 1 Strategic Information and Basic Laws
Chile Business Law Handbook Volume 1 Strategic Information and Basic Laws
China Business Law Handbook Volume 1 Strategic Information and Basic Laws
Colombia Business Law Handbook Volume 1 Strategic Information and Basic Laws
Comoros Business Law Handbook Volume 1 Strategic Information and Basic Laws
Congo Business Law Handbook Volume 1 Strategic Information and Basic Laws
Congo, Democratic Republic Business Law Handbook Volume 1 Strategic Information and Basic Laws
Cook Islands Business Law Handbook Volume 1 Strategic Information and Basic Laws
Costa Rica Business Law Handbook Volume 1 Strategic Information and Basic Laws
Cote d'Ivoire Business Law Handbook Volume 1 Strategic Information and Basic Laws
Croatia Business Law Handbook Volume 1 Strategic Information and Basic Laws
Cuba Business Law Handbook Volume 1 Strategic Information and Basic Laws
Cyprus Business Law Handbook Volume 1 Strategic Information and Basic Laws
Czech Republic Business Law Handbook Volume 1 Strategic Information and Basic Laws
Denmark Business Law Handbook Volume 1 Strategic Information and Basic Laws
Djibouti Business Law Handbook Volume 1 Strategic Information and Basic Laws
Dominica Business Law Handbook Volume 1 Strategic Information and Basic Laws
Dominican Republic Business Law Handbook Volume 1 Strategic Information and Basic Laws
Ecuador Business Law Handbook Volume 1 Strategic Information and Basic Laws
Egypt Business Law Handbook Volume 1 Strategic Information and Basic Laws
El Salvador Business Law Handbook Volume 1 Strategic Information and Basic Laws
Equatorial Guinea Business Law Handbook Volume 1 Strategic Information and Basic Laws
Eritrea Business Law Handbook Volume 1 Strategic Information and Basic Laws
Estonia Business Law Handbook Volume 1 Strategic Information and Basic Laws
Ethiopia Business Law Handbook Volume 1 Strategic Information and Basic Laws
Falkland Islands Business Law Handbook Volume 1 Strategic Information and Basic Laws
Faroes Islands Business Law Handbook Volume 1 Strategic Information and Basic Laws
Fiji Business Law Handbook Volume 1 Strategic Information and Basic Laws
Finland Business Law Handbook Volume 1 Strategic Information and Basic Laws
France Business Law Handbook Volume 1 Strategic Information and Basic Laws
Gabon Business Law Handbook Volume 1 Strategic Information and Basic Laws
Gambia Business Law Handbook Volume 1 Strategic Information and Basic Laws
Georgia Business Law Handbook Volume 1 Strategic Information and Basic Laws
Germany Business Law Handbook Volume 1 Strategic Information and Basic Laws
Ghana Business Law Handbook Volume 1 Strategic Information and Basic Laws
Gibraltar Business Law Handbook Volume 1 Strategic Information and Basic Laws
Greece Business Law Handbook Volume 1 Strategic Information and Basic Laws
Greenland Business Law Handbook Volume 1 Strategic Information and Basic Laws
Grenada Business Law Handbook Volume 1 Strategic Information and Basic Laws
Guam Business Law Handbook Volume 1 Strategic Information and Basic Laws
Guatemala Business Law Handbook Volume 1 Strategic Information and Basic Laws
Guernsey Business Law Handbook Volume 1 Strategic Information and Basic Laws
Guinea Business Law Handbook Volume 1 Strategic Information and Basic Laws

TITLE
Guinea-Bissau Business Law Handbook Volume 1 Strategic Information and Basic Laws
Guyana Business Law Handbook Volume 1 Strategic Information and Basic Laws
Haiti Business Law Handbook Volume 1 Strategic Information and Basic Laws
Honduras Business Law Handbook Volume 1 Strategic Information and Basic Laws
Hungary Business Law Handbook Volume 1 Strategic Information and Basic Laws
Iceland Business Law Handbook Volume 1 Strategic Information and Basic Laws
India Business Law Handbook Volume 1 Strategic Information and Basic Laws
Indonesia Business Law Handbook Volume 1 Strategic Information and Basic Laws
Iran Business Law Handbook Volume 1 Strategic Information and Basic Laws
Iraq Business Law Handbook Volume 1 Strategic Information and Basic Laws
Ireland Business Law Handbook Volume 1 Strategic Information and Basic Laws
Israel Business Law Handbook Volume 1 Strategic Information and Basic Laws
Italy Business Law Handbook Volume 1 Strategic Information and Basic Laws
Jamaica Business Law Handbook Volume 1 Strategic Information and Basic Laws
Japan Business Law Handbook Volume 1 Strategic Information and Basic Laws
Jersey Business Law Handbook Volume 1 Strategic Information and Basic Laws
Jordan Business Law Handbook Volume 1 Strategic Information and Basic Laws
Kazakhstan Business Law Handbook Volume 1 Strategic Information and Basic Laws
Kenya Business Law Handbook Volume 1 Strategic Information and Basic Laws
Kiribati Business Law Handbook Volume 1 Strategic Information and Basic Laws
Korea, North Business Law Handbook Volume 1 Strategic Information and Basic Laws
Korea, South Business Law Handbook Volume 1 Strategic Information and Basic Laws
Kosovo Business Law Handbook Volume 1 Strategic Information and Basic Laws
Kurdistan Business Law Handbook Volume 1 Strategic Information and Basic Laws
Kuwait Business Law Handbook Volume 1 Strategic Information and Basic Laws
Kyrgyzstan Business Law Handbook Volume 1 Strategic Information and Basic Laws
Laos Business Law Handbook Volume 1 Strategic Information and Basic Laws
Latvia Business Law Handbook Volume 1 Strategic Information and Basic Laws
Lebanon Business Law Handbook Volume 1 Strategic Information and Basic Laws
Lesotho Business Law Handbook Volume 1 Strategic Information and Basic Laws
Liberia Business Law Handbook Volume 1 Strategic Information and Basic Laws
Libya Business Law Handbook Volume 1 Strategic Information and Basic Laws
Liechtenstein Business Law Handbook Volume 1 Strategic Information and Basic Laws
Lithuania Business Law Handbook Volume 1 Strategic Information and Basic Laws
Luxembourg Business Law Handbook Volume 1 Strategic Information and Basic Laws
Macao Business Law Handbook Volume 1 Strategic Information and Basic Laws
Macedonia Business Law Handbook Volume 1 Strategic Information and Basic Laws
Madagascar Business Law Handbook Volume 1 Strategic Information and Basic Laws
Madeira Business Law Handbook Volume 1 Strategic Information and Basic Laws
Malawi Business Law Handbook Volume 1 Strategic Information and Basic Laws
Malaysia Business Law Handbook Volume 1 Strategic Information and Basic Laws
Maldives Business Law Handbook Volume 1 Strategic Information and Basic Laws
Mali Business Law Handbook Volume 1 Strategic Information and Basic Laws
Malta Business Law Handbook Volume 1 Strategic Information and Basic Laws
Man Business Law Handbook Volume 1 Strategic Information and Basic Laws
Marshall Islands Business Law Handbook Volume 1 Strategic Information and Basic Laws

TITLE
Mauritania Business Law Handbook Volume 1 Strategic Information and Basic Laws
Mauritius Business Law Handbook Volume 1 Strategic Information and Basic Laws
Mayotte Business Law Handbook Volume 1 Strategic Information and Basic Laws
Mexico Business Law Handbook Volume 1 Strategic Information and Basic Laws
Micronesia Business Law Handbook Volume 1 Strategic Information and Basic Laws
Moldova Business Law Handbook Volume 1 Strategic Information and Basic Laws
Monaco Business Law Handbook Volume 1 Strategic Information and Basic Laws
Mongolia Business Law Handbook Volume 1 Strategic Information and Basic Laws
Montserrat Business Law Handbook Volume 1 Strategic Information and Basic Laws
Montenegro Business Law Handbook Volume 1 Strategic Information and Basic Laws
Morocco Business Law Handbook Volume 1 Strategic Information and Basic Laws
Mozambique Business Law Handbook Volume 1 Strategic Information and Basic Laws
Myanmar Business Law Handbook Volume 1 Strategic Information and Basic Laws
Nagorno-Karabakh Republic Business Law Handbook Volume 1 Strategic Information and Basic Laws
Namibia Business Law Handbook Volume 1 Strategic Information and Basic Laws
Nauru Business Law Handbook Volume 1 Strategic Information and Basic Laws
Nepal Business Law Handbook Volume 1 Strategic Information and Basic Laws
Netherlands Business Law Handbook Volume 1 Strategic Information and Basic Laws
New Caledonia Business Law Handbook Volume 1 Strategic Information and Basic Laws
New Zealand Business Law Handbook Volume 1 Strategic Information and Basic Laws
Nicaragua Business Law Handbook Volume 1 Strategic Information and Basic Laws
Niger Business Law Handbook Volume 1 Strategic Information and Basic Laws
Nigeria Business Law Handbook Volume 1 Strategic Information and Basic Laws
Niue Business Law Handbook Volume 1 Strategic Information and Basic Laws
Northern Cyprus (Turkish Republic of Northern Cyprus) Business Law Handbook Volume 1 Strategic Information and Basic Laws
Northern Mariana Islands Business Law Handbook Volume 1 Strategic Information and Basic Laws
Norway Business Law Handbook Volume 1 Strategic Information and Basic Laws
Oman Business Law Handbook Volume 1 Strategic Information and Basic Laws
Pakistan Business Law Handbook Volume 1 Strategic Information and Basic Laws
Palau Business Law Handbook Volume 1 Strategic Information and Basic Laws
Palestine (West Bank & Gaza) Business Law Handbook Volume 1 Strategic Information and Basic Laws
Panama Business Law Handbook Volume 1 Strategic Information and Basic Laws
Papua New Guinea Business Law Handbook Volume 1 Strategic Information and Basic Laws
Paraguay Business Law Handbook Volume 1 Strategic Information and Basic Laws
Peru Business Law Handbook Volume 1 Strategic Information and Basic Laws
Philippines Business Law Handbook Volume 1 Strategic Information and Basic Laws
Pitcairn Islands Business Law Handbook Volume 1 Strategic Information and Basic Laws
Poland Business Law Handbook Volume 1 Strategic Information and Basic Laws
Polynesia French Business Law Handbook Volume 1 Strategic Information and Basic Laws
Portugal Business Law Handbook Volume 1 Strategic Information and Basic Laws
Qatar Business Law Handbook Volume 1 Strategic Information and Basic Laws
Romania Business Law Handbook Volume 1 Strategic Information and Basic Laws
Russia Business Law Handbook Volume 1 Strategic Information and Basic Laws
Rwanda Business Law Handbook Volume 1 Strategic Information and Basic Laws
Sahrawi Arab Democratic Republic Volume 1 Strategic Information and Developments

TITLE
Saint Kitts and Nevis Business Law Handbook Volume 1 Strategic Information and Basic Laws
Saint Lucia Business Law Handbook Volume 1 Strategic Information and Basic Laws
Saint Vincent and The Grenadines Business Law Handbook Volume 1 Strategic Information and Basic Laws
Samoa (American) A Business Law Handbook Volume 1 Strategic Information and Basic Laws
Samoa (Western) Business Law Handbook Volume 1 Strategic Information and Basic Laws
San Marino Business Law Handbook Volume 1 Strategic Information and Basic Laws
Sao Tome and Principe Business Law Handbook Volume 1 Strategic Information and Basic Laws
Saudi Arabia Business Law Handbook Volume 1 Strategic Information and Basic Laws
Scotland Business Law Handbook Volume 1 Strategic Information and Basic Laws
Senegal Business Law Handbook Volume 1 Strategic Information and Basic Laws
Serbia Business Law Handbook Volume 1 Strategic Information and Basic Laws
Seychelles Business Law Handbook Volume 1 Strategic Information and Basic Laws
Sierra Leone Business Law Handbook Volume 1 Strategic Information and Basic Laws
Singapore Business Law Handbook Volume 1 Strategic Information and Basic Laws
Slovakia Business Law Handbook Volume 1 Strategic Information and Basic Laws
Slovenia Business Law Handbook Volume 1 Strategic Information and Basic Laws
Solomon Islands Business Law Handbook Volume 1 Strategic Information and Basic Laws
Somalia Business Law Handbook Volume 1 Strategic Information and Basic Laws
South Africa Business Law Handbook Volume 1 Strategic Information and Basic Laws
Spain Business Law Handbook Volume 1 Strategic Information and Basic Laws
Sri Lanka Business Law Handbook Volume 1 Strategic Information and Basic Laws
St. Helena Business Law Handbook Volume 1 Strategic Information and Basic Laws
St. Pierre & Miquelon Business Law Handbook Volume 1 Strategic Information and Basic Laws
Sudan (Republic of the Sudan) Business Law Handbook Volume 1 Strategic Information and Basic Laws
Sudan South Business Law Handbook Volume 1 Strategic Information and Basic Laws
Suriname Business Law Handbook Volume 1 Strategic Information and Basic Laws
Swaziland Business Law Handbook Volume 1 Strategic Information and Basic Laws
Sweden Business Law Handbook Volume 1 Strategic Information and Basic Laws
Switzerland Business Law Handbook Volume 1 Strategic Information and Basic Laws
Syria Business Law Handbook Volume 1 Strategic Information and Basic Laws
Taiwan Business Law Handbook Volume 1 Strategic Information and Basic Laws
Tajikistan Business Law Handbook Volume 1 Strategic Information and Basic Laws
Tanzania Business Law Handbook Volume 1 Strategic Information and Basic Laws
Thailand Business Law Handbook Volume 1 Strategic Information and Basic Laws
Timor Leste (Democratic Republic of Timor-Leste) Business Law Handbook Volume 1 Strategic Information and Basic Laws
Togo Business Law Handbook Volume 1 Strategic Information and Basic Laws
Tonga Business Law Handbook Volume 1 Strategic Information and Basic Laws
Trinidad and Tobago Business Law Handbook Volume 1 Strategic Information and Basic Laws
Tunisia Business Law Handbook Volume 1 Strategic Information and Basic Laws
Turkey Business Law Handbook Volume 1 Strategic Information and Basic Laws
Turkmenistan Business Law Handbook Volume 1 Strategic Information and Basic Laws
Turks & Caicos Business Law Handbook Volume 1 Strategic Information and Basic Laws
Tuvalu Business Law Handbook Volume 1 Strategic Information and Basic Laws
Uganda Business Law Handbook Volume 1 Strategic Information and Basic Laws
Ukraine Business Law Handbook Volume 1 Strategic Information and Basic Laws

TITLE
United Arab Emirates Business Law Handbook Volume 1 Strategic Information and Basic Laws
United Kingdom Business Law Handbook Volume 1 Strategic Information and Basic Laws
United States Business Law Handbook Volume 1 Strategic Information and Basic Laws
Uruguay Business Law Handbook Volume 1 Strategic Information and Basic Laws
Uzbekistan Business Law Handbook Volume 1 Strategic Information and Basic Laws
Vanuatu Business Law Handbook Volume 1 Strategic Information and Basic Laws
Vatican City (Holy See) Business Law Handbook Volume 1 Strategic Information and Basic Laws
Venezuela Business Law Handbook Volume 1 Strategic Information and Basic Laws
Vietnam Business Law Handbook Volume 1 Strategic Information and Basic Laws
Virgin Islands, British Business Law Handbook Volume 1 Strategic Information and Basic Laws
Wake Atoll Business Law Handbook Volume 1 Strategic Information and Basic Laws
Wallis & Futuna Business Law Handbook Volume 1 Strategic Information and Basic Laws
Western Sahara Business Law Handbook Volume 1 Strategic Information and Basic Laws
Yemen Business Law Handbook Volume 1 Strategic Information and Basic Laws
Zambia Business Law Handbook Volume 1 Strategic Information and Basic Laws
Zimbabwe Business Law Handbook Volume 1 Strategic Information and Basic Laws

www.ingramcontent.com/pod-product-compliance
Lightning Source LLC
LaVergne TN
LVHW080028210926
848481LV00011B/3129
* 9 7 8 0 7 3 9 7 2 0 5 9 2 *